DAMNED
YANKEE

Missouri Biography Series
William E. Foley, Editor

DAMNED
YANKEE

The Life of General Nathaniel Lyon

CHRISTOPHER PHILLIPS, 1959-

UNIVERSITY OF MISSOURI PRESS
Columbia and London

Copyright © 1990 by
The Curators of the University of Missouri
University of Missouri Press, Columbia, Missouri 65211
Printed and bound in the United States of America

5 4 3 2 1   94 93 92 91 90

Phillips, Christopher, 1950–
    Damned Yankee : the life of General Nathaniel Lyon / Christopher
Phillips.
        p.   cm.—(Missouri Biography Series)
    Includes bibliographical references.
    ISBN 0-8262-0731-6 (alk. paper)
    1. Lyon, Nathaniel, d. 1861.   2. Generals—United States—
Biography.   3. United States. Army—Biography.   4. Missouri—
History—Civil War, 1861–1865.   5. Wilson's Creek, Battle of,
1861.   I. Title.
E467.1.L9P48   1990
973.7'092—dc20   89-20470
    [B]   CIP

∞™ This paper meets the requirements of the American National
Standard for Permanence of Paper for Printed Library Materials,
Z39.48, 1984.

Designer: Liz Fett
Typesetter: Connell-Zeko Type & Graphics
Printer: Thomson-Shore, Inc.
Binder: Thomson-Shore, Inc.
Type face: Sabon

Frontispiece: Capt. Nathaniel Lyon, ca. 1854. Probably taken
en route to Kansas at Webster's Photographic Gallery, Louisville.
Courtesy Missouri Historical Society.

For my grandmother and my great-aunt,
who showed me the cannons

Contents

Abbreviations

AAS	American Antiquarian Society
ATH	Ashford (Connecticut) Town Hall
ChiHS	Chicago Historical Society
CHS	Connecticut Historical Society
CSL	Archives, History and Genealogy Unit, Connecticut State Library
ETH	Eastford (Connecticut) Town Hall
KSHS	Kansas State Historical Society
LOC	Library of Congress
MassHS	Massachusetts Historical Society
MHS	Missouri Historical Society
NYHS	New-York Historical Society
SHSM	Joint Collection, Western Historical Manuscript Collection, Columbia, Missouri/State Historical Society of Missouri Manuscripts
USMA	United States Military Academy Archives/Library
USMHI	United States Military History Institute
WC	Wilson's Creek National Battlefield Archives/Library

Preface

He is called the "savior of Missouri," the man who, through bold, un-compromising actions, kept that neutral border state from leaving the Union in the first year of the Civil War. His death at the battle of Wilson's Creek on August 10, 1861, ensured him fleeting fame as the first Union general to fall on the field of battle, the North's first war hero. Yet today, even among the most avid Civil War aficionados, Nathaniel Lyon's is hardly a household name. He has been all but lost among the war's heroes who have since attained greater stature—Grant, Lee, Jackson, and Sherman, to name but a few. The voluminous annals of scholarly and popular writings on the Civil War—even during the explosion of publications witnessed during the centennial years—have failed to provide much more than a few articles on Lyon. Most often, he has received a page or two on his contribution to the Missouri events in an overarching study of the war.

So what, I have been asked, if not for trivia's sake, makes this little-known character worthy of yet another Civil War biography? I must confess that when starting the project as a Master's thesis, I would have been hard-pressed to answer the question conclusively. In the fall of 1984, after visiting the Wilson's Creek National Battlefield and receiving a presentation of the battle and the entire Missouri situation in the first months of the war, I was left with some nagging questions. With less than five thousand men, and outnumbered at least two to one, why had this man Lyon chosen to attack, much less in the rash manner that he did? Moreover, why had he done so in a state that had officially declared itself neutral, the only slave state to call a secession convention and then vote not to secede? These questions, coupled with the fact that the only biography of the man (which soon proved subjective and often inaccurate) was written in 1862, made Lyon appear a most alluring topic for a thesis, and I plunged in with little more in mind than to bring forth some hitherto-unknown incidents from Lyon's early life that might help to explain his actions in Missouri in 1861. Only after delving into the primary sources did I discover that what wasn't heretofore known about Nathaniel Lyon's life was even more checkered than what was. At that point, his almost inexplicable behavior began at last to make sense.

During and after the thesis, I followed Lyon's life, and my incredulousness grew as I further studied both his often-reckless actions and their attendant results. Yet, just when Lyon's own words and others' reactions to his deeds led me to damn him aloud for his inquisitorial indictments and punishments of those around him, at the Connecticut Archives I stumbled upon a small, oval photograph of a handsome, fresh-faced youth with a mass of curly locks, proudly bedecked in his lieutenant's uniform. As I stared at the photograph, I was overwhelmed by the tangible humanity of the man whom so many had despised. At that moment, Lyon became for me a person—though a perplexing one— and I wanted nothing more than to bring him to life. In the process, I have traced the development of a complex, often tortured mind searching for his own meaning in an incongruent world. And once he had rationalized that role, Lyon would allow nothing or no one to impede his quest to fulfill it, including his army superiors, the United States government, and even the rights and liberties of the populace of an entire state. Because of his own twisted sense of duty, he plunged the politically sensitive state of Missouri into a war in which she herself had chosen not to participate. And in so doing, he helped to precipitate an irrevocable social turmoil in both the state and the city of St. Louis, as well as to reveal the attitudes toward the war of many of those above him who were forced to deal with Lyon's impetuous actions, either by assisting him or resisting him. For these reasons, Nathaniel Lyon's story has for a long while needed to be told.

No book is ever written alone. At every stage of the process, a writer unavoidably makes use of the knowledge, advice, and generosity of others as he fashions an "original" interpretation. Borrowing from Robert Penn Warren's incomparable metaphor in *All The King's Men,* research—like the study of history itself—"is like an enormous spider web and if you touch it, however lightly, at any point, the vibrations ripple to the remotest perimeter . . . ." I fear that in my case, all too often I shredded, rather than rippled, Penn Warren's web. During the various stages of my research and writing, I have incurred more than my share of debts, most of which I cannot repay adequately. To far too few, I offer this small recompense for all that they have done.

I extend thanks to Garold Cole and the rest of the staff at the Milner Library, Illinois State University, as well as the staff of the Main Library at the University of Georgia, for their assistance in locating often-obscure sources and for providing direction in my search for others. V. L. "Gus" Klapp of the Wilson's Creek National Battlefield Park guided me through one of Lyon's account books, and Mr. and Mrs. Dagmar Noll of Eastford, Connecticut, opened the files of the Eastford Historical Society for my inspection, generously sending me photographs and materials before I was able to travel there myself. James Murphy and Fred Bergner of Webster, Massachusetts, followed a blind lead and uncovered Lyon's West Point diploma, long buried in a dusty box in the town hall. Mike Musick and Mike Pilgrim of the National Archives performed feats of magic in leading me to some most valuable sources, though it required a third trip to find them all. Harriet McLoone of the Huntington Library and Marie T. Capps of the United States Military Academy Library Archives remained gracious and helpful, despite my persistently inane questions and requests. Dr. Richard J. Sommers of the United States Military History Institute, archivist extraordinaire, went far beyond the call of duty to send me materials he knew personally to be hidden in his collections, and gave me a most salutary tip when I met him by happenstance in New Orleans at the Southern History Association convention.

I am equally appreciative of the cooperation and courtesies extended me by the Missouri Historical Society, the State Historical Society of Missouri, the American Antiquarian Society, the Kansas State Historical Society, the South Dakota State Historical Society, the Connecticut State Library / Archives, the Connecticut Historical Society, the Massachusetts Historical Society, the Yale University Library, the Tulane University Library, the Valentine Museum, the New-York Historical Society, the New York Public Library, the California State Library, the Chicago Historical Society, the Illinois State Historical Society, the National Archives, and the Library of Congress. The University of Georgia's Office of the Vice President for research provided a generous grant which helped greatly with acquiring illustrations. The *Missouri Historical Review* graciously extended permission to reprint parts of my article published in their journal.

Certain individuals have provided both professional and personal assistance and deserve special thanks. Mark Plummer and L. Moody Simms of Illinois State University guided the project to its initial completion, affording me salutary criticism despite innumerable errors and a taste of champagne I shall forever savor. William McFeely, Emory Thomas, Lester Stephens, and Michele Gillespie each read parts of the draft and helped me iron out some rough spots, both conceptual and mechanical, and along with Kirk Willis lent critical eyes to the do's and don't's of biography. Their enthusiasm and confidence allowed me to persevere despite "complications" (a.k.a. graduate coursework). John Marszalek and Earl Hess served well as readers for the manuscript and provided cogent and necessary criticisms at a point when it needed it most. Rick Boland did a masterful job of copyediting the manuscript, pruning its often faulty prose and questioning its many unclear passages. Finally, William Parrish gave generously of his time and expertise on the subjects of Lyon and Civil War Missouri. A kinder fate could not have befallen me than meeting him in the wilds of Valdosta, Georgia.

Finally, on a personal level, other individuals sustained me throughout the various stages of research and writing. Russ Duncan, as colleague, competitor, and tent-mate, proved an extant role model who never ceased both to challenge and to encourage me, physically as well as mentally. Most of all, however, I thank him for his friendship. My other graduate mates at the University of Georgia—Brian Wills, Glenn Eskew, Randy Patton, Glenna Schroeder, Jon Bryant, Stan Deaton, Steve Moore, Carolyn Bashaw, and Sharon Flanagan—each lent collegial support which cannot be measured in its importance. To my brother, John, I extend gratitude for his generosity and support. In a "technological" sense, this book is as much his as anyone's. To the Browns (my "designated researchers") and the Phillipses, and to the rest of my family, I offer thanks for their unflagging love and confidence. They gave me much more than I can return. And finally, I thank Dulcie, whose tender inspiration provides for me a constant reminder that though Lyon's life ended in 1861, mine didn't.

DAMNED
YANKEE

*Those who enjoy power always arrange matters
so as to give their tyranny an appearance of justice.*

LA FONTAINE, 1668

Prologue

The heat was once again oppressive. Only the day before, the thermometer had registered one hundred degrees in the shade. Coupled with the hothouse humidity of southwestern Missouri, such heat should have paralyzed all activity; even breathing was laborious. The residents of Springfield, long accustomed to this climate, would ordinarily have been inactive on such a day, the dusty streets all but deserted by midafternoon. This day, however, had not proven typical. Despite the heat, the town square was a whirlwind of activity as countless carts, carriages, and wagons were drawn up in disarray in the front of the stores and homes, making passage impossible. Sweating shopkeepers hurriedly loaded merchandise into their respective vehicles, while panic-stricken homeowners did the same with their most treasured possessions. All this was in preparation for an impending exodus from the city. The word was out that a force of Confederates numbering well over ten thousand was encamped on Wilson's Creek, just ten miles to the southwest, and soon would march on the town.[1]

The local populace, a majority of whom were pro-Union, had also heard frightening rumors that the Federal force currently protecting Springfield was outnumbered three to one and had no choice but to retreat to Rolla, 110 miles to the northeast. Fearing the looting that the invaders would inevitably commit if the Federals indeed withdrew, many residents felt that they must follow the army out of town. Therefore, those convinced they must leave hastily gathered what they could before departing for the homes of friends or relatives farther to the north. Some feared their displacement would be a long one.

Late on this afternoon of August 9, 1861, the commander of the Federal army left his rented room on North Jefferson Street, mounted his horse, and rode toward the center of town. When confronted with the

1. Diary of Charles M. Chase, October 3 to October 8, 1861, Charles M. Chase Papers, 1861, SHSM.

frenzied spectacle at the town square, he reined up. Pulling pensively at his unruly red beard, forty-three-year-old Brig. Gen. Nathaniel Lyon watched the commotion in the street. The chaotic scene quickly caused his anger to mount. His features hardened, the wrinkles at the top of his hooked nose deepened, and his small mouth clenched his cigar as tightly as his false teeth would allow. The scene convinced him at last that the course of action decided upon earlier that afternoon at a meeting with his officers was truly the correct one. With firm resolve, he spurred the dapple-gray toward the Federal camp at the edge of town.[2]

Despite being heavily outnumbered, Lyon was not content with merely pulling back and handing the town to the rebels. Considering the circumstances, however, he had until recently seen no other alternative. Since the Army of the West's arrival a week earlier, his pleas for reinforcements had been repeatedly rebuffed by the new department commander in St. Louis, John C. Frémont. Lyon was daily being drained of his forces as their ninety-day enlistments ran out, and without a rail line his force lay precariously far from his supply base in Rolla. Since his spies first brought him news of the linkage of Sterling Price's state troops with a large Confederate force under Ben McCulloch, Lyon had found himself in an unfamiliar state of indecision that was easily apparent to his officers and staff. Even the enlisted men noticed his lack of confidence; to them, it appeared as if their commander were in a daze.[3]

Lyon's subordinates advised him to pull back. Frémont had ordered him to do so as well, but only if Lyon felt incapable of defeating the enemy with the forces he presently had. Lyon had wrestled with all these obviously logical arguments for retreat during the past several days. Combined with debilitating fatigue, they had attenuated his purpose, weakened his resolve. Tonight, however, there was at last some determination in his actions, and as he rode on he thought not of the reasons *for* retreat, but of the reasons *not* to. In his mind, his decision was right, and all of his principles assured him that he would be rewarded by victory. By God, he had vowed to punish these secessionists, and he would not pull back until he made good that pledge. At the officers' meeting, he had

2. Hans Christian Adamson, *Rebellion in Missouri, 1861: Nathaniel Lyon and His Army of the West*, 213–14; Return I. Holcombe and W. S. Adams, *An Account of the Battle of Wilson's Creek, or Oak Hills, Fought Between the Union Troops, Commanded by Gen. N. Lyon, and the Southern Troops, Commanded by Gens. McCulloch and Price, on Saturday, August 10, 1861, in Greene County, Missouri*, 17–18; Eugene F. Ware, *The Lyon Campaign*, 282, 339–40.

3. John M. Schofield, *Forty-six Years in the Army*, 39.

ordered a night march to within striking distance of the Confederate camp. Then, at first light, the army—*his* army—would prey upon the slumbering rebels and mete out their appointed justice.[4]

By the time Lyon and his aides arrived at the camp, black storm clouds had rolled in ominously from the west, obscuring the late evening sun that had dipped low on the horizon. Some time after 6:30 P.M., after delivering a short speech to each company in his force, he ordered the column to move out. The long line of infantry, cavalry, artillery caissons, ammunition wagons, and ambulances moved slowly into the darkening night. Shortly after their departure, a light rain began to fall, turning into a constant drizzle after several hours. The troops began their march with songs and lively conversation, but shortly after 1 A.M., Lyon ordered all talk in the ranks to cease, for they were only a few miles from the enemy's camp. For the next three hours, the march proved extremely cautious, with constant interruptions while scouts reconnoitered the terrain ahead of the column. At 4:15, the troops were halted and told to lay on their arms in a hayfield until daylight, four miles from their slumbering foe.[5]

As the men searched for bedding spots among the numerous limestone outcroppings interspersed on the hillside, Maj. John Schofield, Lyon's aide, found a small, cavelike hollow between two boulders. Dutifully, he asked his commander if he would care to share it with him. Lyon consented, and the two men crawled in and attempted to snatch some much-needed rest. Sleep, however, would come to neither.

Crouching in the darkness, sharing a rubber blanket, each man was too preoccupied with his own thoughts to find rest. Schofield did not understand what could possibly have possessed his commander, with less than five thousand troops, to attack an obviously superior force, and even dare to split his outnumbered army in doing so. Having been an instructor of military science after graduating from West Point, Schofield knew that Lyon's strategy countered every principle that the major had ever taught. He could find no reason for such an audacious move; it defied both logic and sound military principles. But Schofield did not fully understand his commander, this queer little man with an uncontrollable temper who evoked either terror or anger from so many around him. Having known Lyon but for a few months, the major could not

4. Adamson, *Rebellion in Missouri*, 217, 222–23.
5. Ibid., 222–23; Thomas W. Knox, *Camp-fire and Cotton Field: Southern Adventure in Time of War*, 68.

possibly have comprehended his commander's deepest motives, nor understood his complex personality. Yet he knew well enough that once this man made up his mind to do something, no power on earth could dissuade him from that purpose. Lyon would either be right or wrong in his decision; there could be no partial outcome.[6]

Yet the enigma surrounding the diminutive Federal commander traveled far beyond Schofield's bewilderment. Lyon's actions in Missouri between February and August 1861 had aroused strong feelings in both the state and other sections of the country. He had even steeped himself in controversy as far away as Washington, where some—like the president—merely viewed him with misgivings, while others held him with intense distrust. His cyclonic arrival upon the St. Louis scene had taken the entire nation by surprise, and his unbridled adherence to the precepts of the Union had forced a neutral Missouri into a war within itself. Many, like Schofield, wondered who this man was and where he had come from. Those few who were familiar with Lyon's background knew that he had been in the military for two decades, had played an active role in the nation's last war, and also was a participant in the unfolding of one of the nation's most turbulent political controversies. What even Schofield did not realize was that Lyon's actions at the outbreak of the Civil War were the logical consequence of Lyon's violent, dogmatic personality, formulated by his family roots and shaped during a brief yet tempestuous life and career. Schofield did not know enough about Lyon's past or understand his thought processes sufficiently to be able to gauge the general's goals and methods accurately; hence, the major sat in the rain-soaked darkness, brooding about his commander's apparently ill-conceived plan for the morrow's attack.

As the minutes passed, Schofield apologized to his commander for the obviously uncomfortable surroundings he had chosen. After a few seconds, he received a gruff reply, uttered with a distinct nasal twang: "I'm quite alright. Back in Connecticut, where I come from, I was born and bred among rocks."[7]

<hr />

6. Schofield, *Forty-six Years in the Army*, 28–31, 42.
7. Jay Monaghan, *Civil War on the Western Border, 1854–1865*, 169; Augustus Meyers, "Dakota in the Fifties," 129.

I

Born Among the Rocks

On May 25, 1798, Ephraim Lyon struggled for his last breath, then quietly expired at his rural home in the far eastern section of Ashford, Connecticut. Though by New England standards, Ephraim, at sixty-one, was by no means an old man, his death surprised no member of the Lyon family. A lengthy illness had deteriorated the old man's health beyond recovery, and while the family patriarch's early demise grieved all those near him, each recognized that Ephraim had packed a great deal of living into his threescore years.[1]

The third successive member of his branch of the Lyon family to bear his given name, Ephraim settled in Ashford more of necessity than of choice. The colony's earliest settlers had claimed the most desirable farmland, located either in the Connecticut River valley or along the southern coast bordering Long Island Sound. The coastal lands had filled first, followed by the great, fertile river valley. This left only the rocky hills beyond either horizon, and those who came late had little recourse but to purchase lands lying either northwest or northeast of the great valley. Consequently, Ephraim Lyon made his way to Ashford, in Windham County.[2]

Named for the hardwoods that blanketed the area, Ashford was first settled in 1710. Farming was the region's principal occupation. Yet, though Ashford lay on the "Connecticut Path," the main thoroughfare between Boston and Hartford, the community never flourished as an agricultural center. The nearby Natchaug River proved little more than a stream and therefore wholly unnavigable, making production less profitable owing to the high cost of overland transportation to Norwich, the closest outlet to the tidewater ports. Moreover, a combination of steep

1. Connecticut Vital Records, Ashford Township, Barbour Collection, CSL; Will of Ephraim Lyon, Pomfret District Probate Records, CSL.
2. Jarvis M. Morse, *A Neglected Period of Connecticut History, 1818–1850*, 7–8; Ashbel Woodward, *Life of General Nathaniel Lyon*, 350.

hill ranges and marshy lowlands rendered much of the surrounding land useless for farming. Finally, what level land *was* available proved so choked with stones, and the toil required to turn the soil so unremitting, that fields were invariably small and relatively unprofitable, and farms were predominantly self-sufficient. Only a small number of the populace ever achieved a high degree of prosperity. Not surprisingly, few slaves reached Windham County; there was simply no economic reason for them. Yet Ephraim Lyon remained determined to make a life in Ashford, and with youthful energy he cleared a small, hilly tract on the west side of the Natchaug.[3]

A short stint in the Connecticut militia during the Seven Years' War temporarily delayed Ephraim's plans for completing his homestead; but in 1762, shortly after his return to Ashford, he married a local girl, Esther Bennett. Ephraim's patriotic service had helped to ensure him a measure of social respectability in Ashford, and the community soon accepted him into their ranks. Within a year, Esther bore their first child, Nathan, and every second year for the next ten years, another child was added to the growing Lyon brood.[4]

The outbreak of the war for independence interrupted this pattern only briefly. In April 1775, when news of the bloodshed at Lexington and Concord reached Ashford, Ephraim became swept up in the general patriotic fervor. Though thirty-eight, he once again shouldered his flint-lock and enlisted in the fourth company of the Third Connecticut Volunteer Infantry. The colonel of the regiment, Israel Putnam, was a respected tavernkeeper from nearby Brooklyn. Rumor had it that upon hearing of the fight at Concord, Putnam, a former representative to the General Assembly and active member of the local Sons of Liberty, left his plow in the field—still hitched to the mule—and hastened to the scene of operations without even changing clothes. The men of the fifth company elected Thomas Knowlton, a well-liked farmer from western Ashford, as captain of their unit. Ephraim was sufficiently respected by the men of his company to be elected first lieutenant. However, the rigors of military service quickly took their toll on him. Without grown sons to run

3. Morse, *Neglected Period,* 8–9; Allen B. Lincoln, ed., *A Modern History of Windham County, Connecticut,* 235–40; Diane Maher Cameron, *Eastford: The Biography of a New England Town,* 1; U.S. Census, 1790, Windham County, Conn.

4. Connecticut Vital Records, Ashford Township, CSL; Willard Glazier, *Heroes of Three Wars,* 392; Woodward, *Life of Nathaniel Lyon,* 350–51.

the farm, Ephraim resigned his commission after a year and returned home.[5]

Following his return from the war, Ephraim threw all his energy into expanding his farm to keep pace with his rapidly growing family and perhaps to take advantage of the wartime demand for foodstuffs. In addition, he commenced a study of the law. The reasons for his interest in the legal profession are not known, but as early as 1779 he demonstrated a sufficient competency to begin a limited practice in and around Ashford. Country lawyers commanded far less remuneration than those practicing the profession in Boston or New Haven, but Ephraim's practice prospered modestly, and local residents respected his abilities enough to refer to him as "Lawyer Lyon."[6]

As Ephraim's eldest sons, Nathan and Ephraim, Jr., grew to young manhood, he turned over the farm to their capable hands and concentrated on his law practice. The additional income generated by his business allowed him to speculate in land, and by 1789 he had accumulated over four hundred acres worth over $3,600, including a sawmill on the east side of the Natchaug. Though relatively new and worth only about $100, the mill appeared to hold the potential for a lucrative business operation. For this reason alone Ephraim might have looked upon it as a worthwhile investment, but he had another motivation for entering the lumber business: the mill had captured the imagination of his third son, Amasa.[7]

Ephraim appears to have always shared a special affinity with his third son. Amasa, more than any of the other children, grew to emulate his father. He listened entranced to his father's stories of the great war with England and proved to be the only one of Ephraim's sons to display more than passing interest in their father's profession. As the boy matured, Ephraim lodged a considerable amount of trust in his son. Amasa's interest in the mill greatly pleased his father, and though the boy was only

5. Charles J. Hoadly, ed., *The Public Records of Connecticut,* 14:426; "Israel Putnam," *Dictionary of American Biography,* 15:281–82; Woodward, *Life of Nathaniel Lyon,* 18.

6. Receipt for State Rate, prepared by Ephraim Lyon, October 12, 1779, Miscellaneous Manuscripts, MassHS; Will of Ephraim Lyon, Pomfret District Probate Records, CSL; Ashford Township Land Deeds, CSL; Woodward, *Life of Nathaniel Lyon,* 18–20.

7. Woodward, *Life of Nathaniel Lyon,* 350–51; Will of Ephraim Lyon, Pomfret District Probate Records, CSL; Robert J. Taylor, *Colonial Connecticut: A History,* 153.

in his teens, Ephraim felt confident that this fascination involved more than adolescent caprice. Consequently, after Ephraim bought the mill, he allowed Amasa to supervise its operations, though not to the extent that it interfered with his responsibilities on the farm.[8]

Not surprisingly, Amasa inherited the mill at his father's death. Bypassing his two eldest sons, Ephraim made his third son coexecutor of his estate, a genuine display of trust and respect. Each of the four sons inherited a sixth of the real estate (amounting to sixty-six acres each), and the boys would also equally divide Esther's share (totaling 120 acres) upon her death. Because Nathan had already acquired his share of the inheritance and had established his own homestead, Amasa and Ephraim, Jr., tended the family farm. However, Amasa found far more pleasure in working the sawmill and consequently devoted most of his time to its operation. By the turn of the century, Amasa, at age twenty-nine, with land and a small-yet-established business in hand, appeared well on his way to a successful career.[9]

Yet Amasa Lyon appears less conformable to community mores than his father had been. He exhibited a fiercely independent spirit, which the local populace (clinging to the corporatist mentality of most New England communities) often received with less than complete approbation. Always a free thinker, he was rarely diffident about fully articulating his views. On one occasion, he proved a center of contention in local political debate. During the presidential campaign of 1800, in the face of a predominantly Federalist constituency, he dared to campaign actively for the Democratic-Republican candidate Thomas Jefferson. And if this were not enough to raise the ire of the locals, Amasa also proved an infrequent churchgoer.[10]

Partly from residing a hilly and inconvenient four miles from town, and partly from being caught up in his own work, Amasa found little time for church affairs. While never going to the extreme of professing infidelity—at least not publicly—he made well known his belief that two services on Sundays placed too many constraints upon his time. Although the moral restraints that Puritanism placed on society had loosed somewhat in the years following the war for independence, they had by no means relinquished their hold. Despite this pressure, many like

8. Will of Ephraim Lyon, Pomfret Probate Records, CSL; Susan Griggs, *Folklore and Firesides in Pomfret and Hampton,* 157; Nathaniel Lyon, *Last Political Writings of General Nathaniel Lyon, U.S.A.,* 11.

9. Will of Ephraim Lyon, Pomfret District Probate Records, CSL.

10. Woodward, *Life of Nathaniel Lyon,* 20.

Amasa had dropped from the ranks of the more conspicuous churchgoers. Although his unconformable behavior failed to gain him the patronage of his more pious neighbors, it apparently did not cost him his business. His strident personality, however, certainly failed to make him many friends.[11]

Although locals thought Amasa obstinate, even downright odd, his eccentricities did not prevent him from winning the hand of Kezia Knowlton, daughter of a prosperous local farmer and hero in the war for independence, Daniel Knowlton. Both Daniel and his brother, Thomas, were revered locally for their services to the country. Daniel, a veteran of the war with the French and a commissioned lieutenant in the late war, had acted as one of the chief scouts for the New England revolutionary forces. Israel Putnam, by that time a general, once lauded his scout's great value by saying, "Such is his courage and want of fear that I could order him into the mouth of a loaded cannon . . . he alone is worth half a company."[12]

While Daniel achieved fame, Thomas Knowlton earned immortality. After being elected captain of his company, he replaced Israel Putnam as colonel of the Third Connecticut when Putnam rose to the rank of general. At the battle of Bunker Hill he commanded a small force that anchored the American left from behind hay and fence-post defenses to the north of Breed's Hill. This detachment sharply repulsed the initial attack of the British flanking force and compelled the British commander, Gen. William Howe, to alter his battle plan. He recalled the flanking column, put them into line with those troops currently contesting the redoubt on Breed's Hill, and sent repeated assaults against the entrenched forces on that hill. The final attack forced the Americans from the heights, but not before the British had taken nearly 50 percent casualties. Knowlton's men then kept up a sufficient fire to protect the retreating Americans and quite probably saved the entire army. Killed on September 16, 1776, while commanding the rear guard at Harlem Heights, New York, Thomas Knowlton's legacy eclipsed even that of Israel Putnam in the Ashford area.[13]

11. "Eastford Congregational Church Records, 1777–1941," vol. 2, ETH; Will of Amasa Lyon, Ashford Township Probate Records, ATH; Richard J. Purcell, *Connecticut in Transition, 1775–1818*, 7–8; Cameron, *Eastford*, 24–25.

12. Woodward, *Life of Nathaniel Lyon*, 23–24, 354–55; Arthur W. Keith to L. W. Cleaveland, December 8, 1913, Nathaniel Lyon Papers, CHS; Lyon Genealogy, Nathaniel Lyon Papers, CSL.

13. Robert Middlekauff, *The Glorious Cause*, 283, 292, 349; Woodward, *Life of Nathaniel Lyon*, 22. Middlekauff has judged Knowlton "one of the best regimental commanders" in the Continental Army.

Daniel Knowlton's stature in the community could easily have intimidated a potential suitor for his third daughter's hand, especially one with
a somewhat controversial reputation. Amasa, however, was undaunted.
Though Kezia, at twenty-three, was nearly ten years Amasa's junior,
Daniel probably took Ephraim Lyon's reputation into consideration
when he granted his consent to the marriage and set aside a half-acre
tract for a dowry. Amasa and Kezia wed on January 3, 1805, and settled
into the small house next to his mill.[14]

Amasa continued to devote what time he could to the mill, and
during the growing season he assisted with the family farm, now operated jointly by brothers Ephraim, Jr., and James. In May 1805, Amasa
sold some acreage to a brother-in-law, Nathan Burnham, in order to
make improvements on the house and mill. A year later, on Independence Day, Kezia gave birth to their first child, a son, whom they named
Amasa Knowlton. Three years later, she bore a second son, Marcus.
The infant died of unknown causes within ten months of its birth, but
by the spring of 1811 Kezia was again pregnant. The responsibilities of
fatherhood proved a powerful incentive for Amasa. Seeing a need
to provide for his burgeoning family, he made a major career move.
He quit the family farm in favor of a full-time commitment to the
sawmill.[15]

By 1811, Ashford had become the county's second-largest town,
boasting an aggregate population of 2,532. A corresponding increase in
the demand for lumber accompanied the town's growth, as farms continued to be cleared and homes and barns erected. Amasa was hard-
pressed to keep up with demand, and he saw greater potential for his mill
than for his farmland. Besides, he had always enjoyed turning a saw
blade far more than turning the soil. Therefore, Amasa sold to Nathan
the rights to his ninety-six acres, lying primarily on the west side of the
river, in return for a thirty-acre tract owned by Ephraim, lying near the
sawmill on the east side of the Natchaug. In this way, Amasa acquired a
small yet ample homestead and timber acreage near the mill, plus the

14. Woodward, *Life of Nathaniel Lyon,* 354–55; Lyon Genealogy, Nathaniel Lyon
Papers, CSL; Ashford Township Land Records, CSL.

15. Ashford Township Land Records, CSL; Woodward, *Life of Nathaniel Lyon,*
351; U.S. Census, 1810, Windham County, Conn.; Lyon Genealogy, Nathaniel Lyon
Papers, CSL; "Connecticut Headstone Inscriptions," vol. 35 (Eastford), 54–57, Charles
R. Hale Collection, CSL.

capital with which to enhance his lumbering operation. By effecting the transaction with his brothers, Amasa Lyon became a full-time miller.[16]

The land Amasa purchased lay in the southeasternmost section of Ashford, in what was then called the Pilfershire district. This district, according to tradition, was so named for the deceptive proclivities of certain of its former residents who, though apparently keeping neither livestock nor poultry, remained constantly supplied with both. Consequently, Ashford natives assumed the animals had been purloined from neighboring farms. The epithet remained long after the names of the original culprits had been forgotten.[17]

Amasa built his new home in a relatively level clearing adjacent to the Hampton Road. Nestled amid the native maples, ashes, and other hardwoods at the base of the southern tip of the area's dominant ridge, the land was bounded on the east by a large marsh and on the west by a steep, 150-foot declension to the Natchaug. The homesite itself lay just south of a small slough, which Amasa used as a natural hog wallow. Granite stones of all sizes littered the ground, some too mammoth to move. These boulders he simply worked around, while the rocks Amasa was able to pull from the ground served for stone fences to bound his fields and livestock lots. On a slight rise about twenty rods off the main road, Amasa built his new home—a one-story frame and clapboard structure, with a roof pitched sufficiently to allow for a two-chambered sleeping loft. Anchoring the structure, and rising from its center, stood an impressive granite chimney, constructed of stones from the surrounding landscape, and boasting first-floor hearths on three separate sides. Each was capped by a massive, squared hearthstone. The kitchen hearth also contained a small oven, set into the chimney and bricked for heat retention. The finished structure, constructed with hand-crafted nails, received a coat of red iron-oxide paint every year or so. Amasa's sawmill afforded him great advantages in building his home, as well as for the barn and outbuildings that he erected soon after completion of the

16. Ashford Township Land Records, CSL; U.S. Census, 1810, Windham County, Conn.

17. Bruce C. Daniels, *The Connecticut Town: Growth and Development, 1635–1790*, 22–23; Woodward, *Life of Nathaniel Lyon*, 25; Martha F. Child, "The Lion-hearted General," 41; O. W. Gray, *Atlas of Windham and Tolland Counties, Connecticut*, 26. Ashford divided into two separate townships in 1847; the eastern portion (including the Lyon homestead) took the name of Eastford.

house. While no mansion, the Lyon home place drew from its neighbors a healthy respect.[18]

In the next several years, however, Amasa's business fortunes fell upon hard times. Several other sawmills opened near Ashford, and Amasa lost more and more of the local market he had once hoped to capture. Moreover, the town's rapid growth slowed somewhat, and in the next decade the population increased by only about 250, principally from new births. Several of those new offspring hailed from Amasa's own family. Between the fall of 1811 and the spring of 1815, Kezia gave birth to two daughters, Delotia and Sophronia, and a son, Lorenzo. This rapid growth of his family, coupled with lower profits from the sawmill, caused Amasa to reevaluate his career choice. He decided to enter farming again and in May bought a tract of land from his brother Ephraim. Several days later, he and James made a joint purchase of two more tracts, amounting to one hundred acres. He continued to operate the mill, but once more as a sideline to farming.[19]

Rather than embittering him, however, this setback appears instead to have somewhat mollified Amasa's maverick tendencies. Although he never became a model for Ashford society, he began to work within the community more than ever before. However, he could never bring himself to attend church with any regularity. It was Kezia, no doubt pained by Amasa's impiety, who contributed modestly to the annual "sale of the slips." Thus, she ensured the family a pew, though it was located in the back of the church, far from where the congregation's most generous contributors issued forth their weekly praises in conspicuous attendance. Local residents, however, do not appear to have held Amasa's impiety against him any longer. As early as 1832, he had attained sufficient standing in the community to be appointed a local magistrate by the state legislature. Averaging seven to a town, these magistrates acted as justices of the peace, charged with such duties as advising on the executive affairs of the community, assisting with local elections, hearing local civil and criminal cases (not exceeding a nominal sum of money), and performing marriages. This position of authority proved vital in the small, sequestered towns of rural New England, and Amasa soon affixed the custom-

18. Lyon, *Last Political Writings*, 16; Woodward, *Life of Nathaniel Lyon*, 25; "Report of the Commission Appointed to Improve the Burial Place of General Nathaniel Lyon at Eastford, Connecticut," 8; Griggs, *Folklore and Firesides*, 157.

19. U.S. Census, 1810 and 1820, Windham County, Conn.; Woodward, *Life of Nathaniel Lyon*, 351; Ashford Township Land Records, CSL; Cameron, *Eastford*, 3.

ary "Esquire" to his signature as a mark of distinction. However, it had taken time for Amasa to earn this esteem, and his early struggle to rise from the pewter-plate class (which he would never manage to leave) proved agonizing for a man of Amasa Lyon's temperament. Although he eventually gained the respect of his peers, Amasa would never achieve his father's level of success.[20]

Between the fall of 1816 and the spring of 1822, Kezia bore four more children: another daughter, Elizabeth Ann; and then three successive sons. The first of those sons was born on July 14, 1818. After her own older brother, Kezia named the child Nathaniel.[21]

As with his other children, Amasa put young Nathaniel to work around the farm as soon as he could gather eggs or feed the livestock. As he grew older, hours of work in the fields with his father and brothers quickly hardened young Nathaniel's small, sinewy frame. However, free time from chores and other farm responsibilities (sometimes involving work in the fields of neighboring farmers) found him scampering with his brothers to one of the nearby marshes to gig bullfrogs. Growing up in such a rural area (the homestead of the closest neighbor, John Griggs, lay a third of a mile across the marshes to the east) promoted family unity, and the Lyon clan proved no exception. However, much of this familial cohesion developed despite, rather than as a result of, the family's patriarch, for life with Amasa Lyon often proved harsh.[22]

While struggling to regain his economic footing, Amasa demanded much of his sons. To make matters worse, the unexpected death in 1822 of the Lyon's eldest son, Amasa Knowlton, just a month following his sixteenth birthday appears to have markedly soured Amasa's disposition. His younger sons, especially Lorenzo and Nathaniel, bore the brunt of his displaced anger. This is not to say that Amasa did not love his sons.

20. "Eastford Congregational Church Records," vol. 2, ETH; "Connecticut Vital Records," 35:109; Griggs, *Folklore and Firesides,* 157; Will of Amasa Lyon, Ashford Township Probate Records, ATH; Lyon, *Last Political Writings,* 11; J. Griggs and R. Torrey to Lewis Cass, December 1, 1836, United States Military Academy Application File of Nathaniel Lyon, Record Group 94, Records of the Adjutant General's Office, National Archives (hereafter cited as RG 94); Purcell, *Connecticut in Transition,* 132–33; Taylor, *Colonial Connecticut,* 152; Morse, *Neglected Period,* 101; Lincoln, *History of Windham County,* 2:402.

21. Lyon Genealogy, Nathaniel Lyon Papers, CSL; Woodward, *Life of Nathaniel Lyon,* 351, 355.

22. Nathaniel Lyon to Lorenzo Lyon, April 9, 1853, Hoadley Collection, CHS; Lyon, *Last Political Writings,* 17; Gray, *Atlas of Windham and Tolland Counties,* 26.

However, the sorrow of his eldest son's death combined with his frustrating drive to succeed in a calling that he believed was not truly his own weighed heavily upon his shoulders. It does not appear that Amasa could adequately express affection for his remaining sons. As a result, the boys had little chance to regard their father other than as either a taskmaster or disciplinarian. This rigidly defined filial relationship worked lasting effects on young Nathaniel, for it formed the core of his own later perceptions of relationships with—and power over—others in his charge.[23]

In an effort to find warmth in his family, Nathaniel turned to his mother. Kezia offered what Amasa most often could not: a genuine, demonstrable love for all her children. The boy appears to have grown particularly devoted to his mother, and he listened with relish to her stories of the exploits of her father and uncle in the patriot wars. This special relationship became apparent even to many of the local townspeople. A local farmer recalled that "Nathaniel . . . was smart, daring, and resolute, and wonderfully attached to his mother." Most had long before noticed that this young Lyon had inherited many of the typical Knowlton characteristics: close-set eyes, long, thin nose, narrow cleft chin, small, thin mouth, high forehead, and, most noticeably, an unruly crop of red hair. Perhaps a combination of these qualities and her son's small stature served to spark Kezia's obvious endearment to the boy. Yet, while young Nathaniel appeared to be a Knowlton by heredity, he was indeed a Lyon in temperament.[24]

Nathaniel Lyon appears to have been an exceptionally serious child, often to the extent of dourness. Yet, like his father and grandfather, he possessed a short fuse that often exploded with surprising fury beyond all sense of reason. Records from his school years indicate a penchant for fisticuffs; on at least one occasion the boy's temper even provoked him to take on more than one combatant at a time. After he reacted to a practical joke played upon him by some schoolmates, "two or three found themselves suddenly prostrate, with a pair of fists vigorously at work in uncomfortable and dangerous proximity to their person." He seems to have been able to brook neither criticism nor jest, and he appears to have learned early on that a firm resolve and an aggressive

23. Lyon Genealogy, Nathaniel Lyon Papers, CSL; Nathaniel Lyon to John B. Hasler, July 7, 1843, Nathaniel Lyon Papers, AAS.

24. Lyon, *Last Political Writings,* 17; Woodward, *Life of Nathaniel Lyon,* 29; Richard Ketchum, ed., *The American Heritage Book of the Revolution,* 184.

offense could make up for his lack of physical size. For one so young, his perceptions of right and wrong were inordinately rigid—no doubt a reflection of his father's firm hand—and once he made a decision, he clung to it tenaciously. Family legend holds that tales of his Knowlton ancestors, which he had heard for as long as he could remember, influenced the boy early in life to decide upon the military for a career. However, preparation for the military academy depended upon success at the local school.[25]

Like all children in the Pilfershire district, Nathaniel attended the brown clapboard, single-room schoolhouse erected for the use of the residents of the district. As early as 1650, Connecticut law charged town selectmen with making sure that each child be educated, either by their parents or by hired teachers. Rural towns like Ashford did not escape this decree, and each district supported and governed a local school. The Pilfershire schoolmaster was neighbor John Griggs, who served in the same schoolhouse for nearly sixty years and who taught more than three thousand students during his long tenure.[26]

During his school years, Nathaniel Lyon demonstrated a decided aptitude for mathematics. Its rigid rationality was comforting, and he pursued the subject with zeal. He also displayed a natural predilection for declamatory speeches, especially patriotic ones. Stories of the noble Knowltons, coupled with Ephraim Lyon's musket, which hung prominently over the main hearth of the Lyon home (along with Ephraim's cartridge boxes and greatcoat, all of which Amasa inherited from his father), had long ago stimulated both Nathaniel's imagination and love of country. His school, therefore, often served as his patriotic rostrum.[27]

Connecticut schools at this time taught more than basic skills. Morals and manners were an important part of the students' daily "blab" lessons, and instructors placed particular emphasis on the development of character. Indeed, in 1839 the Ashford School Visitors (roughly a nineteenth-century equivalent of a board of education, which was open to all local white males qualified to vote at the town meeting) adopted a set of guidelines vesting the schoolmaster with, among other things, the responsibility to "suppress Vice and immorality among their scholars es-

---

25. Woodward, *Life of Nathaniel Lyon,* 25–27.

26. Griggs, *Folklore and Firesides,* 155–57; Cameron, *Eastford,* 57; Morse, *Neglected Period,* 143–44.

27. Woodward. *Life of Nathaniel Lyon,* 26; Will of Ephraim Lyon, Pomfret District Probate Records, CSL.

pecially lying, profane swearing and quarrelling, and that they punish
exemplary all who are guilty of these crimes while under their care."[28]

These directives merely codified long-standing New England educational practices. Many of the primers used in these schools were replete
with readings designed to instill tangible tenets of republicanism: moral
uprightness, equality, citizenship, and perhaps most of all, civic virtue.
Often effusively patriotic, writings of this sort abounded in the early
years of the republic. Nathaniel's reader, published in 1829, proved no
exception. Its title page read: "The English Reader, or Pieces in Prose
and Verse from the Best Writers Designed to Assist Young Persons to
Read with Propriety and to Improve their Language . . . and to Inculcate
the Most Important Principles of Piety and Virtue."[29]

In early nineteenth-century Connecticut, a virtuous education meant
a pious education. Although the new state constitution, ratified in 1818,
had effectively overthrown the established church and thereby legally
separated it from the state's educational system, the document enjoined
only that no preference be given by law to any one denomination. Hence,
general religious indoctrination continued to be a salient feature of daily
school activities. The Ashford School Visitors "highly recommended that
a portion of the Holy Scriptures be read after the other exercises of the
school and the whole be concluded with prayer." School primers reflected
this philosophy, and along with discourses in patriotism, the students
also received a daily dose of religious indoctrination.[30]

While the lessons of virtue and patriotism were not lost on young
Nathaniel Lyon, religion served only to confuse the boy. During his
formative years his mother had on Sundays carted him and all his other
siblings to church, where he learned of an omniscient and omnipotent
God who ruled the events of the universe with infinite wisdom. In both
church and school he learned that election to God's grace depended upon
his thoughts and especially his actions in this world. His Scripture lessons taught him that "God will bring every deed into judgment, includ-

28. Lincoln, *History of Windham County,* 2:246–47; Morse, *Neglected Period,* 144n.

29. Lyon's School Primer, Nathaniel Lyon File, Eastford Historical Society, ETH;
Sean Wilentz, *Chants Democratic: New York City and the Rise of the American Working
Class, 1788–1850,* 14–15. The primer was used by Lyon between the ages of fourteen
and fifteen, and afterward by his brother Daniel. The book was printed in 1829 by
Lindley Murray, New London, W. and J. Bolles and Collins and Hanway, New York,
Publishers.

30. Morse, *Neglected Period,* 3; Lincoln, *History of Windham County,* 246–47.

ing every hidden thing, whether it is good or evil." And he trembled at the thought that the Creator's divine ledger, kept on every Christian soul, would balance in favor of eternal damnation rather than salvation. Nathaniel Lyon absorbed these teachings, yet he lived in a divided world.[31]

If, as he had heard from both lectern and pulpit, salvation depended upon an incessant effort to abide by God's holy precepts, Nathaniel's own father appeared destined for hell. Not only did Amasa Lyon fail to attend church (despite Kezia's efforts to ensure the rest of the family's attendance), but his eldest son's death further strained his confidence in organized religion. In Amasa's mind, the unjust tragedy demonstrated that the Creator acts in the events of man regardless of one's pious actions; his young son could never have deserved such a fate. Kezia found comfort in rationalizing that although the Lord's purposes often seem arcane, his wisdom is indeed just. Amasa, however, found such logic flawed and rejected its most obvious proponent: the Church.

The situation unavoidably affected young Nathaniel. Though too young to understand the arguments fully, he found his father's bitterness unmistakable. As he grew older and ingested more of the teachings of his religion, there developed in him a distinct confusion when trying to harmonize his mother's unwavering devotion to the church and his father's obvious impiety. This dilemma proved intractable to the youth, but served to spark an incipient questioning of the validity of religion and the ultimate role of God in man's existence.

From this background, Nathaniel Lyon emerged, an ambitious young man, driven by a need for discipline in his life, yet plagued by a vexing question: who controlled man's destiny—God, or man himself? As he developed into manhood, his desire for order in his life manifested itself in a growing aspiration to make the military his career and to secure appointment to the United States Military Academy at West Point, New York. Obtaining this, however, presented something of a problem; at the time of his graduation in the spring of 1837, no vacancy presented itself from Nathaniel's home district. However, a vacancy *was* scheduled to open in the western district of Connecticut at that time, and the boy set his sights on procuring that appointment. No doubt the prestige of having his son attend the academy—and the lure of a free education— encouraged Amasa to assist his son in getting it.[32]

31. Lyon to John B. Hasler, December 5, 1840, Nathaniel Lyon Papers, AAS.

32. Woodward, *Life of Nathaniel Lyon,* 28–29; Edward M. Coffman, *The Old Army: A Portrait of the American Army in Peacetime, 1784–1898,* 48.

In November of 1836, before he graduated from his district school, Nathaniel began requesting the recommendations necessary for appointment. His schoolmaster, his Congregational minister, and a former representative to the U.S. House of Representatives each wrote letters to the secretary of war attesting Nathaniel's "fair moral character," lauding his "reputation of a good scholar," and describing how his "talents and application for the acquisition of knowledge will lose nothing in a comparison with any of his peers." However, these testimonials to the young man's solid potential as an officer might not have resulted in appointment were it not for the efforts of one of Amasa's acquaintances, Eastford resident Flagg Keyes, a personal friend of Orrin Holt, U.S. representative from Connecticut's Third Congressional District. Through this connection, Keyes persuaded Congressman Holt to procure Nathaniel's appointment, and the lad received confirmation of it on March 1, 1837. This early lesson on the power of influence left a powerful impression on the young man's mind. On the fifteenth of that month, newly appointed cadet Nathaniel Lyon acknowledged his appointment, "highly gratified, that I have the honor to pledge myself to serve the United States, . . . and I hope I shall be able to prove myself worthy."[33]

33. John Griggs, Reuben Torrey, Andrew T. Judson, Ebenezer Stoddard, C. F. Cleveland, and Ichabod Bulkley to Lewis Cass, October–December 1836, United States Military Academy Application File of Nathaniel Lyon, RG 94; Nathaniel Lyon to Joel Poinsett, March 15, 1837, ibid.; Lincoln, *History of Windham County,* 2:397.

II

The School of the Soldier

Nathaniel Lyon graduated from his district school early in the spring of 1837. Although his tenure at the Pilfershire school had provided him with a strong educational foundation, the thought vexed him that his skills might prove insufficient for a successful cadetship at West Point. In particular, he worried about the June entrance examinations. Driven to succeed academically, and perhaps anticipating the hardships associated with being away from home for a long stretch of time, he convinced his father to enroll him temporarily at the private boarding academy at Brooklyn, about ten miles east of Ashford. In particular, Lyon sought to hone his mathematical skills in preparation for West Point's rigorous curriculum. He understood that the academy stressed that subject above all others.[1]

Lyon need not have feared West Point's entrance exams; in fact, entrance requirements were embarrassingly minimal. Any cadet who had completed the equivalent of a regular school education passed them without difficulty. Lyon proved no exception, and on July 1, 1837, "Plebe" Lyon (as the first-year appointees were called) officially entered the academy with over one hundred other young men. Fifty percent of them would never finish. Many left within the first few weeks, for adjustment to the environment at West Point was an experience a young man would forever remember, usually unpleasantly. In these early years of the academy, a plebe had more to contend with than continually juggling drill sessions and studies. Hazing was the sine qua non of cadetship, and those in the Fourth Class bore the brunt of often-vicious pranks from the entire upper corps of cadets. And if that were not enough, the program denied a cadet leave to return home at any time during his first two years, a regulation that in itself proved a high source of attrition.[2]

1. Ashbel Woodward, *Life of General Nathaniel Lyon,* 27; Stephen E. Ambrose, *Duty, Honor, Country,* 89–90.

2. Ambrose, *Duty, Honor, Country,* 83–84; Woodward, *Life of Nathaniel Lyon,* 32;

At a month under nineteen years of age, Nathaniel Lyon entered West Point still more a boy than a man. Five feet five inches tall and weighing not more than 130 pounds, he was small even by 1837 standards. His sandy red hair and smooth face, however innocent, only belied a firm resolve to succeed as a soldier. However much he strove to prepare himself for those difficult first few months, the realities of cadetship soon managed to call forth in him one foible of youth: homesickness.[3]

Of all the early trials encountered at West Point, Lyon found this period away from his parents (particularly his mother) especially difficult; it certainly proved more trying than his brief sojourn at the Brooklyn Academy. In a letter written home in August 1838, he reflected on the sorely missed comforts of home: "Where it does not conflict too much with interest, a young man should delight to remain with his parents, conferring and receiving happiness from the interchange of kindly offices." Somewhat overwritten (perhaps to impress his parents with his newfound eloquence), the note nonetheless conveys Lyon's sense of loneliness after a long year away from home.[4]

Yet the hardships of West Point did not end after the initial seasoning period; indeed, they had only begun. The entire four-year stay proved grueling for most cadets. In its effort to mold the young men into officers, the academy attempted to instill more than military bearing. Its leaders undertook to produce both soldiers and Christian gentlemen, and in doing so stood in loco parentis over the moral, physical, and even mental aspects of the student's development. This regimen, emphasizing the precepts of "duty, honor, country," sought to turn out the military's finest soldiers. Attaining perfection, however, placed a terrible strain on its cadets.[5]

The travails of a cadet's daily regimen rarely allowed for more than seven hours of sleep a night. However, considering that the demanding schedule forced most to risk demerits by studying well after lights-out simply to stay abreast of their coursework, it is doubtful they found

---

George W. Cullum, *Biographical Register of the Officers and Graduates of the U.S. Military Academy at West Point, N. Y.,* vol. 2, title page. The United States Military Academy was founded in 1802.

3. Register of the Officers and Cadets of the U.S. Military Academy, 1818–1850, USMA; "Memorandum on Missouri," 6, Franklin A. Dick Papers, LOC.

4. Woodward, *Life of Nathaniel Lyon,* 29.

5. Stephen E. Ambrose, "The Monotonous Life," 22; Ambrose, *Duty, Honor, Country,* 66.

regularly even that much rest. Furnishings were spartan, for academy regulations allowed no decorative adornments in the quarters. Cadets never actually saw their monthly pay of twenty-eight dollars; it was placed on account at the commissary from which they bought their sundry necessities. On Sundays (their only day off), cadets' schedules required them to attend church service—much to the chagrin of the bulk of the corps—and any desired trip off the post required an authorized leave from the commandant. Such passes, however, were customarily denied on the grounds that most cadets had exceeded their credit at the commissary. And as post regulations strictly forbade leaving the post without authorization, so did they prohibit the consumption of alcohol. A short sojourn to any of the taverns in nearby Highland Falls proved quite risky, for offenders caught in such establishments would have two grounds for demerit.[6]

No hardship endured by the cadets was perhaps more lamented than the food served in the mess hall. The menu was monotonously simple: boiled meat, boiled potatoes, boiled pudding, bread, and coffee. Stolen poultry from local farmers, brought back to the rooms and cooked in the fireplace, afforded a deviation from the culinary monotony, but even these "hash" sessions were rare. Atypically, however, Cadet Lyon appears to have approved of the food at the academy, even writing home that he was "getting fleshy on Mess Hall fare."[7]

In the place of a summer vacation, cadets at West Point participated in a ten-week summer encampment, during which they engaged in a simulation of field duty. Only after their Third Class (sophomore) year could a cadet apply for furlough to return home during this period, representing the only such opportunity during their tenure at the academy. Most recently promoted Second Class cadets took advantage of this chance to escape cadetship temporarily and left during that time, while the remainder of the corps donned their white summer trousers, pitched their shelter tents on the parade ground, and camped most of the summer there. The encampment tended to be a welcome change from the regular schedule. Lyon, however, opted gladly to return home to Ashford.[8]

Nathaniel Lyon appears for the most part to have weathered the tempests of cadetship quite well. "On the whole," he wrote, "you may

6. Ambrose, "Monotonous Life," 22–23.

7. Ibid., 25–26; Lyon to John B. Hasler, December 5, 1840, Nathaniel Lyon Papers, AAS.

8. Ambrose, "Monotonous Life," 27–28.

consider us a rather comfortable set here . . . . I am not always at leasure to write when I would like to . . . . But I am disposed to make the best I can of a cadet's life; you must therefore consider me pretty well contented." Lyon thrived on the exacting regimen that formed the core of a soldier's existence. Indeed, the strict discipline of military life fulfilled a great part of his search for order. Military discipline afforded him an escape from the incongruities of his past, and a sense of duty now became his guiding force. One acquaintance remembered him to possess "a morbid tenacity for [the] strictest requirements . . . of a punctilious discharge of duty." In the army, he sought a rigid delineation of rights and wrongs; and after an initial "seasoning period" during which he learned those rules, his conduct rankings bear witness to a nearly exemplary soldier. Even during his first year at the academy, Lyon accumulated only thirty-four demerits, a small amount considering the inevitable difficulties of adjusting to the demands West Point exacted from each cadet. However, once he had learned the rules of conduct, Lyon proved nearly a model cadet.[9]

Despite the thirty-four demerits incurred during his Fourth Class year, Lyon still ranked an impressive thirty-ninth in the entire corps of cadets. With only seven demerits in his Third Class year, he stood twentieth, and in his Second Class year, his scant two demerits earned him twelfth in conduct from the entire corps. Indeed, only in his final year of cadetship does Lyon's fiery temper appear to have interfered with his high conduct ranking. In February 1841, after a slight altercation with the officer of the day, Lyon refused to turn over his orders to that officer. For this insubordination, a cadet court-martial "gigged" him for twelve demerits, his only infraction for the entire year. The incident cost him the chance to complete an academic year without demerit (no mean feat for any cadet), and probably also the chance to rank first in conduct for the entire corps of cadets.[10]

Though seemingly insignificant, this incident provides an early yet

9. Lyon to John B. Hasler, December 5, 1840, Nathaniel Lyon Papers, AAS; E. H. E. Jameson, ed., *A Memorial Wreath Containing an Address from the Lyon Monumental Association of St. Louis, Together with the Oration of Gov. B. Gratz Brown, Delivered January 11, 1866; and Remarks on the Life and Services of Gen. Nathaniel Lyon, by Gen. W. T. Sherman, Hon. Daniel S. Dickinson, and Others*, 22; Nathaniel Lyon Demerit Record, Register of Delinquencies, 1838–1842, USMA.

10. Conduct Rankings, Register of Officers and Cadets, 1838–1841, USMA; Nathaniel Lyon Demerit Record, Register of Delinquencies, 1838–1842, USMA.

important insight into Lyon's character. As Lyon's high conduct rankings attest, in three and a half years at West Point he had demonstrated the ability not just to conform to the mental demands of military discipline, but to excel in doing so. In maintaining a sense of military duty, underpinned by the academy's vaunted maxim, cadets were often forced to circumscribe their own desires and beliefs in order to succeed as soldiers. The confrontation with the other cadet reveals a perceptible limit to which Lyon was willing to carry West Point's philosophy of duty. Though the details of the incident are incomplete, it is apparent that Lyon was confronted with a situation that forced him to choose between what he had been taught to be fealty and what he believed to be injustice. In a fit of rage, Lyon placed his own sense of rightness over the military's—or anyone else's. Hence, in matters of extreme personal importance, Lyon, and Lyon alone, would dictate the terms of duty to which he would subscribe. While as yet Lyon's perception of duty as a rule conformed with that of the military, this early altercation is a harbinger of what would become his increasing predilection to reverse the pattern and conform the military's idea of duty to his own.

However well Lyon mastered army regimentation, his academic successes came only with considerable exertion. Although he grasped most mathematical concepts with ease, his skills proved insufficient to ensure an easy comprehension of calculus, a critical part of the Third Class curriculum. The inventors of the study, he lamented to his parents, "introduced it into the course of academic instruction for the torture of students . . . much to the sorrow of the unfortunate students thereby made to suffer." Despite his problems, Lyon must have possessed a decided proficiency even to study the subject, for the mathematics department allowed only the best cadets into the upper sections of calculus. Unlike his professors, however, Lyon did not appreciate the honor bestowed on him.[11]

During his upper-class years, Lyon ranked near the bottom of his class in both drawing and infantry tactics and proved only average in chemistry, ethics, and geology. However, in natural philosophy, artillery, and especially in Professor Dennis Hart Mahan's course in engineering (the most important of the academy's upper-level courses, and which included in its scope the sub-study "The Science of War"), he demonstrated prowess that placed him near the top of his class. In a letter to his

11. Woodward, *Life of Nathaniel Lyon*, 30; Ambrose, *Duty, Honor, Country*, 93–94.

brother-in-law John B. Hasler (recently married to his sister Sophronia), Lyon mused that his architectural skills, learned in his study of engineering, had ably prepared him for "building a Shoemaker's shop [Hasler's trade] on scientific principles . . . ." Indeed, in overall class standing, or "order of general merit," determined by a combination of coursework (of which mathematics held far greater weight than other subjects), demerits, and the annual year-ending examinations, Lyon climbed from eighteenth in his Fourth Class year to thirteenth in his Third Class year. At the end of his Second Class year, he ranked eleventh of the remaining fifty-five cadets in his class.[12]

However, Nathaniel Lyon enjoyed a rare luxury that served to lighten both his academic and emotional loads. During his cadetship, his first cousin, Lt. Miner Knowlton (Kezia's younger sister's son), held the position of assistant professor of artillery and cavalry at West Point. Knowlton, an 1829 graduate of the academy, had served as an instructor there since 1832 and currently taught artillery. Fourteen years older than Lyon, he became a sort of mentor for the young cadet, assisting him with his course work, offering his home as a refuge from the drudgery of cadet life, and affording him succor with which to endure—and survive—the grind of becoming an officer in the United States Army.[13]

Not blessed with the natural scholastic abilities of his fellow New Englanders Zealous Tower of Massachusetts and Horatio Wright of Connecticut (one of whom dominated the top position in every course during their Fourth Class year), Lyon worked assiduously to succeed as he did. He found little time for frivolities, helping to keep his discipline record clean. During his four years, he checked out books infrequently from the post library, and only those pertaining directly to his classes. While Ulysses Grant, two years behind Lyon at the academy, lost himself in novels when free time presented itself, Lyon kept to his studies. However, if Nathaniel Lyon was both a serious student and soldier, he was also no prude. Although no record exists indicating an especially close friendship with any other cadet, he appears to have been accepted by his peers. When opportunities for social gaieties occasionally presented themselves—especially at the holidays—Lyon usually attended. During

12. Official Register of Officers and Cadets, 1838–1841, USMA; William S. McFeely, *Grant: A Biography*, 15; Lyon to Hasler, December 5, 1840, AAS; Ambrose, *Duty, Honor, Country*, 73–74.

13. Woodward, *Life of Nathaniel Lyon*, 225–26; Cullum, *Biographical Register*, 1:426.

the Christmas season of his First Class year, Cadet Lyon related one such gala event:

> On Christmas' and New Year's eve we had a fancy ball, in which cadets alone took part, appearing in such characters as suited their taste, and acting their respective parts with success. Our company was graced by the presence of the prince, the military chieftain, the sage, the scholar, the peasant, the quaker, the waiter, the beggar, and even the fool. Every thing passed off in excellent order, each making such remarks, and acting in such manner as the assumed character required.[14]

As graduation drew near, Lyon looked forward to leaving West Point. Ironically, as facile as the entrance exams had been, the final examinations proved exceptionally strenuous. After making his final recitation on June 4, he expected to take the last of the examinations on or near the twentieth of that month and to leave for Ashford following graduation ceremonies shortly thereafter. He had, however, several options available to him. Knowlton had requested that Lyon stay the summer at the academy and assist him in his department of instruction, the prospect of which Lyon found agreeable, but he worried that the army would extend his time through the fall or longer if he chose to remain. This he did not want, for he knew that teaching at the Point would afford the slowest method of advancement. Lyon's ambition raced far beyond a life of pedagogy. However, spending the summer with his cousin appealed to him, so he resolved to consult with his parents before deciding the matter.[15]

His second choice, made solely by himself, proved more provocative. Because of his high class rank, the government offered Lyon the choice of which branch of the military he wished to enter. Custom dictated that the highest-ranking graduates entered the Engineering Corps, while those at the lower end would be relegated to the Infantry. However, Lyon realized that advancement in the Engineers Corps was nearly as sluggish as in teaching. He therefore allowed his ambition to prevail when he made the maverick decision, no doubt raising the eyebrows of both classmates and teachers, to receive his commission in the Infantry.[16]

14. Official Register of Officers and Cadets, 1838-1841, USMA; Record of Books Borrowed by Cadet Nathaniel Lyon, Library Circulations Records, 1836-1841, USMA; McFeely, *Grant*, 16-17; Woodward, *Life of Nathaniel Lyon*, 31-32.

15. Lyon to Hasler, June 3, 1841, Nathaniel Lyon Papers, AAS; Ambrose, *Duty, Honor, Country*, 80, 104.

16. Thomas L. Connelly, *The Marble Man: Robert E. Lee and His Image in Ameri-*

While his first two decisions proved manageable enough, a third plagued him—whether to remain in the military after graduation, or to return to Ashford and civilian life. Despite an eight-year service commitment, a continual excess of academy graduates over army vacancies had all but ensured that there would be no penalty for noncompliance. Moreover, the prospect of doubling his salary as a civil engineer, coupled with a much faster rate of promotion compared to the military's, proved an enticing lure for Lyon to give up his commission. "Never in my life," he wrote his sister, "have I been so vexed as since I have been obliged to contemplate this subject." Although this confession would seem uncharacteristic considering his burning ambition for a military career, Lyon appears to have been consumed by an even hotter fire—love.[17]

Little evidence remains to provide any details of the relationship, and one can only speculate on the identity of Lyon's "one absorbing object," with whom all other matters were "of little importance in comparison." She does not appear to have been a resident of Ashford, yet Lyon was enamored of her. One citation illuminates the passion he evinced for the mysterious "Miss Tot." In a letter to John Hasler, he quotes a poem that, in his own opinion, "gives but a poor index to the more intense feelings":

> It is with earnest & beseeching tone,
> Our Prayer is breathed before Creation's throne,
> That this Dear Pledge of love may live to know
> Each joy that this World's Treasury can bestow . . . .

Awash with doggerel, this candid confession, articulated to an only recently made family member, attests to the strength of Lyon's feelings for the young woman. It is quite feasible that a desire to pursue the relationship, coupled with an ambition that sought both adventure and advancement, compelled him ultimately to reject Knowlton's offer to teach at West Point. Though details are sketchy, one thing is clear: the courtship was still aflame—at least in Lyon's mind—in the fall, when he commenced his tour of duty. Therefore, after graduating from the academy on June 22, 1841 (a respectable eleventh in a class of fifty-two), Lyon returned to Ashford, where he spent the summer "with infinite

can Society, 8–9; Ambrose, Duty, Honor, Country, 144; Woodward, Life of Nathaniel Lyon, 32; United States Military Academy Diploma of Nathaniel Lyon, Chester C. Corbin Public Library, Webster, Mass.

17. Edward M. Coffman, The Old Army: A Portrait of the American Army in Peacetime, 1784–1898, 47, 49–50; Lyon to Hasler, June 3, 1841, Nathaniel Lyon Papers, AAS.

satisfaction," and on July 1, shortly after his arrival home, he was promoted to the rank of second lieutenant, U.S. Army.[18]

It was not until September that Lieutenant Lyon received any further correspondence regarding his military future. Yet within a fortnight of the reception of his commission as a second lieutenant came orders, dated September 2, instructing him that he had been assigned to Company I, Second U.S. Infantry. It further read that he had until the last day of November to join his unit at Fort Russell, on the east tip of Lake Orange, about forty miles southwest of Picolata, East Florida, where it was currently engaged in actions against the Seminole Indians. As appears typical, however, the letter failed to provide even a clue as to how the young officer was to get to his post, so on November 2 he wrote to the Adjutant General's Office for instructions. He received a prompt response, but the late date of the correspondences caused him to be unable to arrive according to the schedule of his original directives. Near the end of November, he caught a train for New York, where he boarded a steamer bound for Savannah, Georgia. After a brief stop there, he arrived at Picolata, only to learn that his unit had moved to Fort Shannon, near Palatka, another twenty miles down the St. Johns River. On December 6, 1841, he reached Palatka and reported belatedly for duty.[19]

Lyon arrived in Florida both homesick and uninspired by the strange country. Territorial Florida was a land of few people and fewer settlements. Palatka—comprised of little more than a hospital, barracks for soldiers, and a large stable, surrounded by eight blockhouses for protection—remained the only settlement of any significance south of Jacksonville. Having never before been out of the Northeast, Lyon regarded this new land as the fringe of the entire world, rather than just that of the eastern United States. The inescapable ennui of the place quickly dampened the green lieutenant's enthusiasm for his new career. However, the exigencies of the service soon replaced these feelings with a burden of responsibility, for on Christmas Day, just over a fortnight after his arrival, he assumed command of Company I, which since November 11

18. Lyon to Hasler, January 17, 1842, Nathaniel Lyon Papers, AAS; United States Military Academy Diploma of Nathaniel Lyon, Chester C. Corbin Public Library, Webster, Mass.; Roger Jones to Lyon, November 10, 1841, Letters Sent, RG 94.

19. Returns of the Second Infantry Regiment (hereafter cited as Returns), July 1841, RG 94; Coffman, *The Old Army*, 62; Roger Jones to Lyon, November 10, 1841, Letters Sent, RG 94; Francis P. Prucha, *Guide to the Military Posts of the United States, 1789–1895*, 142.

had been led by an interim commander. Because of an abnormally high
number of officer resignations during the preceding five years (owing to
low pay and the unpopularity of the most recent war with the Semi-
noles), there was a decided shortage of officers in Florida. Lyon's assignment resulted from this shortage, and since he was the only regular
officer commissioned to his unit, the responsibility for its leadership
naturally devolved upon him. He would continue to act in this capacity
throughout his six-month tour of duty in Florida. However, much to his
chagrin, Lyon's stay in the swamplands of northern Florida proved relatively uneventful.[20]

By the time of Lyon's arrival in Florida, little remained of the recrudescence of hostilities dubbed the Second Seminole War. After more than six
years, the army had finally succeeded in subduing most of the small
bands of natives who, though heavily outnumbered, made good use of
the swamps in deftly evading attempts to capture or destroy them. However, by January 1, 1842, few Indians remained in the Florida Territory,
the rest having been forcibly removed to the territory reserved for them
west of the Mississippi River. By this time, military expeditions were
limited to minor patrols to seek out any remaining "renegades." These
rarely lasted more than a few days. Although Lyon led several of these
forays around Lake George, he participated in no engagement with the
Indians. In fact, the closest he came to meeting a native band proved to be
a sighting of "three Canoes with Indians in them on the opposite side of
the Lake, but could not get at them." While Companies B and K celebrated their capture of the last remaining Seminole chief, Halleck-
Tuskenuggee, and his band, Lyon shared no part in the glory.[21]

Indeed, Lyon appears for the most part to have disliked his tour of
duty in the "swampy land of misquittoes & aligators." This was due in
part to his repugnance at the rampant deceit and corruption involved in
the hostilities, whereby civilian employees of the government secretly
aided the Indians, army interpreters and guides sold ammunition covert-

20. Lyon to Hasler, January 17, 1842, Nathaniel Lyon Papers, AAS; Sidney Walter
Martin, *Florida During the Territorial Days*, 190–91; Returns, December 1841, RG 94;
Coffman, *The Old Army*, 51–52. Capt. A. B. Eaton was furloughed from his post in
1838, and his successor, 1st Lt. Marsena R. Patrick, was sent to Tampa, Florida, on
November 11, 1841. Hence, when Lyon reported for duty, he was eligible for immediate
command, but was allowed a short seasoning period before assuming it.

21. Martin, *Florida*, 238; Lyon to Hasler, January 17, 1842, Nathaniel Lyon Papers,
AAS; Nathaniel Lyon to George W. Cullum, January 1, 1860, Nathaniel Lyon File,
USMA.

ly to the enemy, and Spanish provocateurs located on the coast circulated propaganda about both sides. Adding more to his disenchantment, however, was frustration stemming from an impatient belief that his military schooling, of which he was both proud and confident, was somehow being wasted by what he deemed an insignificant assignment. Although he was trained for war, he had failed to encounter it in these God-forsaken swamps. The weather proved the only saving grace of his tenure in Florida; the territory's winter climate he found "charming." Nevertheless, he was not unrelieved when, on May 26, 1842, his brief tour of duty in the Florida hammocks ended and Lyon and his company left Palatka and boarded a transport ship bound for New York.[22]

After disembarking briefly at Fort Hamilton, in the harbor of New York City, the unit proceeded to the Niagara frontier and arrived at the Madison Barracks army installation, located on the remote yet beautiful eastern shore of Lake Ontario at Sackets Harbor, New York. For most of the officers and men, the garrison duty proved a welcome relief from the rigors of the Florida campaign. Nathaniel Lyon, however, found his first year at the post as stormy as Lake Ontario itself.[23]

Initially, life at Madison Barracks does not appear to have disagreed with Lyon. Indeed, the fort not only offered comforts far outweighing those of the rude quarters he had been forced to occupy in Florida; it proved far more aesthetically pleasing as well. The central parade ground occupied about forty acres, enclosed on three sides by officers' quarters and barracks. The limestone buildings each measured about 250 feet in length and boasted neat piazzas on both floors of their front facades. The fourth side of the compound opened to Ontario's expanse, offering both a breathtaking view and a prevailing breeze off the great lake. When not drilling twice daily, logging reports, or leading evening parade, Lyon found ample time to pursue personal endeavors. To keep him company, he purchased a dog, which he named (quite enlightenedly) Tasso, for the Italian Renaissance poet. Indeed, Lyon appears to have been content with his return to the Northeast. Writing home of his stay on Lake Ontario (no doubt to placate his mother), he remarked, "We are well situated here with many respectable and intelligent citizens around us. . . . We have balls occasionally in town and parties in garrison. . . . I

22. Child, "The Lionhearted General," 41; Lyon to Hasler, January 17, 1842, Nathaniel Lyon Papers, AAS; Returns, May 1842, RG 94; Woodward, *Life of Nathaniel Lyon,* 60.
23. Woodward, *Life of Nathaniel Lyon,* 60.

always go to church twice on Sunday and sometimes at evening in the week."[24]

During his leisure hours, Lieutenant Lyon dabbled in both the study of law—his grandfather's and, to a certain extent, his father's profession—and the study of moral philosophy, a favorite subject at the academy. The logic he found stimulating; the diversion, welcome. And though this knowledge of the law proved mere dilettantism, the two subjects combined to ossify further his views on life and its daily trials. In Lyon's mind, every question must have an answer, and these subjects helped him to eliminate the gray areas of man's existence. Moreover, they lent themselves well to Lyon's natural didactics. Just as he had had no difficulty while still an unmarried cadet in advising his new brother-in-law on the secrets of a successful marriage, he now found great satisfaction in advising a relative on a dispute involving a small claim, or developing an algorithm for an Ashford neighbor to figure the legal value of his property per acre. The story goes that late in his career, while stationed at Fort Riley in the Kansas Territory, Lyon found admittance to the bar of the District Court of Davis County on the condition that he produce a basket of champagne for the examining judge. Evidence exists that at that time he indeed purchased a case of this particular libation, but whether this validates the claim remains open to speculation. In any case, only a year out of West Point, Lyon's increasing dogmatism, coupled with his hair-trigger temper, quickly embroiled him in two portentous controversies, coming surprisingly early in his young professional career.[25]

Lyon remained in command of Company I until August 1842, when 1st Lt. Marsena R. Patrick rejoined the unit from a long furlough. Although placement into and subsequent relinquishment of temporary commands occurs frequently in the military, the arrival of the new company commander must have been a humbling experience for the impet-

24. Returns, May to June 1842, RG 94; John W. Barber and Henry Howe, eds., *Historical Collections of the State of New York,* 211; Lyon to Lorenzo Lyon, July 25, 1848, Nathaniel Lyon Papers, CSL; Lyon to John W. Trowbridge, July 7, 1843, Nathaniel Lyon Papers, AAS; Woodward, *Life of Nathaniel Lyon,* 61; Coffman, *The Old Army,* 78–79. In 1841, the army made church attendance mandatory at all posts.

25. Woodward, *Life of Nathaniel Lyon,* 62; Lyon to Hasler, December 5, 1840, Nathaniel Lyon Papers, AAS; James Humphrey, "The Country West of Topeka Prior to 1865," 295; Lyon to John W. Trowbridge, July 7, 1843, Nathaniel Lyon Papers, AAS; Personal Account Book of Captain Nathaniel Lyon, September 1858 to May 1861, Nathaniel Lyon File, WC.

uous young second lieutenant, who had led the company since his arrival in Florida. Perhaps a strong feeling of discomfiture can partially explain why Lyon allowed his temper, effectively repressed at West Point, to rage now uncontrolled, marring his budding career record with a first serious blemish.[26]

On August 15, shortly after the arrival of Lieutenant Patrick, Lyon participated with the company in battalion drill on the parade grounds. After the regimental commander, Maj. Joseph Plympton, had dismissed the troops to their individual company commanders, Lyon took Company I for extra drilling while other units either were dismissed for the afternoon or were themselves participating in extra drilling. Perhaps Lieutenant Patrick had been absent during the battalion drill or had instructed Lyon to drill the troops; regardless, Lyon at that time was in command of the company.[27]

As Lieutenant Lyon held his company at attention, their weapons at "order arms," four privates who had been absent from both company roll call and battalion drill fell into line. Spying their arrival, Lyon ordered these privates to step forward several paces from the rest of the company. They would now have a special drill session as punishment for their tardiness while the rest of the company watched, barked the lieutenant.[28]

One of the stragglers, Pvt. Samuel Kelly, a recently arrived emigrant from Ireland, appears to have been particularly unhappy about this private drill. He also was drunk. As Lyon stepped to the right of the company to speak with its sergeant, William Stewart, Kelly growled—in a voice intended for Lyon to hear—that if he could not drill in the ranks, he was not going to drill at all.[29]

Lyon's visage, already crimson from the day's drill in the late summer sun, quickly became redder. He turned and stamped across the front of the company to Kelly's immediate right. He then drew his sword and asked the discordant private to repeat himself. Kelly, his speech slightly slurred, stated that he would be damned if he would drill. Instantly, Lyon's temper exploded. With visceral savageness, he struck the man a

26. Returns, August 1842, RG 94.
27. Court Martial Proceedings of Second Lieutenant Nathaniel Lyon, December 28, 1842, to January 7, 1843, pp. 9–10, File DD196, Record Group 153, Records of the Judge Advocate General (Army), National Archives (hereafter cited as RG 153).
28. Ibid., 40.
29. Ibid., 10, 13–14, 21.

backhanded blow across the face with the flat of his sword and followed it with at least two more blows to the neck and shoulders. Unprepared for the violence of Lyon's assault, Kelly reached out instinctively with his left hand and pushed against his attacker's chest to ward off further punishment.[30]

Simultaneously, shouts came from the ranks encouraging Kelly to "run the bastard through" with his bayonet, fixed to the end of his musket. Now thoroughly enraged at the contempt his command seemed to share for him and at the fact that an inebriated enlisted man had dared to touch an officer, Lyon lost all sense of reason. He grabbed Kelly's bayonet to prevent him from using it against him and struck the private repeatedly across the face with his sword, drawing blood from both his forehead and chin. At this point in the fracas, Sergeant Stewart rushed from his place in the line, grabbed Kelly by the collar of his fatigue blouse, and wrestled him to the ground.[31]

Major Plympton was walking to his quarters after dismissing the regiment when he was alerted to the problem in I Company. Hastening to the scene, he arrived at the head of the company in time to see Stewart collaring Kelly. Quickly ascertaining from Lyon the problem, he tersely reminded the lieutenant that the parade ground was not the place to discipline a soldier, especially one under the influence of alcohol. He then ordered Lyon to remove the private to the guardhouse.[32]

Having regained his senses after the violent assault, Kelly became more boisterous than ever. He began to affront the lieutenant verbally, calling him a "scoundrel and a coward, he had proved himself so in Florida," and peppered his insults with profanity. While being escorted to the guardhouse, Kelly announced to all who could hear that he would have revenge.[33]

Perhaps at this point the incident might have ended, but Lyon's hot temper still flared, and, to make matters worse, the regimental commander had reprimanded him publicly. Thoroughly piqued, Lyon intended to teach this insolent sot a lesson in respect he would not soon forget.

Once at the guardhouse, Lyon, who was officer of the day (and therefore responsible for both the prisoners and the guard detail), demanded

30. Ibid., 10.
31. Ibid., 32.
32. Ibid., 4–5.
33. Ibid., 13, 34, 44.

some rope from the sergeant of the guard, Edward Hoey. The guard-house contained none, since its ample number of cells could securely confine any prisoner. Lyon, however, appeared determined to do more than merely jail Kelly. He ordered Sergeant Hoey to send a corporal to the quartermaster's storeroom to bring a rope. During the runner's short absence, Kelly continued to berate Lyon, vowing among other things to shoot the lieutenant dead when he found the chance. While maintaining an outward calmness, Lyon allowed his anger to mount.[34]

After the corporal returned with the rope, Lyon instructed Hoey to lay the private on his stomach and tie both his hands securely behind his back. He then ordered the sergeant to draw Kelly's feet to his hands and lash all four of the prisoner's limbs together. The unnatural position caused the ropes to pull tightly on Kelly's wrists and ankles, and within seconds the private cried out in pain, and in anger. Hoey ordered Kelly to be silent, but the private continued unabated, vowing that he would "have satisfaction for this, if it [were] to be found." Lyon responded by ordering him to be gagged with a stick.[35]

In his twenty-six years in the army, Edward Hoey had seen only a handful of soldiers tied and gagged, and then only in extraordinary cases of mutinous behavior. Never before had the sergeant seen a man bound in the manner that Lyon chose for Kelly. Hoey realized immediately that Kelly's punishment was for Lyon's personal satisfaction rather than to prevent the private from injuring those around him. He said nothing, however, as Lyon held the prisoner in bondage on the road in front of the guardhouse.[36]

After about twenty minutes, Hoey was called away briefly from the scene. When he returned, several local citizens chatted with Lyon while Kelly remained face down on the road. Upon the sergeant's return, Lyon reported to Plympton's office to explain the circumstances surrounding the incident. He failed to mention, however, that Private Kelly remained bound, gagged, and in great discomfort. After Lyon returned to the guardhouse, he ordered the prisoner released and confined to a cell. All told, Kelly had been tied up for more than an hour.[37]

The army dealt harshly with Kelly's actions in the incident. In November, he received a court-martial for mutinous behavior and a sen-

34. Ibid., 13, 25–26.
35. Ibid., 26, 29.
36. Ibid., 28–29.
37. Ibid., 26–28, 30.

tence of six months in the guardhouse, without pay, and with ball and chain attached to his leg. He spent two months of the sentence in solitary confinement on rations of bread and water.[38]

Officials did not overlook Lyon's behavior, but the chain of events that transpired as a result of his actions can only be speculated upon. Lyon's superiors investigated his unusual treatment of Private Kelly at the guardhouse and found his actions highly inappropriate. On December 13, the Adjutant General's Office notified Lyon that his presence was required at a general court-martial, scheduled to begin at Madison Barracks on December 28. The charge, preferred by Brig. Gen. John Wool, commander of the 5th Military Department: illegal, arbitrary, and unmilitary conduct.[39]

During the course of the testimony, Lyon countered with obstinacy the charges against him. At one point, he strongly objected to the testimony of a witness for the prosecution, Pvt. John Gillespie, accusing him of being an infidel. Considering Lyon's own doubts about God and religion, this remonstrance seems highly ironic. Conducting his own defense, the custom in military court-martials, Lyon directed a separate line of questioning to ascertain the man's religious convictions. The examination, however, proved inconclusive, and the court overruled Lyon's objection to the witness's testimony. At another point in the trial, Lyon attempted to have the entire proceedings of Kelly's court-martial admitted as evidence in his defense. The court also denied this request, which no doubt enraged the fiery lieutenant even further.[40]

Lyon's loudest objection, however, was to the introduction of testimony concerning his treatment of Kelly at the guardhouse. Arguing that Kelly had been released to his charge by Major Plympton, Lyon believed he could deal with his prisoner "in such a manner as necessity required, not inconsistent with the rules, and custom of service—and such conduct being supposed to have the knowledge and sanction of the Commanding Officer." The court, however, again refused to sustain Lyon's remonstrance.[41]

After ten days of testimony, the court (consisting of ten officers) reached a verdict: Lieutenant Lyon was guilty as charged. His sentence: "To be suspended from rank and command for *five* calendar months;

38. Ibid., 8.
39. Ibid., 1.
40. Ibid., 14–17, 30–31.
41. Ibid., 25.

and during his suspension to be confined to the limits of the station where he now is, or may be, for that term." Whether Lyon's sentence included a suspension of pay remains unclear.[42]

After rendering the court's decision, its president, Bvt. Maj. T. L. Gardner, imparted the reasons behind the court's ruling. Believing it lenient due to Kelly's "outrageous conduct . . . and especially his apparent determination to kill or injure the prisoner [Lyon]," Gardner stated that the basis for the decision against Lyon was not "the error of his requiring and forcing a drunken man to drill instead of sending him to the guard house." Rather, "the worst portion of the prisoner's conduct was his unnecessary severity to Kelly at the guard house." Having rendered its decision, the court adjourned.[43]

However, Lyon was far too impetuous to accept what he deemed a miscarriage of justice, and he soon set about currying favor with the judges. Although Lyon believed passionately that his rights had been violated, he suppressed his emotions during the next several months in order to convince the court members that he sincerely regretted his violent actions. His histrionics appear to have worked. By early March, four members of the court who presided over his case had signed a letter of recommendation stating that "an apparent error in judgment on the part of the prisoner" had been made and that a remission of the sentence appeared warranted. Accordingly, on March 23, Lyon received orders from the Adjutant General's Office in Washington restoring him to rank and command. After Pvt. Samuel Kelly had served his six months in confinement, the army discharged him on April 20 on the grounds that he was an illegal alien. Undoubtedly, Lyon gained a certain satisfaction from that action. Given the circumstances, it is quite feasible that he even had a hand in it, but no proof of that has been found.[44]

Any satisfaction that might have stemmed from Lyon's own reinstatement and Kelly's subsequent cashiering proved short-lived. On April 11, 1843, Amasa Lyon died at age seventy-one. His illness had lasted only a week, and Lyon recalled that the cause of his death had been "the Lung-fever"—most likely pneumonia. He applied immediately for a thirty-day furlough and returned home to Ashford.[45]

Not surprisingly, given his distant relationship with his father and the

42. Ibid., 2–3, 47.
43. Ibid., 47–48.
44. Ibid., 49; Returns, April 1843, RG 94.
45. Lyon Genealogy, Nathaniel Lyon Papers, CSL.

fact that he had been removed from the family for the past six years, Lyon appears to have been relatively unmoved by Amasa's demise. His few written acknowledgments emote only manufactured feelings that appear more sententious than genuine and invariably gravitate around a concern for his mother's health and well-being. Since Lyon chose a profession other than farming, Amasa bequeathed to him no land, but stipulated that his share of the estate was to come from that left to the other boys. Lyon left Ashford with the matter unsettled. Such a somber trip home might easily have given him pause to reflect more calmly upon the recent unpleasant events and accept the judgment as just in light of his own rashness. However, Nathaniel Lyon's single-mindedness ensured that any reflections he might have had would only illuminate the court's malfeasance, and he returned to Sackets Harbor intent upon vengeance.[46]

By July, Lyon found himself again under arrest and confined to quarters, awaiting a court of inquiry for misconduct. In late January, while relieved of command for the Kelly incident, he had demonstrated extreme impatience by requesting printed copies of the proceedings of his court-martial. Lyon not only wrote the secretary of war, James M. Porter, for copies, but also attempted to speed matters by writing former attorney general John J. Crittenden for assistance in obtaining the report. For this breach of military protocol regarding official correspondence, he received censure from the Adjutant General's Office. After his copy arrived in early March (the only such duplication of the original), Lyon vented his anger by having printed in pamphlet form the entire trial proceedings. He then distributed copies to those he knew to be sympathetic to his cause. How many pamphlets Lyon distributed remains unknown, but one found its way to the Adjutant General's Office, resulting in the lieutenant's arrest on July 24. The army charged him with disseminating the confidential transcripts of a military court-martial. The court contacted Miner Knowlton as a witness for the prosecution because Lyon had sent him one of the pamphlets. After Lyon was confined to quarters for a month, the charges were apparently dropped, and Lyon gained his release on August 27, 1843. His action, however, could not have ingratiated him with his superiors.[47]

46. Woodward, *Life of Nathaniel Lyon,* 201; Lyon to John W. Trowbridge, July 7, 1843, Nathaniel Lyon Papers, AAS; Will of Amasa Lyon, Ashford Township Probate Records, ATH.

47. Returns, July 1843, RG 94; Adjutant General's Office to Lyon, February 27,

The remainder of Lyon's stay at Madison Barracks appears to have passed without incident. During these four years, he took advantage of the relative proximity to home and returned to Ashford three times on leaves of absence. However, during this time, he also came to a weighty decision. Perhaps it stemmed from a painful termination of his relationship with "Miss Tot"; we know that the affair ended, but the details remain intractable. Or it might well be, as one writer has charged, that his exposure to military life caused him to realize that the itinerant life of a soldier could never lend itself satisfactorily to a life that he could share with a woman. His exact motivations are unknown, but the consciousness of his decision is clear: Lyon resolved never to marry.[48]

This is not to imply that he had no interest in the prospect of matrimony. Indeed, Lyon held a high regard for members of the opposite sex—and for marriage—which would continue for his entire life. "You may tell Mother," he wrote to his nephew from Kansas later in his career, "we have also some pretty young Ladies, to whom I am devoting my self with more than usual gallantry, and though I do not expect to be devoured by a consuming flame, should this happen I will give a dire account of my distress." And considering Lyon's decisiveness, it is doubtful that imposing upon himself even an edict as doctrinaire as this proved particularly painful; however, the reaction at home appears to have been far less phlegmatic. He seems to have broken the news to his mother while on furlough in the summer of 1844, and her obviously unfavorable response prompted him to write her in defense of his decision immediately upon his return to Sackets Harbor. "And as to love," he penned, "if indeed I be blind mad or foolish I trust reason will not be inactive in asserting its authority & under these circumstances I do not anticipate any immediate change in my condition." Though his family disapproved, Lyon held to his decision with characteristic pugnaciousness.[49]

Before he left Madison Barracks, Lyon for several months participated in recruitment for the army in New York City, an assignment he found quite satisfying. He thought the city exciting, and the time away from his

---

1843, Letters Sent, RG 94; Adjutant General's Office to Miner Knowlton, July 28, 1843, ibid.

48. Returns, September 1843 to June 1846, RG 94; Griggs, *Folklore and Firesides,* 157.

49. Lyon to John A. Hasler, November 17, 1859, Harry H. Ensign Collection, Yale University Library; Lyon to Mother, August 24, 1844, Nathaniel Lyon Papers, AAS; Lyon to Sister, December 30, 1844, ibid.

post at Sackets Harbor proved particularly refreshing. Though it would appear that his pamphlet stunt appeased his sense of justice (or at least enough so to prevent a recurrence of any problems like those during his first year at Sackets Harbor), Lyon's intransigence found vent once more before leaving New York State.[50]

In July 1846, after being stationed at Madison Barracks for just over four years, Lyon and Company I received transfer to Fort Columbus, on Governors Island in the harbor of New York City. Although his duration at this post would last just one month, he managed to again become a source of controversy. Shortly after the arrival of the company, its commander, Capt. Amos B. Eaton, resigned from the service. Apparently unaware of the plans of his superior, Lyon entered the office of Major Plympton, the regimental commander, where a private serving as the major's secretary was transcribing a copy of a letter written by the major. In the letter, Plympton stated that he wished to place 1st Lt. James W. Penrose, currently with a unit other than Company I, in command of that company as Eaton's successor. Unaware that Lyon possessed no knowledge of Plympton's intent, the private innocently asked the lieutenant whether he should yet remove Eaton's name from the company rolls. Although Lyon did not yet understand the details, he sensed immediately that the private had made a faux pas. Guilefully, he asked the young man to what he was referring. The soldier replied that the matter was in reference to the letter he was at the moment copying. Unable to contain himself, Lyon snatched the letter and quickly left the building, despite the appeals of the incredulous private.[51]

Events accelerated rapidly. The private promptly informed Major Plympton (the same officer who had been Lyon's superior during his earlier altercations) of the lieutenant's act, and the major in turn reported the incident to the Adjutant General's Office. Concomitantly, he required Lyon to submit without delay an explanation of the incident. The lieutenant complied, but not without also expressing his view that the promotion of Lieutenant Penrose to the command of Lyon's "rightful" company represented a "violation of the usages of the service and of the positive prohibitus of Paragraphs 49 and 52 of Gen'l Army Regulations and necessarily carries with it (to all external appearances) reflections

50. Returns, September 1843 to June 1846, RG 94; Lyon to Mother, August 24, 1844, Nathaniel Lyon Papers, AAS.

51. Returns, July 1846, RG 94; Francis P. Prucha, *Guide to the Military Posts,* 67; Lyon to Roger Jones, July 30, 1846, to August 9, 1846, Letters Received, RG 94.

and imputations mortifying to my feelings and disparaging to my qualifications and conduct as an officer." Lyon's protests, aside from further alienating his regimental commander, went unheeded. Considering Lyon's record, Plympton placed little confidence in the abilities of a junior officer so rash and troublesome. In August, Penrose received command of I Company, Second Infantry.[52]

For such a short duration in the army, Second Lieutenant Lyon had suffered more than his share of controversy, most of it his own doing. At this point, Lyon himself realized that his military career appeared destined for a dead end. He had reaped disfavor from his superiors, had already been passed over for command promotion, and had earned a black mark on his record from his early court-martial and subsequent actions. By this time, Lyon had resolved that at the end of his mandatory tour of duty he would leave the army and return to private life. However, at this bleakest juncture in time, Providence—and John Tyler—seemed to intervene on Nathaniel Lyon's behalf, and by the most fortuitous of all possible means. They graced him with a war.[53]

52. Lyon to Roger Jones, August 9, 1846, Letters Received, RG 94.
53. Lyon to Mother, undated, Nathaniel Lyon File, NYHS.

III

The Apostate

The war with Mexico provided Lyon with the chance to start his moribund career afresh and to redeem all of his past misdeeds. Although he did not then recognize the opportunity, and although he appears at times to have resisted this good fortune with all his might, in Mexico he found rebirth.

Tensions between the United States and Mexico rose steadily during the decade following the conclusion of the war for Texas's independence. In May 1846, after both the Tyler and Polk administrations had placed "graduated pressure" upon the Mexican government, fighting erupted along the Rio Grande. This was a product of a long series of incidents over, among other things, the disputed territory between that river and the Nueces. The latest tensions with Mexico had actually begun in 1841 when John Tyler became president upon William Henry Harrison's death. Led by the new president, the administration had renewed with determination the attempt to annex the Texas republic, which had claimed independence since the defeat of Santa Anna at San Jacinto. In May 1844, the government sent an "army of occupation" to Louisiana, ostensibly poised to retaliate against Mexican aggressions after Tyler submitted (and Congress approved) a bill for Texas annexation. Lyon believed all along that the government intended to extend its borders forcibly to the Pacific. He decried the forced acquisition of Mexican territory in order to expand the blessings of American liberty, though this put him in direct opposition to the more accepted Democratic philosophy. The movement of troops in 1844 prompted Lyon to accuse the president of unabashed warmongering:

> John Tyler has virtually declared war with Mexico by sending troops to the Texan Frontier. . . . Such high-handed proceedings are not likely to affect us at present, but, in the final issue, will inevitably involve the United States in hostilities. It is to be hoped that the originator of these rash movements may receive a suitable reward for his madness and folly.[1]

1. Lyon to Sister, December 30, 1844, Nathaniel Lyon Papers, AAS; Robert Selph

Ironically, after the election of James K. Polk, an apparently unobtrusive compromise candidate who unexpectedly carried the 1844 election over Whig favorite Henry Clay, Lyon saw no offings of further aggression toward Mexico. In the winter of that year, while still at Sackets Harbor, he wrote that he believed all "danger" of a manufactured war with Mexico had passed, and he dismissed further talk of it as idle rumors. However, the new president proved an obstinate expansionist and vowed to annex both the Oregon Territory (then jointly occupied by the United States and Great Britain) and California, which belonged to Mexico. And Polk was narrow-minded enough to go to war for either. As it turned out, the fated bloodshed began on the Rio Grande.[2]

Despite his strident opposition to the administration's apparent instigation of a war with Mexico, Lyon was strangely reticent once fighting actually broke out. Indeed, when it came to the business of war, Lyon proved ready for action. He wrote to his mother in July 1846 that the "prospects of War with Mexico are now pretty fair." Two months later his unit received orders to proceed to that front with the rest of the Second Infantry. The regiment was formed into two battalions, left and right, and on the trip Lyon acted as assistant commissary of supply. As the troops left Fort Columbus aboard transport steamers, most, like Lyon, were at once enthusiastic and anxious about the months ahead.[3]

On the first day of October, the ships navigated the treacherous pass between Brazos and Padre islands, located at the mouth of the Rio Grande. Once past this obstacle, the troops made a rough landing in sight of Point Isabel, located on a high bluff three miles to the northwest. After encamping for several days, they marched inland to the river, where they loaded onto river steamers and set out for the interior. The convoy stopped briefly in Matamoros, near the site of the initial firefight that had prompted Zachary Taylor's famous telegram to President Polk: "Hostilities may now be considered as commenced." Continuing ninety miles upriver to the Mexican village of Camargo, they debarked on the evening of October 8 and marched to Camp Brady, located near the

---

Henry, *The Story of the Mexican War*, 15; John Edward Weems, *To Conquer a Peace*, 21.

2. Weems, *To Conquer a Peace*, 22, 26–27; Lyon to Sister, December 30, 1844, Nathaniel Lyon Papers, AAS.

3. Lyon to Mother, July 11, 1846, Nathaniel Lyon Papers, AAS; Returns, September 1846, RG 94.

town. Most were confident that this would be only a short stay before they "conquered a peace" in Mexico.[4]

By November, Lyon had lost none of his sense of the war's adventure. Impatient for action, he blithely reminded Hasler to inform Sophronia that he was "flourishing on the plains of Mexico & that she must look to the top of some newspaper not yet printed & probably never will be to see my name appear as the hero of some big Mexican fight." Privately, however, he harbored different aspirations. His experience at Sackets Harbor had left his hunger for advancement unsatiated, and though he had initially opposed the prospect of war with Mexico, once it had actually broken out he embraced it as a chance for personal gain. His unbridled ambition, coupled with natural impetuosity, soon manifested themselves in chronic criticism of his superiors and their actions. Lyon had exhibited a strong tendency toward such behavior at Madison Barracks, yet it had then limited itself to isolated displays of recalcitrance. In Mexico, however, his attacks became personal, and they ranged widely among leaders of the army and the government. The first object of Lyon's scorn was the army of invasion's overall commander, Zachary Taylor.[5]

The Second Infantry arrived in Camargo only after Taylor's force had moved up the Rio Grande and cleared all Mexican opposition as far as that city. Camargo was to serve the army as a base of supply for an interior movement toward the immediate target, Monterey. By the time Lyon arrived in Camargo, Taylor had moved south with his army and had already defeated the Mexican army at Monterey and captured the city, thus effectively clearing the northeastern section of Mexico. While Taylor became an immediate hero north of the border, Lyon found fault with Old Rough and Ready's methods. In securing Monterey, Taylor had led an assault on the city that was tactically disgraceful and had been criticized by many of his subordinates. Though he had neither met Taylor nor witnessed his dubious attack, Lyon proved one of the most vociferous critics: ". . . I find a general expression of indignation & contempt that Genl Taylor should have rashly rushed his men into the centre of a Fortified Town whose streets were lined with armed men

4. Lyon to John B. Hasler, November 4, 1846, Nathaniel Lyon Papers, AAS; Lyon to S. B. Chase, November 21, 1846, Nathaniel Lyon Papers, CHS; Weems, *To Conquer a Peace,* 113; Returns, October 1846, RG 94.

5. Lyon to Hasler, February 28, 1847, Nathaniel Lyon Papers, AAS; Lyon to Hasler, April 5, 1848, ibid; Lyon to Hasler, November 4, 1846, ibid.; Lyon to S. B. Chase, November 21, 1846, Nathaniel Lyon Papers, CHS.

from the basement to the tops of the roofs—here of course nothing but massacre & murder could follow & resulted in a most inhuman sacrifice of human life & the entire escape of the enemy."[6]

Moreover, Lyon criticized the general strategy of the army's operations in Mexico. He saw no benefit in pacifying the small border towns of northern Mexico, for "their loss is hardly felt." This "child-like, blind fool-hardy madness" he placed squarely upon Taylor's shoulders. Thenceforth, in Lyon's dogmatic mind, Taylor's perceived mistake became inextricably fused with a general condemnation of the man himself. By the time Lyon actually met the general in December, his view had become so skewed that he saw only the general's faults. To Lyon (and most others), Taylor's manner appeared "uncerimonious, . . . his dress & manners & habits being of an off hand informal kind." To command respect, one had to act—or at least look—commanding. In Taylor, Lyon beheld nothing that should educe such respect, especially from him. Zachary Taylor, however, would not prove the sole focus of Lyon's contempt.[7]

In early December, several months after Taylor secured Monterey and signed an armistice widely criticized for its generous terms, four companies of the Second Infantry (including Lyon and I Company) and a regiment of Tennessee volunteers received orders to report to that city. Leaving on the afternoon of December 8, the column marched for two weeks through "a small shrubbery higher than a man's head & every where covered with thorns, . . . all go[ing] under the name of 'Chapparal.'" The men passed then to "a cultivated & thickly settled country, having fields of heavy crops of corn & sugar cane." The march averaged between twelve and fifteen miles a day, but the hot sun coupled with a paucity of palatable drinking water caused much suffering. Having taken the eastern route to Monterey, the column reached Montemorelos on the afternoon of December 17. They bivouacked with the remainder of the Second Infantry, a part of the brigade under the command of Col. William S. Harney, and the brigade under Col. Persifor F. Smith. The division was directed by Gen. David Twiggs, and Taylor himself accompanied the command.[8]

6. Weems, *To Conquer a Peace,* 166, 205–6; Henry, *The Mexican War,* 80–81, 92; Lyon to Hasler, November 4, 1846, Nathaniel Lyon Papers, AAS.

7. Lyon to S. B. Chase, November 21, 1846, Nathaniel Lyon Papers, CHS; Mexican War Journal of Lieutenant Nathaniel Lyon, December 8, 1846, to August 19, 1847 (hereafter cited as Lyon Diary), Nathaniel Lyon Papers, CSL, entry of December 23, 1846.

8. Lyon Diary, December 8 to December 17, 1846, Nathaniel Lyon Papers, CSL; Lyon to Hasler, November 4, 1846, Nathaniel Lyon Papers, AAS; Henry, *The Mexican War,* 185.

On the evening of their arrival, a panicky message came from Gen. William J. Worth, commanding a division at Monterey, alerting General Taylor to reports that Santa Anna was approaching the city with a sizable force. Taylor placed his force in motion at daybreak the next morning and made the fifty-five-mile march in three days. Shortly after their arrival, however, Lyon learned that the reports Worth had heard were unfounded and that the march was thus unnecessary. Grumbling, the troops encamped outside Monterey. However, unknown to most of the combatants, a change in strategy would shortly call them from the northern theater of war to participate in an invasion of the eastern coast of the Mexican nation.[9]

Gen. Winfield Scott, the new commander of the army of invasion, arrived in Mexico in late autumn. Polk had only begrudgingly given Scott command of the army after receiving word of Taylor's dubious armistice. Scott, who had sought the appointment fervidly, barely masked his eagerness when he brought word to Taylor that the Virginian's overland campaign had been subordinated to a new plan. With the full sanction of the government, Scott would launch an amphibious assault on the port of Vera Cruz. In November, shortly after a U.S. Navy squadron had secured the city of Tampico, Scott ordered a base of operations set up in the coastal city. The following month, he ordered four thousand of Taylor's six thousand troops to be marched to Tampico, where they would be transported by sea to participate in the assault on the Vera Cruz defenses. Lyon had heard only rumors of such events when, on the rainy morning of December 23, he and his company departed for Tampico—and for what many hoped would be some long-awaited action.[10]

Only after three weeks of hard marching did Lyon hear confirmation of rumors that their destination was indeed Tampico. A week later, the column arrived tired and footsore in that coastal city. Despite the circumstances that had prompted the move, he hastily approved both the new strategy and the new supreme commander, believing Scott would avoid "the same blind fool hardy course" that he was convinced Taylor would have pursued. Before the column had arrived in Tampico, Taylor had taken the dragoons and cavalry and headed west for Saltillo, while the infantry continued to push southward to Tampico. Once there, the

9. Lyon Diary, December 18 to December 22, 1846, Nathaniel Lyon Papers, CSL.

10. Weems, *To Conquer a Peace*, 245–47, 276–78; Lyon Diary, December 23 and December 28, 1846, Nathaniel Lyon Papers, CSL.

infantry encamped outside the city and for the next four weeks enjoyed the sights of the temperate Mexican port.[11]

During his stay on the coast, Lyon became acquainted with Tampico and was impressed by its "profuse vegitation . . . . Lemons of good quality grow plenty in the woods—Bananna, Cocoa, Plantain & other fruits of a tropical clime." The lush tropical setting provided a striking contrast to the austere surroundings of northern Mexico. Yet Lyon's regard for the city's purely Mexican characteristics ended with the exotic scenery. He found Tampico pleasant only because of its decidedly more "civilized" air. Lyon believed the city's true beauty lay in its American-style houses, wide, paved streets, and population "made up mostly of Foreigners." In his eyes, those inhabitants were "civil, well behaved & more intelligent than elsewhere in Mexico." Saddled with a certain amount of New England insularity (he once remarked that "we New Englanders *are* a little clannish"), Lyon often found foreign surroundings difficult to accept. Although Tampico's "American" appearance might have slightly assuaged Lyon's narrowness, he found in the city far more substantial grounds for criticism. To Lyon, the entire servile structure of Mexican society was deplorable.[12]

Growing up in rural Connecticut, Lyon had learned at an early age to deprecate slavery, yet never in those years had he actually witnessed the institution. Neither the Lyons nor the Knowltons had ever owned even one slave, and by the time of Lyon's birth not one bondsman resided within the boundaries of Windham County. It is conceivable that he caught a brief glimpse of thralldom in practice while passing through Savannah, but on this one can only speculate. Moreover, no evidence remains of his having any contact with it while stationed in Florida. His first true exposure to the realities of servility came upon his arrival in Mexico. "It is a singular fact & one entirely unknown to me till my arrival in the country," he wrote from Camargo, "that Slavery the scourge & curse of humanity exists here & in a servile form." Lyon could discern no palpable difference between the peonage practiced in Mexico and the chattel slavery practiced in the Southern states. One centered on debt, the other on color; both created a condition of per-

11. Lyon Diary, December 23, 1846, to January 23, 1847, Nathaniel Lyon Papers, CSL; Lyon to Hasler, November 4, 1846, Nathaniel Lyon Papers, AAS.

12. Lyon Diary, January 23, 1847, Nathaniel Lyon Papers, CSL; *Address on the Death of Gen. Nathaniel Lyon, Delivered at Manhattan [Kansas], September 26th, 1861, By Rev. George D. Henderson, Chaplain at Fort Riley,* 6.

petuity. Yet Lyon's opposition to peonage stemmed not from any sympathy for its victims; he looked upon the Mexican people as no more than "debased savages" and "degraded mongrels." Instead, Lyon found the whole society stagnated and retarded when compared to the modern, industrial standards of the northeastern United States, an obvious result of its servile institution. He railed against it with characteristic lack of restraint: ". . . Nowhere is aristocracy seen in so indolent, ignorant & dependant condition & nowhere is slavery so servile & depraved. Indeed [in] all their social & political institutions this people are radically deranged & have not within themselves the elements & powers of rectification & the present war is no doubt one of means of Providence designed to work a reformation."[13]

Yet Lyon did not limit his criticism of the Mexican social structure to its abusive practice of servility. He perceived its depravity as running much deeper, and his reasoning found root in a nagging doubt that he carried from his own childhood. Lyon had come to believe that the true bane of Mexican society—and, for that matter, of *all* societies—was the obsequious practice of organized religion.

Never had Lyon's perceptions of the sanctity of religion been unclouded. His father's irreverent example had left as unmistakable an impression on him as it had on his older brother, Lorenzo, who by 1846 had followed in his father's footsteps and ceased to attend church. Although Lyon had, while stationed at both West Point and Madison Barracks, continued to send assurances to both his mother and his sisters that he attended church regularly and participated in occasional sermons when itinerant lecturers traveled to camp, these pledges belied his growing confusion on the subject. Lyon had never seriously doubted God's existence, yet he became increasingly convinced that religion served only to delude men from a true relationship with him. Owing to his strict, New England Congregational background, a decision to reject religion without renouncing God could not be made in haste. The two were inextricably entwined. Giving up the church, according to dogma, was tantamount to abandoning any hope of salvation. This dilemma had weighed increasingly heavy upon Lyon during these years as he searched for an answer.[14]

13. Lyon to Hasler, November 4, 1846, Nathaniel Lyon Papers, AAS; Lyon to Hasler, February 28, 1847, ibid.; Lyon to Hasler, October 24, 1847, ibid.; Lyon to S. B. Chase, November 21, 1846, Nathaniel Lyon Papers, CHS.
14. Lyon to Mother, July 11, 1846, Nathaniel Lyon Papers, AAS; Lyon to Mother, August 24, 1844, ibid.

In the summer of 1843, Lyon was introduced to a philosophy that would change his concept of God and religion. "Animal magnetism," he wrote to his brother-in-law, John W. Trowbridge, "is considerably the rage about this country & I am becoming a convert to the faith . . . ." In 1775, Franz Mesmer, a Viennese physician, had posited that by tapping an invisible energy that emanates from God and pulses through all living things, a phenomenon he called animal magnetism, one could cure any human ailment. However, this "science" (often called "Mesmerism") assisted far more Americans of the nineteenth century to reformulate their own religious understanding than ever received any physical healing. Because God's spirit permeated all things in Nature, including man, animal magnetism provided the nexus between the human and spiritual realms. What proved particularly alluring to theologians—and to Lyon— was that the hypothesis supplanted the Calvinist God, a rigid predeterminer of human action, with a deity far more impersonal and less omnipotent. This new Creator acted directly only in rare and miraculous cases. Moreover, the concept of animal magnetism implicitly lent the power of human reason much greater weight. Rather than scrutinize all human thoughts and actions, God now inspired them, giving far more rein to man's natural intuition. This message came as soothing relief to many who questioned their often-unfulfilling weekly sermons.[15]

Lyon grasped this new philosophy eagerly. He had been looking for some time for a more rational concept of God, one that would provide sanctification for his father's impiety. Animal magnetism allowed him a first firm step in that direction. Moreover, it furnished him with a justification for jettisoning his own religious faith. Reason—not dogma— would bring man closer to his Creator. The next summer, after informing his mother of his plans to abstain from marriage, Lyon also proclaimed that though he firmly believed in the Creator, he harbored grave doubts that organized worship held a viable place in God's ethereal design. "As to Religeon I hope I am not blind mad nor foolish either in embracing or rejecting it & must therefore beg you to trust to a proper exercise of my intellectual powers which with the aid of divine truth I yet hope may direct me in a proper channel." His experience in Mexico would harden such impious leanings into a vicelike inflexibility.[16]

The focal point of Lyon's religious contempt became in these years the

15. Lyon to J. W. Trowbridge, July 7, 1843, Nathaniel Lyon Papers, AAS; Robert C. Fuller, *Mesmerism and the American Cure of Souls,* 1-3, 85-88.
16. Lyon to Mother, July 11, 1846, Nathaniel Lyon Papers, AAS; Lyon to Mother, August 24, 1844, ibid.

Roman Catholic Church. His Protestant foundation had taught him long before to distrust the doctrines of the Catholic faith, so his eyes were not widened significantly by the "Idolatrous tendency" of the Mexican people. What struck him now most inimically were the effects that several centuries of Catholic domination had obviously wrought upon the Mexican people and their culture. Though "the independence of Mexico [had] broken the link of Jesuitism & popery binding it to European despotism," the irreversible effects of "the wealth & power of that monster" were manifest. Peonage, poverty, and cultural stagnation represented obvious alluvia of Spanish Catholic domination. Lyon attributed what he perceived as rampant crime and corruption to the State's protection of the church, thus rendering a situation whereby "individuals may commit whatever crimes & if they do not find sanction they find acquittal in the forms of their religeon & believe 'that clerical absolution is divine justification.'" Lyon concluded peremptorily that "the depravity of the people seemed the natural fruit of a corrupt priesthood." In his eyes, the populace's "degraded blindness filled with superstitious awe for the transcendent qualities & heavenly powers of their priests" only fed a tendency toward avarice and profligacy. By taking what little money was available to their impoverished parishioners and using it for such nefarious purposes as keeping concubines, these "hypocritical scoundrals . . . in the name of God" sapped the life from the Mexican populace. Lyon found the entire situation loathsome.[17]

Lyon's condemnation of the Mexican Catholics gave rein to the general renunciation of religion that he had struggled to make for the past few years. At last, it now became clear to him. What he saw in Mexico could not possibly have been part of the Creator's plan for mankind. God had indeed created man, but man had created religion, and he had done a damn poor job of it. Priests—or, for that matter, clergymen of *any* denomination—could be everywhere as debased as they were in Mexico, for their "exalted purpose" only augmented their own aggrandizement at the expense of the society they purported to serve so faithfully. "If this be the religeon of Christ," he wrote, "I am ready to vote the saviour of mankind an illustrious humbug but so great are the abuses of almost every denomination of Christians when possessed of a monop-

17. Lyon Diary, December 17, 1846, Nathaniel Lyon Papers, CSL; Lyon to Hasler, October 24, 1847, Nathaniel Lyon Papers, AAS; Ashbel Woodward, *Life of General Nathaniel Lyon*, 93.

oly of power that I am inclined to believe the religeon of Christ no where exists . . . ."[18]

Lyon's apparent solution to his one question of faith managed only to give rise to another of equal perplexity, however. If one must jettison all tenets of religion in order to gain a true relationship with God, he posited, so must one reject any previously held notions of him, for they had come invariably from the misguided teachings of the church. Hence, Lyon was left to formulate an entirely new, undistorted perception of the Creator. How, if at all, did God act in the lives of men? What was his purpose in placing men upon the earth, and how must one serve him while in this life? To these questions, Lyon as yet had found no answers, but it would be only a matter of time before he forged a judgment.

Lyon found his reflections on Mexican society abruptly interrupted when, after a month in Tampico, the expedition for Vera Cruz commenced. After arriving in Tampico on February 19, Winfield Scott had ordered the immediate embarkation of all troops. A deluge of orders soon flooded the Second Infantry's camp, and they moved the next day to the mouth of the Panuco River to begin embarkation. However, for want of transports they waited there four days before Lyon's company and three others eventually boarded the transport ship *Ellerslie* and headed for Vera Cruz. After bucking strong headwinds for several days, the fleet organized briefly off Lobos Island, about fifty miles south of Tampico, to await the arrival of the remainder of the expedition. The fleet, numbering some one hundred vessels, left Lobos late in the afternoon of March 2, and at sunset two days later arrived at the harbor of Vera Cruz. Enough light remained for those on the ships to see the city and the massive castle of San Juan de Ulúa protecting its harbor. To this point, Lyon had not learned the plans for attack, and like many others he grew impatient for a first taste of real battle. Writing to Hasler in Ashford, he ranted, "You might expect an attack on your pious City as soon as the Mexicans would one on their coast."[19]

Organized with Bennet Riley's brigade of Twiggs's division, the Second Infantry spent several days on board ship before disembarking late on the evening of March 9. They did so after spending the entire day watching nervously as the bulk of the force—three divisions numbering

18. Lyon to Hasler, October 24, 1847, Nathaniel Lyon Papers, AAS.
19. Lyon Diary, February 20 to March 4, 1847, Nathaniel Lyon Papers, CSL; Lyon to Hasler, February 28, 1847, Nathaniel Lyon Papers, AAS; Weems, *To Conquer a Peace,* 327.

12,603 men—beached before them. However, a rather shrewd plan allowed for a bloodless landing. Rather than challenge the Mexican defenders drawn up in strength around the Vera Cruz harbor, the American fleet rendezvoused in the harbor of Anton Lizardo, twenty miles below Vera Cruz. All troops transferred to fourteen naval vessels and five military steamers for ease of landing, then moved north to Sacrificios Island, a few miles out of range of the San Juan de Ulúa guns. While the rest of the fleet returned to Vera Cruz to "invite attention," landing parties for the American troops made a relatively unopposed landing off Sacrificios. After laying on their arms until morning, all three divisions were able to move the next day to the south side of the city, incurring few casualties. Twiggs's division did not engage on that day, but instead moved behind Worth's division as a reserve force. In the predawn gloom of March 11, they received orders to move to a position north of the city, and by early morning they succeeded in completing the encirclement of Vera Cruz. The assault on the city seemed imminent. At last, Lyon was in a position to lead men into battle.[20]

However, the assault did not allow infantry officers to test their mettle. Instead, a protracted siege reduced the city, carried on primarily by the heavy siege artillery brought with the transports. By March 27, the Mexican command found itself with no recourse but to surrender. During the siege, the division command had positioned Lyon and the Second Infantry astride the Jalapa road to prevent any force from falling upon the rear of the American army. They remained at this position throughout the siege, engaging only slightly in the actual fighting yet witnessing much of the action.[21]

On April 8, orders arrived instructing Twiggs's division to begin an advance toward Jalapa. For the next several days, through breathless and debilitating heat, the column struggled to a point nearly thirty miles inland, meeting only limited resistance in the increasingly mountainous country. On the twelfth, the advance drew up before a series of escarpments about eight miles from Jalapa. Subsequent reconnoitering determined that the road ahead wound between mountains on which a force of Mexican troops was strongly entrenched. If the advance were to continue, the defenses would have to be cleared. In the following days,

---

20. Lyon Diary, March 5 to March 11, 1847, Nathaniel Lyon Papers, CSL; Lyon to Hasler, February 28, 1847, Nathaniel Lyon Papers, AAS; Weems, *To Conquer a Peace,* 324–33.

21. Lyon Diary, March 11 to March 29, 1847, Nathaniel Lyon Papers, CSL.

while the high command pondered the situation, the army rested at the south edge of the mountains.[22]

On April 16, while Lyon remained in camp near the small village of El Plan del Rio, he received notice of his promotion to first lieutenant, with a new responsibility as commander of Company D of the Second Infantry. In his diary, Lyon noted only this: "Receive my promotion to day as 1st Lt. & assume command of Co. 'D.'" Although the significance of the day is lost in Lyon's laconic diary entry, its import to his military career cannot be overlooked. This was his first promotion since leaving West Point, and it came after he had determined to leave the service following his term of enlistment. Considering the course Lyon's career had taken prior to his journey to Mexico, the outbreak of the war loomed ever more important.[23]

The next day, Twiggs's division carried the main strike in the battle for Cerro Gordo (also known as El Telegrafo), a seven-hundred-foot, chaparral-covered height that was topped by the remains of a visual telegraph tower once used to communicate between Vera Cruz and the city of Mexico. A daring American flanking maneuver carried seemingly impregnable defensive positions by clearing the Mexican defenders from La Atalaya, a sizable mountain lying to the east of El Telegrafo. In securing this height, the Americans rendered the positions around the tower indefensible, thus compelling the Mexicans' withdrawal. On the second day of the fight, Lyon first actually led men into battle, and his company took an active part in the movement to the rear side of Cerro Gordo. At sundown on April 18, the American advance reached the village of Encerro, eight miles west of Cerro Gordo on the stone-paved National Road. Estimated Mexican losses were heavy: more than one thousand killed and wounded, and over three thousand captured. The American forces took only 417 casualties. The jubilant forces pushed on to Jalapa the next day and settled in for a deserved rest.[24]

The whole of the army remained for over a month at Jalapa to await supplies. This hiatus allowed many to rejuvenate after experiencing their

22. Weems, *To Conquer a Peace*, 360–61; Lyon Diary, April 8 to April 15, 1847, Nathaniel Lyon Papers, CSL.

23. Weems, *To Conquer a Peace*, 365; Returns, April 1847, RG 94; Lyon Diary, April 16, 1847, Nathaniel Lyon Papers, CSL.

24. Woodward, *Life of Nathaniel Lyon*, 90; K. Jack Bauer, *The Mexican War, 1846–1848*, 263–68; Lyon Diary, April 18, 1847, Nathaniel Lyon Papers, CSL; Henry, *Mexican War*, 282–87; Weems, *To Conquer a Peace*, 361–67.

first taste of battle. Like many others, Lyon found Jalapa a welcome respite. Its elevated climate seemed to him "a continual spring," and its oak trees and cultivated fields—divided by stone fences—reminded him of New England. Perhaps most important to him was the fact that the people were uncorrupted by the system of peonage he had seen elsewhere; the city boasted much industry and thriving businesses, an immediate indication of a more "civilized" culture. "The people seem industrious & happy & many are intelligent & with good tastes surround themselves with the comforts & luxuries of civilized life." Accordingly, Lyon found the women in Jalapa the most striking he had seen in Mexico. Taking a room in town, Lyon experienced the luxury of both a roof over his head and a real bed for the first time since his departure from New York the previous September. Lyon's time in Jalapa only reinforced his belief that servility ruined human society.[25]

The American forces left Jalapa on May 22, and after a week's march of 110 miles halted at the city of Puebla. This stop proved much lengthier—three months—but it served two purposes. First, only about half of the original force that had landed in Vera Cruz now presented itself for duty. Although battle casualties had proved relatively light, disease and desertion had decimated the army's ranks, and Scott needed reinforcements desperately. Therefore, the army waited in Puebla for their arrival. Second, the high command harbored some hopes that a peace settlement could be effected since it was obvious to them (as they believed it certainly should have been to the Mexicans) that the American forces could not be stopped. The halt allowed for a temporary cease-fire during the negotiations. However, a settlement failed to materialize, and the army prepared for the final push on the Mexican capital.[26]

Finally leaving Puebla on August 7, with reinforcements that increased the size of the American army to more than ten thousand, the column advanced along the National Road toward the valley of Mexico. Encountering no resistance, it climbed sinuously upward through the mountains. Upon reaching the crest of the mountain range at Cordova, the troops looked down upon the oval plain of Mexico. Although Lyon could not see "the ultimatum of our military aspirations," the city of Mexico lay at the far end of the forty-three-mile valley. On the fifteenth, the column reached Lake Tezcuco, which was surrounded by the first

25. Lyon Diary, April 19 to May 29, 1847, Nathaniel Lyon Papers, CSL.
26. Returns, April and May 1847, RG 94; Woodward, *Life of Nathaniel Lyon,* 93; Lyon to Hasler, October 24, 1847, Nathaniel Lyon Papers, AAS; Lyon Diary, August 7, 1847, Nathaniel Lyon Papers, CSL; Weems, *To Conquer a Peace,* 383–85.

manned defenses they had encountered since taking those at Cerro Gordo. As the forces halted before the towering cone of El Peñon, scouts reconnoitered for four days the seemingly impregnable system of defenses. The area below El Peñon was covered by marshes, and the only passage to the city from that direction was a causeway mounded up above the waters. However, this causeway passed directly beneath the three-hundred-foot peak, bristling with Mexican guns. Wisely the commanders determined to move to the southern end of the city, passing around Lakes Chalco and Xochimilco. Santa Anna, again in command of the Mexican forces, countered this move by hastily fortifying the areas south of the city. He deployed a small force near the village of San Geronimo, with its strongest concentration around the convent and bridge at Churubusco, approximately three miles south of the capital city.[27]

Late on the afternoon of August 19, the two armies met on the high plateau near San Geronimo in the first of several key battles for the city of Mexico. Twiggs's division moved to the southwest of the town and lightly engaged a force of nearly seven thousand troops under the command of Gen. Gabriel Valencia, which occupied a strong fortification called Contreras. As the lines clashed, Riley's brigade's only action was a brief encounter with a charging force of Mexican lancers, whom they drove off after a sharp firefight. The skirmishing ended shortly after dark when a hard rain set in, but at around 3:00 A.M. the brigade slipped quietly around the Mexicans' right flank and lay on their arms the rest of the night. They were now in an advantageous position to cut off any retreat from the planned early morning assault on the entrenchments. However, before the sun cleared the mountains to the east of the city, Twiggs's division left its position, scaled the steep hill before the Mexican camp, and attacked. The ensuing hand-to-hand struggle lasted only seventeen minutes before the Americans carried the works, suffering only sixty casualties while inflicting losses of over fifteen hundred killed, wounded, and captured. In addition, they captured twenty-two pieces of artillery. Those Mexican defenders who managed to escape fled toward the defenses at Churubusco, two miles to the northeast. However, the fighting on this day had just begun.[28]

After a brief pause for regrouping, the Americans drove on toward the

27. Lyon to Hasler, October 24, 1847, Nathaniel Lyon Papers, AAS; Weems, *To Conquer a Peace*, 392–97.

28. Lyon to Hasler, October 24, 1847, Nathaniel Lyon Papers, CSL; Woodward, *Life of Nathaniel Lyon*, 92; Henry, *Mexican War*, 326–37.

town of Churubusco, where Worth's brigade on the right had already
engaged the Mexican defenders hotly at the strongly fortified bridge over
the Rio Churubusco canal. Not only was the brigade taking a beating
from the half-dozen guns at the bridge, but it also was receiving fire on
its flank from the defenses surrounding the convent of San Mateo. In
order to relieve Worth, Twiggs's division received orders to assault the
convent. Although Lyon feared that the large fields of corn standing
before the defenses would likely impede a successful assault, he led his
company gamely into the storm. As suspected, the corn caused great
difficulty for the men; they were forced to grope blindly through it while
enduring a constant fire from both small arms and artillery. Casualties
mounted quickly.[29]

While Lyon and much of Riley's brigade remained pinned down in the
corn, all three American divisions reached the scene and bore down upon
the defenses. Their weight proved too much for the Mexican defenders
to bear. After about an hour and a half of sanguinary fighting, the attack
managed to punch through the line of defense at the bridge. Outflanked,
the troops defending the convent quickly gave way. Soon, the entire
Mexican force, many short of ammunition, broke and fled toward the
city to the north, leaving over eleven hundred prisoners and fourteen
pieces of cannon. The road lay open to the gates of the Mexican capital.[30]

Rather than relish the glory of the victories at Contreras and Churubusco, Lyon found fault with his commanders. He inveighed against the
needless loss of life at the battle at Churubusco, his scorn deriving primarily from the hot fire his brigade had received in the fight. He believed
the works could have been easily bypassed, achieving the same result by
maneuver rather than by bloodshed. In his eyes, the day's principal
malefactor was Gen. William Worth, who Lyon was convinced had deliberately brought on the battle. "Having no share in the glory of Contreras," he charged, "[Worth] determined to bring his division into action
under whatever disadvantages." Lyon ranted, "With the characteristic
stupidity of that stupid Officer a great & unnecessary sacrifice of life was
occasioned equaled nowhere in this war except in his own 'butt head'
attack upon Churubusco." Lyon also protested the apparent lack of
resolve on the part of the high command for not pursuing the attack after
the Mexicans had retreated toward the city. "Had we advanced that

29. Lyon to Hasler, October 24, 1847, Nathaniel Lyon Papers, AAS; Woodward, *Life
of Nathaniel Lyon,* 117; Henry, *Mexican War,* 339–40.

30. Henry, *Mexican War,* 340–41; Lyon to Hasler, October 24, 1847, Nathaniel
Lyon Papers, AAS.

night," he posited, "we should have made the City ours without the loss of five men more. But imagine (if you can) our surprise & indignation when instead of advancing we were halted . . . ." Although he understood that the purpose of this temporary armistice was to attempt peace negotiations, Lyon remained unsympathetic. His uncontrolled anger at the whole situation obstructed all logic. "The prospects of peace are as distant as ever & it is to be hoped our Gov't will make no more useless sacrifice of life in this stupid twaddle about peace." In his blind rage, Lyon could not decide whether he wanted war or peace.[31]

Swiftly he reached a decision on the matter. As a groundswell of opposition to the peace negotiations emerged among the army officers currently engaged in the fighting, Lyon's voice of dissent echoed loudly. The rigors of battle convinced him that peace without total victory would be a travesty. Although he had once considered the taking of Mexican territory immoral, he now considered the thought of relinquishing claims so hard won to be "imbecility." "Mexico," he observed, "affects indignity at the idea of losing a small portion of the large conquests we have made, and taking advantage of time, perfects her fortifications." When negotiations proved ineffectual, Lyon remarked derisively that Scott had "at last blundered into the idea that he was being deceived & consequently the Armistice terminated," much to his and the other officers' satisfaction. By September 7, the push toward the Mexican capital was resumed.[32]

Lyon was directly involved in neither the battle of El Molino del Ray nor Chapultepec, but with the rest of the Second Infantry he entered the city of Mexico on the morning of September 14, 1847. City authorities had given American commanders reports that Santa Anna's forces had withdrawn from the city, and the column started forward expecting a peaceful entry. Haughtily, they passed through the Belen Gate, the southeastern entrance to the Mexican capital, and shortly thereafter entered the city itself. At this point, the troops abruptly found that their visit would not be welcomed with open arms. "As we advanced toward the center of the City," Lyon recalled, "we were fired upon in every direction from tops of houses, windows, balconies & street corners. This street fight continued through out the day . . . ."[33]

31. Woodward, *Life of Nathaniel Lyon,* 118; Lyon to Hasler, October 24, 1847, Nathaniel Lyon Papers, AAS.

32. Returns, 1847 Year End Report, RG 94, filed by Capt. Thompson Morris; Lyon to Hasler, October 24, 1847, Nathaniel Lyon Papers, AAS.

33. Returns, 1847 Year End Report, RG 94; Woodward, *Life of Nathaniel Lyon,*

After such an extremely successful campaign fought against great topographical adversities, this chaotic street fighting proved a most anticlimactic end, especially for Lyon. As he endeavored to direct his company's fire against its ubiquitous assailants, a spent ball struck him in the leg. Luckily, the wound proved slight and failed to incapacitate him at that time. However, his subsequent exertions caused it to become inflamed, and he was forced from duty for a few days. In this rather insignificant manner, Lyon proved himself a false prophet; he had indeed made the newspapers as a Mexican war "hero."[34]

Yet Lyon's actions in battle gained him more than a mere line in his hometown newspaper's casualty report. He had caught the eye of his regimental commander, who recommended him "to the *special notice* of Colonel Riley." Although it would not be conferred upon him until September of the next year, his "gallant and meritorious conduct in the battles of Contreras and Churubusco" earned him a promotion to brevet captain. It would seem that his irascibility, while a detriment to his success as a peacetime officer, could be a great advantage to him as a leader in time of war.[35]

It is interesting to note that in all the battles in which Lyon participated, his only comments on his feelings toward death emerge in his frequent diatribes against his superiors. His journal and letters were often replete with reports, in grim detail, of the deaths of comrades in arms, but his descriptions appear devoid of emotion. At Vera Cruz, he related almost clinically that "balls continue coming from Town—one of which passed through our Ranks & Killed Brevet Capt Alburtes by knocking off the skull & the Brains were scattered out on the ground . . . ." Again a few days later: "The ball passed through the center of the body of the Sergt and thro' the neck of the other man—the Sergt soon died & the man is likely to recover." Nowhere appears any emotive reaction to war's carnage and inhumanity, to the scenes that few soldiers failed to consider the most evocative of their lives. Lyon's only mention of

124; Lyon to Hasler, October 24, 1847, Nathaniel Lyon Papers, AAS.

34. Lyon to George W. Cullum, October 16, 1855, Nathaniel Lyon File, USMA; Woodward, *Life of Nathaniel Lyon*, 125.

35. Woodward, *Life of Nathaniel Lyon*, 120, 122; Returns, September 1848, RG 94; Roger Jones to Lyon, September 18, 1848, Letters Sent, RG 94. Perhaps significantly, Lyon's "special mention" was delivered not by the regular regimental commander, Maj. James Plympton, but rather by the acting commander, Capt. Thompson Morris. One cannot help but wonder, given past circumstances, whether Plympton would have been so quick to recommend Lyon for promotion.

his own wound comes in a brief sentence written in 1855; he does not appear even to have written home about it. One cannot view his ravings about his superiors, though they often pass judgment on their abilities in terms of loss of life, as a genuine concern for human suffering. He used this argument merely as a gauge by which officers should be measured. There is no pathos—only anger.[36]

Lyon's apparent insensitivity to death most likely stems from his personal obsession with duty. He thrived on the discipline at West Point, for it demanded from the individual the strictest requirements in discharging that duty. He despised Florida, for it had not allowed him to perform effectively his responsibility to the country: exterminating the Seminole menace. And he proved relentless toward those who failed to perform that duty. At Sackets Harbor, Private Kelly bore the brunt of Lyon's incipient fanatical treatment of those whom he considered "unfaithful," and Lyon determined to resign from the service when he had been punished for what he considered a faithful performance of his duty. For the soldier, death was simply another duty, and Lyon could evince no emotion when men performed theirs; there was no sense in it. As one of his men remembered of Lyon, "His idea was duty; every soldier was to him a mere machine; it was not the 'duty' of a soldier to think . . . ." In years to come, Lyon would expand his own role to ensuring that men faithfully discharged their various duties.[37]

Lyon remained with his unit in the Mexican capital until November, when he volunteered for escort duty to Vera Cruz. Happy to leave the city, he could not "call to mind a single attraction for which he would wish to stay longer." Yet he found the rest of Mexico as unpleasant as he found its capital city. Marauding bands of guerrillas had taken over the countryside since the surrender of the capital, and they turned both Puebla and Jalapa into havens for terror and destruction. By the spring of 1848, he looked anxiously for peace so that the army of occupation could leave. "Peace to Mexico & all the world we will breathe to this heaven forsaken people," he wrote, "while love for our country & a burning desire to see its wealthy & happy shores shall fill our hearts." At last, in July 1848, the Second Infantry received orders to report to Vera

36. Lyon Diary, March 11 to March 15, 1847, Nathaniel Lyon Papers, CSL; Lyon to George W. Cullum, October 16, 1855, Nathaniel Lyon File, USMA.

37. E. H. E. Jameson, ed., *A Memorial Wreath Containing an Address from the Lyon Monumental Association of St. Louis . . . ,* 22–23; Eugene F. Ware, *The Lyon Campaign,* 311.

Cruz for transport back to the United States. On July 8, Lyon and his company boarded the vessel *Robert Parker* and set sail happily for New Orleans.[38]

38. Woodward, *Life of Nathaniel Lyon,* 134; Returns, November 1847 to July 1848, RG 94; Lyon to Hasler, November 16, 1847, Nathaniel Lyon Papers, AAS; Lyon to Hasler, April 5, 1848, ibid.

IV

Justice for the Unjust

After only nine days at sea, Lyon's ship anchored at the gulf port of Pascagoula, Mississippi. Most on board expected to remain for an extended encampment to discharge any veterans whose enlistments had expired and to recruit new soldiers to fill their ranks. Within days of their arrival, however, orders from Washington instructed them to proceed immediately up the Mississippi River to Jefferson Barracks, the West's largest military post, located at St. Louis. After organizing and outfitting the regiment, the Second Infantry would then proceed by foot to the scene of its newest assignment: California. On the night of July 24, Lyon and his company boarded the steamer *A. R. Hetzel,* bound for New Orleans, and the next day transferred to the riverboat *Sultana* for the trip up the muddy river.[1]

Lyon had never before seen the Mississippi. The mighty river—"this great outlet of the glorious and thriving West"—impressed him, yet he was surprised at the lack of prosperous settlements along the river. Perhaps he envisioned the urban centers of the West to be similar to the established cities of the nation's eastern coast. With the notable exception of New Orleans, however, the western cities were fairly new and had a decidedly western look: unpolished, often haphazardly built, and dirty. This was especially true of the river cities. However, while the West proved less than he expected, Lyon was far from disappointed with what he saw. On the contrary, he intended to seek his fortune in California.[2]

Although he had never been there, Lyon perceived the western states and territories as the outlet for American growth, and to him that growth centered upon economics. He believed that the burgeoning frontier offered opportunities for rapid advancement that could not be found in the East. He was keenly aware of the struggle his father had faced in provid-

1. Ashbel Woodward, *Life of General Nathaniel Lyon,* 137–38; Returns, July to August 1848, RG 94; Lyon to Lorenzo Lyon, July 25, 1848, Nathaniel Lyon Papers, CHS.
2. Woodward, *Life of Nathaniel Lyon,* 137–38; Returns, July to August 1848, RG 94.

ing for his family, and Lyon vowed silently never to fall into the same trap. Imbued with the free-labor ideology, Lyon had always possessed an acute business sense. On many occasions he sent words of advice to his brothers suggesting paths they should take to ensure the greatest profitability from their pecuniary endeavors. His brother Daniel, who had inherited the family mill from Amasa and was currently running it (apparently without great success), Lyon accused of "waywardness," advising him to "get up in the morning and attend to his business during the day and go to bed at night." To brother Lorenzo, Lyon sent congratulations on the purchase of Eastford's first power thresher, but admonished him to "find good employment" with it lest its value be lost. Ironically, Lyon cautioned his brother-in-law John Hasler about moving his shoe manufacturing business to St. Louis. Although Lyon believed as early as 1843 that the West held great profit potential, he thought that that source could be tapped most lucratively by those engaged in the distribution of goods, not in their manufacture. He therefore advised against Hasler's relocation. And now it was time for Lyon to follow his own advice. He had built up a sufficient amount of capital from his seven years of officer's pay, and California, recently ceded by Mexico to the United States as one term of the Treaty of Guadalupe-Hidalgo, appeared to Lyon the ripest area for profit in the country. Even before news of the discovery of gold reached the rest of the nation, Lyon had determined to sate his own *auri sacra fames* with California land.[3]

While still on the ship from Pascagoula, Lyon began penning his brothers a letter informing them of his decision to buy land in California. He had inherited from his father the rights to a share in the acreage Amasa left to the other boys, and just before leaving for Mexico he had acquired three tracts from them worth over four hundred dollars. Now, he offered to sell them back to Lorenzo and Daniel. "My object," he wrote, "will be to look to all kinds of enterprises & speculations that may give encouragement but my present contemplations are to purchase lands either with a view to a permanent future residence myself or to sell at such advantage as the emigration to the country & its improvement may warrant." Because the regiment was scheduled to leave soon, Lyon needed to liquidate his assets as quickly as possible and expected his brothers to oblige immediately. As it turned out, army command coun-

3. Lyon to John B. Hasler, February 27, 1847, Nathaniel Lyon Papers, AAS; Lyon to Lorenzo Lyon, October 16, 1843, ibid.; Lyon to Hasler, October 16, 1843, ibid.; Lyon to Lorenzo Lyon, April 9, 1853, Nathaniel Lyon Papers, CHS; Allen B. Lincoln, ed., *A Modern History of Windham County, Connecticut,* 2:396–97.

termanded the order for the Second Infantry to march cross-country to California in favor of sending it by sea. After a month at Jefferson Barracks, the unit was shipped via Cincinnati and Sandusky, Ohio, to Fort Hamilton in the harbor of New York City. Lyon saw this as an opportunity to settle his matters at home and requested a twenty-day leave of absence prior to movement. He was granted this leave to begin on September 1, the same day the regiment left for New York. On September 15, Lyon reached Eastford.[4]

Lyon harbored an additional reason for returning home. On his last visit, almost three years earlier, his brash promulgations about marriage and religion had left his mother in appreciable emotional turmoil. While at that moment the force of his own rhetoric had precluded all thoughts of its long-term effects, Lyon had since regretted the pain that his statements had obviously inflicted. Writing to his sister, he confessed, "I found Mother rather low & failing in health & very low & depressed in spirits. I left her with a deep impression I should never meet her again on earth . . . ." His guilt led him often to send her small sums of money, though her own fiercely independent spirit caused her to resist such "charity" and on at least one occasion forced him to send the money to Hasler so that she would not apprehend its true benefactor. He worried, particularly in winter, about her living alone on the home place. Plagued by rheumatism, she was not in the best of health, and he believed that she should sell the farm to one of the boys and take up residence with one of her daughters. All these concerns had weighed upon him these past few years. Therefore, upon arriving at home, he was palpably relieved that his mother, at sixty-seven, seemed to be "in tolerable health, and not much suffering from the weight of years as much as, in her advanced age, might be expected." Although he proved unable to convince Lorenzo and Daniel to buy his lands, he did manage to convince Kezia to leave the home place and live with his sister, Elizabeth, and her family in Ashford. Moreover, on September 18, he received confirmation of his promotion to brevet captain.[5]

4. Lyon to Lorenzo Lyon, July 25, 1848, Nathaniel Lyon Papers, CHS; Ashford Township Land Records, CSL; Will of Amasa Lyon, Ashford Township Probate Records, ATH; Returns, September 1848, RG 94; Woodward, *Life of Nathaniel Lyon,* 138.

5. Lyon to Hasler, November 4, 1846, Nathaniel Lyon Papers, AAS; Lyon to Mother, July 11, 1846, ibid.; Lyon to Hasler, December 30, 1844, ibid.; Lyon to Mother, undated, Nathaniel Lyon File, NYHS; Woodward, *Life of Nathaniel Lyon,* 140; Ashford Township Land Records, CSL; U.S. Census, 1850, Windham County, Conn.; Lyon to Roger Jones, September 18, 1848, Letters Received, RG 94.

After nearly a month at home, he packed his gear, leashed Tasso, and on October 8 reported back to Fort Hamilton. A month later, Lyon and two of the regiment's companies, along with all the troops' baggage, boarded the sea transport *Rome,* while the remaining five companies loaded aboard the *Iowa.* The two vessels would carry the troops southward through the Strait of Magellan, at the tip of South America, and then again northward along the Pacific coast of the two continents to Monterey, the California capital. Compared to the length of this trip, the sea journey to Mexico would seem inconsequential. Commanded by Gen. Bennet Riley, the Second Infantry set sail on November 8 for the newly acquired territory of California.[6]

During the voyage, Lyon acted as both the assistant commissary of subsistence and the regiment's assistant quartermaster. The weighty responsibilities allowed him to relinquish temporarily his duties as company commander. The winter seas proved rather rough through the first part of their voyage, hampering the efforts of those on board to acclimate themselves to ocean travel. Under normal circumstances, those who had experienced the voyages to and from Mexico would have been much better off than the newest members of the regiment. The tempestuousness of the ocean, however, negated any intestinal advantages anyone might once have held. The discomfort of seasickness no doubt had passed by the time the ship passed through the two majestic hills of Cape Frio, marking the entrance to the harbor of Rio de Janeiro. On Christmas Eve the ships anchored, and commanders allowed their men liberty to take in the city's holiday sights, their first excursion onto dry land in over a month and a half. Lyon took advantage of the tropical climate during the Christmas season to explore the city. He was impressed with its Portuguese architecture, fashioned predominantly of granite, and with the towering mountains that formed the backdrop to the glittering city. Rio proved an enjoyable first stop, and on January 2, 1849, the ships pulled out of the harbor and began the second leg of their long journey.[7]

As they sailed farther south, the climate grew progressively colder. Fog shrouded visibility, often for days at a time. The ships lost contact with one another, and though Lyon reported that the *Rome* had been in front of the *Iowa* when they left Rio, the latter ship had been in port for

6. Returns, September 1848 to January 1849, RG 94; Lyon to Lorenzo Lyon, July 25, 1848, Nathaniel Lyon Papers, CHS; Woodward, *Life of Nathaniel Lyon,* 140.

7. Returns, November to December 1848, RG 94; Woodward, *Life of Nathaniel Lyon,* 140–43.

two days by the time the *Rome* anchored in Valparaiso, Chile, on February 9. Again they stopped for a few days in the port city, nestled in the shadow of Mount Aconcagua, the highest peak in South America. By the sixteenth, the ships were again under sail. For the final leg of the voyage, warm weather returned, the seas calmed, and the reason behind the appellation "Pacific" at last became apparent. On April 6, after six arduous months at sea, the *Rome* sailed into the harbor of Monterey, California. The *Iowa* followed a week later. For most of the next four-and-a-half years, Lyon would be stationed at various posts on the United States's westernmost frontier.[8]

For over half a decade prior to Lyon's arrival, the territory of California had been the scene of revolution, war, and, most recently, rampant lawlessness resulting from the discovery of gold along the Sacramento River. In the summer of 1846, even before receiving confirmation of an official declaration of war against Mexico, an enigmatic young regular army officer who led an exploring expedition to the Pacific coast, Capt. John C. Frémont, had instigated a farcical "Bear Flag Revolt," intended to free the territory from Mexican rule. He then brashly proclaimed the independence of the "California Republic." In September, as the war in Mexico had just begun to unfold, a combined land and sea operation under Commodore Robert Stockton secured Los Angeles for the United States, only to lose it as a rash of interior counterrevolutions broke out against the invading American forces. Separate movements by forces under Frémont and Gen. Stephen Watts Kearny, fresh from capturing Santa Fe, succeeded in securing California for the United States. Because the impetuous Frémont refused to recognize Kearny's authority over Stockton's, the general had him court-martialed for disobeying his orders.[9]

Since that turbulent time, California had been ruled by a territorial government hard-pressed to maintain civil order. Initially, law enforcement had devolved upon local authorities, but the discovery of gold in 1848 rendered that practice unfeasible. Aspiring prospectors soon poured into the territory and quickly set up mining and panning operations along the streams that gushed from the mountains. These "Gold Rushers" (predominantly single men or those who had left their spouses

8. Woodward, *Life of Nathaniel Lyon,* 143–45; Returns, February and April 1849, RG 94.

9. K. Jack Bauer, *The Mexican War, 1846–1848,* 164–77; Otis A. Singletary, *The Mexican War,* 63–70; Robert L. Turkoly-Joczik, "Fremont and the Western Department," 365.

behind) created a precarious situation as boom towns sprang up near the gold-producing streams. Without an effective system of law enforcement, disorder, corruption, and violence in the towns quickly became pandemic, and federal troops were needed in the area to regain stability. The army therefore dispatched the Second Infantry to assist with these police details.[10]

General Riley assumed the office of territorial governor upon his arrival at the capital, Monterey, and he soon parceled out the Second Infantry to sundry posts in the territory. However, he did so only hesitantly. The lure of gold quickly eroded even the army's effectiveness. Desertion among its recruits had markedly thinned the ranks of those who had arrived prior to the Second Infantry. Consequently, Riley tried to keep away from the mining towns as many of his men as he could. Lyon was one of those detailed for other duties. A week after his arrival, he and D Company received orders to move to the small army post at San Diego. Half of the company would serve as an escort detachment to accompany the government commissioners vested with the duty of laying out a new boundary between the United States and Mexico following the Treaty of Guadalupe Hidalgo. The other half, including Lyon, would remain in San Diego and begin the enlargement of its military post. Lyon would act as constructing quartermaster for the operation.[11]

Because San Diego lay so far from San Francisco, the army's source of supply on the Pacific coast, future operations in the southern part of the territory would depend upon the construction of a distribution center there. In January 1847, when the army first occupied the small post, San Diego was little more than a tiny port, comprised of an adobe enclosure and a few rude houses. In comparison to the military installation at Monterey, with its wharves, customs house, and seaside homes, the post was rather minuscule. Plans for the new San Diego Barracks, with its magazine, corral, barracks, stockade, and six-hundred-foot wharf, would alter the site drastically.[12]

The languor of military bureaucracy, however, forced a lengthy delay in the fort's construction. Because of the extended wait for materials (the frame for the barracks structure was being shipped by sea from Maine), Lyon's station in San Diego was interrupted by a six-month tour of duty at Benicia Barracks, on the San Pablo Bay near San Francisco. In January

10. Hardy Kemp, *About Nathaniel Lyon, Brigadier General, United States Army Volunteers and Wilson's Creek*, 36–38; Returns, April 1849, RG 94.
11. Returns, April 1849, RG 94; George Ruhlen, "San Diego Barracks," 7–9.
12. Bauer, *The Mexican War,* 234; Ruhlen, "San Diego Barracks," 8–9.

1850, however, he returned to the port on the Mexican border and commenced immediately to supervise the work on the depot buildings. Lyon proved a most capable quartermaster and construction supervisor; his punctiliousness and keen attention to detail ensured the completion of the endeavor without hitch. Upon completion of the main barracks, Lyon found himself so pleased with the work that he gave a great ball in the building, inviting dignitaries from as far away as Los Angeles. Indeed, Lyon enjoyed his stay in San Diego. "We have been having very gay times here of late," he wrote to an acquaintance that spring, "in the way of dancing[,] Picknics . . . & if I were not on the point of leaving I am afraid I might be susseptible to the delicate affections of the heart under the piercing flashes & musical note of Castilian origin . . . ."[13]

During Lyon's garrison in San Diego, he was captivated by both the climate and the setting of the town. Though he believed that at present "Cal'a is in a terrible condition in regard to the moral & legal organization of its people & men" (largely as a result of the vigilance committees that plagued San Francisco and the lawlessness of the mining towns), Lyon became convinced of the potential for settlement in San Diego. The barracks had been built near the center of the old town of San Diego, but the post caused a new town to spring up around it with surprising rapidity. Governmental buildings associated with the military post were located in New Town, and by all appearances San Diego would soon be a thriving community. Despite believing that he might soon be transferred, Lyon began to think that San Diego might prove an enjoyable—and lucrative—permanent home at the conclusion of his military career. "Indeed," he wrote, "all things considered, this is the most pleasant place for a residence . . . ." Surmising that his chance for California profit was now at hand, and having already paid fifteen hundred dollars for ten lots of property near Benicia while on duty there, he purchased a small lot near the beach in New Town and had a house built on the lot. His total investment came to five hundred dollars.[14]

13. Ruhlen, "San Diego Barracks," 9–10; William Heath Davis, *Seventy-five Years in California*, 336; Lyon to A. Fisdale, April 30, 1850, Nathaniel Lyon File, SHSM.

14. Woodward, *Life of Nathaniel Lyon*, 163–64; Ruhlen, "San Diego Barracks," 10; Andrew F. Rolle, "William Heath Davis and the Founding of American San Diego," 36, 46n; Lyon Account Book, WC; Estate Inventory of Nathaniel Lyon, Eastford Township Probate Records, CSL. Lyon purchased ten lots in New York of the Pacific for fifteen hundred dollars while stationed in San Francisco. His house in San Diego cost five hundred dollars and was rented after he was transferred and not able to use it. Lyon believed in the value of real estate, and at his death he owned property in California, Iowa, Virginia, Kansas, Illinois, and Nebraska totaling in excess of one thousand acres.

Although until the spring of 1850 Lyon had enjoyed no active field duty in California, the idle time allowed him to cultivate his growing infatuation with the territory. His health had flourished in the "exceedingly fine" southern California climate, which allowed him to enjoy vegetables from his garden as early as April. Although his duty in San Diego proved uneventful, it had been enjoyable. He now believed that his decision to reenlist was a good one, at least for the moment. Writing to his mother, he confessed candidly that he had at one time contemplated leaving the army to tend to her needs, but that his own "pride & ambition, . . . the bane of the human heart & barrier to the perfection of human nature," now prevented him from doing so. He valued too much "the advantages I possess in the service to be willing to relinquish them for uncertain consequences." Indeed, he was so convinced of the future of California that he wrote to his older brother Lorenzo, exhorting him to move his family to the area:

> I am sure you would be well content if once settled here, but this is a great job and I am not disposed to urge it upon you . . . . If this should strike you favourably, and you seriously feel disposed to undertake it, and find you can make arrangements satisfactory, I will volunteer any assistance in my power towards bringing about the result. I should like much to see you well located in this country . . . .

In Lyon's mind, his own destiny lay on the sun coast.[15]

Two isolated Indian incidents in northern California involving the deaths of several white settlers and an army officer provided Lyon's first steps toward fulfilling that destiny. In June 1849, army command sent Bvt. Capt. William H. Warner, an 1836 graduate of West Point serving as a topographical engineer, to survey the mountain passes at the headwaters of the Sacramento River for a proposed transcontinental railroad line. On September 26, the party fell prey to a Pit River Indian ambush, and Warner was killed. At roughly the same time, residents from the vicinity of Clear Lake, about seventy miles northwest of Benicia, reported that a loose confederation of Indians encamped near the lake had murdered two white settlers. Despite reports acknowledging that the victims, Andrew Kelsey and his partner, Charles Stone, had in many ways precipitated the tragedy, and despite the fact that the relationship between white settlers and the Indians around Clear Lake had always

---

15. Nathaniel Lyon to Lorenzo Lyon, April 9, 1853, Hoadley Collection, CHS; Lyon to Mother, undated, Nathaniel Lyon File, NYHS.

been pacific, the two unrelated events in such close conjunction prompted the government into swift, punitive action.[16]

Immediately following the incident, a company of dragoons commanded by Lt. John W. Robinson moved promptly from their camp at Sonoma to Clear Lake, but found that the Indians had retreated onto several of the islands in the lake, rendering further pursuit impossible without boats. Muddy winter conditions delayed the organization of a second expedition until spring. The expressed purpose of this mission, however, as conveyed through the territorial governor himself, was "to chastise the authors of both outrages . . . and to strike them promptly and heavily." Riley ordered that the force be led by Maj. Washington Seawell. However, on the eve of its departure, Seawell received orders from President Pierce to attend a court-martial scheduled to convene in Oregon, leaving him unable to lead the expedition. Because Lyon was presently on temporary quartermaster assignment at Monterey and an immediate replacement was needed, "the lot fell most happily on Brevet Captain Nathaniel Lyon . . . ." After receiving department commander Persifor F. Smith's orders, Lyon left Monterey on April 30 and arrived at Benecia four days later. On May 6, the expedition marched northward.[17]

Lyon's plan of campaign was first to march across the rugged country to Clear Lake, where they would attack the tribes encamped on its shores. From there, they would continue to the northeast to the Pit River, near the border of the Oregon Territory, where Warner was killed, to adequately "call those Indians to an account before returning." Lyon made no mistake in interpreting Smith's orders. He understood fully that by instructing him "to ascertain with certainty the offenders, and to strike them promptly and heavily," Lyon's commander wished him to

16. George W. Cullum, *Biographical Register of the Officers and Graduates of the U.S. Military Academy at West Point, N. Y.,* 1:635; William H. Goetzmann, *Army Exploration in the American West, 1803–1863,* 250–53; Edwin A. Sherman, "Sherman Was There—The Recollections of Edwin A. Sherman," 49–51; Max Radin, ed., "The Stone and Kelsey 'Massacre' on the Shores of Clear Lake in 1849: The Indian Viewpoint," 266–69. Judging by the oppressive methods with which Stone and Kelsey dealt with the local Indians, their deaths were not completely unprovoked.

17. Woodward, *Life of Nathaniel Lyon,* 165–67; Cullum, *Biographical Register,* 1:635; Francis P. Prucha, *Guide to the Military Posts of the United States, 1789–1895,* 108; Lyon to E. R. S. Canby, May 22, 1850, Letters Received, RG 94; Lyon to A. Fisdale, April 30, 1850, Nathaniel Lyon File, SHSM; Returns, January to May 1850, RG 94; P. F. Smith to Irwin McDowell, May 25, 1850, *Executive Documents of the Senate of the United States,* 2d sess., 31st Congress, vol. 1, part 2, doc. 1 (hereafter cited as Senate Executive Document), 78.

seek out the tribes involved in the murders and deal them a telling blow. Traditional modes of justice could not apply here; "debased savages" would neither understand nor comply. Lyon had seen this in Florida but was unable to share adequately in the action there. Now, Lyon possessed power, the power to punish. The army had made it his duty. He could hardly contain his excitement when he wrote to a friend upon his departure from Monterey: "[That] this solution of it [the Indian problem] may be a successful one is of course my highest hope at present & if opportunity affords I will give you some account of us in the rout."[18]

After a five-day march, the column reached the south end of the lake, from which they intended to launch their attack with three whale boats they had transported on wagons. The Indians, however, had learned of the impending assault and fled to a small island at the northern end of the lake, nearly thirty miles away. Lyon sent the company of dragoons around the western length of the lake to pin the tribe on the island, then pursued around the east with the infantry. Because there was no way to cross the lake in one trip with the boats they had brought, Lyon was forced to improvise. After the column arrived at the north end on the afternoon of the fourteenth, Lyon sent the dragoons to take positions on the shores facing the island to prevent any retreat. He then had one of the three heavy transport wagons dismantled and lashed to its frame the three ten-oar whale boats. The next morning, with the dragoons in position, the troops crossed to the back side of the island on the manufactured transport vessel. The natives put up a brief defense, but the infantry quickly gained firing positions on the island. The four hundred defenders, hidden in the rush along the shore, quickly scattered, many plunging into the thick tule growing just offshore.[19]

His sense of duty feverish, Lyon intended now to complete his "punitive" attack. He ordered his men to sling their cartridge boxes around their necks, fix bayonets, and follow their quarry into the reeds, "to pursue and destroy as far as possible." A murky red soon clouded the blue lake water along the shoreline as the soldiers plunged into the tule and, in water in many places shoulder high, butchered summarily between sixty and one hundred braves hiding there. Yet, as with Kelly at Madison Barracks, Lyon's vengeance by this time overrode all sense of

18. Lyon to A. Fisdale, April 30, 1850, Nathaniel Lyon File, SHSM.
19. Lyon to E. R. S. Canby, May 2, 1850, Letters Received, RG 94; P. F. Smith to Irwin McDowell, May 25, 1850, Senate Executive Document, 78.

reason. Possessed by his own power, he then turned his men on the women and children of the island camp. The scene turned from savage to macabre. As native women pleaded for mercy, they and their offspring were bayoneted or shot to death, their bodies then dumped into the lake. Grotesque images emerge: jubilant soldiers swaggering toward the lake with babies impaled upon their uplifted bayonets, shrieking squaws and children diving into the lake to drown themselves rather than suffer death at the hands of the men in blue, old men hanged, their bodies then burned with the rest of the camp. The day's massacre consumed between two hundred and four hundred Indians, without a single loss to Lyon's force.[20]

His apparent bloodlust for the moment sated, Lyon now turned his attention to the true purpose of his mission: to find the murderers of Captain Warner. He sent out a detail that succeeded in capturing two local Indians who informed the federal commander that the tribes that had killed Warner were now located along the Russian River, to the west of Clear Lake. The next day, the column proceeded in that direction. Upon reaching the Russian River, the expedition moved southward for about twenty miles, and early on the morning of May 19 their captured guide led them to the camp of one of the tribes they believed to be the culprits. The Indians had gathered on a small, wooded island in the midst of a large slough, and Lyon formed his men so as to surround the natives completely. After his sanguinary work at Clear Lake, Lyon could not possibly have harbored any intentions of showing quarter to these supposed marauders, and he ordered his men to advance immediately. Because escape was impossible, the island, in Lyon's own graphic words, "soon became a perfect slaughter pen, as they continued to fight with great resolution and vigor till every jungle was routed." Few of the tribe's more than one hundred natives survived the attack. Lyon's force incurred a loss of but two wounded.[21]

Following orders from headquarters, Lyon ordered his force to retrace their steps up the Russian River and head east to the Pit River. However, they located neither the second tribe involved in Warner's murder nor the

20. Radin, "Stone and Kelsey Massacre," 270–73; Lyon to E. R. S. Canby, May 22, 1850, Letters Received, RG 94; P. F. Smith to Irwin McDowell, May 25, 1850, Senate Executive Document, 78–79. The site of the battle, no longer surrounded by water, is known locally as Bloody Hill.

21. Woodward, *Life of Nathaniel Lyon*, 165–67; Lyon to E. R. S. Canby, May 22, 1850, Letters Received, RG 94; P. F. Smith to Irwin McDowell, May 25, 1850, Senate Executive Document, 78–79.

captain's remains. By August, Lyon was satisfied that no further good would come from the mission, and perhaps that the guilty parties had received a just punishment—either directly or vicariously—for their transgressions. He believed that his mission—and duty—had both been fulfilled completely. Achieving his objectives, however, had been quite fatiguing. The expedition had already covered more than 250 arduous miles over particularly rough country, and the men still faced a long march back to Benicia, over 125 miles away. When they arrived there in September, they had been in the field for nearly five months, and for the remainder of the year Lyon and the rest of the expeditionary force found rest and recuperation in garrison. For his services, Lyon received special commendation from Persifor F. Smith, who expressed his "highest praise of Captain Lyon's conduct." In addition, Lyon's official report of the expedition was heard in the United States Senate, where both its explicit detail and the officer's meritorious service to his country against an obviously dangerous and subversive Indian "menace" were met with warm approbation.[22]

As in Mexico, field duty had allowed Lyon to act on his own impulses, and his natural impetuosity lent itself perfectly to a limited command. Yet in California, Lyon exhibited a ferocity that bordered on sadism. This behavior appears to have been linked to what had evolved as Lyon's twisted perception of punishment. As demonstrated both in the Kelly incident and with the Clear Lake tribes, Lyon apparently viewed the meting out of justice to be the ultimate purpose of power. Those who did wrong must be brought to account for their sins. And in Lyon's peremptory mind, no venial offenses existed; all sins were mortal. Therefore, punishment must perforce be harsh, for it was not merely expiation; it was justice. As St. Augustine once wrote, "Punishment is justice for the unjust." Whether or not Lyon was familiar with the quotation matters not: he now embodied its message. And to him, he who possessed power determined who was unjust. Lyon craved such power. Yet by this time, he had carried his view one step further.

Whereas in Mexico Lyon had been unable to formulate God's role in man's life, in California he began to place him in perspective. And his image of the Creator fit unavoidably into Lyon's own perception of duty, power, and justice. As a boy, Lyon believed that God was omniscient and omnipotent; he had even made it a point to remind Hasler, upon Har-

22. Woodward, *Life of Nathaniel Lyon,* 176–80; Returns, April to December 1850; P. F. Smith to Irwin McDowell, May 25, 1850, Senate Executive Document, 78–79.

rison's victory over Van Buren in the 1840 presidential campaign, that "this appears to be one instance of the many, by which it seems the Creator som[e]times administers his laws; —by introducing evil that good may come." Lyon no longer believed such nonsense. God's hand did not guide the daily events of man, as church dogma had long maintained. Rather, intervention on his part came only upon a man's death. Then, the Creator looked judiciously at the divine ledger, determining the servant's eternal reward or punishment. By rejecting the myth of predestination, Lyon renounced his own Calvinist background. His was not a benevolent, merciful God, but one who justly rewarded and punished. As a witness in a court-martial several years later, Lyon promulgated publicly his views of God: "I do believe in the obligations of an oath, and in the existence of an overruling power that will punish falsehood with respect to a future state of rewards and punishments. I must say I have no positive conviction or reasons for belief."[23]

Although by his own admission his reasoning had no "positive" foundation, it nonetheless became evident to Lyon precisely how God's power was exercised on earth. It emanated neither from the church nor the ministry; the corruption of the institution demonstrated that all too clearly. No, God's will could be exerted only by those rare individuals who not only possessed the perspicacity to unfetter themselves from the obsequious tenets of their faith and to develop a true relationship with him, but who also wielded enough power among men to mete out his justice. Lyon believed that he was one of those rare individuals.

Because, as animal magnetism had convinced him, God's power was present in every man, reason was, in effect, divinely inspired. And because Lyon's God was one of reward and punishment, then Lyon's punishments—rationally wrought—were themselves ethereally sanctioned. Lyon saw himself in nearly Hegelian terms: a divine instrument for the purpose of eradicating the world's wrongs, not by the impotent Word, but by judgment and thorough punishment. Yet he jettisoned the dynamic role of Providence in man's destiny and replaced it with a sense of duty so strong that it exempted him from the ordinary canons of human conduct. From this point forward, Lyon's vision transcended an obsession with duty, honor, and country; his became a crusade.[24]

23. Lyon to Hasler, December 5, 1840, Nathaniel Lyon Papers, AAS; Transcripts of the Court-Martial of Bvt. Col. William R. Montgomery, September to December 1855, RG 153.
24. Edward C. Smith, *The Borderland in the Civil War,* 129; James Peckham, *General Nathaniel Lyon and Missouri in 1861,* 63.

Lyon shared time in the next year between San Diego and Fort Miller, situated in the San Joaquin Valley. In June, he received notice of his promotion to the rank of full captain, primarily as a result of his decisive actions with the Indians in northern California. The promotion greatly satisfied him, for it vindicated his own beliefs on rewards and punishment. He had done right; he had adequately punished the Indians. Therefore he received a reward, both for their wrongfulness and for his own rightness. It was divinely ordained. However, in January 1852, Lyon received news that jolted him from his newfound euphoria.[25]

On the twenty-fourth, a letter arrived from Lyon's sister informing him that his mother had gone insane. The news left Lyon thunderstruck. How could a benevolent God allow such a cruel fate for someone who had worshiped and served him her entire life? Although he had so recently begun to understand the ways of God, he was nonetheless bitter. At first, it simply made no sense. Agonizing, he wrote, "I have attempted to reflect upon and revolve this subject in my mind for the last twenty-four hours, but with swelling heart and maddening brain, I am lost in the absorbing thought, that Mother is wandering in clouds of mental darkness. O Mother, my dear Mother . . . . O Heaven, where is thy mercy!"[26]

Her illness appeared life-threatening, so Lyon applied immediately for leave. Within a week, he was granted one for sixty days, and on February 9, 1852, he left on a clipper ship, bound for the isthmus of Panama. After crossing the isthmus, he boarded another clipper for New York. Unknown to him, his mother had died even before he left the camp. He did not discover this fact until he arrived in Eastford, over a month later, after she had already received burial. The cause of death, he learned, was apoplexy, and her temporary madness was attributed to the hemorrhaging in her brain, not to any decay of her mind. The news proved somewhat relieving to Lyon, for much of his own mental acuteness he attributed to his mother's strong will. Yet with his strong attachment to her, the death caused him particular pain. "No more," he wrote, "her deep earnest look of devoted love; no more her tears of solicitude and sympathy . . . ."[27]

Because Kezia had named Lyon executor of her estate, he needed to

25. Returns, September 1851, RG 94; Woodward, *Life of Nathaniel Lyon,* 194; Captain's Commission of Nathaniel Lyon, June 11, 1851, Nathaniel Lyon Papers, CSL.

26. Woodward, *Life of Nathaniel Lyon,* 196.

27. Lyon Genealogy, Nathaniel Lyon Papers, CSL; Lyon to Mother, undated, Nathaniel Lyon File, NYHS; Woodward, *Life of Nathaniel Lyon,* 200.

remain in the East for both legal matters and personal consolation. He applied for and received a six-month extension of his leave. During this time, he saw relatives in and around Eastford and traveled about the eastern seaboard to visit relatives. He spent the majority of his time, however, in Burlington, New Jersey, visiting Miner Knowlton. The time helped him to reemphasize that his mother's unpleasant death was not prompted by God, who had no control over her life, but solely her afterlife. In the latter, Lyon felt confident that the Creator would reward her, of all his servants, justly.[28]

By September, he had written several letters requesting to be reassigned to California but was frustrated by a lack of response. Now officially a full captain, Lyon believed that he was entitled to the respect and benefits of that rank, and he displayed great impatience with military bureaucracy. Reporting to Fort Columbus, he received his duty assignment with another brigade that was to sail for the territory. However, he was piqued at the fact that he had no specific duties with the unit. Convinced that permission to return was given "more as an accommodation than through any demands of the service, and under such circumstances [he] would prefer to return privately," Lyon requested an additional month's leave in order to do so, and on October 5, 1852, boarded a steamer bound for the isthmus of Panama.[29]

His trip proved long and crowded, with over seven hundred persons crammed onto the steamship *Georgia,* "badly supplied with seats," thus causing him to pass "whole days without being able to sit down at all, except when at meals, or some Lady acquaintance gave up her seat." Upon reaching the isthmus, Lyon took the rickety, American-owned Panama railroad across the narrow body of land and embarked at the Pacific onto another steamer for the seventeen-day trip to San Francisco. After an absence of nearly ten months, he arrived there on November 6 and soon repaired to Fort Miller, where he rejoined Company D.[30]

28. Will of Kezia Lyon, Eastford Township Probate Records, CSL; Nathaniel Lyon to Roger Jones and Samuel Cooper, March 31, 1852, to August 31, 1852, Letters Received, RG 94.

29. Lyon to Sister, October 5, 1852, Nathaniel Lyon Papers, CHS; Lyon to Samuel Cooper, September 1, 1852, to September 27, 1852, Letters Received, RG 94; Lyon to Danford Knowlton, November 10, 1852, Nathaniel Lyon File, Eastford Historical Society, ETH.

30. Lyon to Sister, October 5, 1852, Nathaniel Lyon Papers, CHS; Lyon to Danford Knowlton, November 10, 1852, Nathaniel Lyon File, Eastford Historical Society, ETH; Returns, November 1852, RG 94.

For the next eight months, Lyon spent time at both Fort Miller and Benicia. He then traveled to Fort Lane, on the Rogue River in the Oregon Territory. Hostilities with the Indians in the valley prompted the trip, but by the time the expedition arrived, the difficulties had subsided. The remainder of the time passed without incident. In October, Lyon returned again to Benicia on special assignment. By the time he retraced his 450-mile journey (much of which he traversed on a narrow mule path), he received unexpected orders that he and his company were to return for duty on the East Coast. He regretted having to leave, for he found the country both beautiful and interesting, and he vowed to return when it proved feasible. Therefore, rather than sell his house in San Diego, he opted to rent it. In early December, he embarked on the steamer *Golden Gate,* destined for Panama and then New York. For the second time, he spent a Christmas on the ocean. Although he looked forward to some day returning to California, he would never again see the newest American state.[31]

Upon his arrival in New York on January 9, 1854, Lyon requested permission to travel to Washington in hopes of clearing up what appeared to be a discrepancy in his accounts with the Treasury Department. While serving in the army's disbursing department in California, he had been charged with a great amount of financial and property responsibilities, some of which were disputed by treasury auditors. Apparently Lyon's clerk in California had not adequately itemized a pay voucher for transportation expenses incurred by the company, and the Treasury Department demanded submission of written statements and receipts from those involved. This situation was particularly maddening for Lyon, for as a rule he was scrupulous with all details. Because he was relatively close to Washington, Lyon felt it necessary to attend to the "vexatious little things" while the chance was at hand and applied for approval. The secretary of war, Jefferson Davis, granted him "a reasonable and necessary period" in which to settle his financial affairs, so on January 11 he caught a train bound for the capital, where he took a room at the posh Willard's Hotel and hoped for a short stay.[32]

31. Woodward, *Life of Nathaniel Lyon,* 203; Returns, December 1853, RG 94; Prucha, *Military Posts,* 84; Allan Rutherford to D. W. Shurtliff, June 24, 1887, Nathaniel Lyon Papers, CSL.

32. Lyon to Miner Knowlton, July 27, 1854, Nathaniel Lyon File, KSHS; Lyon to Colonel Abercombie, January 23, 1854, Letters Received, RG 94; Returns, January to February 1854, RG 94; Samuel Cooper to Lyon, February 6, 1854, Letters Sent, AGO, RG 94.

Straightening out the nettlesome mess, however, took most of the month of February, thus forcing him to delay his return to Fort Hamilton. By the time he arrived, his company had already left for Jefferson Barracks in St. Louis, so he "repaired there as direct as possible." After stopping in Buffalo to pay his respects to the family of Gen. Bennet Riley, who had recently died, he arrived in St. Louis on March 16. The troops settled in for what most thought would be a summer-long stay. Lyon found Jefferson Barracks "a most unhealthy place, and the Quarters are shockingly out of repair." A recent epidemic of cholera worried him, so he was not displeased when, a month later, the unit found itself again displaced. Moving first by boat up the Missouri River to Fort Leavenworth, Kansas Territory, the unit traveled from there by foot to Fort Riley, over 120 miles to the west. The column consisted of Companies B and C, under the overall command of Maj. William R. Montgomery. The tired, footsore group arrived at the fort on the morning of May 13, placing themselves in the midst of what would soon become the most controversial area of the entire nation. This section of the country would soon be known as "Bleeding Kansas," a fitting sobriquet for the storm that would begin to rage in the territory that same year. And at its vortex would be Nathaniel Lyon, his outlook on the nation's woes solidifying as a result of his experiences on the strife-ridden prairie.[33]

33. Louise Barry, "Kansas Before 1854: A Revised Annals—Part 22," 1.

Lt. Nathaniel Lyon, ca. 1845. The only known photograph of Lyon in early life. Previously unpublished. Courtesy Archives, History, and Genealogy Unit, Connecticut State Library.

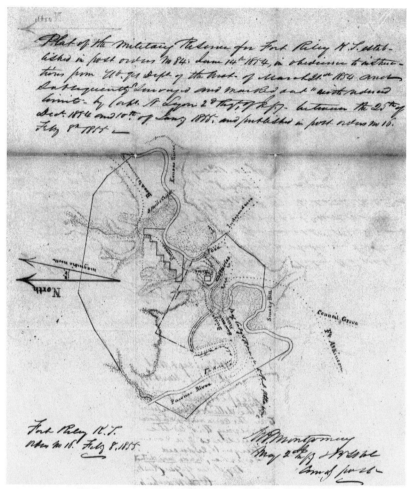

Original plat of the military reserve for Fort Riley, Kansas Territory. Surveyed by Lyon and submitted by post commander William R. Montgomery. Pawnee (a mile downriver from the fort) has been included in the reserve. Courtesy National Archives.

Claiborne Fox Jackson. Pro-secession governor of Missouri in 1861. Courtesy Missouri Historical Society.

Francis P. Blair, Jr. Leader of the radical Unionist faction in St. Louis in 1861.

Gen. William S. Harney, ca. 1863. Commander of the Department of the West in 1861, with headquarters in St. Louis. Courtesy Missouri Historical Society.

Daniel M. Frost, ca. 1862. Commander of the Missouri State Guard for the district that included St. Louis. Shown here as a Confederate brigadier general, Frost surrendered to Lyon at Camp Jackson. Courtesy Missouri Historical Society.

Lindell Grove, St. Louis. The open pasture in the foreground was the scene of the Camp Jackson affair, May 10, 1861. Courtesy Missouri Historical Society.

Rioting in St. Louis streets following the Camp Jackson affair. From *Harper's Weekly*. Courtesy Hargrett Rare Book and Manuscript Library, University of Georgia Libraries.

V

A Sense of Duty

Fort Riley is located in the "upper country," on the western edge of the Flint Hills, a belt of low hills and limestone ridges in the eastern section of Kansas. Tall cottonwoods lined the rivers and streams, their height and verdancy providing definition to an otherwise indistinguishable prairie landscape. In 1854, the fort was situated at the confluence of the Smoky Hill and Republican forks, which together form the Kansas River (known as the Kaw in the early days of the territory). The river then flows slowly eastward across the rolling land until it joins the wide Missouri near what was then the new settlement of Westport Landing.[1]

When Lyon arrived at Fort Riley, the post was just over a year old and consisted primarily of temporary wooden buildings with little other than barracks to distinguish it as a military post. Congress had not yet appropriated enough funds to develop the fort more fully, so its permanent installations progressed at a snail's pace. Lyon and the other officers received only a single room each in which to live, rather than standard quarters. Yet even in its incomplete state, the fort was the center of activity in this sparsely settled section of the country, and therefore was an important post. It would grow increasingly so as the next several years passed.[2]

Lyon's initial stay at Fort Riley would last just over a year. During that short time, his explosive temperament would again rage out of control. In his scrupulous mind, everything—from politics to personal relationships—was either black or white, right or wrong; there was no middle ground on any issue. It would seem that Lyon's personal revelations in Mexico and California had become an obsession, and his time in Kansas

1. James Larson, *Sergeant Larson, 4th Cav.*, 71.
2. George W. Martin, "The Territorial and Military Combine at Fort Riley," 365; Louise Barry, "Kansas Before 1854," 29; Lyon to Miner Knowlton, July 27, 1854, Nathaniel Lyon File, KSHS. The post was established on May 17, 1853, by Capt. C. S. Lovell and several companies of the Sixth Infantry. It was originally called Camp Centre.

served as the first forum for his newly formed views, though often to the chagrin of those around him.

Lyon had always had a penchant for baiting individuals, yet his often-rash statements were limited to close acquaintances or relatives, and only those whom he respected intellectually. John Hasler appears to have been one of his favorite sparring partners. As far back as Lyon's West Point days, he had argued politics with his brother-in-law. A Democrat by heritage, Lyon took particular delight in chiding Hasler, a Whig, about being "an advocate of Whig principles, . . . for to entertain such views whether prompted by self interest or popular delusion[,] I can but consider a defect which I had not supposed formed a part of your character." He applauded with vigor the 1852 election of Franklin Pierce over the "reckless & desperate" Winfield Scott. In addition, the bulk of Lyon's execrations of the Catholic religion he made to Hasler, all the while knowing that his brother-in-law practiced that very faith. He went so far as to ask Hasler if his son (Lyon's nephew) would grow up "to be a Catholic pagan or a protestant worshiper of the true god?" Yet while the words seem strong, the bickering seems to have been somewhat good-natured, and Hasler does not appear to have taken any more than he gave. However, in Kansas, Lyon's baiting of those around him became malicious.[3]

Dr. William A. Hammond, post surgeon at Fort Riley, has provided perhaps the most valuable set of contemporary recollections of Lyon's personality during his time in Kansas. Hammond, later the army's surgeon general, had the dubious distinction of being perhaps Lyon's closest acquaintance at Fort Riley. Though he wrote his impressions of his friend long after Lyon's death, Hammond's assessment of the New England officer seems both unbiased and remarkably accurate: "I have never in the whole course of my life met with a man as fearless and uncompromising in the expression of his opinions, and at the same time so intolerant of the views of others, as was he. If he had lived four hundred years ago he would have been burned at the stake as a pestilent and altogether incorrigible person, whose removal was demanded in the interests of the peace of society."[4]

3. Lyon to John B. Hasler, December 5, 1840, Nathaniel Lyon Papers, AAS; Lyon to Hasler, April 5, 1848, ibid.; Lyon to Lorenzo Lyon, April 9, 1853, Nathaniel Lyon Papers, CHS.
4. Hammond, "Brigadier-General Nathaniel Lyon, U.S.A.—Personal Recollections," 237–38.

Hammond recalled that Lyon dominated conversations, not allowing the listener to get in a word, even if he were anxious to express his views. Lyon liked "nothing so much as a good listener, . . . his ideas flowing with surprising rapidity, and his words being uttered at a rate of speed that would have kept the most skillful stenographer in full action." Yet Lyon's obsession with his own opinions allowed little room for dissent. Said Hammond:

> He was intolerant of opposition, unmindful of the many obligatory courtesies of life, prone to inject the most unpopular opinions at times and places when he knew they would be unwelcome, and enforcing them with all the bitterness and vehemence of which he was capable; easily aroused to a degree of anger that was almost insane in its manifestations; narrow-minded; prejudiced, mentally unbalanced, and yet with all this, honest to the core . . . .[5]

Lyon's inflexible convictions and hidebound opinions often "were of so obtrusive a character that they made him enemies on all sides." And in Kansas, he found a target for his attacks that only augmented such animosity: slavery. In the years preceding Lyon's transfer to Kansas, the debate over slavery as it applied to the territories had steadily accelerated. Although Henry Clay's Compromise of 1850 apparently quelled the storm that arose over the lands ceded to the United States after the war with Mexico (illustrated most notably by the Wilmot Proviso), Lewis Cass's principle of "popular sovereignty," giving residents of the new lands the power to decide for themselves whether to allow slavery within their borders, soon took on a life of its own.

Early in 1854, the slavery issue rose again to national attention when powerful Illinois senator Stephen Douglas supported a bill that would allow popular sovereignty to determine the status of the unorganized territories north of Missouri. In itself, the bill might not have created a major stir had it not threatened to abrogate the Missouri Compromise of 1820–1821. The territory—which Douglas proposed to be organized as two territories, Kansas and Nebraska—comprised a part of the Louisiana Purchase, where, with the exception of the state of Missouri, slavery was prohibited north of the 36° 30' parallel. With his incentive being the construction of a transcontinental railroad from Chicago, Douglas believed that in order to secure this route rather than one farther south (and gain the support of Southern Democrats), he must maintain

---

5. Ibid., 239; Hammond, "Recollections of General Nathaniel Lyon," 416.

the balance between free and slave states. Popular sovereignty then took precedence over what Douglas considered an arbitrary and outmoded line of demarcation. The Little Giant's proposal won almost unanimous support from Southern Whigs and Democrats and a marginal amount of Northern Democrats. However, its narrow passage in May 1854 set off a howl of protest from those who held sacred the terms of the Missouri Compromise.[6]

Nathaniel Lyon was one of those who howled the loudest. He was outraged that the party of the Democracy would dare support a bill that would overturn the compromise which had been in effect literally all of his life. Before the bill had even passed, Lyon fulminated, "That d———d Nebraska iniquity has blighted all wholesome action on the part of Congress, and will I predict, blight Mr. Pierce and his administration, proportionately to the depth and rankness of the corruption in which the scheme originated." By that summer, Lyon accused both Pierce ("the bigoted ignoramus") and Douglas of "subserviency to the slave interest," and he predicted that "the time was not far distant when they would be held up to the execration of all lovers of freedom." Although Douglas's demagoguery (with which he had committed "prostitution to the de-mands of the slave power") bore the brunt of most of Lyon's vehemence, by his own words he looked elsewhere for the root of the evil. That root he found in the Southern states. Douglas's doctrine of popular sov-ereignty served as "but a weak illustration of the humiliating depth to which Mr. Douglas has gone in the slime of his own putrescence, before the flash and roar of his southern masters." In his anger, Lyon began to lash out at Southerners for their crimes against the nation, committed in the name of slavery, the greatest of all evils. "If it were in my power to break up our relations and union," he wrote, "with a power, that does not regard its promise and pledges, in its blind avarice to propogate and extend a blighting curse and degrading sin, I would do so at once, and declare our glorious Union at an end." For the moment, he would have to settle for contemplating the withdrawal of his support from Douglas's party.[7]

    6. Robert W. Johannsen, *Stephen A. Douglas,* 390–434 passim.
    7. Lyon to George Patrick, April 14, 1854, Jefferson Barracks Papers, MHS; Stephen B. Oates, "Nathaniel Lyon—A Personality Profile," 15; Lyon to Miner Knowlton, July 27, 1854, Nathaniel Lyon File, KSHS; Lyon, *Last Political Writings of General Nathaniel Lyon, U.S.A.,* 132–33; Lyon to Lorenzo Lyon, June 11, 1854, Nathaniel Lyon Papers, CSL.

Lyon's outspokenness often resulted in violent arguments. In these cases, his temper would rage out of control, and he would unleash a stream of invectives, "gesticulating violently and stammering over his words in a way that rendered them almost incoherent." On one occasion, Lyon's outbursts over the nation's woes nearly forced a confrontation for which he had not bargained. At a dinner party given by Capt. Richard H. Anderson, an officer at the fort and a native South Carolinian, Lyon launched unexpectedly into an envenomed harangue against the South and its people. Although there were seated at the table Northern men who shared Lyon's views, Hammond recalled that "all were dumbfounded at the violence and virulence of Lyon's attack." Although Anderson remained calm throughout, the onslaught left him deeply offended. Later that evening, after the guests had left, Anderson found Lyon at his quarters and confronted him with the threat of physical violence. Had no other officers been present to step between the two, it undoubtedly would have come to that. However, the interruption only forced Anderson to seek satisfaction in the more traditional Southern method: he challenged his antagonist to a duel.[8]

Though Lyon's fighting blood ran hot, he was at first unwilling to accept the challenge, ostensibly on the grounds that it was illegal and that it went against all of his scruples. However, Hammond convinced him that his offense had been too injurious to Anderson's person for the matter to die peacefully, so Lyon resolved to accept the duel. Since custom granted him the choice of terms, Lyon announced brashly that he would ask for pistols—across a table. Appalled, Hammond somehow dissuaded him from this audacious course, and upon the advice of a council of officers, Lyon formally apologized to the captain. His apology, however, stiffly delivered and without a handshake, reeked of disingenuousness. Yet Lyon realized that he had acted wrongly and therefore accepted his humiliating punishment.[9]

Not only had Lyon's personal convictions hardened, but he also now found pleasure in promulgating his unorthodox religious beliefs. On one summer evening, after a particularly hot day, some of the officers and their wives were enjoying the cool night breeze on one of the officers' piazzas. Hammond, just arrived at the post, did not yet know Lyon. Though the conversation appears to have been light and pleasant, it

8. Hammond, "Brigadier-General Nathaniel Lyon," 240, 243.
9. Ibid., 240–42.

gradually turned to theological subjects. This provided Lyon an opportunity to voice his newly won convictions. Fully aware that he was in the
company of several Christian ladies, he proclaimed tersely "that he was
an infidel, and perhaps even an atheist, and that Socrates was a nobler
man than Jesus." This blasphemy horrified the entire group and prompted Hammond hastily to defend the doctrines of the Christian faith.
Upon his completion, Lyon rose from his seat, face reddened and steely
eyes flashing. He fumed that if the good doctor truly believed such rot,
then he had nothing further to say to him and promptly stormed out.

Later, when discussing the matter with Hammond on much friendlier
terms, Lyon stated that the doctrines of religion had not a shred of proof
to support them. Most men, Lyon posited, believed in their religious
precepts simply because "someone in whom he had confidence told him
they were true." "If men and women could get rid of their early preju-
dices," he continued, "and would look at Scripture exactly as they would
at any other collection of stories, the Christian religion would not stand a
day."[10]

Perhaps also contributing to his acrimony was Lyon's marital status.
Though he had sworn off marriage, this was not for lack of interest in the
female of the species, for Lyon maintained both a great respect for
women and a distinct eye for beauty. While in Mexico and California, he
had been impressed by the ladies, many of whom seemed to be of
"excellent character and disposition. They are beautiful in form and
features, transcendently graceful . . . ." However, he added that he
would probably not fall in love with a Mexican señorita, for he preferred
"to behold the fair faces of American ladies, so pure and bright, so
beautiful and lovely, that if I do not lose my senses altogether, I shall
certainly lose all recollection of the ladies of Mexico."[11]

Lyon often wrote of his respect for female acquaintances. Indeed, in
his letters one can detect a certain amount of longing for "the delicate
affections of the heart." He was certainly not unreceptive to the *idea* of
marriage; however, the strength of his own convictions precluded him
from the institution. In a letter to Miner Knowlton (also a bachelor), the
subject turned to the prospect of matrimony. In the letter, Lyon told his
cousin that he had shared one of Knowlton's previous letters with a
mutual acquaintance, Lyon's post commander, Colonel Montgomery. In

10. Ibid., 237–38.
11. Ashbel Woodward, *Life of General Nathaniel Lyon,* 136.

Lyon's letter, Montgomery sent wishes for Knowlton to be rid of the "crusty disposition" that kept him from enjoying the "sweets of matrimonial life." To that wish, Lyon added somewhat acridly, "I hardly know whether to join him in those wishes concerning yourself,—you will probably consider all my sympathy due to my own case, without extending any to yours."[12]

Yet while Lyon may have held great regard for the ladies, they do not appear to have held him in the same regard. A female resident of Boonville, Missouri, reflected upon her impressions of Lyon after meeting him in the summer of 1861: "He was a very ugly man, nothing spirited or imposing about him. He had frizzly flaxen hair, a tolerably fine forehead, small blue-gray eyes and a mass of red whiskers . . . . The picture of Lyons [sic] in Harper [Harper's Weekly] is infinitely better looking than he is . . . ."[13]

If his appearance was not pleasing to women, Lyon's mannerisms in their presence seem to have been even less so. That same Boonville woman "thought he was the most bashful man I had ever seen, [who] blushed to the tips of his ears when introduced to the ladies." It is quite likely that Lyon was somewhat frustrated by both his marital situation and his lack of decorum around women, thus kindling his own "crusty disposition." At least one of his men appears to have considered that the case. Lyon "never had the softening influence of a home," he observed, "as he was an old bachelor and therefor[e] cranky."[14]

And it was the soldiers who suffered most from his rancorous temperament. Lyon was an unmerciful disciplinarian, moving one of his men to recall that "to the men of his company he is a tyrant and every man hates the very sight of him." Although he maintained a stern, almost paternal bearing with his command (his regulars referred to him somewhat sardonically as "Daddy"), he punished them for even the least infringement of rules. While other units recognized Lyon's company as being exceptionally well drilled, their commander continually found fault with them; therefore he punished. His attitude toward discipline, however, stemmed from his twisted conception of authority and duty. A

12. Lyon to A. Fisdale, April 30, 1850, Nathaniel Lyon File, SHSM; Lyon to Miner Knowlton, July 27, 1854, Nathaniel Lyon File, KSHS.

13. Sallie Yeatman Thompson to Charles Anderson, December 11, 1861, Ovenshine Collection, USMHI.

14. Ibid.; Merrill J. Mattes, ed., "Patrolling the Santa Fe Trail: Reminiscences of John S. Kirwan," 585.

later incident, occurring in November 1855, provides perhaps the most accurate insight into Lyon's perception of his role as a military officer. Pvt. John S. Kirwan, a young cavalryman transferred to Fort Riley only one day earlier, drew guard duty at Post Number One. His primary responsibility was to guard two soldiers being disciplined in typical Lyon fashion: each was sentenced to march while carrying a knapsack loaded with thirty pounds of bricks each day, from dawn to dusk, for a month. One of the prisoners, thirsty from his exertions, asked Kirwan for permission to draw a bucket of water from the well at the end of the post. Empathizing with the poor wretch, the inexperienced Kirwan agreed, and the men gratefully shed their heavy packs and drew their fill of the cool water.[15]

Just as they were rebuckling the brick-laden packs, the officer of the day rounded the corner of the guardhouse. It was Lyon. Kirwan had never met the little captain but perceived his trouble immediately and came to a full salute. Lyon ignored the recognition of rank, strode to a position directly in his front, and peered upward into his face. "How long have you been in the service, sir?" he snapped. In just one day at the fort, Kirwan had already heard of Lyon's reputation and knew that he would have to think fast in order to extract himself from the potentially grave situation. Knowing that a batch of raw recruits had recently entered the camp and that some had been assigned to his company, Kirwan promptly lied. "Two weeks, sir," he replied. Lyon turned to the sergeant of the guard, standing at attention nearby, and asked for confirmation of this fact. The sergeant, realizing the unpleasant consequences of Kirwan's act, also lied on the private's behalf. His eyes flashing gray, then blue, Lyon turned again to Kirwan, studied his face, and growled, "It is a good thing for you, that you are a recruit, or I would punish you properly, sir, for letting that prisoner take off his knapsack, sir." As God's punitive proxy, Lyon let no mistake go unnoticed.[16]

Lyon's draconian punishments were widely known in the ranks, earning for him a reputation as "the most tyrannical officer in the Army." In fact, by 1855, a story circulated among the enlisted men of Lyon's palpable enjoyment of the mere threat of punishment. Upon the arrival of a new group of recruits, Lyon lined them up and, starting from the right, commenced questioning each of them. Facing the first, he asked stiffly, in

    15. Augustus Meyers, "Dakota in the Fifties," 176–77; Mattes, "Patrolling the Santa Fe Trail," 585; Franc B. Wilkie, *Pen and Powder,* 29.
    16. Mattes, "Patrolling the Santa Fe Trail," 584–85; Wilkie, *Pen and Powder,* 29.

his nasal, New England twang, "How long have you been in the service, sir?" After the man's response, Lyon queried, "Have you ever been punished, sir?" The new private, by now noticeably nervous, answered that he had not. Lyon then leaned close to the private, his hooked nose just inches from the young man's quivering face. "Well, sir," he hissed, "I will punish you, sir, I will punish you properly, sir." Then, drawing back and stepping to the next recruit, Lyon in turn asked him if *he* had been punished. This private, having taken in the line of questioning with the man on his left and not about to give the same answer, responded that he had indeed been punished. Not missing a beat, Lyon then snapped, "You were not punished properly, sir, I will punish you properly, sir." This continued the entire length of the line, with each man learning that he had yet to be punished properly and that the only man who could do so was Captain Lyon himself.[17]

And Lyon could—and often did—aptly back up his boast. For minor infractions, his most common punitive measure was to march the offender back and forth across the parade grounds while carrying two or three pieces of cordwood on his shoulder. This could last hours or days on end, and one frequent visitor to the fort remarked that there seemed to be a constant supply of these men trudging off their painful penance. Lyon seldom court-martialed his men; instead, his irrational temper generally prompted more irregular, often sadistic, punishments. On at least one occasion, he forced a miscreant to march bare-headed under a particularly hot sun across the parade ground with honey in his hair and a barrel over his shoulders to keep him from shooing away the swarm of biting prairie flies. Or Lyon might tie an offender to the spare wheel of a caisson, his back to the hub, and either leave him there for several painful hours or, in more serious cases, take him for a short yet torturous ride over the rutted roads outside the fort. After witnessing one of his privates beating a dog, in a fit of rage Lyon reportedly kicked the soldier savagely in the stomach, then forced the man to get down on his knees and beg the dog's forgiveness. And while Lyon was not above using profanity in his rages, his fits came and passed so quickly and violently that he rarely had the time to use it. In any case, he did not need profanity to augment the severity with which he treated those under him.[18]

17. Mattes, "Patrolling the Santa Fe Trail," 584–85; Meyers, "Dakota in the Fifties," 176–77.

18. Mattes, "Patrolling the Santa Fe Trail," 585; "Statement of Theo. Weischsel-baum, of Ogden, Riley Cty., July 17, 1908," 568; Oates, "Nathaniel Lyon—A Person-

By his actions, it would appear that Lyon deliberately culled the antipathy of his troops. There is little doubt that he recognized its presence. On more than one occasion, he almost boasted to his troops, "I know you all hate me and if we should ever go into battle I would get the first bullet; but as long as I command I will make you toe the mark." The savagery of Lyon's methods, however, soon prompted response from the ranks. Within months of Lyon's arrival at Fort Riley, an enlisted man, Sgt. Charles Hutton, leveled formal charges against his commanding officer for his abnormally harsh treatment. The exact nature of the incident is unknown, but Lyon's actions apparently warranted an official reprimand from a court of inquiry. "It is much to be regretted," found the court, "that after so many admonitions and orders on the subject, there should be a continuation of arbitrary conduct on the part of some Officers of the Army, as developed in this case. The attention of Captain N. Lyon, 2d Infantry, is particularly directed to . . . the mode of punishment of non-commissioned officers . . . ." Lyon protested without result the "animadversions" directed against him; however, the incident serves to illuminate the severity with which Lyon inflicted punishment upon his troops. As before, with the Kelly incident, reprimands alone failed to curb what appears to have been a nearly psychopathic appetite for inflicting pain.[19]

However, the Hutton affair effected more than written admonishment. Lyon's brutality had garnered the attention of his immediate superior, William Montgomery. Although Montgomery was himself thought to be somewhat of a martinet, the post commander found the actions of his next-in-command beyond the bounds of reasonable behavior. Therefore, shortly after the Hutton incident, "in order to restrain capricious and improper punishment of the men of this command," and to curb "the Captain's proclivity to severity," Montgomery issued an order prohibiting punishment other than confinement without prior sanction of the commanding officer. Lyon was furious. He could not abide any restriction upon his modes of punishment, for his—and the men's—duty

ality Profile," 15; Meyers, "Dakota in the Fifties," 176–77; Charles W. Goodlander, *Memoirs and Recollections of C. W. Goodlander,* 62; Wilkie, *Pen and Powder,* 29.

19. Larson, *Sergeant Larson,* 71; General Order No. 23, September 15, 1854, Orders and Special Orders, Department of the West, Record Group 393, Records of the United States Army Continental Commands, 1821–1920, National Archives (hereafter cited as RG 393); Lyon to F. N. Page, October 18, 1854, Letters Received, Department of the West, box 2, RG 393.

called for them. Though he complained to department headquarters that Montgomery's order "arrested the administration of justice under his command, and weakened the incentives to discipline and the proper discharge of their [the command's] duties," his remonstrances were returned unheeded. Hence, Lyon began scheming for Montgomery's removal.[20]

Because Montgomery forbade punishments *other* than confinement, Lyon began confining men for even minor infractions. He went so far as to take one teamster from his wagon and lock him up while the team remained hitched. Montgomery again intervened and on January 11 issued an order prohibiting confinement for men on extra or daily duty, except in flagrant cases. Lyon then lost control of his temper and for the next three days disobeyed summarily each order Montgomery gave him. The post commander then arrested his subordinate, only to realize that the small command made Lyon's presence indispensable. Montgomery quickly released him in return for the promise of better future behavior. However, in February, when Montgomery clapped three of Lyon's men in irons, a recrudescence of their feud erupted, and Lyon preferred court-martial charges against his commander, ironically, for the cruelty of his punishments. While this series of events illustrates a great animosity developing between the two antagonists, Lyon had not yet played his trump card, one that Montgomery knew well that his subordinate held. By late spring, Lyon's streak of vindictiveness, mixed with his dangerous temper, had led him to play that card, producing an imbroglio that reached all the way to the president.[21]

The seed for Lyon's plan for revenge was planted even before he and his entourage were transferred to Fort Riley. While still at Fort Leavenworth, Montgomery received orders that, upon his arrival at the new fort, he should establish the boundary lines for the post reserve. The post commander, however, did not begin surveying the reserve lines immediately. Instead, he opted to designate arbitrarily that the original lines would encompass an area ten by eighteen miles, measured from the exact

20. William R. Montgomery to O. F. Winship, March 14, 1855, Letters Received, Department of the West, box 2, RG 393; Charges and Specifications against Montgomery, preferred by Lyon, April 3, 1855, Letters Received, Department of the West, box 2, RG 393.
21. Post Order No. 4, January 11, 1855, Letters Received, Department of the West, box 2, RG 393; Montgomery to O. F. Winship, January 22, 1855, ibid.; Lyon to Irwin McDowell, May 21, 1855, David Rice Atchison Papers, SHSM.

center of the parade ground, and running five miles both north and south and nine miles both east and west. This amount of land was ample to allow an "extent sufficient to afford all the advantages of timber, fuel, hay, and other requisites for a military post." At this point, however, he had established no permanent lines.[22]

Montgomery's estimation of the amount of land needed for the post created great problems for many local settlers, as the intended reserve swallowed up portions of their lands. On September 4, 1854, a delegation presented the colonel with a formal request to exclude a 320-acre portion of the reserve for a town site a mile downriver so that settlers might have a navigable point for shipping and receiving. This area lay directly on the road to Fort Leavenworth and looked to be a perfect spot for a future town. In retrospect, this request appears equitable, and, considering that the boundaries were still unofficial, a viable solution could have been easily achieved. However, political graft soon succeeded in muddying the waters of the upper Kaw.[23]

On June 29, 1854, President Pierce had appointed as Kansas's first territorial governor Andrew H. Reeder, an antislavery lawyer from Pennsylvania. Before journeying to Kansas, Reeder remained at his home in Easton to take care of personal business. However, well in advance of his arrival he sent to the territory "an army of would-be officeholders and land speculators from his native state." The new governor, already thinking of future profits, instructed these men to obtain a "view" of the country and to select a potential site for the territorial capital.[24]

Taking a steamer from Westport, Missouri, the group found the Kaw River navigable to its source. Nearby sat Fort Riley. Navigation was crucial to Reeder's intended location for the capital since the governor planned to develop steamboat traffic to the proposed site, adding greatly to its potential for growth. Because of its central location in the territory (though not at this early date its population), the site below the fort appeared even more attractive as a capital city.[25]

22. Transcripts of the Court-Martial of Bvt. Col. William R. Montgomery, September to December 1855, RG 153, 2.

23. E. Francis Mezick, Anthony Grable, R. C. Miller, Robert Wilson, John Heth, and John N. Dyer to Montgomery, September 4, 1854, Letters Received, Department of the West, box 2, RG 393.

24. Jay Monaghan, *Civil War on the Western Border, 1854–1865,* 13; Henry Shindler, "First Capital of Kansas," 333; William E. Treadway, "The Guilded Age in Kansas," 3.

25. Treadway, "Guilded Age in Kansas," 3.

No evidence exists indicating that at this time Reeder's envoys made any promises to Colonel Montgomery regarding the governor's intention to seat the territory's capital there. However, the scouts *did* intimate that nothing could be done if the military reservation encompassed the ground most suitable for building a town. It so happened that that site was exactly where the local residents had petitioned for exclusion only days earlier. Montgomery was sharp enough to see that he could add considerably to his salary. On September 20, Montgomery replied to the local assemblage that the site in question was not essential to the requirements of the command and consented to exclude it from the reserve.[26]

Montgomery saw no violation in excluding the town from the reserve, for he had always believed his boundaries to be provisional, and he had not yet sent an official plat to Washington. One week later, the colonel informed a select few about the governor's intentions for the capital, and the group quickly formed the Pawnee Town Association. They honored Montgomery and his good business fortune by electing him president, and the list of charter members included Lyon, Governor Reeder, and twenty others from the post and the settlement.[27]

Reeder's inclusion in the association makes it appear that he gave his "scouts" official power to select a site. In any case, the members wasted little time acquiring the land in and around Pawnee. Every man involved understood fully the financial potential of the Pawnee site if it proved to become the territorial capital. Soon after the formation of the company, the site was surveyed and platted, and the speculators began selling town lots for ten dollars each.[28]

By the time Governor Reeder reported to his post at Fort Leavenworth on October 7, each man in the association claimed land in or around the town. Soon after his arrival, Reeder took a "tour of inspection" through

26. Shindler, "First Capital of Kansas," 333; Montgomery to Robert Wilson, John Heth, R. C. Miller, and Others, September 20, 1854, Letters Received, Department of the West, box 2, RG 393.

27. Shindler, "First Capital of Kansas," 333; "Extinct Geographical Locations," 485.

28. James McClure, "Taking the Census in 1855," 230; George W. Martin, "The Territorial and Military Combine at Fort Riley," 373n; "Extinct Geographical Locations," 485. The list of members of the Pawnee Town Site Association reads as follows: Col. W. R. Montgomery, W. A. Hammond, C. S. Lovell, Ed. Johnson, N. Lyon, M. T. Pope, R. F. Hunter, E. A. Ogden, M. Mills, G. M. R. Hudson, James Simons, D. H. Vinton, Alden Sargent, J. T. Schaaff, H. Rich, W. S. Murphy, Robert Wilson, J. N. Dyer, R. C. Miller, A. H. Reeder, A. J. Isaacks, I. B. Donalson, Rush Elmore, and L. W. Johnson.

the territory, though his main purpose was to visit the Pawnee site. Thoroughly satisfied by its location, he met with the Town Company and, to the exuberance of those involved, indicated that Pawnee would indeed become the next territorial capital. Reeder then made a stipulation that would later prove to be his undoing. He insisted that the company secure for him a choice 160-acre claim adjoining the east side of the town site. Though a family of settlers presently occupied the site, Montgomery assured the governor that the matter would quickly be resolved.[29]

Once Reeder returned to Fort Leavenworth, he began promoting the future capital to new settlers, and such a large number of them came to Pawnee to stake their claim that the area immediately surrounding the town was quickly parceled out. One such free-soiler, Stephen B. White, on Reeder's advice moved to Pawnee and bought his land from Nathaniel Lyon.[30]

Like all the other Town Association members, Lyon speculated actively in the Pawnee lands. He was, however, somewhat selective in his sales. Lyon's antislavery convictions prompted him to limit his sales to free-soilers, for he would not sell consciously to those intent upon bringing the institution into Kansas. He took the Whites to his property several miles south of town and "pointed out . . . the beauties and advantages of his claim . . . one of earth's beauty spots." Although he had chosen it for himself, Lyon said to them, he would sell it, for "a soldier has no use for land, except enough to bury one." Considering his substantial land holdings in California, this statement appears duplicitous. Yet Lyon would go even further than deceit to ensure the continued profitability of Pawnee: he would break the law.[31]

On November 10, Reeder called for territorial elections, allowing only those in residence to participate in choosing the territory's delegate to Congress. The casting of ballots by government employees and military personnel not owning property in Kansas was illegal, and election judges were to enforce this mandate. However, the government had taken no territorial census prior to the election, so the actual number of registered voters proved impossible to ascertain. Hence, voting fraud ran rampant, due primarily to the struggle for power between the slavery men and the free-soilers. In the ninth district, encompassing Fort Riley,

29. McClure, "Taking the Census in 1855," 230.
30. Ibid.
31. Mrs. S. B. White, "My First Days in Kansas," 550–51.

however, another important issue was at stake. The election of a free-soil delegate would make the town of Pawnee especially attractive to settlers of that persuasion. This is exactly what Lyon wanted, so he personally eradicated all potential impediments.[32]

The district's voting place was the home of Thomas Reynolds, who was present during the day's voting. He suspected immediately that something was amiss when one of the election judges proved to be a wagon master at the fort. He became convinced that his suspicions were correct when he recognized men from Riley casting ballots. He recalled, "I objected . . . to the men from the fort voting, or acting as judges of election, and they overruled me. Captain Lyon said I should not stay in the country unless I would go with them. I took it that they meant I must not oppose Pawnee, or having a free State."[33]

In this instance, Lyon was willing to overstep a territorial mandate in order to satisfy his own sense of justice. To him, it was far better to allow free-state soldiers to vote in the election than to submit obsequiously to the widespread fraud being committed by the proslavery voters who were crossing the borders from Missouri. Or was this attempt to protect the "respectable dignity" of the free-soilers as noble as it appears? Lyon and the other officers had an admitted stake in the town of Pawnee and knew of its imminent importance, if it were allowed to boom. To Reynolds and others, there was no other conclusion than that the members of the Town Association and those at the fort were in league with the governor in ensuring the future of Pawnee. As Reynolds charged, "It is hard to avoid the conclusion that they and others interested in promoting the town of Pawnee favored this voting of government employees."[34]

By viewing his sales promotion, made with plenty of entrepreneurial zeal, as well as his role in the local election, it is obvious that Nathaniel Lyon was far from an unwitting participant in the Pawnee land dealings. Like all the others, he was engaged in land speculation that, though not illegal, employed graft and could very well have involved the sale of government property. The dubiousness of such dealings, however, does not appear to have threatened in Lyon any sense of moral righteousness. Nevertheless, in the next several months, he used exactly that excuse to justify a complete reversal of his stance on the Pawnee land dealings.

32. Russell K. Hickman, "Reeder Administration Inaugurated—Part I," 328n.
33. Ibid.
34. Lyon to Miner Knowlton, July 27, 1854, Nathaniel Lyon File, KSHS; Hickman, "Reeder Administration Inaugurated," 328.

After Reeder had left Fort Riley, Montgomery made repeated efforts to secure the land the governor had selected from the tenants currently occupying the claim. The owners, Thomas Dixon and his three brothers, were reputedly engaged in the illegal sale of whiskey to the soldiers on the post. Though they were never caught selling whiskey, Montgomery considered their presence unwelcome for more than just avaricious reasons. Despite the colonel's persistent attempts to force out the Dixons, the latter refused just as obstinately to relinquish their claim. In mid-December, however, Montgomery hatched an idea to ensure that the land would be vacated.[35]

Two weeks after the territorial elections, Montgomery chose two men to begin officially surveying the boundaries of the reserve that would exclude the Pawnee townsite. He selected Lyon and Maj. Edward Johnson for the detail and included in his instructions the specific direction to *include* the land the Dixons currently occupied. In doing this, Montgomery would make it appear that they were squatting on government property, grounds for immediate eviction. After the army had removed the Dixons, Montgomery would again change the lines to *re-exclude* the site and thus allow Reeder to receive his claim.[36]

The two men worked during the coldest part of the winter and completed the survey on January 10, 1855. Pawnee was growing daily, and to all those involved with its development it appeared that their investments would pay off beyond their wildest dreams. On April 5, Montgomery sent the official plat of the Fort Riley reserve to the secretary of war, Jefferson Davis. Immediately thereafter he gave orders that on the very next morning, Lyon would lead an armed squad to "demolish and destroy the Dixon cabins" and evict the two "liquor-vender" families from their "claim." This act, however, proved a grievous error on Colonel Montgomery's part.[37]

Lyon had become acquainted with the Dixons immediately after their arrival in Pawnee and had helped them to lay claim to the land they were

35. Hardy Kemp, *About Nathaniel Lyon, Brigadier General, United States Army Volunteers and Wilson's Creek,* 58; McClure, "Taking the Census in 1855," 230; Charges and Specifications against Montgomery, April 3, 1855, Letters Received, Department of the West, box 2, RG 393; Montgomery to O. F. Winship, April 4, 1855, ibid.

36. McClure, "Taking the Census in 1855," 230–31n.

37. Ibid., 233; Kemp, *About Nathaniel Lyon,* 56; Montgomery to O. F. Winship, February 20, 1855, Letters Received, Department of the West, box 2, RG 393; Charges and Specifications against Montgomery, April 3, 1855, ibid.

on. Montgomery's orders to remove them therefore angered him, but the post commander was firm in his decision. Lyon had little choice, so at daybreak on March 3 he and the escort reined up at the Dixon homestead. Reluctantly, the captain informed the residents that they had violated federal law by settling on government property and that they now must leave the premises. Thomas Dixon retorted belligerently that they would fight for their rightful land, but Lyon warned that his men were under orders to open fire if fired upon. Under the circumstances, Dixon had no choice but begrudgingly to submit. Lyon ordered chains attached to the several yokes of oxen that accompanied the detail, and in a few minutes the men pulled down all the wooden structures. However, he soon found the Dixons another nearby plot to squat on until he could conceive a better solution. Meanwhile, Lyon's feud with his commander grew even hotter.[38]

Ten days later, Governor Reeder announced that the next session of the legislature, scheduled for July, would meet at the new capital, Pawnee, at the source of the Kaw River. Any illegalities involved in the establishment of Pawnee now appeared to be water under the bridge, and the jubilant members of the Town Association looked forward to being rich men.[39]

However, on April 23, an incident occurred that capped the long series of confrontations between Lyon and Montgomery and signaled the beginning of the end of Pawnee. Assistant Surgeon James Simons, an officer at Fort Riley and a member of the Pawnee Association, had recently transferred to the post with his family and a servant-maid, Sarah Ehern. The young girl had captured the attention of a private in Lyon's company, Robert Allender. The two fell in love, and Allender reported to Lyon for permission to marry the girl and change her post status to that of a laundress. Lyon agreed to the union, and Ehrens then reported to her soon-to-be-former employer to inform him that her services would shortly terminate.[40]

The news chafed Simons for obvious reasons. He went to Montgomery to prevent the loss of his servant, whom he had paid to have transported from the East. After listening to Simons's pleas, Montgomery

38. Hammond, "Personal Recollections," 246; Montgomery to O. F. Winship, April 4, 1855, Letters Received, Department of the West, box 2, RG 393.

39. Shindler, "First Capital of Kansas," 333–34.

40. Montgomery to Samuel Cooper, April 28, 1855, Letters Received, RG 94. This refutes Hammond's statement that Allender was a corporal.

agreed that the marriage should not be allowed. However, there was no official basis on which he could prevent the union. He therefore immediately issued a general order that forbade any further marriages of enlisted men to personal servants, ostensibly on the grounds that there were already too many laundresses on the post.[41]

Hammond was present at Lyon's quarters when an orderly presented the captain with Montgomery's order. Rarely had he seen "a more striking instance of intense rage than he [Lyon] exhibited." His sense of injustice brimming, Lyon determined that there was no law that could prohibit two people from marrying and that he would personally rectify the situation. He summoned the private and excitedly instructed him and his bride-to-be to report to his quarters at eight o'clock that night, where he would personally perform the marriage ceremony.[42]

Montgomery heard of Lyon's insubordination before the night was out. The news infuriated him; coupled as it was with the court-martial charges Lyon had so recently preferred against him, Montgomery had stood for all of the captain's insubordination he could. He promptly ordered the post adjutant to take an armed detail and arrest his refractory subordinate. The detail escorted Lyon to the commandant's office, where Montgomery castigated him at length. He then placed Lyon under guard for fifteen days until the commandant's temper subsided.[43]

Lyon's anger, on the other hand, only mounted. He knew that Montgomery's order prohibiting a man to marry was manifestly illegal and was convinced that his commander had committed an outrage against both his person and his individual rights. It was now his duty to see that his commander was adequately punished for his crime.

Being privy to the inner workings of the Pawnee land fraud, Lyon realized that by blowing the whistle on the scheme, the perfect opportunity for retribution was within his grasp. Yet he had before been hesitant to do so for fear of his own complicity. However, now his own participation in the fraudulent survey of the reserve would be covered by the fact that he was merely following orders. Reporting the illegal actions of his commander *after* carrying out the order would conform perfectly to the army's modus operandi for such matters. Lyon would therefore

41. Hammond, "Personal Recollections," 243–45.
42. Ibid.
43. Ibid.; Montgomery to O. F. Winship, June 14, 1855, Post Files of Fort Pierre, Nebraska Territory, RG 94 (hereafter cited as Post Files); Montgomery to O. F. Winship, April 4, 1855, Letters Received, Department of the West, RG 393.

"wash his own hands and soil [Montgomery's] with alleged criminality."
In his blind rage, the chance for revenge far outweighed his desire for
profit.[44]

While "in trammels" at the fort, Lyon drew up formal charges against
Montgomery accusing him of official misconduct in the designation of
the Fort Riley reserve lines. He then preferred them dutifully to his
commanding officer. Moreover, Lyon filed a personal damages suit
against his commander in the territory's First Judicial District Court,
asking the sum of ten thousand dollars. Lyon was suing Montgomery for
the crime against his person by being wrongfully arrested, harassed, and
imprisoned. He intended to get the full measure of revenge due him.[45]

His subordinate's actions incensed Montgomery, but with his anger
was mixed a bit of apprehension, for he was fully cognizant of Lyon's
complete knowledge of the reserve boundaries. Writing to his commander, Montgomery tried to disparage Lyon's credibility by asking
"what better could be expected of a man who, publicly denies his God—
vilifies religion, denounces and openly despises its faithful and pious
votaries." On the same day that Montgomery sent Lyon's charges to the
Adjutant General's Office, he restored the captain to command of his
company. Recent troubles with the Brulé Sioux in the vicinity of Fort
Pierre, over five hundred miles north in the Nebraska Territory, prompted the army to organize an expedition against the tribe. The Sioux
expedition was scheduled to commence that summer under the leadership of Gen. William S. Harney, and the Second Infantry figured
heavily in the plans for that expedition. The companies moved to Fort
Leavenworth, where, on June 14, they boarded the steamer *Clara* to
proceed up the Missouri River. Because there were so few officers at the
fort, Montgomery felt forced to release Lyon for the expedition, though
no doubt he would have preferred otherwise.[46]

While the trip could have effected a truce between Lyon and Mont-

44. Montgomery to O. F. Winship, April 4, 1855, Letters Received, Department of
the West, box 2, RG 393.

45. Lyon to Mrs. Charles Albright, April 24, 1855, Nathaniel Lyon File, Henry E.
Huntington Library, San Marino, Calif. (hereafter cited as Huntington); Montgomery
to O. F. Winship, June 14, 1855, Post Files; Samuel Cooper to Montgomery, July 28,
1855, Letters Sent, RG 94.

46. Montgomery to O. F. Winship, April 4, 1855, Letters Received, Department of
the West, box 2, RG 393; Montgomery to O. F. Winship, June 14, 1855, Post Files;
Kemp, *About Nathaniel Lyon,* 56; William S. Harney to Lorenzo Thomas, June 2, 1855,
in "Official Correspondence Relating to Fort Pierre," 387.

gomery, it had exactly the opposite result. The animosity between the two men became even more bitter, and the colonel twice arrested his second-in-command for his "increasingly insubordinate and troublesome" behavior and "gross dereliction of duty." Upon arrival at Fort Pierre, Montgomery confined Lyon to quarters. However, when the post commander received a departmental communication requiring both men to proceed to Fort Leavenworth for Montgomery's court-martial, the colonel released Lyon from arrest and duty. The intransigent captain left the post on September 3, just as Harney began his Sioux expedition. Montgomery followed shortly thereafter. Because of the length of the trial, neither man participated in the expedition.[47]

During the summer, two regional newspapers, the *Kansas Herald* and the *Missouri Republican,* printed heated debates over the Pawnee affair. Several key participants, including Lyon and Montgomery themselves, submitted statements on their views of the case. By the time the court-martial commenced on September 24, the newspapers had reported some rather important incidents that altered the complexion of the trial drastically. Unknown to Montgomery at the time, Secretary of War Davis had submitted Montgomery's plat to the president for approval on May 5. There was, however, one major change: Davis had overturned the plat Montgomery had submitted and had *re-included* the land the colonel had excluded from the reserve for the town of Pawnee. Thus, Davis's decision rendered Montgomery's townsite an illegal intrusion on government property. Pierce approved the revised plat the same day. However, this was not the only new development in the case that occurred while Montgomery was in Nebraska.[48]

The territorial legislature met on July 2 at the newly built stone capitol at Pawnee, but adjourned just four days later because of both the lack of sufficient accommodations and the threat of cholera that had broken out in the vicinity. Moreover, the legislature disagreed with Governor Reeder's claim that he had full authority to change the capital site without their approval, adding to their decision to leave. No doubt Reeder's free-soil opinions also increased the discord with the proslavery legislature,

47. Returns, June 1855, RG 94; Robert G. Athearn, *Forts of the Upper Missouri,* 33–37.

48. Montgomery to O. F. Winship, June 17, 1855, Post Files, RG 94; Montgomery to O. F. Winship, September 9, 1855, Post Files, RG 94; Returns, September 1855, RG 94; Montgomery to Samuel Cooper, April 10, 1856, Letters Received, RG 94; Athearn, *Forts of the Upper Missouri,* 41.

and though the governor vetoed the resolution to change the place of meeting, the legislators passed the resolution over his veto. The territorial supreme court upheld its right to do so, and the legislature reconvened to a "temporary seat of government" at Shawnee Mission.[49]

Reeder's woes, however, were far from over. Once the news of Lyon's charges against Montgomery leaked out, information on the governor's involvement in the Pawnee land scam soon followed. As a result, in early August the president removed Reeder from office, amid great celebration by the Kansas legislators. And to make Montgomery's position even worse, on the last day of August the residents of Pawnee were given just over one month to vacate their "squatter's claims" because they were living on government property. On October 10, the federal troops at Fort Riley razed every one of the town's buildings, while former owners and speculators looked on in disbelief.[50]

The events of the summer and fall of 1855 gave Lyon's charges of fraud unmistakable validity. His damning testimony on the speculators' land parceling further deteriorated Montgomery's plea of innocence. On December 8, Pierce signed the confirmation of the court's verdict; Montgomery was found guilty "of deceit and falsehood" and was dismissed from the army. The other officers involved in the Pawnee venture received official reprimands, and Davis made it clear that he could easily have brought any of the other Pawnee speculators to the chopping block. However, Lyon's sacrificial lamb had been proffered and duly slaughtered, and, although it did not necessarily concern him, he had bagged a governor in the process.[51]

Shortly after the conclusion of the trial, Lyon received leave to travel to

49. Lyon to Samuel Cooper, December 27, 1855, Letters Received, RG 94; Shindler, "First Capital of Kansas," 334–35.

50. Kemp, *About Nathaniel Lyon,* 54–55. On April 30, 1855, Thomas S. Jesup, the acting quartermaster general, forwarded Montgomery's plat to Jefferson Davis, the secretary of war. Upon perusing the proposed boundaries, Davis noticed the exclusion of the Pawnee town site but would not approve the exclusion. On May 5, he passed on the plat to President Pierce with his recommendation not to allow the Pawnee exclusion. Pierce signed the proposal with Davis's recommendations, thus condemning the townsite. On the same day, Davis ordered two generals, Sylvester Churchill and Newman Clarke, to proceed to Fort Riley to investigate the land dealings at Pawnee, which they did during the summer of 1855. In their subsequent report to Davis, they recommended that Montgomery's exclusions were justified as they were not necessary to the army's needs. Their findings, however, were moot since the reserve lines had already been signed into law. Montgomery was subsequently brought to trial for fraudulent activities.

51. Alice Nichols, *Bleeding Kansas,* 35–36; Martin, "Territorial and Military Combine at Fort Riley," 368–71.

Chicago to settle the matter of some land he had purchased nearby. After settling the claim, he stayed in the city for a short Christmas vacation. While there, he wrote a long letter to the adjutant general stating the reasons for being "innocently and unexpectedly placed in the awkward position of being an owner in this Town nearly surrounded by the reserve" and of the "criminal" plan of both Montgomery and Reeder to promote the town for the capital.[52]

The letter, if viewed individually, could conceivably absolve Lyon from any dubious intent in his participation in the Pawnee venture. Yet the fact remains that Lyon *was* involved, so much so that he was willing to debauch an election to ensure the most advantageous results for the Pawnee site. His lands *were* partially on the military reserve, but they were situated where they were not completely swallowed by the final boundaries. Lyon was too keen to plead ignorance to the designs of the land company, although he stated as much in his letter. The correspondence from Chicago was at best an effective effort to cover his tracks, and, fortunately for him, the military authorities were apparently satisfied with the trial's outcome. No further prosecutions resulted; Lyon's revenge was complete. He even dropped his own civil suit against Montgomery, although during the months after the court-martial, while it was still pending, it caused the ex-colonel a great deal of consternation. Later in his life, Lyon's vindictiveness toward Montgomery raged on unabated. In a letter to an acquaintance at the outbreak of the Civil War, Lyon reported that rumors had reached him that Montgomery would soon be offered a commission in a newly formed volunteer regiment. Lyon wrote, "His re-appointment will be a great outrage and . . . I will, if made, so expose it [the reasons for his court-martial] over my own name."[53]

Through it all, Nathaniel Lyon emerged virtually unscathed. Because he had brought forth the charges, it would appear that the government had absolved him of all wrongdoing. The entire incident, however, revealed the extent to which Lyon would go to fulfill his own zealous sense of duty, even if that duty proved susceptible to compromise. He was not

52. Lyon to Samuel Cooper, December 27, 1855, Letters Received, AGO, RG 94; Lyon to Robert Ransom, November 29, 1855, Letters Received, Department of the West, box 2, RG 393; Lyon to Winfield S. Hancock, December 18, 1855, ibid.

53. White, "My First Days in Kansas," 551; Lyon to Dr. Scott, March 7, 1861, in Grace Lee Nute, ed., "A Nathaniel Lyon Letter," 143–44; Ezra J. Warner, *Generals in Blue,* 329–30.

above engaging in legally questionable activities to ensure that his personal desires or convictions were carried out. In his rigidly polarized mind, the laws of men were subservient to a code of justice on a much higher plain: his own. Any laws that failed to uphold those high doctrines he would disregard, and those who did not abide by his laws deserved to be punished. Montgomery was proof of this belief. In the next half-decade, Lyon would also prove this to the proslavery faction in Kansas.

VI

Fire and Blood

Although the brutal winter of 1855–1856 slowed movement into the Kansas Territory, strife continued in its eastern section, seemingly impervious to weather conditions. In December, the townsmen of Lawrence, under the direction of Charles Robinson and James H. Lane, feverishly built blockhouses around the town, in hopes of defending it from an "army" of fifteen hundred proslavery advocates led into the territory by Missouri senator David Rice Atchison. Oddly enough, this grandiose show of force originated as a call from the new territorial governor, Wilson Shannon, to the federal troops at Fort Leavenworth for assistance "in executing the laws and preserving the peace and good order in the Territory." The sheriff of Douglas County had been forcibly prevented from arresting a free-soil man accused of threatening violent retaliation against a proslavery settler for an earlier murder of another free-soiler. On December 5, 1855, Atchison's army—mostly Missourians and dragging at least seven cannon—faced the Lawrence palisades. Among the defenders inside were John Brown and his six sons, recently arrived in the territory. If needed, the invaders were fully prepared to level the town. Although this "Wakarusa War" managed to pass without the imminent armed confrontation, its implications infuriated the free-soilers in the territory. The incident served as a touchstone for emotions that for the entire summer had ridden especially high. One of those most deeply affected was Nathaniel Lyon.[1]

As the incident at Lawrence bears witness, the Kansas-Nebraska Act had not solved a problem in Kansas. Rather, it had created another: civil war. When Lyon arrived at Fort Riley just two weeks before the act's passage, his enmity toward it and the Democratic party was already firmly entrenched. However, he had not foreseen the strife that the "Kansas-Nebraska crime" would so rapidly engender. During the next

1. Jay Monaghan, *Civil War on the Western Border, 1854–1865,* 45; Alice Nichols, *Bleeding Kansas,* 57–70.

few months, as he learned of the bitter power struggle between the free-soil and proslavery factions in Kansas further to the east, Lyon's political views quickly swayed. By July 1854, he had already evinced a dislike for the "contemptible arrogance" of the slaveholding states, particularly their haughty attitude toward the Union, which had manifested itself most recently in their steadfast refusal to compromise on the issue of their "peculiar institution" in the territories. The crisis prompted New York senator William H. Seward to predict that an "irrepressible conflict" would result from the territorial question. Lyon averred that the reason for the South's inflexibility was that the natural "deterioration and weakness" of the system "awakened alarm with those who tolerate it, for their own safety, and for that of the institution itself." He believed that slavery would die inevitably by the choice of those who practiced it, and he deplored the aggressiveness with which the slave faction pushed it into Kansas. Yet Lyon was convinced that "the Friends of the Free State cause in Kansas are in good spirits and I believe are fully determined to adopt the only alternative now left to escape from degradation and to fight for their rights." However, while he hoped "to see her properly supported by the honest and manly men of the north & east," he could not wait passively for such an outcome. Hence, Lyon resolved to do all in his power to assist the Kansas free-soilers in preventing the spread of slavery into their territory, especially around Fort Riley.[2]

Despite his fervid antislavery convictions, Lyon was no abolitionist. He abhorred the fact that Southerners used the term to describe all those opposed to the spread of slavery. Lyon regarded most abolitionists as irresponsible rabble-rousers who were equally as culpable for the country's sectionalism as the slave states themselves. Rather than opposing slavery on moral grounds, Lyon's opposition was far more practical. Whereas in Mexico he opposed servitude as a hindrance to a modern, democratic society, he viewed the spread of slavery as a threat to the territories' economic potential for *white* laborers. In embracing the free-labor ideology, Lyon was convinced that those "who have been associated with slaves in their labor have become more or less degraded, and have little idea of the respectable dignity, to which the honest labor of man may be raised." He wanted none of this retardation in the territories:

2. Lyon, *Last Political Writings of General Nathaniel Lyon, U.S.A.,* 171; Lyon to Miner Knowlton, July 27, 1854, Nathaniel Lyon File, KSHS; Lyon to Catharina Hasler, October 29, 1855, Nathaniel Lyon Papers, AAS.

. . . We have opposed its [slavery's] extension into our territories because of its injurious effects upon the free laborer, and consequent diminution of the productions of labor . . . . We are to have a final settlement of this question, by a new construction of the Constitution, giving an express recognition of the right of property in slaves in the States where it now exists, or may hereafter exist.[3]

Yet his posture was far from humanitarian. Although he viewed the practice of human enslavement as a "vicious system," he would not concern himself with the plight of black slaves. "We are not concerned with improving the black race . . . . Our cause is the white man, and not the negro . . . ." In this stance, Lyon mirrored the majority of both the settlers in Kansas and Northerners in general. Although at least half the populace had emigrated from the western states, where with few exceptions slavery had always been illegal, most Kansas homesteaders proved more anti-Negro than antislavery. Viewing the blacks as an inferior race, they held that bringing slaves into the territory would only increase the population of an unwanted breed. Most supported the continuance of slavery where it presently existed but desired to outlaw its spread. Hence the Southern economy would continue to benefit the entire nation, while government protection of the institution would placate Southerners enough to keep them from striving so adamantly to spread slavery to the territories.[4]

Above all else, however, Lyon held the Union itself sacred. This fervid loyalty served as the primary catalyst in the development of his intense hatred for the "slavocracy." Although this hatred took time to swell to its full fury, he became convinced that the sectional conflict was the principal threat to the stability of the Union. That burgeoning conviction persuaded him that slavery was the root of the evil in the nation. Although upon his arrival in Kansas he stated rather mildly that he harbored some "apprehension that serious difficulties will arise upon the slave question in this Territory," only a year later his tone became far less moderate. By the spring of 1855, he was convinced that "the aggressions

3. Lyon, *Last Political Writings,* 191; Lyon to Miner Knowlton, July 27, 1854, Nathaniel Lyon File, KSHS. For a discussion of free-labor ideology, see Eric Foner, *Free Soil, Free Labor, Free Men: The Ideology of the Republican Party Before the Civil War,* 11–39.

4. Lyon, *Last Political Writings,* 140, 192; Eugene H. Berwanger, *The Frontier Against Slavery,* 101, 106.

of the pro-slavery men will not be checked, till a lesson has been taught them in letters of fire and blood."[5]

Although his upbringing imbued him with a strong disapproval of slavery, not until he had been stationed on the Kansas prairie did he actually condemn those who practiced the "peculiar institution." Much to his dismay, he found that most officers at Fort Riley were proslavery (which no doubt spared him great remorse for his actions in ending the Pawnee Association). Yet Lyon's outburst against slavery that resulted in his confrontation with Captain Anderson during the summer of 1854 signaled only the beginning of what would turn into unmitigated hatred by the end of the long winter of 1855–1856.[6]

After returning from Chicago in January 1856 following Montgomery's court-martial, Lyon remained at Fort Leavenworth until May. During that time, he witnessed firsthand the power struggle of which he had been apprised while at Fort Riley. Outraged at the actions of the Missouri border ruffians and the apparent condonation of their actions by the territorial administration, Lyon's antislavery views sharpened even more radically. During that winter, he wrote:

> I have seen so much of the overbearing domination of the pro-slavery people in Kansas towards the free state men, that I am persuaded the latter have either to fight in self-defense, or submit ignobly to the demands of their aggressors. This conduct . . . ought to be effectually rebuked by the indignation of the North . . . . I despair of living peaceably with our southern brethren without constantly making disgraceful concessions. But rest assured this will not always be, and in this view I foresee . . . ultimate sectional strife *which I do not care to delay.* [italics mine][7]

To this point, the Kansas problem had been limited primarily to a struggle for political supremacy. However, beginning in May 1856, the border conflict exploded into violence. A series of encounters succeeded only in further dividing the plains and gave rise to extralegal vigilante and militia groups. In January, the free-state voters held their own territorial elections, resulting in an extralegal legislature and governor, with

5. Lyon to Miner Knowlton, July 27, 1854, Nathaniel Lyon File, KSHS; Ashbel Woodward, *Life of General Nathaniel Lyon,* 210.

6. Lyon to Miner Knowlton, July 27, 1854, Nathaniel Lyon File, KSHS.

7. Lyon to F. N. Page, February 9, 1856, Letters Received, Department of the West, box 4, RG 393; Returns, September 1855 to May 1856, RG 94; Woodward, *Life of Nathaniel Lyon,* 213–14.

their capital at Topeka. The proslavery bordermen denounced this "bogus legislature" immediately and blamed the abolitionist rebels at Lawrence for the outrage because it had been their pernicious conventions,
aimed at repudiating the elected legislature, that had instigated the free-
state elections and the new constitution. When the residents of Lawrence
interfered with a second arrest, made by the same sheriff who was
thwarted in a similar attempt in December, the proslavery voices screamed
for vengeance. For a second time, Atchison and his Missourians answered the call. He led a large contingent across the border toward
Lawrence and encircled the town with seven cannon pointing toward the
Eldridge Hotel, which stood at its center. Two days later, the "army"
marched into surrendered Lawrence, destroyed the newspaper presses
and the hotel, and looted the stores. Only three days following this "sack
of Lawrence," John Brown retaliated by brutally murdering five proslavery settlers along Pottawatomie Creek. The massacre prompted President Pierce to grant Governor Shannon the use of the United States forces
in Kansas to enforce peace and territorial law.[8]

The employment of troops to assist the proslavery legislature in the
enforcement of laws opposed by the free-soil settlers rankled Lyon. He
held the legislature to be illegal because it relied upon nonresident voters
to gain its validity. He believed Pierce's decision to back the proslavery
legislature was recklessly wrought, induced by Northern demagogues
like "the bold, heartless and unscrupulous Douglas." Such imbecility
would only heighten the already-tense situation in the territory. "Men in
Kansas, who would have it a free state," he wrote, "are denied civil and
political rights, and brutally murdered, or otherwise, with their Families
and property, shamefully outraged and driven from the country." The
situation so angered Lyon that he was "quite willing to . . . do [his] share
in the issue" if he was needed to assist in defending the rights of the free-
soilers against the "merciless outrages of the inexorable assassins." However, he did not yet know what form that assistance might take. On one
opinion, though, he held firm—the army was not the answer to the
problem of law enforcement: "Neither section of the country will be
satisfied with the conduct of the army, and its employment under such
circumstances is diametrically opposed to the spirit of our institutions.

8. Monaghan, *Civil War on the Western Border,* 30–33, 46; Nichols, *Bleeding Kansas,* 80–82, 105–9, 113–15.

The move will only cause mischief, as I fear, in the end, and bring it into disfavor with the people."[9]

His repugnance for the entire situation grew so pronounced that he briefly contemplated resigning his commission in the army rather than submit to such moral debasement. However, he was spared from making this decision when he received orders in late May directing him to proceed to Camp Douglas, near Sioux City, Iowa, to act as judge advocate of a dragoon court-martial. A month later, he proceeded up the Missouri River to Fort Pierre, fifteen hundred miles northwest of St. Louis. Lyon had received an assignment to erect a new military post south of Fort Pierre.[10]

Situated on the Missouri's west bank, Fort Pierre was built in 1832 as a trading post for John Jacob Astor's American Fur Company. The company later sold the structure to the government for the use of the military on the northern plains. However, as Gen. William Harney discovered on his 1855 Sioux expedition, Fort Pierre was woefully unsuited as a military post. The small stockade prohibited all troops from residing within its walls, and half the command was therefore stationed at a cantonment five miles upriver from the fort. In addition, its great distance from St. Louis and the chronic unnavigability of the Missouri due to either low or frozen water made transportation of goods both sporadic and expensive. Wood and drinking water had to be transported great distances to the fort, which sat back from the river on a "high rolling prairie." The width of the river at the fort caused a shallow channel, forcing freight to be loaded and unloaded at least three miles downriver. And finally, the crude stockade and flimsily built quarters offered little protection against the fierce cold of the northern latitude, causing great suffering and even death among the troops—especially those at Cantonment Miller. Harsh conditions forced Harney to adapt Indian garb to keep his men from freezing, and scurvy plagued the garrison throughout the season. One winter was enough to convince him that the sparsely settled area did not warrant a military post. He therefore determined to construct one farther south before the arrival of the next long winter.[11]

9. Woodward, *Life of Nathaniel Lyon,* 214–15; Lyon to Lorenzo Lyon, August 23, 1856, Nathaniel Lyon Papers, CSL.

10. Woodward, *Life of Nathaniel Lyon,* 219–20; Returns, March 1856 to May 1857, RG 94; Lyon to Lorenzo Lyon, August 23, 1856, Nathaniel Lyon Papers, CSL; Augustus Meyers, "Dakota in the Fifties," 132–33.

11. Meyers, "Dakota in the Fifties," 132–38; Lyon to D. H. Vinton, August 1, 1855,

Harney selected a site about a hundred miles above the mouth of the L'eau qui-court, or Niobrara, River. An old trading post, Fort Lookout, at one time had been located near the same spot, below the Great Bend of the Missouri River, but was abandoned in 1851 and had since fallen into disrepair. Harney ordered a new fort to be built near that spot, "where the landing is good, the situation fine." Because of Lyon's experience at San Diego Barracks, the army chose him to construct Fort Lookout. He and his command, Companies B and D—278 officers and men—left Fort Pierre in the first week of June and marched southward toward the spot Harney had designated. Traveling away from the river to avoid the numerous creeks and gullies that intersected the plain, they traversed the rolling, often rough, terrain, a landscape Lyon condemned as "unfortunate & repulsive barrenness." Because they had no road, the march took nearly two months. On August 3, Lyon's command halted, and for the next two days he personally searched for the most appropriate site for a post. He selected one a few miles downriver from the old fort, near some woods "on an elevation gently sloping towards the river, which runs and affords good landing near the foot of it." Lacking further orders, Lyon directed "that the name of the Station be continued . . . as 'Fort Lookout' by which it will hereafter be known."[12]

As in San Diego, Lyon proved both a thorough planner and an exacting taskmaster, to the benefit of Fort Lookout's construction. Laying out the fort with generous dimensions (enough for two full regiments), he was determined to get all lines perfectly straight and true. One of his men recalled that Lyon stayed out several nights aligning the post lines by the North Star. He would have it no other way. In the end, however, the log fort was amply suited for the coming winter. Because of the group's late arrival, and because of a significant number of desertions, snow had

Letters Received, Department of the West, box 2, RG 393; D. H. Vinton to T. S. Jesup, March 30, 1855, in "Official Correspondence Relating to Fort Pierre," 383; William S. Harney to Samuel Cooper, March 9, 1856, ibid.; Richmond L. Clow, "General William S. Harney on the Northern Plains," 240–46.

12. Robert G. Athearn, *Forts of the Upper Missouri,* 46; Clow, "General William S. Harney," 245; Harney to Samuel Cooper, March 9, 1856, in "Official Correspondences," 423; Order No. 57, August 3, 1856, ibid., 436; Frederick T. Wilson, "Fort Pierre and Its Neighbors," 288; Meyers, "Dakota in the Fifties," 170–71, 175–76; Lyon to D. H. Vinton, August 1, 1855, Letters Received, Department of the West, box 2, RG 393; Merrill J. Mattes, "Report on Historic Sites in the Fort Randall Reservoir Area, Missouri River, South Dakota," 543–44; Lyon to Samuel Cooper, August 1, 1856, Letters Received, AGO, RG 94; Lyon to George Deas, September 1, 1856, Letters Received, Department of the West, box 4, RG 393.

already collected by the time work was completed in October. Lyon had built for himself a forty-five- by fifteen-foot house, to which he added an addition for a kitchen and for servants. Because of his well-laid plans for both quarters and food, both his men and those who arrived from Fort Pierre after it was abandoned spent the winter comfortably at the fort. Upon the arrival of spring, however, the garrison received orders to dismantle and abandon Fort Lookout and to transfer both themselves and the materials to Fort Randall, about seventy miles south of Fort Lookout. This fort would now become the supply base for future operations to maintain peace with the Sioux.[13]

Lyon perhaps lamented the destruction of his fort, but he had little time for such sentiments. In April, he applied for a leave of absence to return to the East, and on the last day of the month was granted such leave, but the move prevented him from taking advantage of it at that time. Not until June 23 did he board a river steamer bound for St. Louis. In all, he was removed from his post a total of eight months. While on leave, he visited his relatives in New York, New London, and Eastford, but he spent the lion's share of his time in Burlington, New Jersey, with his cousin Miner. Knowlton had been afflicted with a serious breathing disorder for several years, and on his previous visit home Lyon had witnessed one of his cousin's painful attacks. His problem would today require a tracheotomy to relieve the spasms, but in 1857 the procedure was yet in a nascent stage. Physicians advised him that his illness was most likely fatal, and he retired to Burlington to await his demise, but refused to resign his military commission. Lyon's leave, extended in July, expired in December, and he returned to Jefferson Barracks in St. Louis just after Christmas. His trip east would prove to be the last of his life.[14]

13. Meyers, "Dakota in the Fifties," 169–70; Augustus Meyers, *Ten Years in the Ranks, U.S. Army,* 122–29; Lyon to Assistant Adjutant General, Department of the West, August 5, 1856, Letters Received, Department of the West, box 4, RG 393; Lyon to N. H. McLean, September 20, 1856, ibid.; Lyon to F. J. Porter, September 24, 1856, ibid.; Lyon to Samuel Cooper, July 13, 1857, Letters Received, AGO, RG 94; Woodward, *Life of Nathaniel Lyon,* 225; Athearn, *Forts of the Upper Missouri,* 46, 49–50.

14. Lyon to Mrs. J. W. Trowbridge, September 22, 1857, Nathaniel Lyon File, ChiHS; Lyon to John B. Hasler, September 22, 1857, ibid.; George W. Cullum, *Biographical Register of the Officers and Graduates of the U.S. Military Academy at West Point, N.Y.,* 1:426; Special Order No. 34, April 30, 1857, Orders and Special Orders, Department of the West, RG 393; Special Order No. 87, December 5, 1857, ibid.; Special Order No. 10, February 15, 1858, ibid.; Returns, June 1857, RG 94; Lyon to Samuel Cooper, July 13, 1857, Letters Received, AGO, RG 94; Lyon to Samuel Cooper, July 13, 1857, ibid.; Lyon to Miner Knowlton, July 27, 1854, Nathaniel Lyon File, KSHS; Woodward, *Life of*

After wintering in St. Louis, Lyon received orders to report to Fort Leavenworth, where he arrived on May 3. From there he escorted a company of recruits to Fort Randall, where he rejoined his company. A great deal had happened in Kansas since Lyon had left the territory in the spring of 1856, only some of which he was able to keep up with in the eastern newspapers. Three successive governors—Wilson Shannon, Robert J. Walker, and John W. Geary—had resigned because of the deplorable state of affairs in the territory. Walker and Geary had become so frustrated that each had left Kansas with the stated purpose of attending to personal business, but neither ever returned. The newest governor, James W. Denver, assumed the office just before Christmas 1857, while Lyon was at Jefferson Barracks. However, this administrative revolving door was the least of the problems that plagued the territory in Lyon's absence.[15]

A political war raged in Kansas that was as intense as the violent struggle between the free-state and proslavery gangs. Early in 1857, two days after James Buchanan took office as the fifteenth president of the United States, Chief Justice Roger B. Taney handed down the Dred Scott decision, ruling that Congress had no power to prohibit slavery in the territories. In effect, it declared the Missouri Compromise unconstitutional. Although anti-Nebraskans (those who opposed the Kansas-Nebraska Act) decried the decision as obiter dicta (a judicial ruling that was not binding because it was superfluous to the case at hand), it paved the way for a renewal of the power of the slave faction in Kansas. In 1855, free-staters had voted into office both an extralegal governor and legislature. This "bogus legislature" had convened at Topeka but had been recognized by neither the official territorial government nor the national government.

In the summer of 1857, spurred on by the Dred Scott decision and the election of Buchanan, the slave supporters held an election for convention delegates who would draft a constitution to be submitted to Congress as an application for statehood. The free-staters, holding a majority of the population yet without governmental power, refused to participate and boycotted the election. The resulting Lecompton Con-

---

Nathaniel Lyon, 225–26. Knowlton did not in fact succumb early as the doctors had predicted, but outlived his cousin by nearly a decade, dying on Christmas Eve, 1870, at the age of sixty-six.

15. Special Order No. 16, 2 March 1858, Orders and Special Orders Issued, Department of the West, RG 393; Special Order No. 45, April 15, 1858, ibid.; Nichols, Bleeding Kansas, 139–40, 185, 203–5.

stitution, drafted to gain Kansas's admission into the union as a slave state, created a storm of controversy across the nation. Although President Buchanan recommended that Kansas be accepted under the constitution, Stephen A. Douglas broke with his own party and the president. In the summer of 1858, he condemned the Lecompton "swindle" as a usurpation of his own principle of popular sovereignty.[16]

Primarily as a result of Douglas's opposition, and much to the chagrin of Buchanan, Congress voted against the Lecompton Constitution. In its stead it passed the English bill, which required a plebiscite in the territory on the issue of slavery. If the populace voted *for* slavery, immediate statehood would have resulted, with the practice being guaranteed. However, if the people voted *against* slavery, Kansas would remain a territory until it reached sixty thousand in population, when its legislature could submit a new constitution. The year 1858 had seen a peak in Kansas immigration, and the majority of settlers had come from Northern states. Opposed to slavery in their new home, they turned out in large numbers to help defeat the Lecompton Constitution by the overwhelming margin of 11,300 to 1,788. Since the elections of the previous fall had at last given the free-staters a majority in the legislature and a representative in Congress, the question of slavery appeared at last to be settled. Yet Lyon was forced to deal with the bitter strife that surfaced in Kansas as the debate over the Lecompton Constitution raged in Congress.[17]

After being on duty at Fort Randall for less than two weeks, Lyon received new orders summoning him and Company B to report to Fort Leavenworth as soon as practicable. On May 15, 1858, the group boarded the steamer *Camier* and began the familiar journey down the Missouri River. Arriving at the fort on the twenty-sixth, Lyon reported to the post commander, Bvt. Maj. Thomas W. Sherman, who informed him that the government needed troops in Utah to attend to the trouble there with the Mormons. Considering the religious nature of the problems, Lyon no doubt relished the opportunity to impose his own brand of justice on the recalcitrant polygamists, with full imprimatur from his government. He and his two companies were to start immediately for Fort Kearney, 250 miles west on the Platte River, where they would outfit for the rest of the long journey. They left promptly, but a week later a

16. Stephen B. Oates, *With Malice Toward None*, 150–51.
17. Oates, *To Purge This Land with Blood*, 256.

messenger caught up with the column and ordered them to retrace their steps to Leavenworth. Upon their return, Lyon learned the reason for the recall: the border war had again erupted. This time, however, the focal point was not the town of Lawrence, but the border counties in the southeastern section of the state. From Sherman, Lyon learned that his new destination would be the center of the latest storm: Fort Scott.[18]

Although the free-soilers now enjoyed a majority in the legislature, the Lecompton issue and the news of the Dred Scott decision had incited the proslavery forces, especially in the eastern counties. In the spring of 1858, both Linn and Bourbon counties were still heavily proslave, due to the Missouri influence, and in those areas friction never abated. In the fall of 1856, a group of proslavery border ruffians raided the area, destroying crops, stealing horses and cattle, and burning cabins. This move drew retaliation from free-soiler James Montgomery, who crossed into Missouri posing as a schoolmaster and quickly found a job there. For two weeks, he obtained the names of many of those involved in the raid, then quietly left the state. He returned, however, with armed support, and by their hands twenty of the Missourians received the same treatment they had given to residents of Bourbon County. Since that time the guerrilla bands had waged their own private war. Montgomery and his "Jayhawkers" intimidated proslavery settlers, driving a number of them back across the border. His guerrillas appeared to be mainly in control and encountered little resistance in their efforts to clear southeastern Kansas of the slave power. However, by May 1858 events in the area had escalated rapidly.[19]

After the Lecompton crisis prompted a renewal of proslavery activity, many of the settlers Montgomery had once chased from the territory began to return to their relinquished claims. In late March, the murders of two free-soilers near Fort Scott precipitated more retaliatory raids by free-soil gangs. The situation became so untenable that the newest territorial governor, James W. Denver, requested that federal troops be sent to Fort Scott to control the roving marauders. A force of dragoons from Fort Leavenworth rode into an ambush when they reached Fort Scott, and Montgomery quickly received blame for the firing. The dragoon

18. Returns, May 1858, RG 94; "Documentary History of Kansas—Governor Denver's Administration," 502; Ezra J. Warner, *Generals in Blue,* 440–41; Meyers, *Ten Years in the Ranks,* 135–38.

19. Monaghan, *Civil War on the Western Border,* 81; Nichols, *Bleeding Kansas,* 218–20.

commander detached several squads to arrest the outlaw. One of the detachments caught up with the Jayhawkers and engaged in a heated firefight, leaving two federal soldiers dead and four wounded. At this point, additional troops seemed necessary to keep order, and the call went to Lyon on the road to Fort Kearney. On May 19, just before he arrived at Fort Leavenworth, proslavery ruffians executed five free-soilers and wounded another four in an incident along the Marais des Cygnes River in Linn County. The news of the massacre appeared to mandate the need for more troops in the area, and on June 1, Lyon and Companies B and D, accompanied by a section of artillery, left Fort Leavenworth on the week's march to Fort Scott.[20]

Located on the Marmiton River, Fort Scott was no longer a military post. Like Fort Pierre, it had been a frontier post until 1844, when the government purchased it to fill the gap on the Military Road between Forts Leavenworth and Gibson. Nine years later, army command determined that there was no longer any need to maintain the fort, and it held a public auction and sold the wooden post buildings. Since that time, the old post, with a population of about two hundred, had served as the Bourbon County seat and the center of activity in southeastern Kansas. It was also home to the proslavery newspaper, the *Southern Kansan,* read avidly by the local populace, most of whom were former Missourians. The town also became the nucleus of the area's strife. Its two hotels housed opposing free and slave factions, and nightly raids against settlers of the opposing faction often ended with whooping celebrations in the local saloons. The government believed the presence of the army would stabilize the volatile area, and Lyon received the difficult assignment.[21]

Heavy rains delayed the march somewhat, and it took nine days for the column to reach Fort Scott. Lyon noticed that the area below the Big Blue River was for the most part deserted; most of the residents had abandoned their homes because of the border troubles. At Fort Scott, he found over 150 armed men ready to resist invasion from either Lawrence or Missouri. The situation only reinforced his prior contention that the army could not quell the situation. "A body of Government troops," he wrote, "no larger than this here, if employed, must play too insignificant a part to either arrest it or materialy affect the result." Although his

20. Nichols, *Bleeding Kansas,* 223–25; Monaghan, *Civil War on the Western Border,* 103–4; Returns, June 1858, RG 94.

21. Monaghan, *Civil War on the Western Border,* 100–102; Meyers, *Ten Years in the Ranks,* 141–42.

command was perhaps sufficiently strong to contain the immediate situation, he felt that it could do little to counteract the problems of the entire region. Rather, Lyon believed that the key to peace was "a firm and energetic course on the part of the civil authorities, which would inspire the public with confidence in their integrity and resolution of purpose, would secure the concurrence and cooperation of enough good citizens to affect the results desired."[22]

While Lyon was not blind to the turmoil around Fort Scott, his free-soil sentiments had tainted his views, and he placed full blame on the proslavery settlers for the area's strife. In fact, Lyon believed that the presence of the army, by providing protection for the residents in Fort Scott, actually *assisted* those perpetrators of local crimes living in the town. In this way, the troops prevented the administration of the miscreants' much-deserved punishment, both from himself and from those they had wronged. Thus, to those free-soilers he believed he was protecting, "the Gov't and Troops must be placed in a false position and incur a proportionate amount of odium." In one instance, a group of mounted ruffians actually deployed against Lyon's troops, but several well-aimed cannon blasts quickly dispersed them. Though Lyon was highly critical of the expedition, the presence of his troops appeared to stabilize a potentially explosive situation, and the rest of the summer passed rather peacefully. On August 11, he and his command returned from Fort Scott to Fort Leavenworth, and from there they took the sternwheeler *Morton* upriver once again to Fort Randall. Although Lyon was leaving Fort Scott, his involvement with the fort had not yet ended.[23]

Lyon spent the winter at Fort Randall. The mundane daily duties at the fort soon grew irksome, and men became restless from the lack of activity. Traffic on the Missouri River reached its peak during the year, and the men of the garrison eagerly kept abreast of the events of the country by way of the constant stream of boats docking at the fort. Of particular interest—especially to Lyon—was the rise of the Republican party, which ran a presidential candidate, John C. Frémont, in the 1856 campaign. Although Frémont, the celebrated "Pathfinder of the West,"

22. Lyon to T. W. Sherman, July 15, 1858, Letters Received, AGO, RG 94; Lyon to T. W. Sherman, June 10, 1858, Letters Received, Department of the West, box 6, RG 393.

23. Lyon to J. W. Denver, June 13, 1858, Letters Received, Department of the West, box 6, RG 393; Lyon to T. W. Sherman, June 10, 1858, ibid.; Lyon to T. W. Sherman, July 15, 1858, Letters Received, AGO, RG 94; Meyers, *Ten Years in the Ranks*, 143–45.

lost the election, the party steadily gained support, and much of the garrison followed the fall's senatorial elections with great interest. This was due in part to a summer series of debates in Illinois between Democratic powerhouse Stephen A. Douglas and his relatively unknown challenger, Abraham Lincoln, a lawyer and former Whig congressman now carrying the banner of the state's Republican party. Lincoln and his party gained a great deal of publicity and, of more importance, a good amount of respect from his forensic duels with the Little Giant.[24]

The Republican party had made great inroads into many of the Northern states as its main platform appealed to most residents. Originally, the shibboleth of the Republican movement was its opposition to the Kansas-Nebraska Act, but by 1858 its platform had grown into a general stand against the spread of slavery beyond its present boundaries. Most Republicans viewed the situation in Kansas as a tragic mistake, thus proving at least to them that the theory of popular sovereignty was unworkable with an issue as divisive as slavery. Although Douglas continued to insist that the system was the *most* workable, Lincoln's masterful performance in the Illinois debates forced Douglas to so contradict himself on its intent that the theory became too ambiguous to maintain support, and many turned away from his leadership. Although Lincoln lost the senatorial race, "Bleeding Kansas" helped the Republican party develop rapidly into a political force to be reckoned with.[25]

Like many Northern Democrats, Lyon found himself unable to abide his party's platform on slavery in the territories, which sanctioned and supported the Kansas-Nebraska Act. Democratic policy maintained that slavery was a question for the states to decide; it therefore supported Douglas's popular-sovereignty doctrine as a means by which territories could settle their own futures as the majority of their populations saw fit. Kansas proved the litmus test of Lyon's political philosophy, and what he had seen there could not permit him to continue supporting the Democratic party. In 1856, his hatred for the slave faction propelled him into the Republican camp, and like all his other convictions, he grasped the party's standard in a death grip. Writing to his brother, Lyon first articulated his new political loyalties:

So contemptible had the administration become that its friends dared not to

24. Returns, September 1858, RG 94; Athearn, *Forts of the Upper Missouri*, 60.
25. Thomas H. O'Connor, *The Disunited States: The Era of Civil War and Reconstruction,* 90–92; Mark E. Neely, Jr., *The Abraham Lincoln Encyclopedia,* 84–88, 241–43.

nominate Pierce, nor his conspiritor Douglass [*sic*] . . . and Buchanan, by accepting the platform, places himself in the same attitude, and his election would be construed into a willingness, on the part of our people, that slavery should be established in Kansas, and there can be no doubt the same measures to bring this about would be continued . . . . You will see, by these sentiments, my anxiety that you and all our friends should vote the Republican Ticket . . . . the extraordinary circumstances of our country & the weighty events impending force me to urge upon you a rigorous discharge of your duty.[26]

After spending an enjoyably mild winter at Fort Randall, in July 1859 Lyon led an overland expedition to Prairie Dog Creek, a small tributary of the Republican Fork in the Kansas Territory. The Emigrant Road, connecting Fort Leavenworth with the Pike's Peak mines in the far western section of the territory, crossed the stream near its confluence with the Republican Fork. Nearby, the army had established an encampment to protect travelers as they passed through an area populated heavily with Indians. On July 12, the expedition, consisting of Companies B and I, left from Fort Randall for Fort Kearney, lying 180 dusty, scorching miles to the south. The march proved exceedingly difficult in the oppressive weather; the men could endure only fifteen miles of marching per day before being overcome with fatigue. They moved primarily in the early morning, the coolest part of the day, and halted by noon. After a brief stop at Fort Kearney, the exhausted column straggled into the encampment on August 3. Because no westward parties used the route while Lyon was at the camp (most emigrated via Fort Kearney, a more northerly route), he saw little need to continue maintaining the camp. After returning from court-martial duty at Fort Kearney, on September 15 Lyon led the infantry out of camp and wound eastward on the final leg of their journey. After a ten-day march, the column arrived at Fort Riley, two hundred miles to the east.[27]

Those stationed earlier at Fort Riley could not help but be amazed at the changes that had occurred since their last tour of duty. The old wooden buildings had been replaced with new ones of durable lime-

26. Lyon to Lorenzo Lyon, August 23, 1856, Nathaniel Lyon Papers, CSL.

27. Lyon to Lorenzo Lyon, February 22, 1859, Nathaniel Lyon Papers, CSL; Returns, July 1858, August 1859 to September 1859, RG 94; Woodward, *Life of Nathaniel Lyon,* 227; Lyon to Samuel Cooper, August 3, 1859, Letters Received, AGO, RG 94; Lyon to John A. Hasler, November 17, 1859, Harry N. Ensign Autograph Collection, Yale University Library.

stone, and there now were ample barracks and imposing guardhouse towers at each end of the compound. Equally as noticeable was the new mood in the area toward the recent troubles in Kansas. Lyon saw immediately a "subsidence of political animosity, the return of peace and tranquillity, and that too with the ascendency of free state principles." Since he last saw the fort, "a handsome rebuke has in the interval been given to proslavery arrogance, though at a painful sacrifice of valuable life in martyrdom to the cause." The change of political climate at Fort Riley pleased Lyon; he felt it mirrored the general atmosphere in Kansas. He found opportunity again to bait Hasler, who had abandoned his Whig loyalties for the Democratic banner: ". . . All [your] assistance to the profligate proslavery Democracy has not succeeded in forcing slavery in Kansas, which is firmly secured against this blight, in spite of the power and malice of Federal authorities . . . . And now that people seem fairly awake to the moral turpitude in which the Democratic party is involved, they are everywhere abandoning it to its fate . . . ."[28]

In mid-October, shortly after Lyon's arrival at Fort Riley, the post received news of John Brown's raid on the federal arsenal at Harper's Ferry, Virginia. "Osawatomie Brown"—as he was known in Kansas after his bloody antics in the early years of the territory—had seized the arsenal and armory. During a sharp firefight, local militia drove the raiders from the armory and then surrounded them in the village fire-engine house. For thirty-six hours, Brown and his gang of twenty followers held out, until a party of U.S. Marines stormed the engine house and either killed or captured the defenders inside, including Brown himself.

The proceedings of Brown's trial, held in the Charlestown, Virginia, circuit court, captured headlines in newspapers all over the nation. The country's readers anxiously sought out the dailies to read the latest testimonies of what many purported to be the century's most celebrated case. After a month's deliberation, the jury found Brown guilty of conspiracy to incite an insurrection, treason, and murder. On December 2, he was hung. His death created a martyr for Northern abolitionists and a symbol of Yankee machinations for the South, thus widening the growing division between the states.[29]

28. Woodward, *Life of Nathaniel Lyon,* 229; Lyon to John A. Hasler, November 17, 1859, Harry N. Ensign Autograph Collection, Yale University Library.
29. Oates, *To Purge This Land with Blood,* 290–302, 327.

Lyon, however, held no sympathy for "poor old Osawattomie Brown." To him, Brown was a fanatic, a "simpleton [who] deserved his fate." He believed the old man's actions, though brave, would only cause the South to blame the entire North for the insane act of violence, a "false and silly" stance that would cause the South to "make fools of themselves about the matter, as they always do on the subject of slavery." Brown had merely illuminated the folly of abolitionists and the reason to despise them as much as the slave power, or "Shameocracy," itself. With remarkable prescience, Lyon predicted that the Brown affair would "assume other shapes in course of time."[30]

After Lyon served at Fort Riley for the winter, in May 1860 both the post commander, Maj. John Sedgwick, and his second, Bvt. Maj. Henry Wessells (both Connecticut natives), were called to Fort Scott. This left Lyon not only in command, but the sole officer at the post for the entire summer and early fall except one lieutenant, whose illness prevented him from duty. During this time Lyon exhibited traits that are enlightening when viewed in terms of the enigmatic personality he had already demonstrated.[31]

As post commander, Lyon's responsibilities went far beyond simply ordering about squads of enlisted men. The duty required him to keep a detailed record of all receipts and expenditures for his command. This day-by-day account ledger he submitted to army headquarters, and from there it traveled to the Treasury Department in Washington. Such accounting needed precise documentation, and responsibility for its accuracy fell upon the post commander. Each company commander perforce requisitioned all necessities through Lyon, and the urgency of the requests were therefore subject to his discretion. Lyon kept both his post and personal accounts with the New York banking firm of his cousin, Danford Knowlton. Because he kept both accounts with Knowlton's firm, he often wrote personal drafts to cover such post expenses as newspaper and magazine subscriptions, postage stamps, food items, and payments to company laundresses. Although the two balances could

30. Woodward, Life of Nathaniel Lyon, 229; Lyon, Last Political Writings, 128, 185.

31. Cullum, Biographical Register, 1:560–61, 680–81; "John Sedgwick," in Dictionary of American Biography, 16:548; "Henry Wessells," in National Cyclopaedia of American Biography, 12:241; E. H. E. Jameson, ed., A Memorial Wreath Containing an Address from the Lyon Monumental Association of St. Louis . . . , 22–23; Lyon to the Assistant Adjutant General, Department of the West, June 23, 1860, Letters Received, Department of the West, box 9, RG 393.

have easily become hopelessly entangled, Lyon proved a meticulous accountant. He kept separate ledgers for both post and personal expenditures, including even minor expenses and income. Lyon had dealt once before with the Treasury Department on an accounting discrepancy, and the distasteful experience preyed constantly upon his mind when handling post expenses. He would not allow the Treasury Department accountants again to annoy him with alleged inconsistencies in his bookkeeping.[32]

From his account book, one can gain glimpses of Lyon's personal habits and pastimes. He often spent evenings with other officers (at least with those his outspoken opinions had not alienated) enjoying his favorite game, billiards, and kept a constant supply of "cegars." Lyon also had a penchant for candy, purchasing sweets each month in one- and two-pound quantities, to enjoy both at his office and in his quarters. His sweet tooth, however, appears to have caused him serious dental problems. As early as 1855 he complained of having to see a dentist to "work upon my jaws." By 1861, Lyon wore a plate of false teeth.[33]

In the heat of late summer afternoons, Lyon often enjoyed a cool beer from the sutler's springhouse. On infrequent occasions local Germans sold their best lager or ale to the sutler, and the men at the fort opted for this higher-priced libation over the normal brew. One account testifies to Lyon's love of beer. At Fort Lookout during the summer of 1856, he developed a strong hankering for the drink and determined to make several barrels. Lacking proper materials, he sent a detail to gather cactus plants, wild hops, and spruce twigs with which to make his beer. They mashed the ingredients into a pulp, added molasses and vinegar, then brewed it and stored the spruce beer in barrels. However, when it had "aged," the concoction proved so vile that only Lyon would drink it, though he could hardly have enjoyed it. The men at Fort Riley were more fortunate. Parties or special visitors necessitated the purchase of a keg of the home-brewed variety, at $3.00 to $3.50 per barrel, and on very

32. Personal Account Book of Lieutenant Nathaniel Lyon, October 1856 to August 1858, Nathaniel Lyon Papers, CSL; Personal Account Book of Captain Nathaniel Lyon, September 1858 to May 1861 (hereafter cited as Lyon Account Book), Nathaniel Lyon File, WC; Lyon to Danford Knowlton, August 26, 1856, to May 16, 1861, Nathaniel Lyon Papers, CHS.

33. Lyon Account Book, WC; Lyon to Catharina Hasler, October 29, 1855, Nathaniel Lyon Papers, AAS; Estate Inventory of Nathaniel Lyon, Eastford Township Probate Records, CSL.

special occasions the purchase of champagne. And at these fetes, the post commander sprang for the evening's musical entertainment, provided by locals. Indeed, Lyon never lost his enjoyment of parties. During that winter, one resident remembered that Lyon took a keen interest in the lessons a dancing master gave at Fort Scott. In fact, many nights after dancing school Lyon and others retired to the Free State Hotel, where, after first visiting the hotel bar, they wound up the night in stag dances.[34]

Once a month, a theater troupe traveled to the fort to render their dramatics for the men of the post. Lyon was unflagging in his attendance, generally paying to see each of the two nights' performances. He was particularly fond of Shakespearean productions, and his personal repertoire of dialogue appears to have been quite lengthy. In addition to drama, Lyon found comfort in reading poetry. Although he enjoyed Robert Burns, his preference lay in the works of the Irish poet Thomas Moore, whose heroes bespoke many of Lyon's innermost feelings about himself. Tortured by an obsession with solitude, Moore's characters fought an endless battle between craving their isolation and being trapped by it. As victims, their aloneness grew only more acute, and Lyon believed he understood perfectly many of Moore's arcane emotions. Lyon felt the author speaking to *him,* and through Moore's writings he sought to understand better his own obsessions. In Moore, Lyon saw himself: "I feel like one / Who treads alone."[35]

Any solace that Thomas Moore's words might have offered seems to have failed to curb Lyon's eccentricities. If anything, at Fort Riley they grew more pronounced. Because he was the only officer on duty at the post, the burdens of commandant, post adjutant, company commander, and officer of the day devolved entirely upon him. He requested assistance, but none was forthcoming. Yet this mountain of responsibility only augmented Lyon's intense devotion to duty. He moved like a man possessed in fulfilling the duties required of him. One of his men recalled that he never failed to visit the guard twice each night, once at nine o'clock and again after midnight. Yet another related a similar incident illustrating even more graphically Lyon's fanatical sense of duty. Around 2:00 A.M., as James Larson walked his first guard duty since being

34. Lyon Account Book, WC; Meyers, *Ten Years in the Ranks,* 120; Charles W. Goodlander, *Memoirs and Recollections of C. W. Goodlander,* 61–62.

35. Lyon Account Book, WC; James Peckham, *General Nathaniel Lyon and Missouri in 1861,* 61–62; Lurton D. Ingersoll, *Iowa and the Rebellion,* 24; "Extracts from the poems of Thomas Moore," Nathaniel Lyon Papers, AAS.

transferred to Fort Riley, he heard a rustle in the weeds behind him. He turned to see the silhouette of a man leaping from the brush. Reacting quickly, he leveled his rifle and ordered the man to halt and identify himself. It was Lyon. Larson was warned while still in St. Louis of Lyon's reputation as a "perfect military martinet" and his penchant for ensnaring his men with schemes to "catch him doing something wrong." Though Larson had made no mistake in identifying his shadowy assailant, he refused to allow the commandant to pass without the proper countersign. When Lyon failed to provide it, Larson summoned the corporal of the guard, who marched the indignant post commander to the guardhouse. Though the entire command delighted at their commandant's discomfiture, Lyon's motives were self-evident. Had Larson failed Lyon's test by not acting exactly as he did, Lyon would have punished him severely for failing to do his duty.[36]

Lyon also found the opportunity to put his religious convictions to what he considered a beneficial use. As commandant, he used his power to effect the dismissal of the post chaplain, ostensibly on the grounds that he had insulted one of the ladies of the fort. While the minister cried foul, Lyon held the upper hand. He wrote that the minister's dismissal was due to "ungentlemanly and gross conduct," which was "consistent with that of a christian minister under the arrogance of this subtle craft, to presume upon the religious superstition and awe with which it is regarded to obtrude gross improprieties upon persons." A year later, while in St. Louis, Lyon would pen a similar note to a member of that city's Unionist clergy, in which he regretted "the necessity to deplore that the profession he [the minister] much adorns is not always identified with faith and truth, but is, on the contrary, often used as a cloak, with which to war upon the most beneficent institutions of mankind."[37]

Although his normal post duties occupied most of Lyon's waking hours, during the summer of 1860 he found his free moments devoted to an entirely different medium. Beginning in early June, he implemented his literary skills as a contributor to a local weekly newspaper, authoring a series of twenty-four political essays on the upcoming presidential

---

36. Jameson, *Memorial Wreath*, 22–23; Lyon to the Assistant Adjutant General, Department of the West, June 23, 1860, Letters Received, Department of the West, box 9, RG 393; Edward M. Coffman, *The Old Army: A Portrait of the American Army in Peacetime, 1784–1898*, 164–65.

37. Lyon to Samuel Cooper, June 21, 1860, Letters Received, AGO, RG 94; Peckham, *Lyon and Missouri*, 237.

election. The editorials, published in the *Western Kansas Express* of Manhattan, were motivated by the evils he saw in both the nation generally and the Democratic party particularly. They represented the first public announcement of his unequivocal support for the Republican party and its candidate, Abraham Lincoln. However, the thoughts presented in the essays consisted of more than a strong advocation of Lincoln's election. In a style deemed by one historian "dull, heavy, and more than a little prosaic," they synthesized the opinions that Lyon had formulated over the past decade on the nation's woes. He strongly condemned Stephen Douglas for his part in the Kansas-Nebraska Act; blamed Southerners for their uncompromising stance on the practice of slavery; explained his philosophy on slavery and expressed his hostility toward its spread into the territories; and, following the election in November, cited reasons for the Republican victory and caustically criticized Buchanan's proposed amendments to the Constitution. Lyon's essays represented the tour de force of his political philosophies. Yet, while his role as political analyst offered him great satisfaction, in the next few months his contributions to the cause saw far more action than words.[38]

In November 1860, Wessells returned from eastern Kansas with instructions to send Lyon and a sufficient number of troops again to Fort Scott. A rash of recent murders and vigilante retributions had again created the need for additional forces in the area. Wessells informed Lyon that the new commander of the Department of the West, Gen. William S. Harney, had called for Lyon's force for the expressed purpose of capturing the free-state outlaw James Montgomery. Lyon fumed at the news. Although he had missed the Sioux expedition, Lyon knew well the gruff, haughty general with the impeccable white beard. Lyon had served under him both in Florida and in Mexico, when Harney was a colonel and Lyon a lieutenant, and was under the general's command during his brief term at Fort Scott in 1858. Harney was both a native Tennessean and a known slaveholder, and the story circulated that he had once whipped a slave woman to death in St. Louis. Although Harney's duties as a military officer were to keep peace in the turbulent section of the territory, Lyon perceived that he did so with a decided partiality to the proslavery faction. Hence, Lyon branded him a Southern sympathizer.

---

38. Edward C. Smith, *The Borderland in the Civil War*, 129. The editorials are published in their entirety in *Last Political Writings of General Nathaniel Lyon, U.S.A* (New York, 1861).

During Lyon's earlier tour of duty at Fort Scott, Harney had attempted to pin the local troubles entirely on Montgomery's head, and it appeared to Lyon that he was attempting to do so again.[39]

This time, however, Lyon refused to aid in Harney's prejudiced campaign. Since his last visit to Fort Scott, Lyon's convictions to uphold the free-soil movement had grown even stronger. While stationed at Fort Riley, Lyon had repeatedly assisted the free-state settlers on the Kansas prairie. Whenever possible, he provided them with employment or clothing, purchased their crops, and, on at least one occasion, provided his own quarters to a family for temporary lodging. His adoption of the Republican party, however, did more than prompt him to write his essays (which gained for him a fair amount of notoriety among the settlers). He had received initiation into the antislavery group known as the "Wide Awakes," a nationwide organization of Republican supporters who held secret late-night drills and in their distinctive oilcloth capes conducted torchlight marches during the latest presidential campaign in support of their candidate, Abraham Lincoln. Because his membership in the group pledged him to uphold the principles of the Republican cause, Lyon vowed to do so even over the authority of his military superiors. His sense of duty could countenance nothing less. All of these factors defined his thoughts when preparing for the journey to Fort Scott. By the time the boats left Fort Riley on November 28, Lyon resolved exactly how he would defy Gen. William Selby Harney.[40]

Harney had moved the day before with 150 dragoons and a section of artillery from Fort Leavenworth to Fort Scott, with the ostensible purpose of keeping the peace during a public land sale. Lyon and his command debarked from the steamer on November 30 at Camp Silver Lake. While bivouacked at the camp, Lyon received Harney's orders to proceed to Mound City, a small town twenty-three miles northwest of Fort Scott. From that point he was to capture Montgomery, Charles Jennison, and the other local free-state "outlaws." Jennison had taken upon himself the roles of vigilante judge, jury, and executioner and had recently per-

39. William Hutchinson, "Sketches of Kansas Pioneer Experiences," 402–3; Hardy Kemp, *About Nathaniel Lyon, Brigadier General, United States Army Volunteers and Wilson's Creek,* 31; Clow, "General William S. Harney," 130–31; William Wells Brown, *Narrative of William W. Brown, A Fugitive Slave,* 8.

40. Mrs. S. B. White, "My First Days in Kansas," 552; "Reminiscences of Ferdinand Erhardt," Nathaniel Lyon File, KSHS; "Statement of Theo. Weischselbaum," 568; A. H. Tanner, "Early Days of Kansas," 226; Returns, November 1860, RG 94.

formed several public executions of known border ruffians. His atroci-
ties had thus earned him a place on Lyon's arrest list. On December 1,
Lyon ordered his column to advance, and four days later they reached
Mound City.[41]

The next day, Lyon met with free-staters in town and arranged a
meeting with Montgomery. On the night of December 6, Lyon and local
resident William Hutchinson drove a team of horses to the leader's
cabin, five miles west of town, and the three men cordially discussed the
situation. Lyon found Montgomery everything he hoped him to be: "a
man of great earnestness of purpose, of quick apprehension, and great
executive ability . . . a disciple of the higher law doctrines, and feels his
convictions of justice and duty to be his guide, rather than the requirements of law or the constitution." More than ever, Lyon refused to arrest
this man, who echoed so many of his own sentiments. He explained to
Montgomery that in order to avoid court-martial, Lyon must attempt a
capture of the "brigand." The men exchanged hearty laughs and arranged the next day's scenario. Montgomery would leave to see a friend
near Osawatomie before the time that troops were to arrive at Montgomery's "fort," as his cabin was called. It was quite late by the time Lyon
returned to camp, and early the next morning, when the troops arrived
at the cabin, they found it empty of both Montgomery and the stockpile
of arms purported to be housed there. A subsequent search of Jennison's
home revealed just as little. Jennison himself is reputed to have been
standing on a wooded hillock to the rear of the house, laughing at the
ruse. Thus, Lyon's scheme to thwart Harney had worked to perfection.[42]

Harney soon left the area and sent the artillery and dragoons back to
Fort Scott. However, for over two weeks Lyon and his two companies of
infantry were forced to remain encamped near Mound City to assist the
local marshals in arresting Montgomery and crew when they showed up
at their homes. The weather soon grew severe. In their small canvas tents,
the troops endured alternating bouts of snow (six inches on one occasion) and freezing rain, creating a quagmire of mud that only added to
the "superlative wretchedness, and disgust ineffable." Being privy to the
reasons why none of the outlaws could be found, Lyon was particularly

41. Lyon, *Last Political Writings,* 219; Hutchinson, "Sketches of Kansas Pioneer
Experiences," 402; Stephen Z. Starr, *Jennison's Jayhawkers,* 32–35; Returns, December
1860, RG 94.
42. Hutchinson, "Sketches of Kansas Pioneer Experiences," 402–4; Woodward, *Life
of Nathaniel Lyon,* 231–32; William Lyman, "Origin of the Term 'Jayhawker,'" 205.

irritated about being forced to remain under the present conditions in Mound City. Yet he used the time to assist the free-staters in any way possible, even to the extent of breaking the law for the abolitionists' cause. During the time at Mound City, Lyon used the government's own horses to assist a group of fugitive slaves in their flight to Canada. Lyon realized that if he were caught, he would be court-martialed for this blatant violation of the Fugitive Slave Law, yet he was willing to take the risk in order to fulfill his own righteous purpose. And Lyon would remember Harney for his cursed slave-power sympathies.[43]

On December 18, Lyon and his command received orders to report to Fort Scott. They remained there until the end of January 1861. Earlier that month, Harney had withdrawn the dragoons and artillery to Fort Leavenworth, leaving Lyon in command. The area again stabilized as a result of the army's latest arrival, but periodic news reports of a far more foreboding crisis broke the uneasy calm. On December 20, a state convention in South Carolina voted unanimously to secede from the union of states. In the following weeks, five other states from the Deep South voted to leave the Union and scheduled a convention to meet in February to form an entirely separate government. Lyon anticipated such actions soon after Lincoln's election. He resented the fact that he was employed at Fort Scott for what he felt was an unnecessary purpose while the Union was being torn asunder. On January 27, he wrote, "I do not consider troops necessary at all here, and should much prefer to be employed in the legitimate and appropriate service of contributing to stay the idiotic, fratricidal hands now at work to destroy our Government . . . . It is no longer useful to appeal to reason but to the sword . . . ."[44]

Just four days later, fresh orders arrived instructing him and his command to proceed immediately to St. Louis. There they would augment the garrison at the city's federal arsenal. St. Louis was heavily divided in sentiment, and there were far too few troops to protect the installation and its valuable supply of arms and ammunition. Lyon was enthralled about being sent to St. Louis. At last, he could aid in the suppression of what appeared to him to be the beginning of a vast, and treasonous, insurrection. At last, he could impose his own unique brand of justice on

43. Lyon, *Last Political Writings,* 220; Joseph Gardner to George L. Stearns, June 6, 1861, George L. Stearns Collection, KSHS.
44. Woodward, *Life of Nathaniel Lyon,* 233–36; Special Order No. 171, December 18, 1860, Orders and Special Orders Issued, Department of the West, RG 393.

the state that had caused the turmoil he had been forced to witness in Kansas. But in his excitement rang a perceptible tone of fatalism. Before leaving for Fort Leavenworth to embark upon a steamer for St. Louis, Lyon expressed his clearly monomaniacal intentions, which would prove strangely prophetic: "I shall not hesitate to rejoice at the triumph of my principles, though this triumph may involve an issue in which I certainly expect to expose and very likely lose my life. We shall rejoice, though in martyrdom, if need be."[45]

45. Woodward, *Life of Nathaniel Lyon,* 236.

VII

Into the Maelstrom

In 1861, St. Louis was the largest urban center on the upper Mississippi; of the cities along the "Father of Waters," only New Orleans boasted a greater population. Slave traders conducted auctions on the steps of the courthouse, well within sight of the massive system of levees and wharves lining the riverfront of the bustling entrepôt—the major gateway to the burgeoning West. On any given day, one could find the wide, cobblestone levee cluttered with wagons and drays, stacks of casks and sandbags, and skids of unloaded freight, while stevedores loaded or unloaded the docked steamers with rhythmic lethargy. A maze of smokestacks and pulley booms jutted into the sooty sky from the multiple rows of boats tied up daily at the levees. In fact, in 1860 alone over four thousand boats loaded and unloaded at the St. Louis wharf.[1]

Most of the growing city's two- and three-story buildings (along with the sidewalks running in their immediate fronts) were fashioned of red brick, made from clay found in abundance beyond the bluffs rising from the west and south of town. Many of the narrow, cramped streets were macadamized with limestone, making travel much easier during the rainy season. And after the spring rains came the oppressive humidity, thick enough to slice, which trapped the heavy black smoke that belched forth constantly from the steamers on the river and the ever-growing number of factories in the manufacturing district. In winter months, wood smoke from the chimneys of thousands of individual dwellings and businesses only added to the dusky, begriming atmosphere. As one resident remembered, "In still days of the autumn or winter the smoke hung like a pall over the city."[2]

On the evening of February 7, Nathaniel Lyon and his company of eighty infantrymen unloaded from their Pacific Railroad cars at Union

1. Galusha Anderson, *A Border City During the Civil War*, 9; Cyrus B. Plattenburg, "In St. Louis During the 'Crisis,'" 16–17.
2. Anderson, *Border City*, 2–3.

Depot. Knowing only that their assignment would be to buttress the weak defenses of the St. Louis Arsenal, Lyon marched his troops briskly through the cold, moonlit night the four miles southeast to the arsenal compound. In the next few weeks, however, he learned that the situation both in St. Louis and in Missouri was far more complex—and dangerous—than either he or the army had ever imagined.[3]

In the last two decades, St. Louis had enjoyed an increasing economic preeminence in Missouri. Because of its location below the confluence of the Missouri and Mississippi rivers, it had early become the hub of the growing river traffic for the entire West. By 1861, however, St. Louis shippers found the railroad a more reliable and inexpensive mode of transportation, and they therefore began to move their products by rail rather than by water. Because all of Missouri's rail lines save one emanated from St. Louis, the city became even more important to Missouri's economy. Most of the country's rail lines moved east and west, rather than north and south, so the bulk of St. Louis's trade alliances had shifted from New Orleans to New York. For most of the city's merchants and traders, at least, St. Louis's ties were with the North rather than the South.[4]

However, this economic realignment did not reflect Missouri's traditional social hierarchy. Long the center of the state's social and political power, a twelve-county area along the Missouri River known as Little Dixie now found its preeminence challenged by the rising fortunes of St. Louis. Not surprisingly, the wealth and power of those river counties were inextricably fused with the practice of slavery. The region boasted most of Missouri's largest plantations, as well as the state's highest concentration of slaves. Many of those living in the interior—especially in Little Dixie—had long held a special affinity for the South. Their Southern forebears had settled the state, slave-grown cotton and tobacco were its early boom crops, and as late as 1860 more than 60 percent of its total population had been born either in Missouri or another slave state. Many Missourians—whether slaveholding or not—could not release such strong cultural bonds. Yet with the exception of a distinct minority,

3. Ashbel Woodward, *Life of General Nathaniel Lyon,* 236; Lyon to Frank Blair, April 21, 1861, in James Peckham, *General Nathaniel Lyon and Missouri in 1861,* 111; *Missouri Democrat,* February 7, 1861.

4. Douglas L. Craig, "An Examination of the Reasons for Missouri's Decision Not to Secede in 1860," 92–93; Edward C. Smith, *The Borderland in the Civil War,* 21–23; Robert R. Russel, *Economic Aspects of Southern Sectionalism, 1840–1861,* 279.

by 1861 few could boast that their loyalty was more than sentimental. In 1860, the state's slave population made up less than 10 percent of its aggregate; only one in eight Missouri families owned even one slave. A short growing season limited cotton production to the state's southernmost areas, and the price of tobacco proved so low that relatively few engaged in its production. Hence, the two products most conducive to slave labor were by 1860 the most ill-suited to Missouri farmers. Only hemp continued to generate sizable incomes for its Little Dixie producers. Moreover, many—especially those in the Ozark region—held no loyalty at all to the practice. Economic impracticalities, however, did not prevent the debate over slavery from raging within the state's borders. On the contrary, the recent prosperity of St. Louis had merely altered its complexion.[5]

The shift of Missouri's winds of fortune from the plantation owners in Little Dixie to the merchants and manufacturers in St. Louis was indicated by the results of the most recent presidential election. In 1860, 70 percent of the population supported one of the moderate candidates, Stephen Douglas or John Bell. The Republican victor, Abraham Lincoln, ran last in the state, carrying but two counties. One of those was St. Louis. Few in the plantation counties failed to perceive by the election results that St. Louis had become more like the industrial North and less like the rest of the state. And like those Northern cities, St. Louis seemed to have little use for either the South or for slavery. She had therefore gained for many the stigma of being a city of abolitionists, traditionally the most unwelcome reputation in Missouri.[6]

However, Missouri's population could not be divided neatly into a contest pitting slavery supporters against antislavery advocates; the break proved far less clean. Missourians had grown accustomed to slavery versus antislavery rhetoric. Their political leaders had confronted them with the issue since before the compromise that bore the state's name. Since then, the populace had debated slavery with aplomb. Because they could and did argue the matter, Missourians and their politics proved quite different from the states of the Deep South. Hence, this effete subject would not split the state. What now threatened its stability

5. Milton E. Bierbaum, "The Rhetoric of Union or Disunion in Missouri, 1844–1861," 8n, 12–13, 20–23; Robert M. Crisler, "Missouri's 'Little Dixie,'" 131; Sceva B. Laughlin, *Missouri Politics During the Civil War,* 3.

6. Laughlin, *Missouri Politics,* 26; Smith, *Borderland in the Civil War,* 24–29; Bierbaum, "Rhetoric of Union or Disunion," 14–17.

was the question of union or disunion: whether Missouri should remain loyal to the Union or follow the course of many of her "sister states" of the South. Yet precisely because they were so accustomed to the slavery debate, most Missourians were able to remove themselves sufficiently from the emotion of the slavery question to look at the secession crisis more objectively than their Southern brethren. Though many of the state's largest and most powerful slaveowners screamed for immediate secession, most slaveholders feared that rather than saving the practice, secession would prove its death knell. Most Missourians—both pro- and anti-slave—were a conservative lot who looked upon secession as only a last resort. Yet they also feared the coercion of the new Republican government under Abraham Lincoln, whose leadership few Missourians outside St. Louis endorsed. Above all, Missourians wanted to be left alone to decide their state's future, especially by the federal government. "We ask nothing of the gov't at Washington," wrote one resident to a Unionist acquaintance in St. Louis, "but to be left alone. We need not its *protection*—such protection as the wolf offers the lamb."[7]

The division in Missouri's loyalties was compounded by the anomalous situation posed by its political leadership. Although the 1860 state elections had left Breckinridge Democrats with pluralities in both houses of the General Assembly, this was not because the state's sentiments reflected a pro-Southern attitude. Rather, that faction had so long controlled the party machinery that the nominations were made prior to the fissure in the Democratic party that erupted the previous April. Missourians, however, demonstrated their conservatism by voting into the legislature a combined majority of Douglas Democrats and Constitutional Unionists. The state's gubernatorial situation was equally as perplexing.[8]

On January 3, retiring governor Robert M. Stewart delivered his farewell speech to the Missouri General Assembly. Urging conciliation in the face of the rapidly escalating national crisis, Stewart, who was a moderate, condemned both Northern abolitionists and the states of the lower South for creating the deplorable condition that plagued the na-

7. Bierbaum, "Rhetoric of Union or Disunion," 2; William E. Parrish, *Turbulent Partnership: Missouri and the Union, 1861-1865,* 5-6; Walter H. Ryle, *Missouri: Union or Secession,* 166; Laughlin, *Missouri Politics,* 24-27; Johnson B. Clardy to Frank Blair, May 17, 1861, Blair Papers, box 18, LOC; Frank Carr to James O. Broadhead, July 4, 1861, Broadhead Papers, MHS.
8. Ryle, *Missouri: Union or Secession,* 176; Bierbaum, "Rhetoric of Union or Disunion," 339-40.

tion. Because of her central geographic location, Stewart advised that
Missouri take "the high position of armed neutrality" to prevent coercion by either side. On the same day, the state's new governor, Claiborne
Fox Jackson, took office. Although the charismatic Jackson was elected
as a Douglas Democrat, his relatively neutral stance had been merely
political; once elected, his true loyalties became apparent. In his inaugural address, he put himself on record as standing unequivocally for
Southern rights. Although he expressed the hope that the rights of the
states would be preserved within the Union, he stated emphatically that
the destiny of Missouri was synonymous with the slaveholding states.
"Her honor, her interests, and her sympathies," he exhorted, "point alike
in one direction, and determine her to stand by the South."[9]

Jackson believed that Missouri's economic ties with the South drew
her to her sister states, and he was convinced that most of the state's
population was opposed to any "submissionist" conciliation to the "Black
Republican" government. Within days of taking office, he called for the
General Assembly to convene a state convention to "consider the then
existing relations between the government of the United States, the people and governments of the different states, and the government and
people of the state of Missouri." In addition, he called for state legislators to authorize a reorganization of the state militia, as established by
the Militia Act of 1858, to put the state on a firmer defensive footing in
the event of war. Finally, he requested that control of the St. Louis police
force be removed from the Republican mayor's hands and placed into
those of a special board to be appointed by Jackson himself.[10]

Though undeniably the bastion of the state's Republican strength, St.
Louis in 1861 was itself divided in its sentiments. While the city's slave
population was quite low (only 4,346 in 1860), a sizable number of the
city's nearly 200,000 citizens felt a decided loyalty to the South. However, this proslavery populace was but an aggressive minority. Over two-
thirds of St. Louis's population had been born in areas where slavery was
illegal. City residents born in free states outnumbered those born in slave
states other than Missouri by almost three to one. In addition, almost

9. Smith, *Borderland in the Civil War,* 116–19; William B. Hesseltine, *Lincoln and
the War Governors,* 116; Basil W. Duke, *Reminiscences of General Basil W. Duke,
C.S.A.,* 34; Arthur Roy Kirkpatrick, "Missouri on the Eve of the Civil War," 101–3.

10. William H. Lyon, "Claiborne Fox Jackson and the Secession Crisis in Missouri,"
432–34; Kirkpatrick, "Missouri on the Eve," 103, 106; James O. Broadhead, "St. Louis
During the War," Broadhead Papers, MHS; Smith, *Borderland in the Civil War,* 120.

half of the entire city was foreign-born, dominated by a German community that represented the greatest concentration in any city west of the Appalachians. However, while moderates held sway in the city's political affairs and the conservative Union supporters represented the sentiments of most of the city, the activities of its two radical Unionist elements—the Unconditional Unionists and the Germans—tended to overshadow the influence of moderates.[11]

The first of these radical factions proved unwavering in its support of the Union. Many of this group had once been members of the St. Louis chapter of Wide Awakes, the same oil-caped, torchbearing defenders of Republicanism that Lyon joined in Kansas, but they had disbanded following the 1860 election. Recently, however, the secession crisis had roused an even larger number to organize Union clubs around the city in support of the Union. Some of the wards were even reforming their old Wide Awake groups in anticipation of trouble from the disunionists. At least one man recognized the potential strength in attendance at these weekly ward meetings and sought to tap it. And in Frank P. Blair, Jr., the radical Unionists found a most powerful leader.[12]

At forty, Frank Blair was one of the state's most influential Republicans. His father, Francis Preston Blair, Sr., former editor of the esteemed *Congressional Globe,* had been perhaps Andrew Jackson's most trusted "kitchen cabinet" member and was instrumental in the founding of the Republican party in 1856. Although the elder Blair continued to be a salient force in Washington politics, the reins of ascendance had by 1861 passed to his first son. Montgomery Blair, vaunted St. Louis lawyer and judge, had once served a single term as mayor of that city, but his reputation was made as counsel for Dred Scott in the celebrated case heard before the Supreme Court. While he lost the arguably unwinnable case, his intellectual performance left an indelible impression upon Washington political circles, and rumors abounded that he was presently a leading candidate for one of Lincoln's cabinet seats. Frank himself had graduated from Princeton, studied law, and then set up a successful law practice in St. Louis. After serving as a private in the Mexican War, he had returned to St. Louis and entered politics under the tutelage of Thomas Hart Benton. After serving two terms in the state legislature as a

11. William E. Smith, *The Francis Preston Blair Family in Politics,* 2:30; Anderson, *Border City,* 1; William Roed, "Secessionist Strength in Missouri," 417; Smith, *Borderland in the Civil War,* 121; Laughlin, *Missouri Politics,* 4.

12. Broadhead, "St. Louis During the War," Broadhead Papers, MHS; *Missouri Democrat,* January 1, 4–5, 1861.

free-soil Democrat, in 1856 he had joined the ranks of the Republican party. Blair had since been twice elected to the U.S. House of Representatives, in 1856 and again in 1860. During Lincoln's presidential campaign, he was the Illinoisan's stentorian voice in Missouri, and after Lincoln's nomination and subsequent victory effectively split Missouri politics, Blair remained the driving force of the radical Unionists. With his piercing hazel eyes and indefatigable energy, he now strove to whip up enthusiasm in the city for the Union cause by appealing to all elements of Republican support. And Blair intended to entrench his leadership without compromising the Union in any way.[13]

Though he had hitherto advocated a reorganization of the city's Wide Awakes, Blair now sought to capitalize on the organized strength of the Union ward clubs. Learning that the moderate Unionists had scheduled a mass meeting at the courthouse on January 12, Blair surmised that he needed to land the first punch if he was to capture the city's Unionist support. He therefore advertised for a meeting at Washington Hall on the night of January 11 to consolidate the city's Unionist support. Despite the threat that secessionists might break up the gathering (or perhaps because of it), the meeting was well attended; its twelve hundred participants represented one of the largest indoor meetings held in St. Louis to that date. Those present voted to disband the Union ward clubs in favor of a more generic Central Union Club, with branches throughout the city and county and open to any man believing in the primacy of the Union and "refusing only to accept proposals for compromise." Blair realized that to gain the city's full Unionist support, he must enlist more than just Republican strength, yet he was unwilling to concede any aspect of the party's platform on the Union. Moreover, those at the meeting vested Blair with the authority to appoint a Committee of Safety, sanctioned to act with the full power of the Unconditional Unionists. Considering the turnout and the accomplishments of the meeting, Blair could not help but be pleased with the course of events to this point.[14]

13. Robert J. Rombauer, *The Union Cause in St. Louis in 1861*, 105–6; Smith, *Francis Preston Blair Family in Politics*, 19–22; Thomas L. Snead, *The Fight for Missouri from the Election of Lincoln to the Death of Lyon*, 64–65; Burton J. Hendrick, *Lincoln's War Cabinet*, 76–88 passim; Charles M. Harvey, "Missouri from 1849 to 1861," 32; Smith, *Borderland in the Civil War*, 54; Bierbaum, "Rhetoric of Union or Disunion," 301.
14. *Missouri Democrat*, January 9–12, 1861; Broadhead, "St. Louis During the War," Broadhead Papers, MHS; Smith, *Borderland in the Civil War*, 124; Harvey, "Missouri from 1849 to 1861," 31–32; James W. Covington, "The Camp Jackson Affair, 1861," 198; Smith, *Francis Preston Blair Family in Politics*, 2:24.

The next day's grand rally of the Conditional Unionists quickly sobered Blair to the reality of the situation. Fifteen thousand people thronged to the courthouse on Fourth Street, blocking the streets and requiring streetcars to be removed temporarily from that block. Amid scores of flags and bunting lining the buildings along Pine Street, the patriotic speeches delivered by such prominent moderates as Hamilton R. Gamble and Lewis V. Bogy impelled the crowd to adopt resolutions endorsing the Crittenden Compromise, which called for government protection of slavery south of the old Missouri Compromise line. Though he had actively encouraged Republicans not to attend the rally, the huge turnout convinced Blair that refusing to work with the Conditional Unionists would only split the city's sentiments and could conceivably allow the disunionists to carry the upcoming city elections. Hearing his supporters denounced as "Black Republicans," Blair resolved that he must work with the moderates to maintain Unionist solidarity. Yet he was unsatisfied by the decision and sought to maintain his support through the other radical group in St. Louis. Because he did so, he was despised by many both in and out of the city.[15]

As he had done when drumming up support for Lincoln, Blair turned to the city's second radical Unionist group: St. Louis's sizable German population. In them, he found fifty thousand potential allies, most of whom had come to the city in the last decade. Some had been enticed by glowing descriptions of Missouri conveyed by the writings of Gottfried Duden; more, however, had fled homelands torn by revolutions that had rendered unwelcome their own political persuasions, which supported personal liberties and universal manhood suffrage. Consequently, their sentiments were solidly pro-Union. Their strength had carried the county for Lincoln, raising the xenophobic ire of the city's slave faction toward "the lop-eared Dutch" and furthering the already perceptible rift in the city's populace. Yet Blair saw in the Germans far more than a voting bloc.[16]

15. Smith, *Borderland in the Civil War,* 125–27; Snead, *Fight for Missouri,* 57–58; Peckham, *Lyon and Missouri,* 84; Harvey, "Missouri from 1849 to 1861," 35–36; *Missouri Democrat,* January 14, 1861; Broadhead, "St. Louis During the War," Broadhead Papers, MHS.

16. Virgil C. Blum, "The Political and Military Activities of the German Element in St. Louis, 1859–1861," 103; Donnal V. Smith, "The Influence of the Foreign-Born of the Northwest in the Election of 1860," 192–93; Bierbaum, "Rhetoric of Union or Disunion," 17; Charles D. Drake, "Autobiography of Charles D. Drake, 1811–1867," 682, Charles D. Drake File, SHSM.

Since as early as 1855, the Germans had formed their own fellowship societies, though not initially to support the Union. In the time-honored tradition of their homeland, the men of the community had for years met as social clubs for athletic competition, singing, marching, and, of course, beer drinking. The groups were called Turner Societies, or *Turnverein,* and at least five hundred of their ranks had served in the Wide Awakes. On January 1, 1861, the various *Turnverein* held a large meeting to determine their course in the present national crisis. The group passed overwhelmingly a resolution to stand by the Union and defend her at risk of life and property. They quickly organized themselves into military companies and began to drill with wooden rifles, for lack of real muskets. Older members with experience in the Prussian army served as drill instructors, and Turner Hall soon took on the look of a fortress, with barricaded windows and stored supplies and ammunition. They even spread sawdust on the floor to muffle the sound of their tramping feet as they drilled. And Blair was there to help these Germans obtain real firearms. Using his brother's influence in Washington and New York, he procured for the St. Louis *Turnverein* their first shipment of muskets. Because of their Republican loyalties and quasi-military base, the *Turnverein* loomed as a most valuable ally to the Union cause. Blair would do all in his power to secure their help and get them arms.[17]

On the evening of January 8, in response to alarming reports that the *Turnverein* were arming themselves, a group of the city's opposing radical faction met at Washington Hall. Most supported secession, and many showed up convinced they needed to countervail the force said to be rising among their foreign antagonists. However, some attended the meeting out of a belief that by joining with the South, St. Louis would become the Confederacy's preeminent manufacturing city. Amid a sea of blue cockades, those at the meeting passed nine resolutions pledging themselves "to a hearty cooperation with our sister Southern states and such measures as shall be deemed necessary for our mutual protection, against encroachment of northern fanaticism, and the coercion of the Federal government." Included in those measures was the formation of quasi-military companies calling themselves "Minute Men." Numbering about five hundred, much of the group was comprised of young men

17. Rombauer, *Union Cause in St. Louis,* 128–29; Ryle, *Missouri: Union or Secession,* 174–75; Jay Monaghan, *Civil War on the Western Border, 1854–1865,* 124; Frank Blair to Montgomery Blair, January 25, 1861, Blair Papers, box 3, LOC.

from St. Louis's more genteel pro-Southern families. However, there were also members from the poorest of the city's Irish immigrants working on the docks, who feared that the "damned, nigger-loving Black Republicans" would soon free the slaves to take their jobs or drive down their already-low wages. Leaders of the Minute Men soon gained family permission to drill their companies at the old Berthold mansion, on the corner of Fifth and Pine, and the location immediately became their headquarters. These young firebrands, armed mainly with shotguns and pistols, hoped fervently for a chance to both confront the Germans and ensure that the state of Missouri would also join the Confederate nation. After their drill sessions, those of the upper crust celebrated at the Planters' House hotel, the social center for emulative young Southern parvenus. After enough bourbon had loosed their tongues, many boasted that they would soon take the federal arsenal, located along the city's riverfront.[18]

And in the St. Louis Arsenal, the secessionists had their eyes on a most worthy prize. Its sixty thousand muskets, ninety thousand pounds of powder, one-and-a-half million ball cartridges, forty field pieces, siege guns, and machinery for the manufacture of arms represented the largest federal arsenal in the South. Yet guarding the valuable stores housed in the compound was a garrison of a handful of men; the arsenal's commander, Maj. William H. Bell, lamented that he had "only one man to walk the grounds at night to keep out intruders." Equally unprepared for an attack was the federal subtreasury, located downtown, which housed over one million dollars in gold and silver. Between the two installations, the federal government stood to lose a weighty cache quite easily, had it not been for the perspicacity of the assistant U.S. treasurer, Isaac Sturgeon.[19]

Upon learning from Bell of the poor defenses at the arsenal, Sturgeon urgently telegraphed President Buchanan on January 5, alerting him to the woefully unprotected public funds and munitions. Buchanan referred the matter in turn to Winfield Scott, the army's commander-in-

---

18. Broadhead, "St. Louis During the War," Broadhead Papers, MHS; James O. Broadhead to Abiel Leonard, January 6, 1861, Abiel Leonard Papers, MHS; Duke, *Reminiscences,* 37–39; *Missouri Democrat,* January 8–9, 1861; Smith, *Borderland in the Civil War,* 123; Covington, "Camp Jackson Affair," 199; "Memorandum on Missouri," Franklin A. Dick File, LOC; Plattenburg, "St. Louis During the 'Crisis,'" 17.

19. Smith, *Borderland in the Civil War,* 116, 122; Duke, *Reminiscences,* 37; Broadhead, "St. Louis During the War," Broadhead Papers, MHS.

chief, who promptly ordered to St. Louis a detachment of forty men under the command of Lt. William Robinson from their present post at Newport Barracks, Kentucky. Scott placed Robinson and his men "at the disposal of the Assistant Treasurer," who, upon their arrival on January 11, quietly removed the funds from the subtreasury. However, the presence of the small detachment caused great agitation in the city; many of those who learned of the incident from the newspapers believed the troops to be a dreaded vanguard of the federal government's coercion of Missouri. In Jefferson City, where the state's Southern sentiment ran perhaps highest, the General Assembly adopted a resolution that called the sending of troops to St. Louis "insulting to the dignity and patriotism of the State, and calculated to arouse suspicion and distrust on the part of the people toward the Federal Government." The furor prompted the legislators to approve the governor's call for a secession convention, and on January 21, they authorized elections for delegates to be held on February 18. In addition, on January 29, the legislature adopted a set of resolutions that declared that if the federal government should attempt to coerce the South into rejoining the Union, Missouri would aid in resisting any attackers. Those who decried the affairs in St. Louis would soon find their fears fully vindicated.[20]

The security offered by forty soldiers failed to satisfy Frank Blair. Like many others in the city, he had heard talk of the Minute Men's plans to take the arsenal, and he understood fully the great advantage that Southern sympathizers would gain if they defeated his mostly unarmed Germans. Within a week, he twice wrote his brother Montgomery, entreating his assistance in obtaining more reinforcements at the arsenal. In addition, he employed detectives to maintain observation of the installation and enlisted a host of volunteers to assist the garrison in case of attack. Finally, Blair distrusted the loyalties of the arsenal's commandant, William Bell, and intended to do something about it.[21]

Blair's suspicions soon proved well-founded. Major of Ordnance William H. Bell had served the army faithfully since his graduation from West Point in 1820. Since 1858, he had commanded the St. Louis Arsenal. A native North Carolinian, Bell was torn between his loyalty to the federal government, to his home state, and to his present home, Mis-

20. Broadhead, "St. Louis During the War," Broadhead Papers, MHS; Smith, *Borderland in the Civil War,* 123–26; *Missouri Democrat,* January 12, 17, 1861.

21. Frank Blair to Montgomery Blair, January 18, 24, 1861, Blair Papers, box 3, LOC; Smith, *Borderland in the Civil War,* 127.

souri. On January 24, an envoy of Governor Jackson's, Daniel M. Frost, visited Bell at the arsenal. Himself an 1844 West Point graduate, Frost had served in the Mexican War before resigning his commission in 1853. Since then he had engaged in the lumber and fur business in St. Louis, had served a term in the state senate (during which he personally framed the 1858 Militia Act organizing the state militia in the event of war), and was currently a brigadier general in the Missouri militia he had helped to form. In November 1860, Frost had led a militia brigade to the southwestern corner of the state to aid federal authorities at Fort Scott in the suppression and capture of James Montgomery and his free-state Jayhawkers. Though they did not actually participate in the activities, the expedition entrenched Frost's rapport with the militia, a number of whom now bolstered the Minute Men's ranks. Frost proved able to convince the vacillating Bell that according to the doctrine of state sovereignty, Missouri had the right to claim the arsenal since it rested upon her soil. Before the two men parted, Bell agreed not to defend the arsenal if state authorities such as the governor determined to claim it, and he promised not to remove its munitions without first notifying state officials.[22]

Yet Blair did not wait to hear of the meeting before acting on his inclinations. After reports reached him charging that on the night of January 22, Bell had refused to allow Blair's volunteers to enter the arsenal to aid in its defense against an apprehended attack, Blair telegraphed his brother Montgomery. He urgently requested Bell's immediate removal, which Montgomery effected on the same day that Frost met with the arsenal's commandant. Rather than accept transfer to the East, however, Bell chose to resign from the army and retire to his farm outside nearby St. Charles. In his place, army command appointed Bvt. Maj. Peter V. Hagner.[23]

Blair saw the entire incident as an ominous sign. Realizing that his responsibilities as congressman-elect would soon call him from the city, and disturbed by increasing rumors of an imminent attack on the arse-

22. Smith, *Borderland in the Civil War*, 127; George W. Cullum, *Biographical Register of the Officers and Graduates of the U.S. Military Academy at West Point, N.Y.*, 1:248–49; J. Thomas Scharf, *History of Saint Louis City and County*, 2:502; Rombauer, *Union Cause in St. Louis*, 126–28; D. M. Frost to C. F. Jackson, January 24, 1861, in ibid., 142–43; Anderson, *Border City*, 63n; Covington, "Camp Jackson Affair," 198; Joseph G. Knapp, *The Presence of the Past*, 1–4.

23. *Missouri Democrat*, January 24, 1861; Smith, *Borderland in the Civil War*, 127.

nal, which had become so pronounced they had reached the newspapers as far away as New York, he stepped up his efforts to protect the city. On February 1, Blair called together in secret those confidantes he trusted enough to appoint to the Committee of Safety. Included were some of St. Louis's most prominent figures: O. D. Filley, the city's mayor; Samuel T. Glover and James O. Broadhead, two highly respected lawyers; and John How and J. J. Witzig, two of the city's most successful merchants. Yet Blair selected these men for more than their loyalty; each man he appointed to the committee had very powerful political connections. Two (including Filley) were at one time the mayor of St. Louis, and three others were personal acquaintances of the president-elect. Though Blair, Filley, Glover, and Broadhead were each slaveowners, their slaveholding status would in no way hinder their efforts to secure the state for the Union. These men would guide the course of St. Louis's radical Unionists, and they began to meet nearly every night to plan their response to the secessionists' challenge. One of their first decisions was to encourage actively that *all* the city's Union elements arm themselves. Through their efforts, much of St. Louis soon became an armed camp.[24]

In the midst of this widening chasm in the city's population, Lyon and his company arrived in St. Louis. Prompted by Frank's urgent pleas for reinforcements, Montgomery Blair had used his heavy oar to persuade Buchanan to send additional troops to St. Louis. Upon reaching the arsenal, Lyon released his men to the enlisted men's barracks and hastily surveyed the grounds. Covering an area of roughly fifty-six acres, the arsenal compound sat next to the river on low, sloping ground. A massive limestone wall, ten feet high and three feet thick, enclosed the grounds on its land sides, broken only on the west wall by its Carondelet Street entrance: a double-doored gate fashioned ornately of wrought iron and concrete. Along the river's front ran a stout wooden-plank fence, and in its center a water gate opened to the wharf. Inside the walls of the compound was an assortment of buildings, including a foundry, workshops, warehouses, and four stone barracks for enlisted men. Everywhere Lyon looked he saw neat, elongated pyramids of artillery ammunition—shot and shell of all sizes—often limiting passage to designated aisleways between the stone slabs on which the shells were stacked. At

24. Peckham, *Lyon and Missouri,* 46; Printed Sketch of James O. Broadhead, Broadhead Papers, MHS; Broadhead, "St. Louis During the War," ibid.; U.S. Census, 1860, St. Louis County, Slave Schedule.

the center of it all lay the administration building. Exactly when the confrontation took place is not known, but within hours of his arrival in St. Louis, Lyon had already kicked up a row with the arsenal's commandant.[25]

Bvt. Maj. Peter Hagner had held his present post for just over a week, having been transferred from Fort Leavenworth, where he had commanded its arsenal. He was keenly aware of the need for additional defense at the St. Louis Arsenal. Two days earlier he had recommended to the department commander, Gen. William S. Harney, that more men be sent to the compound so that a greater vigilance could be maintained, especially at night. Now he received an entire company. Hagner's career paralleled Lyon's in many ways. An 1836 graduate of West Point, he served with the artillery in the Seminole War and again in the Mexican War, where, like Lyon, he was wounded at the gates of Mexico City. For his gallantry, he received his brevet promotion to major. Hagner gained a full commission as captain of ordnance on July 10, 1851, but his rank of brevet major, received in 1847, superceded his official rank—or so he thought.[26]

When Lyon learned that Hagner's rank was only a brevet, he questioned him brashly about his date of promotion to captain. Once that was learned, Lyon informed the commandant brusquely that according to Article of War 62, his own commission, dated June 11, 1851, gave him overall command of the arsenal. Quickly outraged at the officiousness of the newly arrived captain, Hagner retorted that his rank of brevet major made him the undisputed ranking officer at the arsenal. Lyon then declared that he would not respect a brevet ranking. He refused to be subordinate in this case and would at once take the matter up with General Harney.[27]

After having served under Harney at Fort Scott, Lyon detested having to refer to him for anything, but in this matter he felt confident he would receive satisfaction. He was wrong. Harney also remembered from Kansas the impertinence of his subordinate, and the commander of the

25. Woodward, *Life of Nathaniel Lyon,* 236; Frank Blair to Lyon, April 21, 1861, in Peckham, *Lyon and Missouri,* 111.

26. Cullum, *Biographical Register,* 1:647–48; Peter Hagner to Seth Williams, February 5, 1861, Letters Received, Department of the West, box 10, RG 393; Snead, *Fight for Missouri,* 117–18.

27. Lyon to Frank Blair, February 25, 1861, in Peckham, *Lyon and Missouri,* 67; Cullum, *Biographical Register,* 2:74; Snead, *Fight for Missouri,* 124–25.

politically sensitive Department of the West curtly denied Lyon's demand
for command of the arsenal. Not satisfied with his commander's answer,
Lyon went over his head and wired Washington for a ruling on the
matter. While he waited for an answer, Lyon was forced to retain command of his company only, while Hagner commanded the entire garrison. In the meantime, he began to think of a more effective method of
combatting the problem.[28]

Within days of his arrival in St. Louis, Lyon was introduced to Blair
and the Committee of Safety. A contemporary source claimed that
Lyon's articles in the *Western Kansas Express* had caught the congressman's eye and that Blair had then specifically requested Lyon's
transfer to St. Louis. This, however, cannot be substantiated. In any
case, the acquaintance was struck, and the committee briefed the captain
on the perceived danger to the arsenal from the city's secessionists. Blair
and Lyon were strikingly similar in many ways. Roughly the same age
(Lyon was forty-three and Blair forty), they shared many of the same
antislavery beliefs. Both possessed acerbic wits and reputations for outspokenness easily provoked to violence. Moreover, both were steeped in
controversy. That "when the Blairs go in for a fight, they go in for a
funeral" was nearly axiomatic in Missouri, and Frank fully embodied
the adage. His duels and fistfights were legendary—he had once even
shot a man during an argument in a tavern—and he was as fearless in his
utterances as in his fights. When Lyon met Blair, the two hit it off
immediately. Because of his influence in high places, Blair would quickly
prove the most important acquaintance Lyon had ever made.[29]

At their meeting, Lyon learned just how active both Blair and the
committee had been in organizing for the city's defense. Since the organi-
zational meeting, they had enlisted sixteen companies of Union Guards,
representing over fourteen hundred men. Predominantly Germans, their
growing numbers forced them to expand from Turner's Hall, and they
began drilling in all parts of the city: in foundries, breweries, private
homes, the Yaeger Garden, and even at Washington Hall. Blair had
managed to enlist enough private subscriptions from St. Louis to purchase seventy muskets, but his real coup came by convincing Illinois

28. Snead, *Fight for Missouri*, 124–25; Lyon to Frank Blair, February 25, 1861, in
Peckham, *Lyon and Missouri*, 68.
29. Peckham, *Lyon and Missouri*, 58; Rombauer, *Union Cause in St. Louis*, 150;
Broadhead, "St. Louis During the War," Broadhead Papers, MHS; Leonard B. Wurthman, Jr., "Frank Blair: Lincoln's Congressional Spokesman," 266–68.

governor Richard Yates to send him two hundred muskets from that state's militia. They arrived at Turner's Hall packed in beer barrels and were quickly distributed. Blair also turned to certain local businessmen with powerful connections in the East, who initiated a subscription drive in New York and Boston for musket funds. Blair tried to drill some German companies himself but realized that he lacked the necessary military skills to do so effectively. "I wish I had your West Point educa- tion," he lamented to Montgomery, "I could make good use of it here at this crisis . . . ."[30]

Realizing that a military officer in his camp could gain the munitions his Germans needed to save the city from its secessionists, Blair turned to Lyon. And in the Connecticut captain, he found an ally as passionate in his convictions as himself. Unlike the city's conservative element, Lyon heartily endorsed all that Blair had done. He assured him that if the necessity arose he was ready to assume command of both the arsenal and the Germans to support the government. Muskets, however, Lyon could not yet provide, though he wanted nothing more. However, he hinted that if Blair's influence could effect a favorable solution to the arsenal's pernicious command situation, they might then talk about guns.[31]

After just a few days in St. Louis, Lyon became convinced that both Harney and Hagner were in sympathy with the Southern states. He had believed as much about Harney since their days in Kansas, but his suspi- cions about Hagner surfaced only after being ordered to the arsenal. Hagner was a native Marylander but had moved his family to St. Louis upon being transferred to the city. His wife had been born into a slaveholding family, and many of his closest associates were sympathetic to the Southern cause. Lyon took close note of these facts. After learning that Frost had issued an order on January 8 directing the militia in and around St. Louis to meet upon the pealing of the church bells, he stepped up night vigilance at the arsenal. Indeed, the air became rife with rumors that the arsenal would soon be attacked by the state militia and that an earlier attempt had been aborted only by the wariness of Blair's spies. When Lyon learned that on the night of February 10 many Union of- ficers from both the arsenal and Jefferson Barracks—including Hagner himself—had cavorted with the enemy at a ball thrown by Frost's state

30. Broadhead, "St. Louis During the War," Broadhead Papers, MHS; Scharf, *His-tory of Saint Louis,* 1:457; "Memorandum on Missouri," 8–10, Franklin A. Dick File, LOC; Frank Blair to Montgomery Blair, February 14, 1861, Blair Papers, box 3, LOC.
31. Smith, *Borderland in the Civil War,* 124–25.

militia, he even began keeping a private vigil at the arsenal walls. Although Lyon was able to persuade Hagner on February 16 to move two hundred reinforcements to the arsenal from Jefferson Barracks, located on the extreme south side of town, to provide some much-needed support, he had concluded that Hagner was disloyal. However, the captain waited for a response from Washington so that he could conclusively put Hagner in his place.[32]

Yet Lyon was already working through other channels to secure his place as arsenal commandant. Maj. David Hunter had stopped in St. Louis on his way from Fort Leavenworth to Springfield, Illinois, where as a personal friend he would accompany the first family on its inaugural train ride to Washington. On February 9, Assistant Treasurer Sturgeon met with Hunter at the Subtreasury, trying to convince him that the city needed more troops to ensure its safety. Since his first letter to the War Department, Sturgeon had sent subsequent messages requesting additional troops, but Harney apparently refused to acknowledge any such need. Apparently Lyon burst into the meeting and avowed to Hunter his desire for command at the arsenal "in order to make sure of its protection and defense." Because Hunter was as rabid as Lyon in his defense of the Republican party, the captain's vigor impressed the major, and he promised to discuss the matter with the president-elect on their impending trip.[33]

On February 21, two days before Lincoln and his entourage reached the capital, Lyon received his answer from Washington: Winfield Scott himself had denied his request for command. Lyon was indignant. Once again, "Old Fuss and Feathers" had shown his "sordid spirit of partisanship and favoritism to pets, and personal associates, and toadies." Yet simply accepting an adverse ruling was not in Lyon's nature; he would not be stymied so easily, especially after what had transpired in the city during the last few days. By all indications, secessionist strength was growing daily; in a parade held only two days later, many known Minute Men brigaded brazenly in the street as new members of the First

32. Peckham, *Lyon and Missouri*, 45; Rombauer, *Union Cause in St. Louis*, 153; Snead, *Fight for Missouri*, 125; Ray W. Irwin, "Missouri in Crisis—The Journal of Captain Albert Tracy, 1861," 11–14; Broadhead, "St. Louis During the War," Broadhead Papers, MHS.

33. Ezra J. Warner, *Generals in Blue*, 243–44; Lyon to Frank Blair, February 25, 1861, in Peckham, *Lyon and Missouri*, 66–68; George W. Lay to William S. Harney, May 13, 1861, in Scharf, *History of Saint Louis*, 2:485.

Military District of the Missouri State Guard. Moreover, two of the
Minute Men's leaders, Basil Duke and Coulton Greene, had even received captaincies in the militia. Despite this affrontery, Hagner refused
to comply with Lyon's repeated demands for further fortification of the
arsenal compound. Although on the nineteenth Hagner ordered entrenchments dug and sandbag emplacements erected for the artillery
within the walls, Lyon wanted more. He insisted that Hagner mount
firing platforms on all walls, build sandbag parapets, and place artillery
on parapets along the walls so as to fire *over* them. Lyon was confident
that with the proper defensive works, a force could defend the arsenal
against any number of attackers. Hagner, however, argued that the present force of over four hundred men was sufficient to repel any attempted
breach without additional defensive works. He also refused to allow the
men to fire over the compound walls "so as to endanger, to the least
possible degree, the lives of Residents in the neighborhood—women and
children." Moreover, Hagner believed that such preparations would only
exacerbate the already volatile mood of the city. In this decision, Harney
lent him full support; the department commander believed that the city's
loyal residents would forestall any such attack.[34]

Lyon was infuriated at this complacency. Seething, he called Hagner's
attitude "either imbecility or d——d villainy." Convinced that Hagner's actions were motivated by "covert treachery," Lyon was certain that
he must be replaced for the safety of the arsenal. This belief was only
furthered by Lyon's feelings of injustice regarding Hagner's rank and
Scott's "sordid" ruling. Thus, as he had done on several occasions earlier
in his career, Lyon sought a higher authority by which to gain his desired
end. He had attempted to have Hagner removed through military channels; he now chose to use political influence. And to this end, Lyon
turned to Frank Blair.[35]

Lyon immediately informed Blair of his travails at the arsenal. To
make matters even worse, two days earlier Harney had written a letter to

34. Stephen B. Oates, *With Malice Toward None,* 230; Irwin, "Missouri in Crisis,"
13–15; Lyon to Frank Blair, February 25, 1861, in Peckham, *Lyon and Missouri,* 66–67;
Lyon to Dr. Scott, March 7, 1861, in Grace Lee Nute, ed., "A Nathaniel Lyon Letter,"
142; *Missouri Republican,* February 14, 1861; *Missouri Democrat,* February 23, 1861;
Rombauer, *Union Cause in St. Louis,* 193; Peter V. Hagner to Seth Williams, March 20,
1861, Letters Received, Department of the West, box 10, RG 393; Broadhead, "St.
Louis During the War," Broadhead Papers, MHS.
35. Lyon to Frank Blair, February 25, 1861, in Peckham, *Lyon and Missouri,* 66–68.

Washington stating that all was well in St. Louis and that at present there was no threat of an attack on the arsenal. Lyon feared that even Washington was deluded as to the actual situation in the city. With no defensive works, the arsenal was ripe for the picking. And if that were not distressing enough, Lyon recognized that all the fortifications he could devise would be worthless if the secessionists were able to lay their hands on artillery and place it on the bluffs beyond the town. The arsenal sat on such low ground that cannon either on the bluffs or on the island in the river to its east could command it easily. Lyon saw himself trapped in a nest of vipers.[36]

Blair saw the predicament exactly as did Lyon and agreed that the federal leadership in St. Louis had questionable loyalties. Long suspecting that Harney would be of little use to the city's Unionists, he had as early as January written Montgomery to gain his transfer. Now, he felt sure that his personal acquaintance with the president-elect—whose inauguration lay only days away—could be used to improve the present situation. Satisfied by the decisive victory the city's Union candidates had won in the convention canvass only three days earlier, Blair determined to leave that day for Washington to meet with Mr. Lincoln and enlighten him on the perilous situation in St. Louis. He would attempt to convince Lincoln of the dubious loyalties of both Harney and Hagner and gain for Lyon the command of the arsenal once Lincoln had taken office. When that was accomplished, Blair would take his seat in Congress.[37]

In return, however, Blair exacted a heavy sum: he required that the captain obtain government arms for his Union Guard. Lyon realized, however, that issuing arms to men not even informally mustered into government service was grounds for immediate court-martial. Already on slippery footing with Harney, Lyon could make no such promise. Blair, however, knew that he needed the captain to put his plans into motion, so he sweetened the pot. With his leverage in Washington, he assured Lyon that for any action the captain might take that was irregular and unauthorized, Blair would guarantee complete impunity. In effect, Blair's quid pro quo was a blank check. Lyon grasped Blair's meaning

---

36. William S. Harney to Lorenzo Thomas, February 19, 1861, in *The War of the Rebellion: A Compilation of the Official Records of the Union and Confederate Armies* (hereafter cited as *OR*), series I, 1:654.

37. Rombauer, *Union Cause in St. Louis*, 153–54; *Missouri Republican*, February 22, 1861; Frank Blair to Montgomery Blair, January 18, 1861, Blair Papers, box 3, LOC; Frank Blair to Montgomery Blair, February 9, 1861, ibid.

immediately and eagerly accepted the congressman's terms. He agreed to meet regularly with the various Union Guard elements to teach them drill techniques and supervise their organization. Blair enlisted similar aid from Franz Sigel, a former insurrectionist in Germany who had been forced to flee that country and now directed the German Institute of Education in St. Louis. Sigel possessed a solid military background; before coming to St. Louis, he had taught military science in New York, where he held the rank of major in the state militia. He now enjoyed an immense popularity among the city's Germans. With Lyon's help, Blair had ensured that the Union Guard would have more than just wooden muskets with which to fight. With Lyon and Sigel in charge, Blair left the city on February 21 convinced that his Germans were in good hands.[38]

With the inauguration of Abraham Lincoln on March 4, 1861, as the nation's sixteenth president, the country moved rapidly toward war. A total of seven states had already seceded, and on March 11 those states adopted the constitution of the Confederate States of America. After the inauguration of the "Black Republican," secessionist movements increased dramatically in all the Southern states, threatening to add to the number of states already organized in the new Confederate nation.

Missouri's future, however, continued to hang in the balance, though the conservative results of the convention election (not one avowed secessionist was elected to the convention) had dealt the state's secessionist faction a mighty blow. "I despise your party; I detest your principles," wrote a Waverly, Missouri, resident to the editors of the *Missouri Democrat*, "but I do confess that by your party's exertions you have the State in your hands." However, the convention that commenced in Jefferson City on the last day of February had not yet rendered secession a dead issue. Partly from their cramped quarters, and partly from the rampant spirit of secessionism in the capital, those attending the convention voted to relocate to the more spacious Mercantile Library Hall in St. Louis. Reconvening there on March 4, the change of venue—and of mood— influenced the convention's actions. After long sessions of impassioned debate, the convention adopted on March 9 a series of resolutions stating, among other things, that "*at present* there was no adequate cause to impel Missouri to dissolve her connection with the Federal Union." Missouri's future interests could be best preserved within the framework

38. "Memorandum on Missouri," 9, Franklin A. Dick File, LOC; Rombauer, *Union Cause in St. Louis,* 128, 197–98; Warner, *Generals in Blue,* 447–48.

of the Union. Of the eleven slaveholding states that would eventually call secession conventions, Missouri alone would vote to remain in the Union. The threat of secession was thus conclusively ended. However, the state's ties with the Union were still decidedly precarious.[39]

The effects of Missouri's long political tightrope walk spilled over onto St. Louis. One resident recalled, "Secession was rampant everywhere . . . . In all places the secesh were noisy and undisturbed. The enemies of the Government were rapidly providing themselves with arms and ammunition . . . . To those not in the secret, it seemed as if secession in Missouri was an accomplished fact." Daily disturbances wreaked havoc on the city's business districts. The Minute Men planned one such incident for the day the convention was scheduled to reconvene in St. Louis. Since the date coincided with Lincoln's inauguration, they designed a flag "emblazoned [with] every conceivable thing that was suggestive of a Southern meaning"—a single star, a crescent moon, and a cross on a field of blue—and flew it superciliously over both the Berthold mansion and the dome of the city courthouse. Their plan sought nothing less than to provoke the Union Guard into a violent encounter, thus giving the governor grounds to call out the militia to quell the street fighting. Then, bolstered by the large number of Minute Men who had the month before enlisted in the Missouri State Guard, they would continue and take the arsenal in the process. This grandiose plan failed, however, when only a handful of the city's Unionists appeared angrily at the Berthold gates and then quickly dispersed when a bipartisan committee of the city's leaders appeared and convinced the mob to return to their homes. Nonetheless, the incident briefly threatened the peace of the entire city.[40]

Meanwhile, Frank Blair caught up with Lincoln in Washington and, with the help of David Hunter's earlier prodding, convinced the president of the need for a change in the St. Louis situation. Sensitive to the urgency of keeping border states like Missouri in the Union, and unwill-

39. William H. Lyon, "Claiborne Fox Jackson and the Secession Crisis," 433; *Missouri Democrat,* February 20, 1861; Allen P. Richardson to Broadhead, April 24, 1861, Broadhead Papers, MHS; Broadhead, "St. Louis During the War," ibid.; Parrish, *Turbulent Partnership,* 10–14; Smith, *Borderland in the Civil War,* 132; Bierbaum, "Rhetoric of Union or Disunion," 2, 380.

40. Peckham, *Lyon and Missouri,* 56; Smith, *Borderland in the Civil War,* 150–51; Broadhead, "St. Louis During the War," Broadhead Papers, MHS; Duke, *Reminiscences,* 39–42; *Missouri Democrat,* March 5, 1861; *Missouri Republican,* February 14, 1861; Anderson, *Border City,* 70.

ing to allow the St. Louis Arsenal to fall needlessly, the president overrode Scott's earlier ruling and sent orders to Harney placing Lyon in
command of the defenses at the arsenal. The message, which reached
Harney's office on March 13, greatly displeased the department commander.[41]

William Harney was caught in a grave dilemma. He was a Southern
Unionist who had married into the aristocratic Mullanphy family of St.
Louis, who supported the secessionists. His transfer to St. Louis in
November 1860 was made at his own request, prompted by his intimate
connection with the family's real estate empire. Despite Lyon's suspicions to the contrary, after forty-two years in government service, Harney's allegiance to the federal government was indubitable. Yet he was
torn repeatedly between his military position and the politics of the
family, forcing him to tread lightly when dealing with the situation in the
city. He believed that secession was wrong and that Missouri's economic
interests would keep her in the Union. He wanted nothing to upset the
precarious balance existing in both the city and the state. "I implore my
fellow-citizens of that State," he wrote, "not to be seduced by designing
men to become the instruments of their mad ambition by plunging the
State into the vortex of revolution."[42]

And yet here was Lyon, whose insubordination and persistent demands proved a constant headache to Harney. After the general imposed
a quarantine upon the men at the arsenal to curb an outbreak of small-
pox, he learned that Lyon had ignored his order and on several occasions
had gone into town after hours. Though Harney probably never realized
that Lyon's purpose was to continue his training of the Union Guard, the
general saw clearly that the captain did not appear to respect his authority. He already wished that the army had never sent the contentious little
rabble-rouser into such a combustible situation. Harney had managed to
replace Bell with Hagner, whose malleability greatly satisfied the general. Now, Lyon's fanaticism threatened to disrupt the fragile peace in the
city. The department commander, however, held an ace he now chose to
play, and the card—dealt him from Lyon's own past—appeared to provide the means by which Harney could rid himself of his dangerous
subordinate.[43]

41. Lorenzo Thomas to Harney, March 13, 1861, in OR, I, 1:658.

42. Assistant Adjutant General to Isaac Sturgeon, December 18, 1891, Civil War
Collection, MHS; Harney to John O'Fallon, May 1, 1861, in Logan U. Reavis, The Life
and Military Services of Gen. William Selby Harney, 389–92.

43. Rombauer, Union Cause in St. Louis, 126; Snead, Fight for Missouri, 100; Peter

After reading the War Department's letter thoroughly, Harney dictated another to his adjutant, calling Lyon to a court of inquiry scheduled for April 15 at Fort Leavenworth. While at Fort Riley in 1860, a private in Lyon's company, James Hunter, had starved to death under suspicious circumstances. One of the men at the post then preferred charges stating that the negligence of both Lyon and the post surgeon, M. Mills, had precipitated the tragedy. Whether Lyon's role was deliberate or inadvertent remains uncertain; however, given his reputation for harsh punishment, the army took action to ascertain the truth. Harney had first learned of the incident as early as January 26 and quickly recommended a court of inquiry to the secretary of war. Winfield Scott approved his recommendation only days prior to the arrival of Lincoln's order. Because Harney had already issued the order for the court to convene, he was now understandably hesitant to send the captain the War Department's ruling on the command of the arsenal. However, after pondering the matter for a few days, he formulated a plan to alleviate the problem.[44]

Harney saw in the War Department's pithy message an interpretive loophole. The message stated that Lyon was to take command of the arsenal's *defenses*—no more, no less. So be it, the general thought, and that same day he addressed a letter to Lyon at the arsenal detailing the War Department's orders. He then added his own translation:

> . . . you should not exercise any control over the operations of the Ordnance Department, and you will not, therefore, regard the officers and men of that branch of the service stationed at the arsenal as forming a portion of your command.
>
> The arrangement heretofore made for the accommodation of the troops at the arsenal and for the defense of the place will not be disturbed without the sanction of the commanding general . . . .[45]

According to Harney's "interpretation," Lyon would command only the infantry at the arsenal, while Hagner would retain complete control of the ordnance. Moreover, Lyon would not receive even a scrap of

V. Hagner to Seth Williams, February 20, 1861, Letters Received, Department of the West, box 10, RG 393; Hagner to Williams, February 23, 1861, ibid.; Williams to Hagner, March 23, 1861, Letters Sent, Department of the West, vol. 4, RG 393; *Missouri Democrat,* February 25, 1861.

44. Seth Williams to Lyon, April 9, 1861, Letters Sent, Department of the West, vol. 4, RG 393; Report of the Court of Inquiry of Capt. Nathaniel Lyon, April 9, 1861, Richard Graham Papers, MHS.

45. Seth Williams to Lyon, March 13, 1861, in OR, I, 1:658-59.

material without first requisitioning it from Hagner, and Hagner must then go to Harney for approval. Lyon worried Harney; he was the stick that swatted at the hornets' nest. The general believed that this arrangement would keep his dangerous subordinate at bay until the court of inquiry called him from the city.[46]

Lyon was thunderstruck by Harney's actions. He refused to believe that his commander's interpretation of the War Department's order was in accordance with the president's wishes. Now that he was at last in a position to provide adequate defense for the arsenal, Hagner still held the upper hand. Far worse, Harney had found a way to remove Lyon from the city. Lyon found himself as powerless as before. In desperation, he wrote again to Blair in Washington:

> I am aware that I am indebted to you for changing the command of the troops at this post . . . . But with the orders of General Harney, . . . I fear little has been gained . . . . I have no control over the ordnance department, and therefore cannot take a single round of ammunition, nor a piece of artillery, or any other firearm without the direction of General Harney; . . . I cannot get a hammer, spade, ax, or any needful tool, but upon Major Hagner's concession, or by making requisition upon General Harney and getting his orders . . . . I feel embarrassed, and would be glad of any relief from this anomaly . . . .[47]

While Lyon waited helplessly for Blair's response, visitors to the arsenal compound found a unique situation. There were *two* commanders, one wholly dependent on the other for matériel, and the other entirely unwilling to supply the former with any of it. Moreover, Hagner had lodged an official complaint against the command change at the arsenal, hoping for a new ruling in his favor. Blair soon received not only Lyon's letter, but also several from acquaintances in St. Louis who supported Lyon. The details of Harney's ploy shocked him. He moved immediately, asking his brother Montgomery—Lincoln's new postmaster general—to convince Scott to rescind the court order. He then went about trying to secure an order granting Lyon permission to arm the Union Guard, an order that Harney summarily refused to issue. Again Blair had proven himself Lyon's most valuable ally.[48]

46. Peckham, *Lyon and Missouri,* 74.

47. Lyon to Frank Blair, April 6, 1861, in Peckham, *Lyon and Missouri,* 69–70.

48. Ibid., 71–74; John McElroy, *The Struggle for Missouri,* 60–61; Lyon to Lorenzo Thomas, April 9, 1861, Letters Received, AGO, RG 94; Seth Williams to Peter V. Hagner, March 22, 1861, Letters Sent, Department of the West, vol. 4, RG 393; Franklin A. Dick to Frank Blair, April 2, 1861, Blair Papers, box 39, LOC.

Even without Blair's help, however, political events in St. Louis precluded Lyon's imminent transfer. On April 1, the results of the city's municipal elections reversed the precedent set by the Unionist-dominated February convention elections. The voters ousted Republican mayor O. D. Filley in favor of Constitutional Unionist Daniel G. Taylor, who opposed the administration's perceived policy of coercion toward the seceding states. Taylor defeated Unconditional Unionist John How by over 2,600 votes, thus stripping the city's political power from Republican hands for the first time since 1857. The election results further illustrate the conservatism of St. Louis residents, who perceived from both Lincoln's inaugural address and the army's presence in the city that the Republicans were indeed the warmongers. They therefore voted not to have that party in power in their city. In an effort to avert war, the city's voters cast their ballots for the party they believed more interested in compromise than in war. Many, however, misconstrued the results as an ascendancy of the city's secessionists and feared that their apparent victory would soon lead to conflagration in the streets.[49]

One of those most disturbed by the city's latest power swing was William Harney. Speculation that the Minute Men, with the militia's assistance, planned to take the arsenal was a daily fixture in the city's newspapers, which claimed that the group had even subverted the federal troops stationed at the arsenal. "There is reason to believe," read one editorial, "that many soldiers who have been in town from time to time, have been tampered with by the secessionists and induced to desert, with the view of going South and joining the Southern Confederacy." Harney could not deny that a significant number of men at the arsenal *were* currently being tried by court-martial for desertion. Yet the department commander wanted desperately to be rid of Lyon, especially after the captain's insolence had embarrassed Harney so recently in his own home.[50]

On the evening of April 4, the general had invited the arsenal's officers for a small dinner party. Also attending was Samuel B. Churchill, a respected lawyer and former state senator from St. Louis who was editor of the *St. Louis Bulletin*. Although he did not advocate secession for Missouri, Churchill upheld the South's right to do so. To Harney's horror, Lyon repeatedly challenged Churchill's statements on the state of

49. Snead, *Fight for Missouri*, 94–95; Anderson, *Border City*, 71; Kirkpatrick, "Missouri on the Eve," 108; Harvey, "Missouri from 1849 to 1861," 38; Smith, *Borderland in the Civil War*, 148–49.

50. *Missouri Democrat*, March 31, 1861.

the Union, creating an unpleasant tension among the guests and ruining the dinner. Though the host remained reticent throughout the outburst, Lyon's peevishness left Harney deeply offended. However, though proud and often gruff, Harney was not a rash man, and despite his subordinate's offensive behavior, he found himself beginning to accept the captain's assumptions about the safety of the arsenal. While skeptical of any immediate danger, Harney realized that he needed all the officers in his small command—no matter how unruly—to deal with any potential crisis. Therefore, on April 8, the general telegraphed Washington "that under existing circumstances he deems it important that Capt. Lyon should not leave his command at St. Louis Arsenal to attend the Court of Inquiry." The next day, partly through Blair's influence, an order arrived revoking the call for Lyon's court of inquiry.[51]

Simultaneously, Harney granted Lyon permission to begin fortifying the arsenal and issued orders to Hagner to comply with Lyon's requisitions for materials. He also ordered that all powder and ammunition stored in the Jefferson Barracks magazine be moved to the arsenal. Though plagued by a debilitating bout with fever, Lyon wasted no time in beginning work, for fear that his vacillating commander might change his mind again. He ordered the buildings mined, the tops of the walls sandbagged, ramparts and portholes cut, and banquettes built. He then placed artillery at strategic locations and posted guards at all walls and gates to restrict passage into the compound. The speed with which Lyon accomplished this impressed the Committee of Safety. Lyon realized that his power to act in the impending crisis was far greater than it had been before Harney had granted him the necessary matériel of war. However, he continued to worry that he had too few men with which to man his new defenses effectively.[52]

Though Harney had at last complied with their wishes, both Lyon and the Committee of Safety still harbored grave suspicions about Hagner. On April 4, after the officers at the arsenal were again invited to a ball thrown by the State Guard, Lyon forbade his men to attend, declaring

51. Irwin, "Missouri in Crisis," 15–16; Duke, *Reminiscences,* 51; Report of the Court of Inquiry of Capt. Nathaniel Lyon, April 9, 1861, Richard Graham Papers, MHS.

52. Seth Williams to Lyon, April 9, 1861, Letters Sent, Department of the West, vol. 4, RG 393; Harney to Peter V. Hagner, April 9, 1861, in *OR,* I, 1:662–63; Hagner to Williams, April 9, 1861, Letters Received, Department of the West, box 10, RG 393; Lyon to Williams, March 22, 1861, ibid.; Irwin, "Missouri in Crisis," 14–15; McElroy, *Struggle for Missouri,* 59–60; Peckham, *Lyon and Missouri,* 74.

that "his officers were not to be withdrawn, and his men left to capture by a pretence so shallow." In addition, Hagner failed to move the munitions from Jefferson Barracks, ostensibly on the grounds that there was not enough room at the arsenal. Hagner's actions only fueled Lyon's desire to have him replaced immediately. At a Union Guard drill session, Lyon grumbled that the commandant treated him and his men "like dogs, hardly giving us what is indispensably necessary." He vowed that if he caught Hagner "taking any step to throw the post into the hands of the enemy, I will throw him in the Mississippi river." He then boasted to the committee members that if the necessity arose, the Union Guard would indeed have their guns. Lyon planned for the Germans to be ready to strike the secessionists from the rear if the latter ever attacked the arsenal. When asked about the threat of Hagner procuring the guns for the state's secessionists, Lyon proclaimed boldly, "If he attempts to throw these guns into Jackson's hands, I'll shoot him down like a dog."[53]

During the next week, the entire nation watched tensely the unfolding drama in the harbor of Charleston, South Carolina. The small federal garrison under the command of Maj. Robert Anderson continued to man Fort Sumter, the most visible federal installation still held in Confederate territory. While negotiations were being conducted, the Confederate force surrounded the garrison and refused it provisions. A federal relief expedition had been fired upon earlier in the spring, and a new expedition was leaving from New York to attempt again to supply the garrison. Early on the morning of April 12, the situation erupted. The Confederate guns ringing the harbor commenced firing upon Fort Sumter, forcing its surrender two days later. Subsequently, on April 15, President Lincoln issued a call for seventy-five thousand volunteer troops to combat the obvious rebellion in the South. Large cities and small towns in all states found their recruiting offices jammed with young men trying eagerly to enlist and fight for their country. Entire companies, already equipped and many bedecked in resplendent uniforms, pledged their services to both sides. The quotas established by Lincoln for the states were not enough to encompass the thousands of anxious recruits, and many crossed state lines to enlist in a neighboring state if the quota for their own state was filled. The nation was at war.

53. Irwin, "Missouri in Crisis," 15–16; Peter V. Hagner to Seth Williams, April 9, 1861, Letters Received, Department of the West, box 10, RG 393; Peckham, *Lyon and Missouri,* 75, 93.

In St. Louis, the effects of Fort Sumter were cataclysmic. Secessionist and Union flags flew over all parts of the city—in some cases, directly across the street from one another. Altercations in the street were common, and the activities of both the Minute Men and the Union Guard increased dramatically. Newspapers across the state either supported or vehemently opposed Lincoln's call, exacerbating anti-Republican sentiment in the state. And on April 17, Claiborne Jackson, in his most well-known statement, sent a stinging rejoinder to the president's call for Missouri's quota of troops: "Sir, . . . your requisition in my judgment, is illegal, unconstitutional and revolutionary in its object, inhuman and diabolical, and cannot be complied with. Not one man will the state of Missouri furnish to carry on such an unholy crusade."[54]

The news from Fort Sumter heightened Lyon's sense of outrage. That the secessionists dared attack the forces of his government galled him to the fiber of his being. Not only did the incident confirm his belief that, from the very beginning of the secession crisis, Lincoln should have taken stronger measures, but it also ossified his own self-righteousness. He had already turned away a group of men posing as the grand jury of the city's circuit court when they came to the arsenal asking to inspect it. Now he knew he had done so correctly. Such secessionists no longer posed only a threat to the arsenal; they now were the enemy—*his* enemy. And because he believed the situation in St. Louis mirrored the general crisis of the nation, Lyon determined not to allow the traitors in Missouri to strike first, as the South Carolinians had done at Fort Sumter. He must smite the disunionists a crushing blow. He must punish them for their sins against the nation so severely they could never recover. The fact that Missouri had sided with the Union was immaterial; vengeance now dictated Lyon's actions. It was his duty. It was his obsession. And he welcomed his chance to act:

> I have felt deeply mortified by the humiliating attitude of my country toward traitors who could easily have been put down, and can be now, under proper measures. I do not see how a war is to be avoided . . . . Yet I have no apprehensions about the final triumph of almighty truth, though at the cost of many unnecessary sacrifices. But let them come. I would rather see the country lighted up with the flames of war . . . than that the great rights and hopes of the human race expire before the arrogance of secessionists.[55]

54. Arthur Roy Kirkpatrick, "Missouri in the Early Months of the Civil War," 235.
55. *Missouri Democrat,* April 11–12, 1861; Peckham, *Lyon and Missouri,* 76–77; Woodward, *Life of Nathaniel Lyon,* 242.

Within days of the surrender of Fort Sumter, Daniel Frost, command-ing the local state militia brigade, began openly to support secession. As a result, several of his highest subordinates peremptorily tendered their resignations. One such letter, written by Maj. Frederick Schaefer, reached the newspapers on April 19, airing the dubious loyalties of the State Guard. "I cannot reconcile it with my ideas of military fealty and disci-pline," the letter read, "that a part of your command has hoisted another flag than the only true flag of these United States . . . . The militia of the State of Missouri, who have . . . sworn fidelity and obedience to the Constitution of the United States and of the State of Missouri, should not have dared to unfurl this signal of rebellion and treason."[56]

The resigning officers were not mistaken in their suspicions about their former commander. Only four days earlier, Frost had sent a mes-sage to the governor apprising him of the situation in St. Louis. He warned Jackson that Lyon had greatly strengthened the arsenal's defenses and added, "If Lyon is allowed to go on, it will be but a short time before he will have this town and the commerce of the Mississippi at his mercy." Frost then made a list of suggestions, including sending a messenger to the Confederate capital to procure mortars and siege artillery for an attack on the arsenal. In addition, he suggested that the governor order Frost to form a camp of instruction near the city and authorize him to muster military companies into the service of the state. Two days later, after fashioning his answer to the president, Jackson answered Frost's message. He had already sent agents to Montgomery, Alabama, request-ing that Jefferson Davis send him artillery. However, he was unable to call out the militia before May 6 unless the General Assembly ordered him to do so. It *was* within his rights, though, to order the *commanders* of the militia districts to assemble at a "convenient" location for the purpose of drill and discipline. He therefore authorized Frost to establish his camp at any place within the St. Louis city limits.[57]

During this time, Lyon prepared furiously for his, and the seces-sionists', next moves. Anticipating an assault on the arsenal on the night of April 12, he organized a series of midnight drills to ready his troops. At 11:00 P.M., he called together only his most trusted subordinates—Captains Thomas Sweeny, Rufus Saxton, and Albert Tracy—for a secret

56. Peckham, *Lyon and Missouri*, 103-4; Covington, "Camp Jackson Affair," 200; *Missouri Democrat*, April 19, 22, 1861.

57. Broadhead, "St. Louis During the War," Broadhead Papers, MHS; McElroy, *Struggle for Missouri*, 62-63.

meeting at his quarters. In the dim light of a screened lantern, Lyon gave instructions as to how the arsenal should be defended. Just as the cabal was about to break up, Lyon gathered himself as if to rise, then slammed his fist violently on the table and seethed, "And now, gentlemen, if that man, Hagner, interferes with you in any way, or presumes to give one single order, put him in irons . . . . And if he interferes with *me*, . . . I'll shoot him in his tracks!" Though aghast at the prospect, the officers comprehended that their commander was fully willing to commit this mutiny for his principles. They were understandably relieved when the attack never came.[58]

In addition, Lyon ordered the posting of round-the-clock patrols and pickets outside the arsenal walls so that the garrison would not be surprised. This action outraged many local citizens. However, when members of the city's Board of Police Commissioners (recently appointed by the governor according to the bill that the General Assembly had passed, placing control of the city's police force in his hands) complained to Lyon that the patrols violated city ordinances, Lyon retorted gruffly that the patrols were necessary to maintain the arsenal's safety and refused to withdraw them. Indignant at the captain's rudeness, the board members took up their complaint with General Harney.[59]

Lyon carried his perceived authority even further. On April 16, he wrote to the governor of Illinois, Richard Yates, requesting that he hold Illinois troops in readiness for use at the arsenal in case of attack. Yet Lyon saw that Yates, a strong Lincoln supporter, could provide more than just troops for his—and the Union's—cause. Because Lyon believed the stockpile of arms at the arsenal was far larger than he could ever use, thus rendering the installation a more tempting target than desirable, he requested that Yates requisition a large number of arms to be supplied from the St. Louis arsenal. Lyon would then ship a large portion of them to a safer locale in Illinois. He believed that this was not overstepping his authority, but merely using the opportunities at hand.[60]

While Lyon prepared for the arsenal's immediate defense, the Committee of Safety was occupied with the defense of the city. Since Blair's departure, they had recruited actively for the Union Guard, and the response to Lincoln's call for volunteers indicated that their efforts had

---

58. Irwin, "Missouri in Crisis," 16–18.

59. Peckham, *Lyon and Missouri,* 96–97; Anderson, *Border City,* 73.

60. Lyon to Richard Yates, April 16, 1861, in *OR,* I, 1:667.

paid off handsomely. Within hours, three complete companies of German Turners presented themselves at department headquarters. Within the week, at least fifteen hundred of the city's Unionists would tender their services to the federal government.[61]

On the morning of April 17, as Lyon waited for Yates's reply, Frank Blair returned from Washington. Traveling immediately to the arsenal, he sought out Lyon in his office. To the captain's amazement, Blair produced an order from the War Department authorizing the issuance of five thousand stand of arms to those Union Guards who would enlist in the federal army. Although Blair was exuberant, Lyon's response quickly sobered him; Harney had refused to accept any of the Union Guard who had already sought enlistment. Since the governor refused to comply with Lincoln's call, Harney claimed that he had neither authority nor mustering officer to do so. Lyon knew that the department commander would not risk provoking the secessionists by approving such authorization, as he did not believe they would act upon the arsenal until the state had officially seceded. Although the news raised Blair's temper appreciably, he had little time to vent it. He rushed to meet with the leaders of the Union Guard to prevent them from tendering their services to the governor of Illinois, promising to "admit them and arm them at the earliest possible moment."[62]

Harney learned the next morning of Lyon's authorization for muskets. The police commissioners had already visited him to complain of Lyon's street patrols, and he now feared that his excitable subordinate would overstep his authority and issue guns to the Germans. Though the general had at last acceded to Lyon's claims that the arsenal would be in some danger if the State Guard ever moved artillery to the heights outside town, he was too experienced to allow rash actions to incite any unnecessary conflagration. Harney's entire career illustrated an ability to judge situations and react with sagacity. His decision not to muster the Union Guard proved no different; the state had declared itself neutral, and he had received no authority from the War Department to enlist them.

61. Broadhead, "St. Louis During the War," Broadhead Papers, MHS; "History of the 1st Artillery Regiment," V. Mott Porter Papers, MHS; Rombauer, *Union Cause in St. Louis*, 188–89, 195; *Missouri Democrat*, April 23, 1861.

62. *Missouri Democrat*, April 18, 1861; John Schofield, *Forty-six Years in the Army*, 33; McElroy, *Struggle for Missouri*, 64; Frank Blair to Montgomery Blair, April 20, 1861, Blair Papers, box 3, LOC; Seth Williams to Lyon, April 18, 1861, in *OR*, I, 1:668; "History of the 1st Artillery Regiment," V. Mott Porter Papers, MHS.

Harney wanted no war without due cause; he felt the gravity of his position as both commander and resident too acutely. Therefore, he sent a message to Lyon ordering the withdrawal of all patrols from outside the arsenal limits for fear they would instigate trouble. He then forbade Lyon to issue arms or ammunition to *anyone* without Harney's approval. In addition, he decided to move his quarters to the arsenal to keep a tighter rein on Lyon's impetuosity. Finally, Harney sent a request to the adjutant general that an officer of higher rank be sent to the arsenal to supercede Lyon. "There are reasons," he wrote, "which in my judgment, render it expedient that the change in the command . . . should be made without delay."[63]

Both Lyon and Blair were incensed by Harney's blatant obtuseness—especially Blair. He resolved that he must *force* an immediate change in the city's military leadership. He went promptly to see Harney and informed him that he intended to secure the general's removal from command of the western department. Though indignant at Blair's hauteur, Harney recognized that the congressman's influence in Washington would most likely prove successful. Blair went so far as to discuss desirable locations for Harney's transfer. However, Harney summarily refused to permit Lyon to implement Blair's order to issue arms without himself receiving similar instructions. The next day, Blair set his plans into motion. Addressing a letter to Simon Cameron, the secretary of war, Blair apprised him of the dire situation in St. Louis and of Harney's vacuousness in reacting to it. Although he did not doubt the general's loyalty, Blair believed Harney should be moved to surroundings "less embarrassing" and replaced with someone more alive to the true nature of the situation, perhaps Gen. John Wool. Blair maintained, however, that Hagner was "in league with the secessionists." On April 19 and 20, he penned successive letters to Montgomery Blair imploring him to see Cameron and convince him to act upon Frank's requests. Moreover, he railed against Harney's refusal to allow Lyon to pass out arms because of the lack of an "emergency"—despite Blair's personal order to do so—and asked that Lyon be given authority to muster four regiments for government service, as per Missouri's quota. Convinced that many of the city's telegraph operators were of dubious loyalty, he entrusted the

63. "History of the 1st Artillery Regiment," V. Mott Porter Papers, MHS; William S. Harney to E. D. Townsend, April 16, 1861, in *OR*, I, 1:666–67; Seth Williams to Lyon, April 18, 1861, ibid., 668; Harney to John A. Brownlee, April 22, 1861, ibid., 670; Harney to AGO, April 20, 1861, in Reavis, *Life and Services of Harney*, 354.

letters to a close acquaintance who would deliver them personally to Washington and then lobby Cameron for their implementation. Blair then wired Cameron a second message repeating his requests and instructing him to send any responses to East St. Louis, Illinois, to ensure their safe arrival.[64]

The next day, the War Department's reply to Lyon's request for Illinois troops arrived at the arsenal. To Lyon's elation, Cameron had authorized the transport of two or three regiments "to assist in the defense of the St. Louis Arsenal." Hagner received orders to equip these troops and issue an additional ten thousand stand of arms to an agent of the Illinois governor for the rest of that state's quota of recruits. Lyon breathed a sigh of relief. Even if Harney would not muster troops, with Yates's help he would finally receive the support he needed. At the same time he would dispose of a sizable surplus of arms stored at the arsenal, a target far too tempting to the disunionists. Lyon feared, however, that the aid would arrive too late.[65]

What neither Blair nor Lyon yet realized was that their mustering officer had already arrived in St. Louis. On April 15, the War Department had contacted Lt. John M. Schofield, on leave from the army as a professor of physics at Washington University, detailing him to act as mustering officer for the state of Missouri. Schofield quickly informed Governor Jackson of his presence in the state but received no reply. He then called on Harney to tender his services but received the commander's well-worn argument that he had yet to receive authority to accept volunteers. Though as yet he had found no one to accept his services, Schofield's presence had not gone unnoticed.[66]

On the morning of April 21, news arrived that on the day before, local secessionists had seized the federal arsenal at Liberty, Missouri, just east

64. Frank Blair to Simon Cameron, April 18, 1861, Blair Papers, box 18, LOC; Broadhead, "St. Louis During the War," Broadhead Papers, MHS; Peckham, *Lyon and Missouri*, 109–11; Frank Blair to Montgomery Blair, April 19, 1861, in ibid., 111; Frank Blair to Montgomery Blair, April 20, 1861, Blair Papers, box 3, LOC; Frank Blair to Simon Cameron, April 19, 1861, in OR, I, 1:668–69.

65. McElroy, *Struggle for Missouri*, 64; Simon Cameron to Richard Yates, April 20, 1861, in OR, I, 1:669; Cameron to "Commander of the Arsenal at Saint Louis," April 20, 1861, ibid.

66. James L. McDonough, *Schofield: Union General in the Civil War and Reconstruction*, 10; John Schofield to Lorenzo Thomas, April 20, 1861, John M. Schofield Papers, box 45, LOC; Schofield to C. F. Jackson, April 20, 1861, ibid.; Schofield, *Forty-six Years in the Army*, 32–33; Lyon to Frank Blair, April 21, 1861, in Peckham, *Lyon and Missouri*, 107–9.

of Kansas City. The act secured fifteen hundred stand of arms, eleven thousand pounds of powder, and four small brass cannon for the state's rebels. Far more frightening was the added rumor that on that same night, St. Louis's new mayor had narrowly averted an attack by the Minute Men on the St. Louis Arsenal. The arsenal was in serious jeopardy, Lyon averred, and he and Blair must take immediate action. He had tried twice in the last two days to secure Harney's sanction to enlist volunteers and provide them with arms but was each time rebuked. Now, he and Blair determined to enlist volunteers that night, secretly and without Harney's permission. While preparing for it, Lyon learned of Schofield's presence in the city. He sent word immediately to Blair, who rushed several members of the Committee of Safety to find him and bring him to Blair's office.[67]

Blair's agents soon located Schofield at church and hastened him to Blair. The congressman ascertained the lieutenant's sympathy to their cause and entreated him to see Lyon as quickly as possible. Schofield went immediately to the arsenal. Much to his dismay, however, Lyon saw by the wording of Schofield's orders that the lieutenant had no official authority to arm the men they intended to enlist. Harney and Hagner would no doubt block any efforts to do so once the men were mustered. Lyon worried about the entire mutinous affair; Blair's letters to Washington had not yet prompted an answer, and Lyon knew that when the night's events became known, the department commander would order his immediate arrest and disperse the entire force of ex-officio volunteers. Thereupon, he sent Schofield and Saxton with a note to Blair voicing his concerns: "We do not seem to be starting out right with the instructions Mr. Schofield now has."[68]

When Blair received Lyon's note and his envoys explained their conversation with the captain, Blair thought of another approach. He called for a telegrapher he knew to be trustworthy and dictated a message to the governor of Pennsylvania, Andrew G. Curtin. Knowing that Curtin was

67. Kirkpatrick, "Missouri in the Early Months," 237; Broadhead, "St. Louis During the War," Broadhead Papers, MHS; Floyd C. Shoemaker, *A History of Missouri and Missourians*, 153; Lyon to Seth Williams, April 20, 1861, Letters Received, Department of the West, box 10, RG 393; Lyon to Williams, April 21, 1861, ibid.; Williams to Lyon, April 21, 1861, Letters Sent, Department of the West, vol. 4, RG 393; Lyon to Frank Blair, April 21, 1861, in Peckham, *Lyon and Missouri*, 106–9.

68. Schofield, *Forty-six Years in the Army*, 33–34; Lyon to Frank Blair, April 21, 1861, in Peckham, *Lyon and Missouri*, 107–9; Broadhead, "St. Louis During the War," Broadhead Papers, MHS.

a close acquaintance of Cameron's (also from Pennsylvania), Blair asked that the governor send a messenger to the secretary of war relaying his request that Harney allow Lyon to muster and arm the volunteers. "Our friends distrust Harney very much," he wrote. "He should be superceded immediately . . . ." By chance, Maj. Fitz John Porter was at the time in Harrisburg on a special recruiting assignment for Cameron. Curtin quickly relayed Blair's telegram to Porter, who acted just as promptly. Believing himself "justified to use the means and authority of the Secretary of War and of the General-in-Chief," Porter sent copies of the following telegram to Harney, Lyon, and Blair:

> Captain Nathaniel Lyon, 2d Infantry, is detailed to muster in the troops at St. Louis and to use them for the protection of public property. You will see that they are properly armed and equipped.
>
> By order of Lieutenant General Scott,
> Fitz John Porter, A. A. G.[69]

After sending the wire to Curtin, Blair traveled to the arsenal to meet with Lyon, where that afternoon they received Porter's dispatch with great relief. They planned then for the enlistment of the Union Guard that evening at the arsenal. Those designated to enlist would be given for identification a strip of ribbon on which Lyon's personal seal was impressed in wax. Between 7:30 and 8:30 P.M., under cover of darkness, the officers would come to the main gate on Carondelet Avenue, while the men were to come to the wooden fence gate on the riverfront. Both would gain admittance into the compound upon producing their identification. Schofield would then muster them into the federal service and issue them arms. While members of the Committee of Safety began the elaborate preparations, Blair visited such establishments as the Flora Garten—a Turner Society beer garden—and announced the plans to enthusiastic crowds.[70]

Unfettered of the threat of Harney's interference, Lyon worked as if possessed. As scheduled, the Germans began arriving after dark, and throughout the evening Lyon enlisted and equipped all those who came

69. Peckham, *Lyon and Missouri,* 109–10; Frank Blair to A. G. Curtin, April 21, 1861, Blair Papers, box 3, LOC; Lyon to Lorenzo Thomas, April 27, 1861, in Rombauer, *Union Cause in St. Louis,* 211; Report by Fitz John Porter to Adjutant General, May 1, 1861, Civil War Collection, MHS.
70. Lyon to Frank Blair, April 21, 1861, in Peckham, *Lyon and Missouri,* 111; Broadhead, "St. Louis During the War," Broadhead Papers, MHS.

to the gate. However, at midnight, the arsenal's telegraph receiver clacked a late dispatch from Washington addressed to Lyon. The clerk transcribed the message and found Lyon in the compound, where the captain read the note by lantern. It read: "General Harney has this day been relieved from his command. The Secretary of War directs that you immediately execute the order previously given to arm the loyal citizens, to protect the public property, and execute the laws. Muster four regiments into the service."[71]

Lyon was elated. The Blairs had come through! Montgomery Blair, however, could not boast sole credit for effecting the St. Louis coup. During the past week, cabinet members Edward Bates and Salmon P. Chase also had been deluged with requests from St. Louis acquaintances to give Lyon authority to secure the Union position in the city. The characters behind the telegraph message, however, mattered little to Lyon; he could now commence his night muster with Blair's promised impunity.[72]

As planned, over three hundred Union Guards—composed entirely of German Turners—received induction into the federal service by daybreak. By that afternoon, Lyon had accepted more than seven hundred troops, nearly all of whom had already been armed and posted in positions along the arsenal walls. At last, Lyon felt that the arsenal was safe from immediate danger. Yet his good news had not ended. That morning, another wire arrived from Washington relieving Hagner of command of the arsenal and assigning him to Fort Leavenworth to await further orders. Harney's orders stipulated that command would now "devolve upon the senior officer in the department." Though Lyon was officially only a captain, Hagner's removal placed departmental command squarely in his hands. Both Harney and Hagner, thorns in his side since arriving in St. Louis, had received just punishments. Blair's help had allowed Lyon to see to that. No longer would his plans for the city's defense be hamstrung by their ineptness or treachery, or both. Lyon had power, and power meant punishment. The city's secessionists now stood to feel his full wrath.[73]

71. Lyon to Lorenzo Thomas, April 22, 1861, in Rombauer, *Union Cause in St. Louis,* 211; Lorenzo Thomas to Lyon, April 21, 1861, in *OR,* I, 1:670.

72. O. D. Filley to Montgomery Blair, April 19, 1861, Blair Papers, box 29, LOC; Benjamin Farrar to Salmon P. Chase, April 20, 1861, Civil War Collection, MHS; W. W. Greene to Edward Bates, April 22, 1861, in *OR,* I, 1:671–72; Charles Gibson to Bates, April 22, 1861, ibid., 672–73.

73. "History of the 1st Artillery Regiment," V. Mott Porter Papers, MHS; Lyon to

As per orders, on the evening of April 23 Harney left the city on a train bound for Washington. By that time, the arsenal command had received, sworn in, and armed nearly 1,500 recruits. Before the week was up, that number would rise to 2,500. The volunteers, more than 80 percent of whom were German, enlisted for a three-month term of service. On April 27, the 1st Regiment, Missouri Volunteers—already at full strength—elected Frank Blair as their colonel. The ranks of three other regiments were also nearly filled. Because the great number of recruits had densely crowded the compound, Lyon sent several hundred to the Marine Hospital to take up temporary quarters. Blair wired Washington jubilantly that within the week, Missouri would indeed fulfill her quota.[74]

By general consensus, the Missouri volunteers elected Lyon general of their regiments. Though supportive of Lyon, Blair first offered Missouri's single allotment of brigadier generalships to William T. Sherman, a former army brevet captain who had served for less than a month as the president of St. Louis's Fifth Street Railroad Company. Blair's reasons for offering the position to Sherman instead of Lyon are not clear; it is likely that he owed a political debt to Sherman's brother, Ohio senator John Sherman. The reasons matter little, however, for Sherman declined the offer, and Blair then supported Lyon for the commission. The captain accepted it eagerly. While it is virtually certain that Lyon would soon have been promoted to colonel in the regular army, he was too ambitious to go that route. Volunteer or not, here was the chance for a generalship, for overall command. Lyon could not pass up the opportunity at hand. And in this decision, he received the full support of the German enlistees.[75]

News of the enlistment of the Union Guard rendered the arsenal a hub of activity. "Crowds of curious spectators hover around the inclosure and throng the gateways," read the *Missouri Democrat*, "and hundreds clam-

---

Lorenzo Thomas, April 22, 1861, Thomas J. Sweeny Collection, Huntington; Lyon to Lorenzo Thomas, April 27, 1861, in Rombauer, *Union Cause in St. Louis*, 211; Lorenzo Thomas to William S. Harney, April 21, 1861, in OR, I, 1:669; Special Order No. 57, April 22, 1861, Orders and Special Orders Issued, Department of the West, RG 393.

74. Lyon to Adjutant General, April 23, 1861, Thomas J. Sweeny Collection, Huntington; Reavis, *Life and Services of Harney*, 357; *Missouri Democrat*, April 24, 26, 1861.

75. Lyon to Lorenzo Thomas, April 22, 1861, Thomas J. Sweeny Collection, Huntington; Lyon to Thomas, April 27, 1861, in Rombauer, *Union Cause in St. Louis*, 211; ibid., 226, 349; William T. Sherman, *Memoirs of W. T. Sherman*, 168–71; *Missouri Democrat*, April 4, 1861.

ber upon the walls and into trees in the neighborhood. The balconies, houses, shed tops &c., whence a view of the interior of the Arsenal can be gained, are eagerly and constantly visited by people of both sexes and nearly all ages. The St. Louis Street Railroad Co. is reaping an unusual harvest of half-dimes, as the Bremen and Arsenal cars are generally crowded." However, not all shared in the picnic atmosphere. News that the "damned Dutch" had received government arms caused the sporadic disturbances in the downtown area to become daily occurrences. Some took the form of armed violence; however, clubbings and stonings proved most prevalent. Numerous threats and several actual attacks on his home forced Frank Blair to move his family out of the city. Most of the city looked upon Blair as the leading protagonist in the controversy over the arsenal; Lyon was still but a relatively insignificant character. Unsettling stories abounded that the governor planned to place the artillery seized at the Liberty raid on the hills overlooking the arsenal and that the federal government had approved twenty-five thousand troops from other states to be sent to protect the arsenal. One newspaper even reported that Lyon threatened to shell the city if the Minute Men attacked the arsenal. Such rumors succeeded only in further agitating the city's populace and in prompting the secessionists to employ spies to keep constant watch over the arsenal. Many of those milling about the front of the gate shouted obsenities at the soldiers, attempting to provoke an incident.[76]

On April 24, Capt. James H. Stokes arrived from Illinois and struggled through the crowd to meet with Lyon in his office. He was sent by Governor Yates to secure the ten thousand muskets the government had earlier approved for the Illinois troops, and he had chartered a steamer, the *City of Alton,* which lay tied across the river awaiting the arms. The two men quickly realized, however, that there would be no way to slip the large number of weapons past the Minute Men's spies without creating a riot. Some sort of ruse would be necessary to divert the attention of the secessionists while the weapons were loaded at the arsenal's dock. Perplexed only briefly, Lyon hatched an ingenious plan.[77]

The next day, Lyon circulated a rumor that at some time that night, he would attempt to transport a load of arms on the Fifth Street cars to the

76. *Missouri Democrat,* April 26, 30, 1861; W. W. Greene to Edward Bates, April 22, 1861, in OR, I, 1:671–72.

77. Woodward, *Life of Nathaniel Lyon,* 245.

Tenth Ward Union Guards. Knowing that the spies would spot the activity immediately, Lyon intended to send the cars out at about midnight, gambling that the secessionists would take the bait and stop them. While their attention was thus diverted, Stokes would order his steamer captain to tie at the arsenal landing, without lights or whistles, in order to load the rifles. Their plans set, they waited for nightfall.[78]

At 9:00 P.M., earlier than originally planned, four streetcars moved slowly up Fifth Street. As Lyon hoped, the spies quickly summoned their comrades from the local bars. They rushed to the cars and searched for the guns they were rumored to be carrying but found only an unsuspecting federal officer. Meanwhile, as the secessionists preyed upon the cars, the *City of Alton* docked quietly at the arsenal wharf, and an arsenal detachment under Capt. Harry Stone loaded the cargo of arms. At 4:00 A.M., without the secessionists discovering that they had been duped, the *City of Alton* slipped away and steamed up the Mississippi with more than 20,000 muskets, 5,000 carbines, 500 revolvers, 100,000 cartridges, and other miscellaneous equipment. Retaining only enough small arms for 10,000 men—the number of volunteers both Lyon and Blair felt they could raise from the city—Lyon sent the rest of the arsenal's stockpile aboard the steamer to Alton, Illinois, where it was loaded upon a train bound for Camp Butler, near Springfield. Lyon's ruse had worked to perfection.[79]

Lyon's arms smuggle, reported by the newspapers, received laudatory reviews from much of the city's populace. Since the arms were the primary aim of secessionist machinations, the Unionists reveled in their enemy's discomfiture while the conservatives sighed with relief, hoping that the lack of temptation would ease the city's tensions. Yet the news traveled farther than St. Louis. Attorney General Edward Bates commended Lyon on his great coup. "St. Louis," he wrote, "I am now satisfied, is safe, at least from actual war. The arms being removed, there is no temptation to Gov. Jackson to commit treason for the sake of the arsenal." In addition, volunteers for service flocked to the arsenal from in and around St. Louis in numbers beyond either its capacity to house them or Lyon's quota to accept them. Lyon was so swamped with

78. Peckham, *Lyon and Missouri,* 116.

79. Ibid.; McElroy, *Struggle for Missouri,* 66; Franklin A. Dick to B. J. Lossing, July 6, 1865, Franklin A. Dick File, LOC; "History of the 1st Artillery Regiment," V. Mott Porter Papers, MHS; *Missouri Democrat,* April 27, 1861; Lyon to Lorenzo Thomas, April 30, 1861, in OR, I, 1:675–76.

recruits that he even wired Yates that there was no hurry about sending his troops.[80]

Blair, however, saw the need to enlist all available troops in some form of defense organization. Although Lyon was limited to raising four regiments, Blair sent to Washington a plan for the organization of a Reserve Corps, made up purely of Home Guard regiments, whose jurisdiction would not reach beyond the city limits. These units would ensure the continued defense of the city if Lyon's government volunteers were called away to put down the general rebellion. Though only adjuncts to the federal troops, Blair wanted government arms and officers for them. Because he believed the enlistment of the present regiments had saved St. Louis from being "to-day where Baltimore now is, in the hands of the mob of disunionists," Blair believed the Reserve Corps would secure the future safety of the city. He appealed to Montgomery Blair for support of his plan.[81]

Once again, Montgomery proved successful in implementing Frank's wishes. On May 2, Lyon received a dispatch from the War Department, dated April 30. Addressed to "Capt. Nathaniel Lyon, Commanding Department of the West," it read:

> The President of the United States directs that you enroll in the military service of the United States the loyal citizens of Saint Louis and vicinity, not exceeding, with those heretofore enlisted, ten thousand in number, for the purpose of maintaining the authority of the United States; for the protection of the peaceable inhabitants of Missouri; and you will, if deemed necessary for that purpose . . . proclaim martial law in the city of Saint Louis.
>
> The additional force hereby authorized shall be discharged, in part or in whole, if enlisted, as soon as it appears to you . . . that there is no danger of an attempt on the part of the enemies of the Government to take military possession of the city . . . .

An endorsement by Winfield Scott at the bottom of the letter read: "It is revolutionary times, and therefore I do not object to the irregularity of this. W. S." Immediately below Scott's postscript, in thick, black ink, was scrawled: "Approved, April 30, 1861. A. Lincoln."[82]

80. Edward Bates to James O. Broadhead, May 3, 1861, Broadhead Papers, MHS; Lyon to Benjamin Farrar, April 26, 1861, Civil War Collection, MHS.

81. Frank Blair to Montgomery Blair, April 25, 1861, Blair Papers, box 3, LOC; Frank Blair to Montgomery Blair, April 28, 1861, ibid.; Lyon to Lorenzo Thomas, April 27, 1861, in Rombauer, *Union Cause in St. Louis,* 211; Chester Harding to Lorenzo Thomas, July 7, 1861, Letters Received, Department of the West, box 10, RG 393.

82. Lorenzo Thomas to Nathaniel Lyon, April 30, 1861, in *OR,* I, 1:675.

At last, Lyon had unquestioned authority to act as he saw fit in maintaining peace, not only in the city of St. Louis but in the entire state of Missouri. By orders of the president himself, Lyon was now in a position to use his troops to protect the citizenry from the state's secessionists. Yet he would not stop there. He had vowed to punish the secessionists for their treasonous activities. With such powerful sanction—and with an ally like Blair—his duty called for no less, and he wasted no time in carrying his newly acquired power to its most extreme fruition.

Sterling Price, 1862. A former governor of Missouri, he commanded the Missouri State Guard. Courtesy Special Collections, Howard-Tilton Library, Tulane University.

Pro-Union cartoon depicting events from the battle at Boonville. Courtesy Library of Congress.

Lyon's Army of the West leaves Boonville in pursuit of Jackson's State Guard. From *Harper's Weekly*. Courtesy Hargrett Rare Book and Manuscript Library, University of Georgia Libraries.

John M. Schofield, ca. 1862. Lyon's chief of staff during the Missouri campaign.

Franz Sigel, ca. 1862. Commander of the southwest expedition of Lyon's campaign and popular leader of the German troops from St. Louis.

John C. Frémont. Controversial commander of the Department of the West after Harney's dismissal.

Ben McCulloch. Commander of Arkansas's Confederate forces at Wilson's Creek. Courtesy Valentine Museum, Richmond, Virginia.

Charge of David S. Stanley's federal dragoons at Dug Springs. From *Harper's Weekly*. Courtesy Hargrett Rare Book and Manuscript Library, University of Georgia Libraries.

Henry Lovie's eyewitness sketch of the death of Lyon. Later published as a lithograph in *Frank Leslie's Illustrated Newspaper*. Courtesy Print Collection, Miriam and Ira D. Wallach Division of Art, Prints and Photographs, The New York Public Library, Astor, Lenox and Tilden Foundations.

Nathaniel Lyon, brigadier general of volunteers, 1861. Last known photograph of Lyon, probably taken by W. L. Troxell in St. Louis.

VIII

This Means War

A whirlwind of activity swept the state of Missouri during the first few days of May 1861. On the second, the legislature reassembled in a special session called by the governor for the ostensible purpose of taking "measures to perfect the organization and equipment of the Militia and raise the money to place the State in a proper attitude for defense." The convention's decision to reject secession had effectively tabled debate over Jackson's controversial military bill (called by one resident "the most wicked attempt at military despotism ever known") well before the adjournment five days earlier of the assembly's last session. Yet the governor was determined to force the issue, for he saw his time for action waning rapidly. The legislature appeared to be his best—and last—hope.[1]

Claib Jackson had always been an effective, if less than moderate, politician. The convention's decision that the state should remain neutral placed him in a position of inertness, a posture he found wholly distasteful. Political means had proven ineffective in obtaining the state's secession, but Jackson was a man of action, and his sincere belief that Missouri's destiny lay with the Confederacy prompted him to redouble his efforts after, in his words, the "miserable, base, and cowardly conduct of [the] submission convention." He wrote, "I do not think Missouri should secede today or tomorrow; but I do think it good policy that it should *publicly so declare* . . . . Missouri should act in concert with Tennessee and Kentucky. They are all bound to go out and should go together if possible . . . . Let us then prepare to make our exit." Moreover, the governor now saw Unionist forces in St. Louis growing stonger by the day. He was particularly angered by the fact that a golden oppor-

---

1. John McElroy, *The Struggle for Missouri*, 63; William E. Smith, *The Francis Preston Blair Family in Politics*, 2:30; Samuel T. Glover to Montgomery Blair, February 2, 1861, Blair Papers, box 29, LOC; Charles M. Harvey, "Missouri from 1849 to 1861," 37; Floyd C. Shoemaker, *A History of Missouri and Missourians*, 152.

tunity to seize the St. Louis Arsenal apparently had been squandered. Seemingly overnight, Blair had gathered over three thousand troops, and Lyon had managed to ship the arsenal's entire surplus of arms to Illinois, thus eliminating the main reason for capturing the arsenal. "She [Missouri] ought to have gone out last winter when she could have seized the public arms and public property and defended herself," he lamented to J. W. Tucker, editor of the *State Journal* in St. Louis. "This she had failed to do and must now wait a little while." Now, the governor devised another strategy to set Missouri on the course he believed she ought to take.

Jackson intended to convince the General Assembly that arming the Germans in St. Louis posed a grave threat to the state and represented the federal government's intention to coerce Missouri into the Union. He believed that if he could convince its members to pass his military bill, he could call forth a state militia with such great numbers that it would crush any gambit Blair and Lyon might attempt. Because his response to Lincoln's call was applauded so overwhelmingly by the state's populace, Jackson was confident that his strategy would work. "I want a little time to arm the state," he wrote, "and I am assuming every responsibility to do it with every possible dispatch . . . . Every man in the state is in favor of arming the state. Then let it be done."[2]

Jackson, however, could not wait for the General Assembly to render a decision. To keep pace with the Unionist strength in St. Louis, Jackson saw a dire need to call out the state militia, his greatest organ of support. According to the Militia Act of 1858, the governor possessed the power to call the militia into camp once each year for a week of drill. Therefore, on April 22, Jackson ordered all state militia units to meet in their respective districts on May 3, as prescribed by law. In this way, when the assembly voted to pass the military bill, as he was convinced it would, the state militia would be ready to act immediately upon his orders.[3]

In the interim, Jackson prepared for Missouri's secession through more clandestine channels. His communiqué with Jefferson Davis had

2. C. F. Jackson to J. W. Tucker, April 28, 1861, James O. Broadhead Papers, MHS; Edward C. Smith, *The Borderland in the Civil War,* 132; William H. Lyon, "Claiborne Fox Jackson and the Secession Crisis in Missouri," 423, 434; William E. Parrish, *Turbulent Partnership: Missouri and the Union, 1861–1865,* 20; *Missouri Democrat,* February 8, 1861; Smith, *Francis Preston Blair Family in Politics,* 2:25–26; Lyon to Lorenzo Thomas, April 30, 1861, in *OR,* I, 1:675.

3. Draft of the 1858 Militia Bill, Missouri Militia Collection, MHS; James O. Broadhead, "St. Louis During the War," Broadhead Papers, MHS; *Missouri Democrat,* April 23, 1861; James W. Covington, "The Camp Jackson Affair, 1861," 201.

borne fruit; on April 23 the Confederate president directed that four pieces of artillery be sent from the captured Baton Rouge Arsenal to Frost in St. Louis for use in capturing the arsenal at St. Louis. When three days later Davis wrote again, inquiring whether Missouri could furnish and equip one regiment of infantry for service in Virginia (which had seceded on April 17), Jackson declined reluctantly but insisted that the situation was only temporary. "Missouri can and will put 100,000 men in the field," he assured the Confederate president. "We are using every means to arm our people and until we are prepared must move cautiously." His most fervent hope, however, was that his impassioned speech to open the upcoming legislative session would cajole the lawmakers into overriding the convention's decision to remain in the Union. By voting to secede, they would at last submit to what he perceived to be the true will of Missouri's people.[4]

The state's legislators, however, did not favor secession. Like most Missourians, the majority supported Jackson's rebuke of Lincoln's call because of their adamant opposition to armed coercion of the South. When the session commenced, however, the representatives would not even seriously discuss an issue as radical as secession; it was all they could do to debate the military bill. "The long and short of it in my estimation," lamented Jackson's state treasurer, "is that a very decided majority of the governing influences are in favor of Missouri remaining with the old U.S."[5]

In St. Louis, Daniel M. Frost, the militia district commander, received the news of Jackson's proclamation with great enthusiasm. Although the arsenal was no longer an important target, he felt that the mustering of the militia could effectively counter Lyon's buildup of troops in the city. Though he had desired originally to place his camp on the hills commanding the arsenal (and in the process implant his artillery there as well), Lyon had parried his plan by occupying the heights with infantry and artillery immediately after the arrival of the message from the presi-

4. Robert E. Shalhope, *Sterling Price: Portrait of a Southerner,* 156; Jefferson Davis to C. F. Jackson, April 23, 1861, in Robert J. Rombauer, *The Union Cause in St. Louis in 1861,* 212–13; Thomas L. Snead, *The Fight for Missouri from the Election of Lincoln to the Death of Lyon,* 168; C. F. Jackson to Jefferson Davis, April 28, 1861, in *OR,* I, 1:689–90; Rombauer, *Union Cause in St. Louis,* 214–15; Hans Christian Adamson, *Rebellion in Missouri, 1861: Nathaniel Lyon and His Army of the West,* 3.

5. Shalhope, *Sterling Price,* 156; B. F. Massey to J. F. Snyder, May 31, 1861, John F. Snyder Papers, MHS.

dent that gave him the power to proclaim martial law in the city. Frost then obtained authorization from city officials to use Lindell Grove, a clearing in the woods on high ground at the western edge of the city, for his camp of instruction. Though not strategically located, the grove had ample room for what he hoped would be a large encampment.[6]

On May 6, at 10:00 A.M., militia units from all over the state converged in their various district encampments. Secessionist flags waved exultantly over Jefferson City and other cities throughout the state. In St. Louis, onlookers watched with divided sentiments as the various groups formed at the corner of Washington Avenue and Eleventh Street and marched westward, noticeably raggedly, to Lindell Grove. In honor of the governor, the camp received the name Camp Jackson, and upon the arrival of the baggage wagons, 892 men pitched their tents in company streets. The camp's two main streets were dubbed Davis and Beauregard, for the Confederate president and the commander of the forces that had bombarded Fort Sumter. As brigadier general of the 1st Brigade of Missouri Volunteers, Frost located his headquarters at the intersection of the two streets. The camp soon became the center of social interest, and hundreds of visitors strolled through it each day to find an acquaintance or simply to watch the men drill. Few failed to notice that the troops were donned quite conspicuously in Confederate gray.[7]

Particularly interested in the doings at Camp Jackson was Nathaniel Lyon, and his spies kept him well apprised of the activities in the camp. One (whose powers of observation appear to have been stronger than his spelling) advised him that "thay ar a verry bad lot and very dangerous men . . . think it would be well to go over the ground at Camp Jackson and give it a thorough surch." Moreover, for the past week Lyon had met secretly in late-night conferences with the Committee of Safety and other important Unionists at Franklin Dick's downtown office. Lyon and several others insisted from the start that the camp was filled with traitors and was closely connected to the duplicitous activities of both the governor and his troops in the interior. "There are dayley communic.s held here between some of the Confederate rebels and Gov. Jackson," wrote a Jefferson City resident to James Broadhead. "There is no doubt in my mind of their full intention of making hostile demonstration on the St.

6. Galusha Anderson, *A Border City During the Civil War,* 88–89; Peggy Robbins, "The Battle of Camp Jackson," 37.

7. Covington, "Camp Jackson Affair," 201–3; Military Commissions of D. M. Frost, Fordyce Family Papers, MHS.

Louis arsenal . . . . There is a deep scheme among The rebells to force Missouri out of the Union and a fight for St. Louis would bring about the desired effect." Even more alarming were reports that Frost would be receiving the cannon stolen from the Liberty Arsenal, with which he intended to take the arsenal in St. Louis. Lyon was convinced that Camp Jackson posed an immediate danger to the city.[8]

His distrust was confirmed on May 6, when Frost's aide-de-camp arrived with a message from his commander. Frost claimed that he wished to give his engineers some practical experience at building fortifications, so to practice their craft he planned to move forty of them to the bluff just south of the arsenal. He wished merely to inform Lyon of his motives and hoped that the captain would not be alarmed. Lyon snarled that his only reply to any such activity on the bluff would be immediate cannon fire and promptly ordered the aide out of his office. The incident, however, gave him pause to evaluate the present situation. He had already begun accepting the Home Guard units and within the next few days expected to muster four complete regiments. All were enlisting for a three-month term of duty with the understanding that they would not be called upon for service outside the county without their consent. In addition, a fifth regiment was actively organizing. Eighty percent of these Home Guards were of German parentage. The arsenal was already overflowing with the large number of troops stationed there, forcing Lyon to house many in buildings outside the compound and to remove Blair's regiment to Jefferson Barracks for want of room. Although Lyon was able to arm these enlistees, many were stationed at their homes. There were daily roll calls, drills, and occasional parades, but Blair had run into roadblocks trying to secure funds from the government for uniforms and equipage. Lyon's force hardly looked like an army.[9]

Moreover, as a member of the regular army, Lyon was very suspicious of the effectiveness of these ninety-day volunteers. He had nearly eight

8. J. E. D. Couzins Notes, Broadhead Papers, MHS; "Memorandum on Missouri," 6, Franklin A. Dick File, LOC; Allen P. Richardson to Broadhead, April 24, 1861, Broadhead Papers, MHS.

9. Rombauer, *Union Cause in St. Louis,* 219–21, 349; Lyon to Lorenzo Thomas, April 30, 1861, in *OR,* I, 1:675–76; Chester Harding to Lorenzo Thomas, July 7, 1861, Letters Received, Department of the West, box 10, RG 393; *Missouri Democrat,* May 3, 1861; Frank Blair to Simon Cameron, May 4, 1861, in *OR,* I, 1:679–80; Cameron to Blair, May 9, 1861, ibid., 680–81.

thousand troops at his disposal but had little confidence in their abilities. Yet his spies conceded that the state militia troops at Lindell Grove were as green as his own troops and that his force outnumbered theirs almost nine to one. They were a legally organized body, so he apparently had no legal recourse but to allow them to stay. Yet while his military training told him they posed no great threat, Lyon's *instincts* told him differently. He was less worried about the arsenal's defense than he was incensed by the militia's insolent, openly prosecessionist stance. Thus he made a visceral decision to capture the traitorous camp and all those in it. However, Lyon understood well the gravity of his decision and began taking steps to ensure the success of his coup. Though his vendetta was personal, his actions would not be rash, for he wanted nothing more than to punish the militia properly for their blatant contempt for the Union. And that punishment necessitated thorough planning.[10]

During the next several days, Lyon resumed heavy correspondence with Illinois governor Yates. Convinced that his raw German recruits were "not better prepared to act as soldiers, than almost any other citizens," he worried that they would prove unable to maintain themselves if firing broke out during the capture of Camp Jackson. Perhaps most important, Lyon feared that his coercive plan might incite the general populace of the city to "rise up and get the better of the Union forces." He therefore met on several occasions with Gustave Koerner, the former lieutenant governor of Illinois and still the undisputed leader of the German community in that state. Koerner resided in Belleville and, acting as Yates's envoy, arranged with Lyon for the deployment and transportation of Illinois troops from their camps at Caseyville and Mattoon to act in concert with Lyon's force at—and after—the Camp Jackson affair.[11]

That Lyon was so cautious in his preparations suggests that he understood fully the consequence of the actions he intended to take. Although he was empowered to proclaim martial law in the city, he had no authorization from the government for any offensive military movements, especially against a body legally sanctioned by the still-loyal state of Missouri. And though Lyon was an officer in the United States Army, much of his staff was made up of civilians—local Unionists whom he took into his trust and gave extralegal military commissions. Franklin A.

10. Gustave Koerner to L. U. Reavis, January 3, 1881, L. U. Reavis Collection, ChiHS.
11. Ibid.; Robert P. Howard, *Illinois: A History of the Prairie State*, 190, 222–23.

Dick, a St. Louis lawyer and Lyon's "assistant adjutant general," remembered that they were "irregulars . . . . But we assumed an organization analagous to a legal one." Although he had ample opportunity, Lyon did not announce his plans to the entire Committee of Safety. Besides Koerner and Yates, he informed only Blair, Dick, O. D. Filley, and Chester Harding (his adjutant general) of his plan to take Camp Jackson. Blair went so far as to impetuously wire the governor of Indiana, Oliver P. Morton, to send Lyon troops from that state. Although the War Department promptly countermanded Blair's "orders," Lyon remained determined to follow through with the plan and wanted no slip of the tongue to betray his intentions for St. Louis's traitors.[12]

In the early morning hours of May 9, Lyon's plans for capturing Camp Jackson took an unexpected turn. Well after midnight, the stern-wheeler *J. C. Swon* docked at the St. Louis levee. Among the cargo unloaded were several heavy plank crates marked "Tamaroa marble" and numerous unmarked barrels. Waiting for this cargo was a company of the Brownlee Guards under the command of Capt. John Tobin, who loaded it onto waiting wagons and drays. The procession then moved slowly the six miles to Camp Jackson, where it unloaded its cargo in a thick stand of trees near Frost's headquarters. Some of the deckhands at the levee were Germans, and they quickly reported their observations to Lyon's spies. Those containers, they were sure, held munitions—heavy cannon, shot and shell, mortars, muskets and ammunition—not marble. Early the next morning, one of Lyon's subordinates reported the night's activities to the federal commander.[13]

The deckhands were correct in their suspicions about the *J. C. Swon*'s cargo. Basil Duke and Coulton Greene, acting as envoys for Governor Jackson, had succeeded in obtaining an order from Jefferson Davis authorizing the commandant at the Baton Rouge Arsenal to release to them two twelve-pound howitzers, two thirty-two-pound siege guns, five

12. "Memorandum on Missouri," 1–2, Franklin A. Dick File, LOC; Franklin A. Dick to B. J. Lossing, July 6, 1865, ibid.; Dick to Lossing, August 7, 1865, Civil War Collection, MHS; Oliver P. Morton to Simon Cameron, May 6, 1861, in *OR*, I, 1:680; Cameron to Morton, May 6, 1861, ibid.

13. James Peckham, *General Nathaniel Lyon and Missouri in 1861*, 136, 160; Lyon to Lorenzo Thomas, May 11, 1861, in *OR*, III, 1:4–5; Otto Lademann, "The Capture of Camp Jackson—St. Louis, Missouri, Friday, May 10th, 1861," 71; Lyon to Lorenzo Thomas, May 11, 1861, in *OR*, III, 1:4–5; J. E. D. Couzins Notes, Broadhead Papers, MHS; *Missouri Democrat,* May 10, 1861; "Memorandum on Missouri," 2, Franklin A. Dick File, LOC.

hundred muskets, and a large amount of ammunition for the weapons. After commandeering the *Swon* at New Orleans, they proceeded to Baton Rouge and loaded the guns, which were concealed in crates and barrels. They steamed then to Cairo, where a hasty inspection failed to unmask the secret freight, and pressed on to St. Louis, arriving early on the morning of the ninth. The waiting soldiers then delivered the heavy cargo to Camp Jackson.[14]

Lyon had little doubt of the actual contents of the crates; a militia encampment would have no need for imported marble. He was convinced that the boxes contained arms and ammunition stolen from the Baton Rouge Arsenal and sent to Missouri's secessionists. Lyon first summoned the United States marshal, Daniel A. Rawlings, and demanded that he ascertain the validity of the reports. However, when Rawlings returned claiming that no such shipment had been made to Camp Jackson, Lyon resolved to find out for himself. He concluded that he must personally reconnoiter the camp, yet wanted the militia to know nothing about it. The logistics baffled him until Franklin Dick, also a close confidante of Blair's, concocted a daring plan.[15]

The sentries posted at the main entrance to Camp Jackson were enjoying themselves on the spring afternoon of May 9. The skies were overcast, making their uncomfortable wool uniforms much more tolerable than on other days. Although picket duty was normally an insipid affair, the duty at Camp Jackson had proven far more pleasant. They could view personally the camp's many visitors, and the guards took special delight in furtively eyeing the many beautiful belles of the city being driven constantly through with their important fathers or husbands. To the guards, the entire city seemed to have come to the camp in the last few days.

At about 3:00 P.M., an ornate barouche wheeled toward the entrance, its black driver, William Roberts, driving "deliberately but cautiously." One of the passengers was J. J. Witzig, a prominent local engineer and a member of the Committee of Safety. Next to him an old woman sat stiffly in the low, open carriage. She was wearing a black, bombazine gown, heavy veil, and huge bonnet. The guards quickly concluded that she was Mrs. Mira Alexander, Frank Blair's blind mother-in-law, out for

14. Basil W. Duke, *Reminiscences of General Basil W. Duke, C.S.A.,* 44–50.

15. Peckham, *Lyon and Missouri,* 136; "Memorandum on Missouri," 2–3, Franklin A. Dick File, LOC; C. D. Drake to B. J. Lossing, December 20, 1864, Civil War Collection, MHS.

her daily carriage ride about the city. As Witzig prattled on in his thick German accent about the sights in the camp, the guards graciously allowed the carriage to pass into the camp. Had they looked more closely, they might have noticed that old Mrs. Alexander was wearing military brogans.[16]

Franklin Dick had managed to borrow Mrs. Alexander's shawl, dress, and bonnet and had supplied his own carriage and driver so that Lyon could pose brazenly as the elderly widow and gain entrance into the camp. The captain's slight, angular build allowed him to pass for the old woman, while the heavy veil covered his unruly red beard. In the event he was recognized, however, Lyon clutched two Colt revolvers under a lap robe. No one suspected him, however, and Lyon gained an accurate picture of the camp's layout, the militia currently in attendance, and the number of arms they possessed. Most important, he beheld the unopened boxes reputedly removed from the *J. C. Swon.* After half an hour, Lyon had seen enough and ordered the driver to take him back to the arsenal.[17]

However, upon his return, Lyon was greeted with some thoroughly disagreeable news. Winfield Scott had reinstated General Harney, called so conveniently from the city over a week ago, into his old position, and he was returning to the city. He was scheduled to arrive by train on Sunday evening, May 11. It would seem that Harney had played Lyon's own game by going to a higher authority to overturn what he considered an unjust ruling. Lyon was shocked. He realized that his chance to punish the secessionists would end immediately upon Harney's arrival. Instantly, his entire consciousness was geared toward one purpose: to force the surrender of Camp Jackson before Harney's return, with or without legal justification. Unfortunately, by doing so he would have to forgo waiting for Yates's troops. Lyon sensed that he had no time to lose.[18]

Late that afternoon, Lyon sent messages to each member of the Committee of Safety calling for a meeting at 7:00 that evening in his arsenal

16. Anderson, *Border City,* 92; McElroy, *Struggle for Missouri,* 71–72; "Memorandum on Missouri," 3, Franklin A. Dick File, LOC.

17. C. D. Drake to B. J. Lossing, December 20, 1864, Civil War Collection, MHS; "Memorandum on Missouri," 3, Franklin A. Dick File, LOC; McElroy, *Struggle for Missouri,* 71–72; Rombauer, *Union Cause in St. Louis,* 191; Peckham, *Lyon and Missouri,* 139–40; Covington, "Camp Jackson Affair," 204.

18. Rombauer, *Union Cause in St. Louis,* 225.

office. The overcast skies opened about nightfall, and the committee members arrived at Lyon's upper-floor office amid a driving rain. Pacing the wooden floor, the captain explained the situation as he saw it. His spies had led him to believe that the camp was a "fearful menace" since the newly arrived artillery, when outfitted with caissons, would render his six pieces of artillery (the heaviest of which were but two eight-pound howitzers) wholly ineffective. Because they all knew that the camp was a "nest of traitors," Lyon insisted that it must be eliminated. Impatiently, he proposed to take the camp, arguing that its capture would "force Jackson to recognize [the federal government's] authority, and cease doing those things which were seemingly forcing Missouri into a position of antagonism toward it." He admitted that the act would be treading "upon delicate ground," but he was prepared to take full responsibility for the gambit. Although Lyon left no doubt that he had already determined to take the camp, he desired to consult with the committee and hoped for their acquiescence.[19]

Of the six committee members in attendance, four agreed completely with Lyon. Two others, however, dissented. John How wavered regarding Lyon's rash plan, though apparently he did not strongly disagree with the necessity for some sort of action. Samuel Glover, however, met Lyon's logic with purely legal reasoning. As a lawyer, Glover saw the camp as being lawfully sanctioned by the state for at least the next three days. Moreover, since the national flag was flying over the camp, it was in accordance with the federal government. He agreed that if the munitions from Louisiana were stored at the camp, they were subject to retrieval, but only by legal means: a federal marshal armed with a writ of replevin. Lyon and his troops could assist the marshal, but seizing the camp was manifestly illegal, and Glover refused to assent to Lyon's reckless plan.[20]

Desperate, Lyon played his final hand. He reminded the men of the imminent passage of the military bill currently under debate in the General Assembly. With its passage, the state militia would be a fully funded and permanently sanctioned force that would continue to be dominated by secessionists. Frost could not be allowed to arm the secessionists with government weapons, for that would only aid the governor in leading the

19. Peckham, *Lyon and Missouri,* 137–38; Broadhead, "St. Louis During the War," Broadhead Papers, MHS; Seth Williams to George B. McClellan, May 9, 1861, Letters Sent, Department of the West, vol. 4, RG 393.

20. Peckham, *Lyon and Missouri,* 141; Broadhead, "St. Louis During the War," Broadhead Papers, MHS.

state to join the seceding states. It was not a point of law that was in question but "the supremacy of the Union or Secession authority. The United States flag did not shield loyal Union troops at Fort Sumter, why should the name of the State shield disloyal militia in St. Louis?" Lyon's exhortations caused How to acquiesce, but Glover remained resolute in his opposition. He insisted that a writ of replevin be obtained. Lyon wryly agreed; he had no objection to Glover drawing up the papers. However, he entertained no thoughts of allowing such formalities to interfere with his plan. As he later said to one subordinate, "I have something better than writs; I have powder and ball." The meeting broke up about midnight, but, as Lyon made preparations for the next day's actions, the lights at the arsenal's administration building burned long into the night.[21]

Early on the morning of May 10, Lyon sent orders to the commanders of the volunteer regiments, some of whom were encamped at the Marine Hospital and Jefferson Barracks, and to the various Home Guard commanders, whose units were stationed at their homes throughout the city. They were summoned to proceed immediately with their commands to the arsenal. The converging columns, many of which were not started until after 8:00 A.M., immediately caused the secessionist watchdogs to suspect some sort of hostile action against Camp Jackson. The spies quickly reported the movements to Daniel Frost. The news, however, could not have been very surprising to Frost, for rumors of Lyon's imminent attack had circulated for several days. So pronounced were the reports that Chief of Police James McDonough, appointed by the governor as a member of his police board, had posted patrols near the arsenal and known Home Guard rendezvous buildings. When his sentries reported that German companies were indeed forming and had even received ammunition, and that a number of horses had been taken into the arsenal late the previous afternoon, presumably for hauling artillery, McDonough alerted the board of commissioners. Basil Duke, one of the commissioners and an officer in the State Guard, wasted no time alerting Frost of Lyon's impending movement on his camp.[22]

Whether Lyon knew that his enemies had already ascertained his plans is not known, but he had little time to worry that the element of

21. Rombauer, *Union Cause in St. Louis,* 225; Broadhead, "St. Louis During the War," Broadhead Papers, MHS; *Missouri Democrat,* June 7, 1861.

22. Anderson, *Border City,* 94; Covington, "Camp Jackson Affair," 204; Duke, *Reminiscences,* 50–51; J. Thomas Scharf, *History of Saint Louis City and County,* 2:494.

surprise would not be complete. Organizing even trained troops for a movement such as Lyon's is tedious at best, and often fraught with unforeseen delays. Yet Lyon would ask for even more; with but a few hours' notice he had called upon untried troops, spread throughout the city, to mobilize in the dead of night and move to the arsenal with all possible speed and stealth for an early morning attack. Although his regulars were under marching orders before daybreak, the rest of the operation failed to come off so smoothly. Blair's regiment, stationed at Jefferson Barracks, found their twelve-mile march impeded by the muddy roads created by the night's downpour. The Home Guards straggled in throughout the overcast morning as best they could. Normally excitable, Lyon was on this morning frantic. William T. Sherman (who, sensing something was afoot, had visited the arsenal several times that week) remembered him "running about with his hair in the wind, his pockets full of papers, wild and irregular." However, Lyon was unwilling to move without all of his available troops. He was so obsessed with carrying out his attack before Harney's imminent arrival that by late morning he cared little whether Frost was alerted or not. The risk of open warfare in the middle of an urban center he subordinated to his personal pursuit of vengeance.[23]

Having known Lyon at West Point, Frost perhaps believed that the captain's military training would prevent such a rash act, for he refused to act upon Basil Duke's early morning caveat. By late morning, however, Frost had received enough additional information from his informants to convince him that Lyon was indeed up to something. Though he found it difficult to believe that Lyon would do something so rash, he penned a cautious note to the federal commander:

> Sir—I am constantly in receipt of information that you contemplate an attack upon my camp; whilst I understand you are impressed with the idea that an attack upon the arsenal and United States troops is intended on the part of the militia of Missouri. I am greatly at a loss to know what could justify you in attacking citizens of the United States, who are in the lawful performance of duties devolving upon them, under the Constitution, in organizing and instructing the militia of the State in obedience to her laws, and therefore have been disposed to doubt the correctness of the information I have received.
>
> I would be glad to know from you personally whether there is any truth in the statements that are constantly poured into my ears . . . .

23. "Memorandum on Missouri," 2–3, Franklin A. Dick File, LOC; William T. Sherman, *Memoirs of W. T. Sherman,* 1:172.

Frost sent the message to the arsenal with his chief of staff, Col. John S. Bowen, expecting a written reply from Lyon. His answer arrived in a quite different mode.[24]

Lyon refused even to receive Bowen. Arriving at about 1:00 P.M., just as Lyon's columns were moving from the arsenal, the colonel delivered his note to Lyon's aide, who took it to the federal commander, mounted at the head of the first column on a dapple-gray stallion. Lyon would not read the message. At such a late hour, he cared little for what Frost had to say. Lyon was interested only in organizing his attack, which would proceed in multiple columns along several routes. Two companies remained at the arsenal, while the volunteers, in dark-blue federal uniforms, moved by three separate routes toward Lindell Grove. The Home Guard units marched in four columns, their only semblance to military units being the shining new government muskets and tarred accoutrements each man carried. At about 1:00 P.M., with the once-threatening skies cleared, the seven groups, totaling between six and seven thousand men, started on the six-mile journey to Camp Jackson.[25]

One of the most difficult maneuvers in military science is the coordination of separate forces that are moving on different paths yet are to reach the same destination at approximately the same time. Invariably there are delays or mistakes that confound even the most experienced commanders and troops, much less those who are completely green. Miraculously, though, at about 3:15 P.M. all seven of the columns arrived at Lindell Grove almost simultaneously and quickly surrounded it on three sides, in full view of the encampment. However, because Lyon's troops failed to fill in the south side of the camp as quickly as the other sides, one spectator estimated that at least one-third of the militia escaped in that direction before the federal columns could enclose the entire sixty-acre grounds. Those who ran, however, were jeered derisively by their remaining comrades.

Alerted to the activity at Lindell Grove, throngs of onlookers had followed the Union troops through the streets to the camp, and many

24. Scharf, *History of Saint Louis,* 2:494; D. M. Frost to Lyon, May 10, 1861, in Peckham, *Lyon and Missouri,* 145–46; Rombauer, *Union Cause in St. Louis,* 217.

25. Peckham, *Lyon and Missouri,* 143; Lademann, "Capture of Camp Jackson," 72; Covington, "Camp Jackson Affair," 205; *Missouri Democrat,* May 8–10, 1861. On May 9, 1861, the government bought thirty-six horses to pull the cannon to be used by Lyon in the attack on Camp Jackson. One of those horses, secured by Giles F. Filley, was a dapple-gray stallion, which he earmarked for Lyon's use.

now crowded behind the blue line to watch the show. Still more filled the tops of nearby buildings to take in the entire panorama, oblivious to the potential danger if shooting were to break out. Yet not all were mere spectators. Many of those in the streets had grabbed rifles, pistols, or shotguns and rushed to the camp to assist the state troops when they heard of Lyon's movements. However, they were impeded by two of Lyon's reserve regiments, which he posted east of camp to guard the approaches to it. The armed and agitated civilians milled about the city streets awaiting the outcome of the affair.[26]

Ubiquitous in his efforts to move the columns into their respective positions, Lyon made certain that there were no weak spots in his line. To the east, on elevated ground just beyond the actual encampment, Lyon had his artillery unlimber. From that position, the six guns commanded the entire scene. He directed the commander of his regulars, Capt. Thomas Sweeny, to charge the militia batteries if they opened on any part of his line. Even with so many men, Lyon believed that only the regulars could be counted on, especially against artillery fire. When everything was set exactly as Lyon wanted it, he sent Maj. Ben Farrar to deliver a message to Frost that Lyon had written the night before. Just after Farrar rode off, three loud cheers erupted from the militia camp in what appeared to be a preliminary to their deployment. As a precaution, Sweeny ordered his regulars to move their cartridge boxes around on their belts in case shooting began. All those at the scene waited tensely.[27]

Farrar rode from Lyon's position on the north side across the open meadow and delivered his commander's note to Frost. Already brimming with anger from the injustice of Lyon's action, Frost broke the letter's wax seal and read its icy content:

> Sir—Your command is regarded as evidently hostile to the Government of the United States.
>
> It is for the most part made up of secessionists who have openly avowed their hostility to the General Government, and have been plotting at the seizure of its property and the overthrow of its authority. You are openly in communication with the so-called Southern Confederacy, which is now at war with the United States; and you are receiving at your camp, from said

26. Peckham, *Lyon and Missouri,* 149–50; "Memorandum on Missouri," 3–4, Franklin A. Dick File, LOC; *Missouri Democrat,* May 9, 1861; Scharf, *History of Saint Louis,* 2:497.

27. Peckham, *Lyon and Missouri,* 149–51; "Memorandum on Missouri," 4, Franklin A. Dick File, LOC.

Confederacy and under its flag, large supplies of the material of war, most of which is known to be the property of the United States. These extraordinary preparations plainly indicate none other than the well-known purpose of the Governor of this State, . . . having in direct view hostilities to the General Government and co-operation with its enemies.

In view of these considerations, . . . it is my duty to demand, and I do hereby demand of you, an immediate surrender of your command . . . .[28]

The note gave the militia commander half an hour to comply. Though outraged by Lyon's obvious disregard for state authority, Frost could see that he was in no position to force the issue. After meeting with the other militia officers, he sent Farrar back to Lyon carrying a note asking for a conference between the two men. Lyon read the short missive, flattened the paper on the pommel of his saddle, and on the back scrawled his own peremptory message. Unless he received an unconditional surrender in ten minutes, it read, Lyon would order his men—some now poised less than twenty yards from the camp—to open fire. He then sent the message back to Frost. Upon its receipt, the militia commander believed he had no choice but to submit to Lyon's demands. He sent a final, angry message to the federal commander:

> Sir—I never for a moment conceived the idea that illegal and unconstitutional demands as I have just received from you, would be made by an officer of the United States Army.
>
> I am wholly unprepared to defend my command from this unwarranted attack, and shall, therefore, be forced to comply with your demand.[29]

After a few minutes, a horseman approached the federal command and handed Frost's note to Lyon. He received the message, read it quickly, then announced laconically, "Sweeny, they surrender." As he dismounted from his horse onto Olive Street, many thoughts no doubt ran rapidly through Lyon's mind. He needed to organize the terms of the surrender, the confiscation of weapons, and the escort of hundreds of prisoners back to the arsenal through a crowd growing rapidly in both size and hostility. Apparently, his thoughts raced so quickly that he failed to notice that he was passing quite close to the rear of one of his artillery officers' mounts. Suddenly, the animal wheeled and lashed out with a rear hoof. The blow caught Lyon squarely in the stomach and knocked him completely unconscious. He fell heavily to the ground and lay dou-

28. Peckham, *Lyon and Missouri,* 150–51.
29. Rombauer, *Union Cause in St. Louis,* 232.

bled up, scarcely breathing. As his aides anxiously encircled their fallen commander, trying to revive him, some feared him dead.[30]

At this most inopportune moment, Frost's adjutant, Lt. William Wood, rode up with another message from his commander. Thinking quickly, Sweeny headed off Wood before he could see the stricken federal commander. He directed that the message be placed with him and assured Wood that he would see that it got to Lyon, who was at the moment "occupied." Wood inquired about the government weapons, the mode of evacuation, and whether the militia officers would be allowed to retain their sidearms. Sweeny replied that the officers could retain their sidearms, that the government property would be confiscated, and that his troops would collect and guard all other private property. Wood left without knowing that Lyon lay incapacitated only a few yards away.[31]

A regimental physician attached to one of the nearby German units administered "restoratives" to the stricken federal commander, and after about thirty minutes Lyon had recovered enough to resume command. Pleased with Sweeny's quick decisions, he sent the captain with his two companies of regulars to the camp. After the rest of the command had moved the prisoners to the arsenal, Sweeny's detachment would collect the remaining stores and personal possessions of the militia encampment.

Once Frost's men stacked arms, Lyon gave orders that the militia be given the chance for immediate parole if they would take an oath of allegiance to the federal government. Only ten accepted the offer. Most felt that they had already done so and that taking it again would imply that they had committed a treasonous offense. They therefore opted to be taken prisoners. Although Lyon allowed officers to retain their sidearms, several overzealous German officers demanded that they surrender their swords. Rather than turn them over to the "Dutch swine," several State Guard officers broke their expensive new blades over nearby fence posts.

Considering the size and hostile temperament of the growing crowd, Lyon must have seen the great potential for violence in the streets of west St. Louis. His military training had taught him to avoid at all costs any armed confrontation with civilians in such an emotionally charged atmosphere, and his common sense surely dictated as much. Lyon chose,

30. Peckham, *Lyon and Missouri*, 151–52; "Memorandum on Missouri," 4–5, Franklin A. Dick File, LOC.

31. Peckham, *Lyon and Missouri*, 152; "Memorandum on Missouri," 5, Franklin A. Dick File, LOC.

however, to ignore both his training and his sensibility in order to use Camp Jackson to make a strong, public statement, one that would make his intentions for the city's secessionists unmistakable. In a grandiose show of might, Lyon would march his State Guard prisoners back through the city streets—through the heart of the crowd—to the arsenal. Rather than avoid confrontation, Lyon chose to march squarely into the teeth of it.

For the march back to the arsenal, Lyon split Blair's regiment into two single-ranked columns and placed the 669 captured militia between them. The remaining regiments would fill in behind the prisoners and guard the files. At about 5:30 P.M. the entire procession, with the exception of Sweeny's regulars, began the long march down Olive Street toward the arsenal. Whereas the troops had been silent on the march up, the band now struck up a tune, with drums beating and flags flying.[32]

All along Olive Street, the throngs of onlookers who had followed the troops to Lindell Grove, as well as the many hundreds more who had arrived since the news of the surrender had spread, packed the sidewalks and spilled out into the streets. A great number of the crowd's anti-Unionists jeered and insulted the troops, especially "the Dutch Blackguard." Many had arrived too late to support the militia but were still armed. Many too were drunk. Shouts of "Damn the Dutch!" and "Hurrah for Jeff Davis!" rent the air, while more demonstrative hecklers spat on the columns of volunteers as they marched by.

As the column moved farther from the camp, the crowd's jeering grew louder and more obscene. Soon rocks, brickbats, dirt clods, and other thrown objects began pelting the soldiers. At this inopportune moment, the column was inexplicably halted, perhaps to allow rear units that had fallen behind to catch up. One witness to the riot maintained that during the halt a drunken man, attempting to push through the front of the column to get to the other side of the street, was repulsed by the exasperated Germans. He rose and fired a concealed pistol at the federal troops. Several civilians near him then also fired, though over the heads of the crowd. Although the regulars near the head of the column held their fire, those near the end of the line did not prove so restrained. At least one

32. "Memorandum on Missouri," 5, Franklin A. Dick File, LOC; Scharf, *History of Saint Louis,* 2:496–97; Covington, "Camp Jackson Affair," 207; Peckham, *Lyon and Missouri,* 152–53; Lyon to Lorenzo Thomas, May 11, 1861, in *OR,* III, 1:4–5; Anderson, *Border City,* 98; Sherman, *Memoirs,* 1:173; Lyon to Seth Williams, May 26, 1861, Letters Received, Department of the West, box 10, RG 393.

predominantly German company received more direct fire from an even larger section of the crowd. While trying to restrain his men, Capt. Constantine Blandovski was mortally wounded by the fire. His raw troops responded by shooting at will into the crowd of onlookers. While many spectators ran for their lives, others fell to the ground to evade the whining bullets. In the smoke and confusion, green soldiers were firing at each other, adding to the chaos in the street.

The effect proved contagious, and firing soon erupted along nearly the entire length of the line. William T. Sherman, who upon learning of the militia's surrender unwisely took his son to watch the troops return to the city, soon found himself caught in the fire and threw himself on the ground on top of the boy to protect them both from "the balls cutting the leaves above our heads." At least one man was thrust through with a bayonet after firing at a regimental officer. After several deadly minutes, Lyon and John Schofield (who acted as Lyon's chief aide during the day's action) managed to end the firing, although orders were delayed by the great length of the column. The troops, shaken from the events of the day, arrived back at the arsenal at about dusk. In all, twenty-eight of the crowd were killed and as many as seventy-five others wounded in the brief "massacre." Two of the federal soldiers and three militia prisoners were also killed, while several others were wounded. Through it all, the German band at the head of the column had continued to play.

In his public statement, published in Monday's papers, Lyon refused to accept responsibility for the tragedy. "If innocent men, women, and children," he wrote, "whose curiosity placed them in a dangerous position, suffered with the guilty, it is no fault of the troops." He believed that the fault lay with those who dared to challenge the authority of the government and threaten its stability. As it was his duty to take the camp, so it was the duty of his soldiers to ensure the success of their mission— no matter the cost.[33]

The Camp Jackson affair and its aftermath produced a state of wild alarm in St. Louis. Sara Jane Full Hill remembered that she was quietly sewing in her home near the militia camp when she heard the sound of musket fire. Although many of her neighbors went out to watch what

33. Scharf, *History of Saint Louis,* 2:497–500; Lyon to Lorenzo Thomas, May 11, 1861, in *OR,* III, 1:4–5; *Missouri Democrat,* May 13, 1861; Sherman, *Memoirs,* 1:173–74; Peckham, *Lyon and Missouri,* 153–56; Covington, "Camp Jackson Affair," 208–11; Anderson, *Border City,* 97; Peggy Robbins, "The Battle of Camp Jackson," 41–42; Anderson, *Border City,* 99.

they believed would be more military drills, the shouts and cries in the distance soon made her "aware of something unusual occurring. Soon a neighbor, Mrs. Kempin, an Englishwoman and a secession sympathizer, rushed in wildly excited, crying, 'The Black Dutch! The Black Dutch are killing them all. They are shooting women and children in cold blood . . . .' She was almost incoherent with fright." Chilling rumors circulated freely that the federals had declared martial law in the city and that the Germans would soon seek reprisals on known secessionists for the insults they had taken during the day. Citizens filled the streets in search of news of the tragedy, many heading for speeches being given by prominent local politicians. The largest gathering was in front of the Planters' House, where pro-Southern speakers harangued the German troops and federal leaders for their bloodlust. Uriel Wright, one of the strongest opponents of secession at the recent convention, now declared, "If Unionism means such atrocious deeds as I have witnessed in St. Louis, I am no longer a Union man."

Still others fled the city (as many as ten thousand in the days following Camp Jackson, estimated one correspondent), fearing their lives were in danger from the "murdering Dutch." Steamers filled with refugees left the riverfront for safer environs, while carriages, drays, and wagons commanded exorbitant prices during these hours of panic. Frightened homeowners fastened shutters and doused their lights, while saloons, restaurants, and other businesses closed because of the crowds of armed men roaming the streets. Squads of police were posted at busy street corners, and the police chief placed the offices of local Republican and German newspapers under heavy guard, protecting them from certain destruction. Only a platoon of thirty policemen under the command of Chief James McDonough, armed with muskets and fixed bayonets, saved the offices of the *Missouri Democrat*. Before the night's terror subsided, angry mobs had murdered at least three residents of German extraction. A heavy rainfall late in the evening helped quell the disturbances, but it took until morning for an uneasy calm to settle over the city.[34]

Word of the Camp Jackson affair electrified the entire state. At least

34. Covington, "Camp Jackson Affair," 212; Anderson, *Border City*, 101–8; Lademann, "Capture of Camp Jackson," 74; Lyon to Lorenzo Thomas, May 12, 1861, in *OR*, III, 1:9; Mark M. Krug, ed., *Mrs. Hill's Journal: Civil War Reminiscences, By Sarah Jane Full Hill*, 13–18; Parrish, *Turbulent Partnership*, 24; Broadhead, "St. Louis During the War," Broadhead Papers, MHS; Scharf, *History of Saint Louis*, 2:500–501; Thomas W. Knox, *Camp-Fire and Cotton Field: Southern Adventure in Time of War*, 32.

one wire to the governor, reputedly from J. W. Tucker, editor of the *State Journal* in St. Louis, informed him of "Blair taking Frost." The news placed Jefferson City in a state of excitement as early as 3:00 P.M. Prompted by subsequent rumors that three of Blair's volunteer regiments were marching on Jefferson City, nearly two thousand men mustered under the secession flag. Moreover, about midnight, Jackson ordered the bells in the Missouri capital's church spires to ring, calling an emergency session of the General Assembly. The members of the legislature arrived armed and fearful, and within fifteen minutes of the start of the session, both houses passed the long-debated military bill. The unprecedented act gave the governor sweeping military powers "to Suppress Rebellion and Repel Invasion." Many residents and even several members of the legislature hastily moved their families across the river from the city. "The name of Colonel F. P. Blair," read the afternoon's *Missouri Democrat,* "seems to strike terror to all—the Governor, the officers, and the Assembly." Jackson sent out several State Guard companies with orders to burn the bridges leading into the capital if the patrols spotted any troops. None materialized, but the nervous troops still partially destroyed the Osage River bridge. "The rain of *perfect teror has* commenced," wrote one resident. "They are terably alarmed."[35]

Continued rain failed to prevent a recurrence of bloodshed in St. Louis the following day. While Mayor Daniel Taylor attempted to preserve the peace by issuing a proclamation requesting that saloon owners close their establishments "during the continuance of the present excitement," Tucker's *State Journal* kept tempers high with its disparaging editorials. "*This man Lyon,* alias 'Numidian Lyon' alias 'Lyon the murderer,'" began one such indictment. In one incident, Charles Stifel's Home Guard regiment was fired upon as it returned from the arsenal to its barracks on the north side of the city. It returned fire, and in the ensuing melee twelve persons were killed, including two soldiers. St. Louis was a powderkeg ready to explode.

Lyon's initial efforts seemed only to exacerbate the volatile situation. The regulars brought the captured stores from Camp Jackson through the city streets to the arsenal, and Lyon insisted that troops be stationed at the Pacific Railroad depot to prevent rural militia from moving to the

35. Kirkpatrick, "Missouri on the Eve," 239–40; Parrish, *Turbulent Partnership,* 24–25; Broadhead, "St. Louis During the War," Broadhead Papers, MHS; Allen P. Richardson to Broadhead, May 11, 1861, ibid.; *Missouri Democrat,* May 11, 1861.

city. In an effort to control the spreading violence, Lyon placed Sweeny in command of the Home Guard, hoping that his regular army training would bring some discipline to the unpredictable volunteers. In addition, Lyon released all prisoners upon the administration of a verbal oath to the men in the ranks and a signed oath to all the State Guard officers. Although Frost, in anticipation of Harney's return, prepared a letter of protest to the department commander concerning the "additional indignity" of being forced to take the superfluous oaths, all but one of the militia were eager enough to return home that they took them prior to Harney's arrival. To avoid further confrontation, Lyon sent the parolees around the city on a steamer and debarked them at the upper levee.[36]

William Harney arrived in the city late that afternoon amid the tumultuous aftermath of the Camp Jackson affair. Aghast at the turmoil in the streets, he personally viewed Stifel's Home Guard exchanging shots with its assailants. Hastening to his home, he met that afternoon with several "old acquaintances," including such leading St. Louis conservatives as Robert Campbell, James E. Yeatman, and ex-mayor Washington King. From them, he received a briefing on Lyon's reckless act, and they pleaded with Harney to somehow rid the city of the red-headed menace. Surprisingly, Harney demurred. Although he disapproved of the rioting that he had witnessed in the streets, Harney did not take a strong stand against his subordinate's coup. However, he pledged either to disband the Home Guards or at the very least to remove them to Jefferson Barracks, as they appeared to be "the sole cause of irritation and disturbance" in the city. This minor concession, however, failed to placate the conservatives.[37]

The next morning, May 12, Harney met with Blair and informed him of his intention to disarm or remove the Home Guards from the city limits. Blair was undaunted. He showed Harney his order, signed by the

36. Peckham, *Lyon and Missouri,* 158–59, 162–63, 190; Scharf, *History of Saint Louis,* 2:509; Lyon to "Commanding Officers of the U.S. Reserve Corps," May 11, 1861, Thomas J. Sweeny Collection, Huntington; Lyon to Seth Williams, May 17, 1861, Letters Received, Department of the West, box 10, RG 393; Lyon to Williams, May 26, 1861, ibid.; Unsigned report, undated, Abiel Leonard Papers, MHS; D. M. Frost to Harney, May 11, 1861, in Logan U. Reavis, *The Life and Military Services of Gen. William Selby Harney,* 359–61.

37. Harney to War Department, May 13, 1861, in Reavis, *Life and Services of Harney,* 361–62; John McNeil to L. U. Reavis, February 27, 1878, ibid., 385–86; Ashbel Woodward, *Life of General Nathaniel Lyon,* 260; Peckham, *Lyon and Missouri,* 181, 184, 191.

president, authorizing the enlistment of the locals in defense of the city and giving Lyon command over them. Harney had no power to override the president's wishes. After a long and heated conversation, the general at last assented to his lack of authority. That afternoon, he issued a public statement trying to ameliorate the city's situation. He announced that he regretted the "deplorable state of things existing here," but the "past cannot be recalled. I can only deal with the present and the future." Harney promised to "carefully abstain from the exercise of any unnecessary powers" and to resort to martial law only as a last resort. Furthermore, if troops were needed to keep peace, he would use only regulars, not locals. However, he conceded that he had "no authority to change the location of the 'Home Guards.'"[38]

The reasons for Harney's apparent change of attitude can only be inferred. Despite returning to the city in the midst of the general conflagration he had tried so desperately to avoid, he appeared now actually to *condone* Lyon's actions. In his report to the army, Harney went so far as to say that "the conduct of Captain Lyon on the occasion meets with my entire approval." Although most of the people of St. Louis credited Harney with restoring peace to the city, the conservative politicos failed to understand his mild stance toward Lyon. Since Harney had brushed so recently with dismissal for lack of resolve, it is more than plausible that the general was reluctant to again challenge Blair and his "machine." Yet, if his behavior was staged, it seems to have worked. After visiting with the general, Illinois senator Lyman Trumbull wrote confidently to an acquaintance, "Harney was not quite up to the mark on his first arrival, but I think has come to it now."[39]

Privately, however, Harney held somewhat different sentiments about the affair. Although he acknowledged that at Camp Jackson there were "indisputably clear . . . evidences of its treasonable purposes," Harney believed Lyon had too zealously applied Lincoln's proclamation "ordering the dispersion of all armed rebels hostile to the United States" in pursuit of his own "high and imperative duty." However, Harney's recent

38. Frank Blair to Montgomery Blair, May 20, 1861, Blair Papers, box 3, LOC; John McNeil to L. U. Reavis, February 27, 1878, in Reavis, *Life and Services of Harney,* 386; Peckham, *Lyon and Missouri,* 184.

39. Harney to E. D. Townsend, May 13, 1861, in OR, I, 3:369–70; T. T. Gantt to Harney, May 14, 1861, in Reavis, *Life and Services of Harney,* 365–67; Lyman Trumbull to James P. Doolittle, May 16, 1861, in Duane Mowry, ed., "A Statesman's Letters of the Civil War Period," 47; Lucy Hutchinson to Robert M. Hutchinson, May 22, 1861, Civil War Collection, MHS.

trip to Washington had persuaded him that he must publicly uphold his government's right to take such drastic measures if deemed necessary— even to the extent of feigning support for Lyon's rash actions at Camp Jackson. "His action in the premises I recognize, therefore," he wrote to an acquaintance, "as imposing upon me the obligation of assuming the consequences of his proceedings so far as to abstain from pursuing any course which, by implication, might throw a doubt upon the sufficiency of his authority." However, Harney resolved that if he could not disarm the Home Guard, he would attempt to neutralize them by refusing to allow them to act in concert with either the regulars or volunteers. In effect, Harney attempted to ensure that he would never again have need to call them out.[40]

Despite Harney's efforts to bring the city back on a sound footing, the effects of Camp Jackson were in many ways irreversible. Tactically, Lyon's coup achieved its intended results. It eliminated the threat posed to the arsenal by the organized and armed body of militia, many of whom were known secessionists. It allowed him to confiscate the federal arms shipped from the Baton Rouge arsenal, especially the heavy artillery pieces that would have rendered untenable the arsenal's defense. Finally, the Camp Jackson affair quashed secessionist spirit in the city. "It operated like a poultice," recalled James Broadhead, "the inflammation has been drawn out of a great number of men who were heretofore rampant secessionists . . . ." A pro-Southern resident bemoaned the state of affairs following Lyon's attack: "We are so bound down by military despotism here . . . that we hardly dare say our souls are our own for fear our loved ones may be cut off forever in expression of opinion in favor of the South . . . . Those soldiers who were liberated on parole are threatened every day with re-arrest. Our city is almost as silent as the grave . . . . We are bound down hand and foot under a slavery worse than Egyptian." When the newspapers reported that Yates's Illinois troops were encamped across the river at various locations, one resident's despair was complete. "Frank Blair is Dictator," he lamented, "he had assembled troops from all parts of Illinois . . . all within an hour's ride and if the slightest show of resistance is made we will be crushed out."[41]

40. Harney to Judge [Samuel] Treat, May 15, 1861, in Reavis, *Life and Services of Harney,* 369–70; Lyon to Seth Williams, May 20, 1861, Letters Received, Department of the West, box 10, RG 393.

41. Broadhead to Edwin Draper, May 21, 1861, Broadhead Papers, MHS; Lucy

On a strategic level, however, Camp Jackson would prove, as one historian has termed it, a "colossal blunder." The vote of the state convention had already rendered Lyon's actions a fait accompli, and thus wholly unnecessary. The actions of the secessionists were a mere chimera of the true sentiment of the state. Although the relationship was tenuous, Missouri had shown for the Union. However, she had stated in no uncertain terms that she would tolerate no coercion by the federal government. By representing that government as a coercive power, Lyon changed the relationship, as well as the attitudes of those who had previously maintained a shoestring loyalty to the Union. The most immediate effect was that the legislature passed the military bill, thus arming the state for war. Despite the governor's efforts, it is doubtful that such a drastic measure would have passed prior to a full-scale invasion by one of the two opposing armies. And while Camp Jackson cowed St. Louis's secessionists, the result was just the opposite in much of Missouri's interior. Rather than becoming intimidated, thousands of those most disaffected flocked in patriotic rage to recruiting stations for the State Guard. Three Camp Jackson parolees raised forty men who traveled south to enlist in the Confederate army, seeking to liberate their home city and state from the "Goths and Vandels" who had taken control. "My blood boils in my veins," wrote one resident, "when I think of the position of Missouri—held in the Union at the point of Dutchmen's bayonets—I feel outraged . . . but the sullen submission of downtrodden men will be avenged the more terribly in the days of their uprising—may I live to see that day." Another wrote, "The time has arrived when every patriot ought to show his hand, acting in stern and harmonious action, until the iron heel of the despot shall be removed from the neck of Missouri." Still another sent a ringing indictment to James Broadhead: "I see your name coupled with those of Lyon, Blair, How and others, whome all honest Missourians curse with a deep and bitter hatred . . . ." M. Jeff Thompson quickly offered his services to the State Guard, then wrote caustically that he "proposed a plan to the *Council of War,* to make a *speedy and bloodless peace,*" which was "to *burn all the breweries*

Hutchinson to Robert Hutchinson, May 22, 1861, Civil War Collection, MHS; Unsigned, May 20, 1861, ibid.; Richard Yates to John McClernand, May 15, 1861, in William B. Hesseltine, *Lincoln and the War Governors,* 216. What the resident did not realize was that Governor Yates positioned his troops near St. Louis to defend Illinois against invasion from Missouri's secessionists in the event that Lyon's attack on Camp Jackson ended in defeat and subsequent conflagration.

and declare *Lager beer to be contraband of war.* But this means the DUTCH will all *die in a week,* and the yankees will then run from the state." Thompson's sentiment rang throughout the state. Lyon's victory at Camp Jackson would soon prove Pyrrhic, for he and Blair—through their own blind ambitions—had plunged Missouri into the vortex of war.[42]

In St. Louis, Harney's apparent change of attitude led some of the city's leading moderates to meet in the mayor's office on the night of May 11 to decide the best course for its continued safety. In the backs of their minds, most wished to eliminate Lyon from the St. Louis scene, though one committee member maintains that the subject was never directly discussed. The committee selected James E. Yeatman, a local banker and one of the group's more politically influential members, to leave on the next train for Washington to "represent to the President what they considered injurious to the government" and to urge Lincoln to disarm the Home Guard as "there was likely to be engendered a feeling of bitterness and hostility which would . . . bring about a fude of nationalities which would last through long years to come." The men would wire ahead to Hamilton Gamble, already in Pennsylvania, and implore him to join Yeatman in Washington. Together the two would then call on Attorney General Edward Bates, in whom the moderates felt confident they would find a sympathetic ear in a place high enough to counter Blair's juggernaut.[43]

When word of the meeting leaked out, one of the first ears it caught was Franklin Dick's, who quickly surmised that the committee must have concluded to depose Lyon. Hurriedly he conferred with Blair, and the two decided that Dick must travel to Washington and meet with Montgomery Blair in Lyon's defense. Blair then alerted Lyon, who all along had refused to believe that Harney genuinely supported him. The general's return disgusted Lyon thoroughly. He believed that Harney was in league with the moderates to thwart any future plans he might lay. Lyon

---

42. Shoemaker, *History of Missouri,* 154; Unsigned, May 20, 1861, Civil War Collection, MHS; Lucy Hutchinson to Robert Hutchinson, May 22, 1861, ibid.; M. Jeff Thompson to Charles M. Thompson, May 29, 1861, ibid.; William C. Lane to Sterling Price, June 3, 1861, William Carr Lane Papers, MHS; J. D. McKown to Son, May 29, 1861, McKown Papers, SHSM; "Reminiscences of Patrick Ahearn," Mrs. Jesse P. Henry Papers, MHS; Frank Carr to Broadhead, July 4, 1861, Broadhead Papers, MHS; "Diary of Elvira A. W. Scott," 78–79, Elvira A. W. Scott File, SHSM.

43. Peckham, *Lyon and Missouri,* 191–94; James Yeatman to Hamilton R. Gamble, June 23, 1863, Hamilton R. Gamble Papers, MHS.

wrote to Washington that the old general once again "embarrasses, in the most painful manner, the execution of the plans I had contemplated." Having tasted power, Lyon could not abide anyone riding herd on him in Missouri. Yet even he feared that his Camp Jackson affair had been a move far too radical for the administration and that he now had "many enemies in high places." Accordingly, Lyon convinced Dr. Charles Bernays, editor of the *Anzeiger des Westens,* one of the city's German newspapers, to travel to the nation's capital on his behalf. Bernays was a close personal friend of the president, and because he supported Lyon, he agreed to try to convince Lincoln that the capture of the rebel camp had indeed been justified. In addition, Lyon requested that Bernays secure an order again removing Harney from command. Thus, the race to reach Lincoln was on.[44]

Yeatman and Gamble reached Washington a day ahead of Dick and met immediately with Bates. The attorney general, proud of his Whig conservatism, had been a successful lawyer and politician in Missouri since 1814. When Bates had failed to receive the Republican nomination for president, Lincoln had named him to his cabinet, its first member from west of the Mississippi. Bates was particularly concerned with the volatile political situation of his home state. In an April 15 memorandum to the president, Bates had outlined his suggestions for the nation's defense, arguing that "the safety of St. Louis ought to be ensured" even ahead of the protection of the federal capital. Yet Bates would not be as easily moved to call for Lyon's removal as the St. Louis moderates believed.[45]

Since early in the secession crisis, Bates had kept in touch with the Committee of Safety and wholly approved of its efforts to keep peace in St. Louis. Had the Camp Jackson affair occurred earlier, Bates would probably have condemned Lyon for a needless violation of state law and public peace. However, by early May, Bates's thinking was closer to the president's: the federal government must act swiftly and decisively to crush the rebellion by the Southern states. Therefore, he upheld Lin-

---

44. Lyon to Lorenzo Thomas, May 12, 1861, in OR, III, 1:9; Peckham, *Lyon and Missouri,* 194–201; Parrish, *Turbulent Partnership,* 27; *Westliche Post,* June 5, 1861, in Steven Rowan and James Neal Primm, eds., *Germans for a Free Missouri: Translations from the St. Louis Radical Press, 1857–1862,* 253–54.

45. Hendrick, *Lincoln's War Cabinet,* 56–60; Howard K. Beale, ed., *The Diary of Edward Bates,* 182–83; Franklin A. Dick to Benjamin Farrar, May 16, 1861, in Peckham, *Lyon and Missouri,* 195–96.

coln's use of implied power to suspend the writ of habeas corpus and, upon hearing of Camp Jackson, Lyon's use of his own implied authority. Barton Bates, who kept his father apprised of the situation in St. Louis, also supported Lyon's vigorous actions, no doubt influencing Bates's stance. And perhaps as important, Bates still owed Frank Blair a large political debt for Blair's unqualified support prior to the 1860 Republican nominating convention. The scholarly Bates would not be pushed hastily into withdrawing his support for strong measures in his home state, even by his old law partner and brother-in-law, Hamilton Gamble.[46]

Upon his arrival in Washington, Franklin Dick rushed to the postmaster general's office and hurriedly delivered to Montgomery Blair the message from Frank Blair. Armed with a lengthy correspondence endorsing Lyon and Camp Jackson that was signed by each member of the Committee of Safety, Dick insisted upon Lyon's importance in St. Louis and condemned Harney for trying to effect the captain's ouster. The two went immediately to the White House and found the president in conference with Bates, Secretary of the Interior Caleb Smith, and Secretary of War Simon Cameron. Yeatman and Gamble had already met with Bates, and though unable to convince him to remove Lyon, they had managed to persuade him to defend Harney's competence as commander in St. Louis. When the newest St. Louis contingent arrived, Lincoln invited Dick to air his views. His unqualified defense of Lyon favorably impressed the president, but Dick's message only solidified what Lincoln was already beginning to believe.

While publicly upholding Missouri's neutrality in an effort to keep it and the other border slave states loyal to the Union, the president had become increasingly convinced that strong measures would be necessary to ensure that outcome. This was revolution, and if necessary, revolutionary measures must be employed to suppress it. Rather than lose the border by inaction (thus costing him, in his words, "the whole game"), Lincoln had already opted for action in Maryland. The question now was whether the forceful tactics that had worked there would work as well in Missouri. In Lyon's favor, the president relied upon the Blairs to appraise the situation in Missouri, and both they and Bates supported Lyon's retention in St. Louis. Therefore, though the capture of Camp

46. Marvin C. Cain, *Lincoln's Attorney General: Edward Bates of Missouri*, 19, 138–40, 143–44; Barton Bates to Edward Bates, June 3, 1861, Bates Family Papers, MHS; Milton E. Bierbaum, "The Rhetoric of Union or Disunion in Missouri, 1844–1861," 301.

Jackson directly contradicted Lincoln's pledge against federal coercion of Missouri, the president was willing to risk keeping Lyon, who was obviously ready to fight for the Union, in the event that Harney proved unable to handle a future escalation in Missouri.[47]

While Dick spoke, Montgomery Blair drafted a memo removing Harney as commander of the Department of the West for a second time. Simultaneously, it promoted Lyon to the rank of brigadier general of volunteers. However, Lincoln did not immediately sign the note. While he was inclined to keep him, the president was a prudent man, and he worried about Lyon. Was he truly the best man for the situation, or would he prove merely a loose cannon? He had not completely made up his mind. Because of Bates's opposition, and because fellow Illinoisan Lyman Trumbull had visited personally with Harney, Blair, and Lyon shortly after Camp Jackson and believed the department commander was now truly alive to the situation, Lincoln instead sent the note on to Winfield Scott for his opinion.[48]

Later that night, Scott mistakenly turned the memorandum into a special order. There was some difficulty in promoting Lyon to his new rank in the volunteers since it was necessary to excuse him from duty in the regular army with a leave of absence. Montgomery Blair apparently convinced Cameron of the need for the irregular request, and the secretary of war had cleared the way for Lyon's promotion. By early the next morning, the Adjutant General's Office had readied Special Order no. 135. Moreover, Blair had, with great difficulty, convinced Cameron to grant Frank Blair the power of discretion in presenting Harney with his leave of absence. He should deliver it, wrote the postmaster general, "only, if in his judge it is now deemed advisable to relieve him from command." Montgomery believed that Harney suffered most from weak judgment, and that in using his authority, Frank must use extreme caution.[49]

When Lincoln heard that Scott had issued the order to relieve Harney,

47. Franklin A. Dick to Benjamin Farrar, May 16, 1861, Blair Papers, box 39, LOC; Broadhead, "St. Louis During the War," Broadhead Papers, MHS; Stephen B. Oates, *With Malice Toward None*, 254–56; Bruce Catton, "Lincoln's Difficult Decisions," 6–7.

48. Franklin A. Dick to Benjamin Farrar, May 16, 1861, Blair Papers, box 39, LOC; Lyman Trumbull to James R. Doolittle, May 16, 1861, in Mowry, "A Statesman's Letters," 47.

49. Franklin A. Dick to Benjamin Farrar, May 16, 1861, Blair Papers, box 39, LOC; Dick to Farrar, May 17, 1861, ibid.; Montgomery Blair to Frank Blair, May 17, 1861, ibid.

he was taken aback. He had not intended for Scott to send the order without his own final confirmation. Lincoln seriously doubted the propriety of giving Frank Blair the power to make such an important decision. Missouri was too vital a state, and since Blair and the other radicals scorned Harney so adamantly, he worried that Frank Blair was too close to the subject to be objective. Many were convinced that the general was genuinely interested in keeping peace in the explosive city, even if his beliefs on the safety of the arsenal seemed naively complacent. Harney could prove to be an important ally in the coming war, and Lincoln wanted to ensure that the general's loyalties—like those of Missouri itself—would not swing to the South. Moreover, the president worried about the appearance of vacillation in the eyes of the St. Louis public by relieving, reinstating, and again relieving Harney. Lincoln needed to make a quick decision.

After pondering the vexing question overnight, on May 18 the president wrote a letter to Frank Blair in which he requested that Blair use discretion in serving Harney with the notice. While he did not countermand Scott's orders, he wanted Blair to be absolutely sure of his decision before acting. By allowing Blair to retain the power of discretion, Lincoln would appease the radicals clamoring for Harney's removal. At the same time, he would make clear to Blair the gravity of his responsibility in the president's eyes. "Still," Lincoln maintained, "if in your judgment, it is *indispensable,* let it be so."[50]

As the opposing emissaries sparred over Lyon and Harney in Washington, Harney's about-face in St. Louis continued to shock the city's conservatives. On May 14, he issued a public proclamation condemning the military bill as "an indirect secession ordinance" that "cannot and ought not to be upheld or regarded by the good citizens of Missouri." Most dramatic, however, was the fact that though he avoided "comment upon the official conduct of my predecessor in command of this department," Harney fully supported Lyon's capture of Camp Jackson. "No Government in the world," he wrote, "would be entitled to respect that would tolerate for a moment such openly treasonable preparations." Moreover, on the day prior to his proclamation he sent a message to Winfield Scott stating that he approved of "Captain Lyon's conduct in capturing the State troops." Finally, in attempting to maintain order in

50. Abraham Lincoln to Frank Blair, May 18, 1861, in Peckham, *Lyon and Missouri,* 210.

the city, Harney had rankled many of the conservatives by stationing volunteer troops at various points. Harney was attempting to pacify the turmoil in the city, yet his methods seemed dictated by radicals, not conservatives.[51]

Lyon did nothing to allay the moderates' fears when, on May 15, he ordered a small detachment to the town of Potosi, sixty-five miles southwest of St. Louis, to arrest secessionists who were harassing local Unionists. The company released all but nine of the fifty-six they arrested, but they confiscated a large quantity of lead and a secessionist flag, which they took to the arsenal. Moreover, on May 18, he sent a similar mission through Hillsboro and Ironton, where it took more prisoners and confiscated more lead. By moving outside his sphere of influence in St. Louis, Lyon ruffled the feathers of even more of the state's secessionists.[52]

Foremost among them was former Missouri governor Sterling Price. A veteran of the Mexican War, Price had chaired the state's secession convention, but while not favoring secession, he supported slavery. Loyal to his state, Price opposed Lyon's coercive actions in St. Louis but had angered Governor Jackson with his moderate stance. However, the Camp Jackson affair quickly drove Price from the conservative ranks, and he immediately tendered his services to the governor as commander of the Missouri State Guard. Jackson at first distrusted Price, but his lieutenant governor, Thomas C. Reynolds, convinced him that a man of Price's stature could prove most beneficial to their cause, both militarily and politically. Buoyed by the encouraging number of enlistments in the Jefferson City State Guard, on May 12 Jackson granted Price the command. Price's first action was to order the militia's eight brigadier generals to organize the men in their respective districts and hold them in readiness for defense against further federal incursions.[53]

The governor believed that Camp Jackson had precluded any further possibility of peaceful secession. Accordingly, he wanted time to recruit and train the state militia and to solicit aid from the Confederate government. Above all, Jackson needed time, and Lyon appeared far too aggressive to leave things to chance. Realizing that Harney was interested in conciliation, Jackson believed that his only chance to buy such pre-

51. Proclamation of W. S. Harney, May 14, 1861, in OR, I, 3:371–72; Snead, *Fight for Missouri*, 177–79; *Missouri Democrat*, May 17, 1861.
52. Nelson Cole to Lyon, May 16, 1861, in OR, III, 1:10–11; Lyon to Seth Williams, May 23, 1861, Letters Received, Department of the West, box 10, RG 393.
53. Shalhope, *Sterling Price*, 159; Albert Castel, *General Sterling Price and the Civil War in the West*, 14; Parrish, *Turbulent Partnership*, 26.

cious time was to dupe the old general into some form of agreement of neutrality. He had no intention, however, of honoring any such arrangement. Jackson sent overtures of peace to both the department commander and the Committee of Safety, promising to disband the State Guard if Harney would assert that he entertained no hostile intention of marching on the state capital. He then requested a meeting between the two men for the sake of peace. At the same time, Thomas Reynolds—impatient with the governor's apparent placidity—took it upon himself to leave for Richmond, Virginia, to gain Confederate military assistance.[54]

At Harney's invitation, Jackson agreed to a May 20 meeting in St. Louis. The governor, however, would not personally attend; for more than a month, he avoided travel to the city for fear of being arrested for treason. Perhaps he knew that his fears were justified, for Edward Bates had indeed instructed U.S. Attorney James Broadhead to draw up a warrant for the governor's arrest. Though Broadhead had the papers in hand, upon learning of the intended meeting he opted to wait until after the results of the meeting with Harney became known before serving them. Jackson, however, refused to take such a chance, and in his stead sent Major General Price to meet with the federal commander.[55]

The two men met at Harney's 10th Street office. Harney found Price most congenial and placed confidence in the former governor's "honor and integrity," in the "purity of his motives, and in his loyalty to the Government." Neither man believed that coercion was the best policy for Missouri, and they agreed on the need for the state's continued neutrality. They drafted a formal agreement that the state would assume responsibility for keeping order in Missouri, and that so long as order was maintained, Harney would take no military action that might provoke conflict between state and federal forces. This, they felt, was the best course for Missouri's future. Pleased by the agreement, in the next few days both men grew more confident that the pact had indeed tranquilized the troubled state.[56]

On the same day that Harney and Price met, the letters from Wash-

54. Gerald Gannon, "The Harney-Price Agreement," 42; Snead, Fight for Missouri, 185–87; Allen P. Richardson to Broadhead, May 20, 1861, Broadhead Papers, MHS.

55. Gannon, "Harney-Price Agreement," 42; Snead, Fight for Missouri, 185–87; Allen P. Richardson to Broadhead, April 24, 1861, Broadhead Papers, MHS; Edward Bates to Broadhead, May 3, 1861, ibid.; Broadhead to Edwin Draper, May 21, 1861, ibid.

56. Shalhope, Sterling Price, 161; Harney to John O'Fallon, May 1, 1861, in Reavis, Life and Services of Harney, 388–92; Harney to Lorenzo Thomas, June 5, 1861, in OR, I, 3:383; Harney to E. D. Townsend, May 29, 1861, ibid., 376.

ington arrived at Frank Blair's office, making official Lyon's promotion. Lyon happened to be present at the time, and he expressed his utmost thanks to Blair for all his efforts. Blair took Montgomery Blair's directives about Harney with all seriousness and pocketed the dismissal orders. Despite criticisms that the old general was "no match for the men he is dealing with in cunning and sharpness," and that he would "lose his head so far as to confound the essential distinctions between loyalty and treason," Blair was convinced that Harney was "doing good service" and believed that "we shall make him serviceable to us in the end." For the moment, at least, he saw no reason to force him to leave the city.[57]

On May 22, the afternoon newspapers published the Harney-Price agreement. The agreement elicited generally favorable responses from the state's moderates, and the *Missouri Democrat* congratulated the two men "upon the recovery of a little common sense." Lyon and Blair, however, were sickened by what they considered to be Harney's craven condescension to the secessionists. Yet the news surprised neither man, for Harney had earlier intimated that he intended to make the agreement, against the advice of Blair and several other radicals. "All our Union people are disgusted with this treaty," Lyon wrote to Miner Knowlton, "and Gen. Harney gets roundly scolded; for it is regarded only a trick of the secession Governor, to gain time, get arms and prepare again for war . . . . The very Government against which the secessionists have been so long and are still conspiring, is thus used to shield them from the just consequences of their own treachery." Those "just consequences" Lyon was unable to dole out while Harney remained in command. Impetuously, he demanded that Blair serve the general his notice without any further delay.[58]

Yet Lyon had other reasons for wanting to send his commander packing. Besides the fact that Harney had effectively rendered the Home Guard a shadow force, he had also ordered Lyon to cease all citizen searches, a precaution Lyon considered essential to maintaining peace. Similarly, he had even ordered Lyon to discontinue searching riverboats for munitions and to release the *J. C. Swon,* the boat used to transport the illegal arms to Camp Jackson, which Lyon had captured on May 22

57. Peckham, *Lyon and Missouri,* 209–10; T. T. Gantt to Montgomery, May 21, 1861, Blair Papers, box 29, LOC; Frank Blair to Montgomery Blair, May 20, 1861, Blair Papers, box 3, LOC; Frank Blair to Montgomery Blair, May 22, 1861, ibid.
58. Frank Blair to Montgomery Blair, May 25, 1861, Blair Papers, box 3, LOC; Allen P. Richardson to Broadhead, May 24, 1861, Broadhead Papers, MHS; Lyon to Miner Knowlton, May 26, 1861, in Woodward, *Life of Nathaniel Lyon,* 260–61.

thirty miles south of the city. Moreover, Harney refused to heed requests that commissioned United States officers be allowed to lead the untrained volunteer and Home Guard regiments, a denial even Blair regarded as "damned absurdity." Finally, the general had curtailed Lyon's irregular purchases of supplies that were not requisitioned through the department. Because Lyon did not trust the quartermaster, Maj. Justus McKinstry, he had avoided dealing with him while Harney was away. Now Harney was effectively currying favor with the press, the public, and the government, while also interfering with Lyon's plans for protecting the city and state.[59]

Although Blair agreed completely with Lyon's remonstrances against the department commmander, he felt obligated to abide by Lincoln's wishes. Blair held immense respect for the president and wanted to allow Harney the opportunity to put his policy to the test. However, while Blair genuinely hoped that it would work, in the next week it became obvious that it would not. Daily telegrams soon flooded the desks of Blair, Lyon, and the Committee of Safety, claiming secessionist depredations against Unionists across the state. Moreover, despite the agreement, the buildup of men and arms in secessionist camps continued unabated. Other wires reported rumors of invasion from both the recently seceded state of Arkansas and the Indian Territory. Some of the messages claimed that the Harney-Price arrangement was merely a subterfuge, intended to afford the governor time "to arm the state and place it in a condition successfully to resist the Federal authority." The reports were so strong that they became known even in Washington, prompting the president to direct a letter to Harney ordering him to use any necessary force to suppress partisan activities against loyal citizens: "The authority of the United States is paramount; and whenever it is apparent that a movement, whether by color of State authority or not, is hostile, you will not hesitate to put it down." Blair was quickly beginning to lean toward Lyon's pleas for the department commander's removal.[60]

59. Seth Williams to Lyon, May 19, 1861, Letters Sent, Department of the West, vol. 4, RG 393; Williams to Lyon, May 25, 1861, ibid.; Williams to Lyon, May 17, 1861, ibid.; Williams to Lyon, May 24, 1861, ibid.; Williams to Lyon, May 27, 1861, ibid.; Woodward, *Life of Nathaniel Lyon,* 262; Frank Blair to Montgomery Blair, May 2, 1861, Blair Papers, box 3, LOC; Lyon to Williams, May 20, 1861, Letters Received, Department of the West, box 10, RG 393; Lyon to Williams, May 23, 1861, ibid.; Benjamin Farrar to Montgomery Blair, May 29, 1861, in Reavis, *Life and Services of Harney,* 377–78; Edward G. Longacre, "A Profile of General Justus McKinstry," 15–16.

60. Peckham, *Lyon and Missouri,* 210–19; Lorenzo Thomas to W. S. Harney, May 27, 1861, in ibid., 220; Edward C. Smith, *Borderland in the Civil War,* 248–49; Frank

On May 26, Harney's death knell sounded. A fully armed and outfitted company of Zouaves, resplendent in their outlandish vests and bil-
lowing pantaloons, offered their services to the department commander
and to the United States government. After interviewing the officers for
just a few moments, the general advised them wearily to return to their
homes since the government had enough troops already. Insulted by
Harney's perplexing attitude, the men reported immediately to the arsenal and sought out Lyon, who found the entire situation untenable.
Angry, he said to them: "You are a fine-looking body of men, and no
doubt ought to be accepted. But General Harney has the power; I have
not. Had I the authority, I would take you, and all others presenting
themselves. I'd finish this business up at once, by putting the traitors in
such a position they could not organize . . . ."

At that moment, Lyon resolved that Harney's vacuousness must no
longer be allowed to impede the Union cause. The state was in great
jeopardy of being lost to the governor's growing ranks of secessionists,
and every day that Harney remained in office gave the traitors added life.
Lyon advised the group to write to the secretary of war for authority to
be mustered, and he promised that he and Blair would do the same.
Concluding his interview with the Zouave leaders, he reassured them,
"You had better keep up your spirits and organization. The present state
of affairs cannot last long."[61]

Lyon was right. On the evening of May 30, Benjamin Farrar was
ushered into Harney's home and delivered the War Department's correspondence of May 16, relieving the general of command of the Department of the West. Earlier in the day, Blair had written a long letter to the
president justifying his actions. In it he defended Lyon's attack on Camp
Jackson, where he believed the captain saw "formidable preparations
which were being made by the authorities to commence war upon the
United States, and knowing that these preparations had long been on
foot, and extended to all parts of the State, [Lyon] felt it to be his duty to
strike a decisive blow at the enemy, at a time when his forces were
relatively so much the larger . . . ."[62]

Blair to Montgomery Blair, May 25, 1861, Blair Papers, box 3, LOC; Richard C.
Vaughn to Broadhead, May 30, 1861, Broadhead Papers, MHS; *Missouri Democrat,*
May 22, 1861.

    61. Peckham, *Lyon and Missouri,* 220–21.

    62. Harney to Lorenzo Thomas, May 31, 1861, in *OR,* I, 3:381; Peckham, *Lyon and
Missouri,* 222–25; Special Order no. 135, May 16, 1861, in Reavis, *Life and Services of
Harney,* 381.

Harney's initial reaction to the letter was disbelief. He was convinced that his agreement with Price had already proven effective, that he had secured a "bloodless victory" for the state, and that the reports from the interior were for the most part fabrications. Judging by Price's response to his letters, the former governor appeared to be upholding the agreement, thus guaranteeing peace in Missouri. The general sent a letter to Washington the following morning, insisting that "it was not the intention of the President I should be relieved." By that afternoon, he realized the truth. Harney's disbelief then turned to anger. After reputedly tearing up the note, he retired to his farm in Jefferson County to await further orders. A week later, he fired off a virulent letter to the adjutant general in which he defended his actions in pursuit of peace and protested against such an "unmerited disgrace [inflicted] upon a true and loyal soldier." He then requested a transfer to California. His remonstrances, however, apparently went unheard. Harney remained on his farm, waiting for orders, as the state he had fought so hard to keep out of war sundered before his disbelieving eyes.[63]

Blair's decision, however, received nearly full support in Washington, with the notable exception of Edward Bates. Wary of Lyon's temerity when making decisions, the attorney general advocated that Missouri be placed under the jurisdiction of the commander of the Department of the Ohio, Brig. Gen. George B. McClellan, despite the fact that he was currently stationed in western Virginia. Although this would mean a revamping of the military's departmental structure, Bates found a sympathetic ear in Winfield Scott, the army's commander-in-chief. While that decision was going through political channels, though, Lyon officially accepted the command Harney had been forced to leave.[64]

The word of Harney's latest demise quickly spread throughout Missouri. Many saw it as an apocalyptic premonition of the state's future. "Uncle Abe will begin to see that politics and war are two different things," wrote a disgruntled Missourian. "They have thrown overboard good officers such as Wool and Hearny to make room for a set of political popguns." Another proved far less restrained: ". . . a Captain

63. Harney to Lorenzo Thomas, May 31, 1861, in OR, I, 3:381; Harney to Thomas, June 5, 1861, ibid.; Harney to Sterling Price, May 24 to May 27, 1861, ibid., 378–80; Price to Harney, May 24 to May 29, 1861, ibid., 379–81; T. T. Gantt to Montgomery Blair, May 31, 1861, Blair Papers, box 29, LOC; Scharf, History of Saint Louis, 2:521.
64. Montgomery Blair to Frank Blair, June 4, 1861, in Peckham, Lyon and Missouri, 225–27; Smith, Borderland in the Civil War, 256; General Order no. 5, May 31, 1861, General Orders, Department of the West, 58–61, RG 393.

goes out with 8000 Hessians, surrounds and captures without bloodshed less than 700 men!!! (More than 10 to 1) His Hessians shoot down
and bayonet some 30 men, women & children, & presto—he is made a
brigadier General!!! For his brave & gallant Exploits!!!? Pshaw, it is
disgusting, nauseating . . . ." Others, however, heralded the news with
elation. "I look upon [it] as the most favorable symptom thus far in the
west," hailed one Unionist. "With such a man as this for a commander
over the western division, what may we not hope for the future[?]"[65]

The news prompted Jackson and Price to alter their strategies for fear
that Lyon would act before the militia was prepared adequately. With
only one thousand poorly armed and disorganized troops at their immediate disposal, they were powerless to resist Lyon if he marched on the
capital. Jackson wanted time to prepare more actively for secession,
while Price needed to prepare for the state's defense. He issued a proclamation to all militia commanders stating that despite the federal change
of command, the Harney-Price agreement was still in force and that any
rumors of federal military movements were unfounded. He hoped that
the statement would calm any local unrest that might develop at the news
Lyon had assumed command in Missouri. At the same time that Price's
statement was made public, he sent orders to his subordinate commanders hastening their preparations for active service. Although he deplored
the thought of war, Price would not be caught unprepared for it if Lyon
was so mad as to bring bloodshed to the interior.[66]

Lyon quickly mustered those troops denied enlistment under Harney.
By June 1, Lyon had a fighting total of 10,730 volunteers and Home
Guards, and he planned to add to it by authorizing the recruitment of
Home Guards in interior towns. Moreover, he reenlisted several of his
volunteer regiments for three-year terms of service. The volunteers continued to drill at both the arsenal and Jefferson Barracks, and the Home
Guard at their various locations around the city; the volunteers stationed
at the reservoir even staged a sham battle, complete with blank cartridges. Efforts to raise funds in the East for Home Guard munitions had
proved successful; by June 8, they had received over fourteen thousand
dollars, six thousand from New York City alone. All the units raised in

65. Anthony W. Smith to Father and Mother, July 29, 1861, Anthony W. Smith
Papers, MHS; Joseph E. Elder to Broadhead, June 18, 1861, Broadhead Papers, MHS;
Joseph Gardner to George L. Stearns, June 6, 1861, George L. Stearns Collection,
KSHS; John M. Richardson to O. D. Filley, June 4, 1861, Blair Papers, box 18, LOC.
66. Gannon, "Harney-Price Agreement," 45; Shalhope, *Sterling Price,* 164.

St. Louis had been fully equipped by private funds, and the Home Guard were now outfitted in gray flannel shirts and dark-blue trousers and kepis. In the midst of his preparations, Lyon took time to pose for a portrait at the downtown studio of noted St. Louis photographer W. L. Troxell, adorned in his newly acquired brigadier's uniform.[67]

Harney's second removal and the subsequent resumption of military preparations in St. Louis sent many of the city's conservative Unionists into a state of alarm. Lyon and Blair were now in complete command, and their zealous policy would undoubtedly drive the state to secession or, worse still, to its own civil war. In a state still officially neutral, this was a frightening prospect. In an effort to preserve peace, some of the more influential moderates persuaded Jackson and Price to request a meeting with Lyon and Blair. Similarly, other moderates urged the federal leaders to meet with the state officials. A series of correspondences ensued, throughout which Lyon insisted that the meeting be held in St. Louis. Because Jackson still feared arrest for treason, the federal commander guaranteed the governor's party safe passage to and from the city until midnight on June 12. One advisor, however, reproved Price for even considering such a meeting, and especially for catering to Lyon. "It is a most ill advised proposition," he snapped. "Let the abolitionist chief communicate with *you* . . . ." Despite such warnings, on the afternoon of the tenth, the governor's entourage left Jefferson City in a private railroad car bound for St. Louis.[68]

Upon reaching the city, the party registered at the sumptuous Planters' House hotel, next to the courthouse, which had played host to so many important meetings in St. Louis politics. The next morning, June 11, Jackson sent a message to Lyon notifying him that their party had arrived and was anxious to meet with him. Lyon returned the note, saying that he would send a carriage for Jackson's party to transport them to the arsenal. Already indignant over Lyon's insistence that the meeting be held in St. Louis, Jackson became even more piqued that a man of his

67. Lyon to Josiah Hunt, June 1, 1861, Thomas J. Sweeny Collection, Huntington; Special Order no. 1, June 8, 1861, ibid.; *Missouri Democrat,* May 27, 29, and June 8, 1861; Lyon Account Book, Nathaniel Lyon File, WC.

68. Gannon, "Harney-Price Agreement," 45; Lyon to C. F. Jackson, June 8, 1861, in McElroy, *Struggle for Missouri,* 109; Shalhope, *Sterling Price,* 164–65; Smith, *Borderland in the Civil War,* 251; *Missouri Democrat,* June 12, 1861; William C. Lane to Sterling Price, June 3, 1861, William Carr Lane Papers, MHS; Snead, *Fight for Missouri,* 197–98.

stature should be forced to travel to see a mere army captain. He demanded that the conference take place at the Planters' House. Only begrudgingly did Lyon consent, and at 11:00 A.M. he arrived, accompanied by Blair and an aide, Maj. Horace Conant.[69]

The trio proceeded to the governor's opulent suite, where they met Jackson, Price, and the governor's private secretary, Thomas Snead. The scene was memorable. The group seated themselves around a heavy, oval table, made of dark mahogany and covered by a marble top. Jackson and Blair were similarly dressed in dark broadcloth coats, white shirts, and black silk neckties. Price sat resplendent in his Mexican War dress uniform, complete with cocked and ostrich-plumed hat, sword, sash, and tall cavalry boots. Lyon provided a striking contrast to Price's regalia in his brigadier's uniform and sash, with worn infantry belt, dented sword scabbard, and unadorned black felt slouch hat.[70]

Lyon opened the conference by announcing that the discussion on the part of the federal government "would be conducted by Colonel Blair, who enjoyed its confidence in the very highest degree, and was authorized to speak for it." Jackson then began speaking for the state, and his propositions amounted to an offer of strict neutrality. He was willing to disband the State Guard and discontinue organizing and arming militia companies, although the state granted him the power to do so. He would also curtail all future importations of arms and munitions into the state and guarantee the protection of the rights of all citizens of the state, regardless of political loyalties. Finally, he agreed to prevent the entry of Confederate troops into Missouri, namely those in Arkansas. In return, the governor wanted guarantees that Blair and Lyon would disarm all existing Home Guard units and pledge not to occupy any state localities other than those already held by federal troops.[71]

For his part, Price stressed adherence to his agreement with Harney, stating that in his opinion there was no reason for the pact to be scrapped merely because of Harney's demise. He pledged his support for the precepts of the agreement and hoped that Lyon felt the same. Surprisingly, Blair interjected only infrequently, and not at all during Price's remarks.[72]

69. Shalhope, *Sterling Price,* 165.

70. Ibid.; Estate Inventory of Nathaniel Lyon, Eastford Township Probate Records, CSL.

71. Snead, *Fight for Missouri,* 198; Shalhope, *Sterling Price,* 165; Smith, *Borderland in the Civil War,* 252.

72. Shalhope, *Sterling Price,* 165; Snead, *Fight for Missouri,* 198–99.

After listening to the conversation for half an hour, all the while puffing nervously on a cigar and pulling pensively at his beard, Lyon began to take an active part in the discussion. Within minutes, he dominated it. Perhaps impatient with Blair's reticence, he could not suppress his deep hatred for the secessionists, which would not permit him to take a passive role in the most important debate of his life. Lyon began questioning the governor sharply on points that to him seemed incongruent. Without a State Guard, how would Jackson "protect" the state's residents when he had not done so *with* one? Moreover, how could Jackson properly punish those who now perpetrated crimes against the government without any means of doing so? And most important, the mere suggestion of "preventing" Confederate troops from entering the state was to Lyon all but an admission of disloyalty and sympathy with the seceded states. Lyon had early on been convinced of the governor's duplicity; by now, Jackson could not possibly convince Lyon that his truest desire was for neutrality when he asked openly for secession and had schemed subversively to get it.[73]

Lyon likened his duty to that of the president's in handling the situation in Maryland. He would maintain neutrality by force rather than allow even a chance for secession to breed. He refused to countenance any limitations upon the authority of the federal government, which included being told where not to station troops. Lyon was far too aroused to remain sitting for long, one leg crossed stiffly over the other, and he rose frequently, speaking deliberately and emphasizing words such as *my* and *to*. When making an important point, he would raise his right hand, then bring it down convulsively, forefinger extended; yet only rarely did he raise his voice above the firm tone with which he conducted the entire session.[74]

At this moment, the years of frustration raged up from deep inside Lyon. All the adversities he had been forced to suffer now found immediate focus, filling him with indomitable purpose. For the past decade, he had watched as the slavocracy's constant usurpations took the country steadily toward ruin. He had witnessed the lurid scenes on the Kansas prairie, which he deemed to be the direct result of previous pandering to the slave power by the federal government. To Lyon, Republican ascen-

73. Snead, *Fight for Missouri*, 198–99; Shalhope, *Sterling Price*, 165; *Missouri Democrat*, June 12, 1861; Lyon to Miner Knowlton, May 26, 1861, in Woodward, *Life of Nathaniel Lyon*, 260–62.

74. Adamson, *Rebellion in Missouri*, 111–12; Smith, *Borderland in the Civil War*, 252.

dancy signaled the end of such folly, and the current administration now faced the residuum of the former administrations' inertness. The Missouri secessionists would be coddled no longer. Previously, Lyon had been unable to prevent their machinations because of his subordination to others who were either too nescient to understand or too corrupt to do anything about it. Though he couched his objections to Jackson's proposals in terms of federal authority, in truth Lyon now refused to accept any restriction of his own omnipotence. Once, he had had no power. Now, Lyon was *the* power. His duty was not—and never had been—to make peace with the secessionists. His duty, his calling, was to punish them. No one else knew how. And now, no one could stop him. God was in him.

After four hours of heated debate, Lyon punched out his cigar. Cheeks flushed, he began speaking in a particularly deliberate tone:

> Governor Jackson, no man in the state of Missouri has been more desirous of preserving peace than myself. Heretofore Missouri has only felt the fostering care of the federal government, which has raised her from the condition of a feeble French colony to that of an empire state. Now, however, from a failure on the part of the chief Executive to comply with constitutional requirements, I fear she will be made to feel its power.

Rising stiffly from his seat, he squared his shoulders and stared directly at the governor, pale blue eyes flashing. "Better, sir, far better," he continued, "that the blood of every man, woman, and child within the limits of the State should flow, than that she should defy the federal government." Grabbing his hat, he stated bluntly, in his flat, New England twang, "This means war. In an hour one of my officers will call for you and conduct you out of my lines."[75]

With that, he turned on the heels of his boots and strode briskly from the room, sword clattering. The remaining men sat in stunned silence, shocked at both the audacity and the intensity of Lyon's final statement. Yet even Blair knew that the time for talking had abruptly and unceremoniously ended. The men rose, shook hands, and parted, each silently anxious about the fate awaiting both the state and themselves. Nathaniel Lyon had forced war upon Missouri.[76]

75. *Missouri Democrat,* July 2, 1861; Peckham, *Lyon and Missouri,* 248; Snead, *Fight for Missouri,* 199–200.
76. Snead, *Fight for Missouri,* 199–200.

IX

The Grand Steeple Chase

Governor Jackson and General Price took Lyon's declaration of war with dead seriousness. Choosing not to wait for Lyon's promised escort, they hastily packed their bags, hurried to Union Depot, and by six o'clock that evening had impressed a locomotive to carry them to Jefferson City. Arriving in the capital at 2:00 A.M., Price immediately sent a company of the State Guard (including the governor's own son) to the railroad bridge over the Gasconade River to burn the expanse and cut the telegraph wires. The rest of the night they spent drafting a proclamation explaining the breakdown of the Planters' House conference, warning of federal intent to occupy the state, and calling to its defense fifty thousand able-bodied men. The announcement reached the presses the next morning.[1]

Jackson and Price had gauged their adversary's next move perfectly. With amazing celerity, Lyon was preparing to execute a campaign to both subdue Missouri's secessionists and capture the State Guard. Upon receipt of a copy of the governor's proclamation, Lyon called together his leading aides and subordinates for a conference. Believing the proclamation tantamount to a declaration of war, Lyon, Schofield, and Blair quickly planned a pincer movement designed to paralyze the state's secessionists. Lyon would lead the first Union force along the Missouri River to Jefferson City, where it would scatter the secessionist forces currently forming around the capital. In doing so, he would occupy the river cities, thus controlling all river traffic and preventing the secessionists north of the Missouri from joining with those south of it. Lyon would then move southward, chasing the State Guard toward Springfield, in the southwestern portion of the state.

Simultaneously, a second column under Thomas Sweeny would move by rail to Rolla, securing the southern branch of the Pacific Railroad to

---

1. John McElroy, *The Struggle for Missouri*, 118–19; *Missouri Democrat*, June 12–14, 1861; Depositions of Martin Loughlin and Michael H. Cohen, Notes on Trial of J. W. Tucker, 5, 17, James O. Broadhead Papers, MHS.

that point. Sweeny would then march his force toward Springfield, establishing a cordon of posts between there and Rolla, the nearest railroad terminus, thereby providing a safe line of communication and supply. By moving swiftly, Sweeny could effectively cut off any avenue of retreat for the State Guard and prevent any link-up with the Confederate troops reputed to be building in northern Arkansas. The pincers would close somewhere north of Springfield, trapping the fleeing Jackson and the entire force of traitors. Thus, Lyon could secure the state.[2]

With the extensive preparations necessary to launch the campaign, it is remarkable that Lyon moved so quickly. On the eleventh, as a result of the efforts of the Committee of Safety, Lyon received authority from the War Department to enlist as many additional troops as he deemed necessary, and he was authorized five thousand additional stand of arms with which to equip them. Schofield was detailed to remain in St. Louis to complete the task. Lyon had already commandeered four steamers—the *Iatan,* the *City of Louisiana,* the *A. McDowell,* and the *J. C. Swon* (which Lyon refused to release, despite Harney's order to do so)—and had outfitted their wheelhouses and decks with sandbags to protect the pilots and troops against enemy fire from the shore. He then hastily gathered all available camp equipage (of which he was woefully short), provisions, and ammunition and ordered several locomotives commandeered and the tracks cleared to Rolla for Sweeny's troops. At the last minute, however, Sweeny was forced to remain in St. Louis to complete the indispensable task of organizing the matériel, supplies, and provisions that had to be sent to Springfield as the eventual destination of both of the campaign's columns. In his stead, Col. Franz Sigel, the bespectacled patriarch of the German soldiers, commanded the southwestern expedition.[3]

As a final preparation, Lyon designated Lt. Col. Chester Harding to act as adjutant general in St. Louis during the campaign. Harding would serve as a vital liaison with Washington for both Lyon and Sigel. At

2. McElroy, *Struggle for Missouri,* 121; Lyon to George McClellan, June 22, 1861, in *OR,* III, 1:11–12; Hans Christian Adamson, *Rebellion in Missouri, 1861: Nathaniel Lyon and His Army of the West,* 116.

3. Frank Blair to Montgomery Blair, June 11, 1861, Broadhead Papers, MHS; O. D. Filley to Gideon Welles, June 12, 1861, ibid.; Simon Cameron to Lyon, June 11, 1861, ibid.; *New York Times,* June 19, 1861; John M. Schofield, *Forty-six Years in the Army,* 34–35; Frank Moore, ed., *Rebellion Record: A Diary of American Events,* 1:76; James Peckham, *General Nathaniel Lyon and Missouri in 1861,* 254; Adamson, *Rebellion in Missouri,* 119, 121–22.

11:00 A.M., only twenty-four hours after Jackson's proclamation reached the general public, the left wing of Lyon's expeditionary force, under the command of Lt. Col. George Andrews, left St. Louis on board the *Iatan.* Three hours later, Lyon and the right wing left aboard the *J. C. Swon,* followed by the *A. McDowell,* the expedition's primary supply boat. One detachment of troops moved westward on the Pacific Railroad to Hermann to await the arrival of the *City of Louisiana,* which would transport them from there to Jefferson City. In all, Lyon had just over two thousand troops. Later that night, the bulk of Sigel's command, numbering about five hundred, left Union Depot en route to Rolla.[4]

After anchoring overnight just west of St. Charles, the convoy steamed carefully upriver all the next day, the troops often being forced to disembark to move over sandbars. In case of sniping, Lyon stationed marksmen on all boats. They proved unneeded. One spirited recruit recalled that "every Bluff & grocery & log cabin & settlement greeted us cheer on cheer—men, women & children in emulation with handkerchiefs & flags waving, until we would round a turn & so lose sight of them—We also cheered ourselves hoarse & returned the Ladies' Salutes." Though they anticipated sharpshooters or artillery at every bend, they found the reputed secessionist districts "silent as the grave." Having encountered no resistance, at 2:00 P.M. on the fifteenth the convoy steamed into the Jefferson City wharf at the foot of the capitol building, whose towering presence the Union troops had seen more than six miles downriver.[5]

An enthusiastic crowd was on hand to greet the boats as they docked, and Lyon soon learned that the governor had been able to assemble for the city's defense only 120 men from its heavily German and predominantly pro-Union populace. After Price had convinced Jackson that the capital was indefensible, the governor had hastily gathered as much personal property and papers as he could, and then on the evening before Lyon reached the city Price had fled on the steamer *White Cloud,* followed closely by many of the pro-Southern legislators. It was rumored that he had moved upriver about fifty miles to Boonville, one of two river towns at which Price had directed area State Guard units to assemble, and where several thousand troops were reputed to be feverishly erecting defenses on the high river bluffs. Lyon decided to press on to Boonville as

4. Peckham, *Lyon and Missouri,* 254–55; *New York Times,* June 19 and July 10, 1861.

5. McElroy, *Struggle for Missouri,* 121; Adamson, *Rebellion in Missouri,* 119; James E. Love to Molly, June 18, 1861, James E. Love Papers, MHS.

quickly as possible, but he would rest his troops for the night in Jefferson City. He ordered several companies at the arsenal to march immediately for the Gasconade River to repair the bridge and open communications between St. Louis and Jefferson City. Lyon then marched his troops up the steep streets to the deserted capital building, occupied it, and raised the U.S. flag. Thus, bloodlessly, the Missouri capital fell. Although not recognized immediately, the importance of Lyon's coup would soon enough be understood.[6]

When Jackson and his entourage arrived at Boonville, they found the city defended by several hundred State Guardsmen rather than several thousand, and though their numbers were growing by the hour, nearly all were untrained and armed primarily with shotguns and squirrel rifles. Many lacked weapons completely. Under the overall command of Brig. Gen. John B. Clark, the largest regiment was headed by the governor's cavalier nephew, John S. Marmaduke, a recent West Point graduate whose uncorrected nearsightedness caused a chronic habit of squinting. Inexperience did nothing to dampen the spirits of the militia recruits, however, and Camp Bacon, four miles east of Boonville, soon took on a carnival-like atmosphere as the troops waited undaunted for the arrival of Lyon and his Germans.

The state's militia commander, however, was far less confident of success. Sterling Price realized that aside from his troops' greenness, he had no artillery of sufficient size to obstruct river traffic. Price hoped that the Boonville troops could provide at best an effective delaying action while he organized the other body of militia currently gathering at Lexington. Suffering from a debilitating bout with diarrhea, on June 13 the State Guard's commander left Boonville in the governor's hands and returned to his home in Keytesville, some sixty miles upriver. Before he left, he urged holding Boonville as long as possible and then withdrawing to the southwest if it became necessary. Price was wholly unprepared for the swiftness of Lyon's next move.[7]

Leaving three companies under the command of Col. Henry Boernstein to guard the capital, Lyon embarked the remaining 1,700 troops at

6. McElroy, *Struggle for Missouri*, 121; *Missouri Democrat*, June 15, 1861; Thomas W. Knox, *Camp-Fire and Cotton Field: Southern Adventure in Time of War*, 43–44.

7. Albert Castel, *General Sterling Price and the Civil War in the West*, 4, 25–26; *Missouri Democrat*, June 27, 1861; Paul Rorvig, "The Significant Skirmish—The Battle of Boonville, June 17, 1861," unpublished paper presented at the Missouri Conference on History, March 17, 1989, 7–8.

2:00 P.M. on the sixteenth and proceeded up the Missouri toward Boon-ville. Though his troops were eager for a fight with the rebels, the federal commander was less animated. He remained in his cabin, accepting few visitors, save Blair. Progress was again slow because of low water, and late that night the convoy was still fifteen miles from Boonville. After anchoring for a few hours, Lyon ordered an early start, and by 6:00 A.M. the boats had reached Rocheport, just ten miles below their destination. During a brief stop, Lyon learned that the militia was preparing defenses a few miles upriver, well below Boonville. The news forced Lyon to adjust his plans. Creeping upriver, he ordered the troops disembarked on the south shore about eight miles below Boonville, where the level river bottom sloped gradually to steep, wooded bluffs a half-mile away. Leaving a company of infantry and an eight-inch howitzer aboard the *McDowell* with orders to move upriver and shell the rebel camp, the column marched two miles along the bottom, then ascended the winding river road leading toward Boonville.[8]

Upon learning of Lyon's landing, Governor Jackson ordered Mar-maduke to move forward from Camp Bacon and engage the Union force. Though strongly opposed to fighting on this ground with untrained troops, the young militia colonel sent up a detachment of skirmishers, who engaged in a brief firefight with the advancing federals before being quickly dispersed. Once the Union line had reached the crest of the ridge, it became apparent that the State Guard's main line of defense lay across a steep valley on the brow of a subsequent ridge, three hundred yards distant. Occupying a farm lane and fence line running roughly perpendicular to the river road, Marmaduke had anchored his line on a brick farmhouse owned by William M. Adams, sitting at the junction of the two roads. Inside the house were perched crack militia sharpshoot-ers. Lyon ordered his troops to press onward.

Quickly, the air was filled with "balls flying thick and fast" as the two lines closed. Because of the moving battle, some sections of Lyon's force were far in advance of others, preventing the entire weight of the federal line from coming to bear. Regardless, the inexperience of the State Guard and the effective fire of the federal artillery battery under the command of James Totten—a profane, hard-drinking officer with whom Lyon had served in Mexico, and who even then had earned great respect

8. *Missouri Democrat,* June 17, 1861; Peckham, *Lyon and Missouri,* 269–70; McEl-roy, *Struggle for Missouri,* 125; Knox, *Camp-Fire and Cotton Field,* 43–44.

from Lyon—combined to dislodge the defenders quickly. Two cannon balls smashed through the walls of the Adams house, scattering the sharpshooters positioned inside. After just twenty minutes, the entire militia force was running pell-mell back toward Boonville, five miles distant. Lyon pushed onward, capturing the abandoned State Guard camp, which yielded a large supply of shoes, arms, and blankets, and as an added bonus two pieces of artillery that had never fired a shot. Casualties were light, each side suffering two killed and less than ten wounded, but sixty of the State Guard surrendered as well. Lyon occupied Boonville later that morning, after its mayor formally surrendered the city. By that time, Jackson (who had watched the entire debacle from a nearby hill) and the remnants of his shattered forces had begun a headlong flight toward the southwestern corner of the state. There the deposed governor hoped to find an Arkansas force prepared to come to the aid of his beleaguered state.[9]

Heralding what they touted as a smashing victory at Boonville, the newspapers portrayed Lyon as a paladin of Union courage. Prior to the battle, he was known only in Missouri. Now, however, his name became well known beyond the state's borders. No less than four major newspapers sent correspondents to cover the Lyon campaign, two from New York. Similarly, the papers both in and out of the state gleefully ridiculed Jackson and the State Guard for the embarrassing defeat. Price's incapacitation, however, proved the most attractive focus for editorial sarcasm, and one writer took full advantage of the incident:

> One of Gov. Jackson's organs in Missouri says that it pities the U.S. troops. It seems that Gen. Price pitied them at the battle near Boonville. His bowels were moved for them.
>
> "Follow me, lads," the General cried,
> "I'll bet you'll smell gunpowder,"
> They followed, and, they say, enjoyed
> An odor somewhat louder.[10]

While Unionists hailed Lyon's victory, many Missourians decried the past month's apocalyptic turn of events. War had moved into their midst,

9. Lyon to George McClellan, June 30, 1861, in OR, III, 1:12–14; Castel, General Sterling Price, 26; McElroy, Struggle for Missouri, 123–25; Lyon to John B. Hasler, February 28, 1847, Nathaniel Lyon Papers, AAS; New York Tribune, June 24, 1861; Rorvig, "Significant Skirmish," 10–13; Peckham, Lyon and Missouri, 269–73.

10. Missouri Democrat, June 27, 1861.

and many sought to understand the shattering of peace. "Missouri is in a deplorable condition," lamented one resident. "We have civil war in our very midst . . . . Men seem to have lost their reason and gone mad— here we are constantly in dread of an insurrection or some other rupture . . . ." Still others placed blame squarely on shoulders that wore federal blue. "I am now convinced that it was the fixed purpose of Blair and others from the beginning to create these troubles in order to make capital out of their suppression," wrote another Missourian. "Blair is already receiving plaudits throughout the North for the energy he had displayed in suppressing rebellion in Missouri when you and I know there would have been none but for the efforts of himself and his coadjutors in creating it."[11]

Had Lyon's campaign ended at this point, it would have been viewed as an unquestioned success. With lightning speed, he had chased the secessionist governor and many of his conspiratorial legislators from their seat of power, effectively eliminating any chance of them further promoting the state's secession in the General Assembly. In addition, he had captured both the state treasurer, Alfred W. Morrison, and the attorney general, J. Proctor Knott, along with a large amount of currency and treasury records. Then, with scant losses, he had dispersed a sizable force of the State Guard, the primary threat to federal authority in Missouri, and blocked a large contingent of future recruits from reaching the main body of pro-Southern forces. Price lamented later that Lyon's swift actions had forced him to leave behind between five and ten thousand recruits in central and northern Missouri. Lyon's remarkable success prompted the *New York Times* to laud his strong moves: "Gen. Lyon . . . is evidently the right man in the right place . . . . Nowhere else has treason met so nearly the exact treatment it deserves as in Missouri."[12]

Moreover, from a military standpoint, the movement of Lyon's wing of the campaign had alone accomplished all that was strategically necessary to secure Missouri. By occupying the Missouri River line, Lyon controlled most of the state's population, agriculture, industry, and wealth. Perhaps equally important, control of the river gained for the Union the means of preventing the South from ever wresting Missouri

11. Loundes H. Davis to Mary B. Hall, June 28, 1861, Civil War Collection, MHS; H. S. Turner to "Dear General," July 15, 1861, ibid.

12. Arthur Roy Kirkpatrick, "The Admission of Missouri to the Confederacy," 368; *Missouri Democrat,* June 17, 1861; Sterling Price to Jefferson Davis, in *OR,* I, 3:734–36; *New York Times,* June 20, 1861.

from her hands. The rapid transportation afforded by the Missouri River allowed the army to concentrate superior forces quickly at any point between St. Louis and Fort Leavenworth should a Confederate invasion ever materialize. Thus, Lyon's campaign had already given the federal government all it needed strategically to keep Missouri in the Union.[13]

Whether Lyon recognized the strategic importance of his coup is not known. Even if he had, it would have mattered little. For despite his successes and the praise he had received, Lyon was not yet satisfied. Believing that he had been "too mild" with the secessionists, he intended now to "deal summarily" with Jackson's fleeing force. Yet doing so properly would mean more than capturing the state capital and sending the State Guard into wild flight. As a correspondent covering the Missouri campaign recalled, Lyon denounced the treason of the secessionists and "asserted with vehemence that no punishment was too great for that crime." At all costs—and above and beyond any strategic considerations—Lyon was determined to see that requisite punishment was inflicted for the secessionists' crimes. He was no longer directing a military campaign; Lyon was now leading a punitive crusade.[14]

However, Lyon's hasty move on Jefferson City had afforded time only to gather enough supplies to carry his troops that far. A cross-country move to Springfield, without benefit of a railroad, would require a complete reassemblage of supplies and transportation for the journey. And with only 1,700 men and an entire river to garrison, Lyon was in need of reinforcements. All of this would take time. Therefore, Lyon prepared to remain at Boonville until his force was ready.

The day following the engagement at Boonville, Price arrived at Lexington from his home, still weak from his illness. Assembled were the combined commands of two brigadier generals, James S. Rains and William Y. Slack, numbering between five and six thousand militia, who had just learned of the defeat of the State Guard at Boonville. Price then learned some equally distressing news: federal troops were approaching quickly from Fort Leavenworth to the west. Believing Lexington now untenable, Price took command of the troops and ordered his men to prepare to march. Rains would lead the column southward toward

13. Albert Castel, "A New View of the Battle of Pea Ridge," 149; Franc P. Wilkie, *Pen and Powder,* 29.

14. Lyon to Colonel White, July 4, 1861, Civil War Collection, MHS.

Lamar, just north of Joplin, where they might effect a junction with Jackson and Clark. Price and his staff would then ride on to Arkansas and seek out the commander of the Confederate troops there, Brig. Gen. Ben McCulloch, and ask for his aid. Within hours, Price had the column moving south.[15]

At the same time, Lyon issued a stern proclamation to the people of Missouri citing the reasons for his expedition to Boonville. He condemned the state officials for violating the Harney-Price agreement and claimed that their organization had "upon a large scale the means of warfare . . . , having made a declaration of war." He explained that he had paroled many of those captured in the engagement because of their immature ages, and he gave warning that as the new commander of the Department of the West, he would no longer afford any laxness to those who took up arms against the federal government, a luxury they had enjoyed under the former department commander. Lyon then "invited" those persons to "return to their homes and relinquish their hostile attitude to the General Government" without further "molestation for past occurrences." Later in the day, he sent word to Maj. Samuel D. Sturgis at Fort Leavenworth to march his command, consisting of two recently mustered regiments of Kansas infantry totaling twenty-two hundred troops, to Clinton, Missouri, where they would link with Lyon's column in pursuit of Jackson. Expecting to leave by June 26, Lyon awaited both the arrival of his supply boats (accompanied by reinforcements from Jefferson Barracks) and the 1st Iowa Volunteers, who boasted an aggregate of over nine hundred able-bodied troops. Though his campaign appeared to be shaping up well, his satisfaction was mixed with an appreciable amount of apprehension.[16]

On June 18, Lyon received a distressing wire via Chester Harding that threatened to halt abruptly his ambitious campaign plan. On June 6, under steady pressure from both Attorney General Bates and General Scott, the War Department issued orders adding the state of Missouri to

15. Castel, *General Sterling Price,* 26; Robert E. Shalhope, *Sterling Price: Portrait of a Southerner,* 167.

16. McElroy, *Struggle for Missouri,* 125–26; "Proclamation to the People of Missouri," in Peckham, *Lyon and Missouri,* 274–75; Albert Castel, *A Frontier State at War: Kansas, 1861,* 45; Mark A. Plummer, *Frontier Governor: Samuel J. Crawford of Kansas,* 10; Adamson, *Rebellion in Missouri,* 129; Lyon to George McClellan, June 22, 1861, in *OR,* III, 1:11–12; Peckham, *Lyon and Missouri,* 255–56; Ray W. Irwin, ed., "Missouri in Crisis—The Journal of Captain Albert Tracy, 1861," 157.

the Military Department of the Ohio. Its commander, Maj. Gen. George B. McClellan, was currently headquartered at Cincinnati, over four hundred miles away. For some reason, the two men most directly affected, Lyon and McClellan, were not notified of the decision until sometime around the eighteenth.[17]

The wire upset both Lyon and Blair, who commanded both a brigade and his regiment of volunteers on the campaign. Neither understood how McClellan was to take charge effectively of the situation in Missouri from such a great distance. More important, each worried that McClellan would not support the continuation of Lyon's campaign. What left Blair seething, however, was that it appeared that the Missouri moderates had convinced Bates to undermine all that Blair had accomplished on Lyon's behalf. It seemed that each time Blair was able to clear Lyon's path to what they both knew was the most effective method of dealing with the Missouri secessionists, those meddling conservatives somehow reblocked it.

However, as soon as Montgomery Blair had learned of the War Department's decision, he had sought actively to have it overturned. On June 18, the postmaster general sent an emissary to attempt to persuade Scott to change his mind, but the effort proved unsuccessful. Not satisfied, he wrote Bates with the same purpose but heard nothing in reply. Francis Preston Blair, Sr., on the other hand, had more luck. Personally visiting the general-in-chief at his office, the elder Blair learned some interesting information. McClellan had responded to the change in command by in effect handing Missouri back to Lyon, with orders to "carry out such views in respect to Missouri as seem most advantageous—very much as if he were in charge of a separate department." McClellan, in the midst of preparing for his own campaign in western Virginia, was not anxious to be saddled with the added burden of another state, especially one west of the Mississippi. He did not even possess a map of the state's counties, much less a working knowledge of the situation there. Unable to relinquish command of the state outright, he did the next best thing: he opted for status quo. Old Man Blair could not have been more pleased, and he wrote immediately to his son in Boonville, informing him of the news. He and Montgomery realized, however, that Lyon's de

17. General Order no. 30, June 6, 1861, in OR, I, 3:384; George McClellan to Chester Harding, June 18, 1861, ibid., 385; Lyon to Chester Harding, June 18, 1861, ibid.

facto authority was still quite tenuous, and they intended to continue their efforts to change the Missouri command structure.[18]

At the same time, Frank Blair faced a difficult decision, and the opposition to Lyon in Washington and elsewhere probably helped him to make it. The next session of Congress was scheduled to convene on July 4, and as an elected member of the House of Representatives from Missouri, he was required to be present. However, he currently held a high position of command in the most important military campaign the state had ever seen. He was forced to decide how best to serve the country, the president, and, after the latest of Scott's decisions, his ally Lyon. Somewhat painfully, he resolved to return to Washington to espouse Lyon's reinstatement. Accordingly, the command of the Third Brigade and the 1st Missouri passed to Lt. Col. George Andrews. On June 22, Blair left Camp Cameron (the Army of the West's camp at the county fairgrounds east of Boonville, named in honor of the secretary of war) for a second round with the Washington bureaucracy.[19]

Despite Lyon's herculean efforts, he could not meet his June 26 target date for departure from Boonville. Numerous delays occurred in the arrival of supplies and reinforcements at Camp Cameron, and assembling an adequate supply train proved nearly impossible. Angered by Lyon's penchant for ignoring military supply regulations, Quartermaster Chief Justus McKinstry had confiscated most of the wagons and mules procured by Sweeny for Lyon and had also discharged most of the civilian teamsters. This forced Lyon to try to gather what makeshift transportation he could from the interior. Unfortunately, the best wagons and horses from around Boonville had been confiscated by the State Guard, and the various vehicles that Lyon managed to collect proved insufficient to handle the number of men in his army. Only one small, two-horse wagon was allotted to each company, and the amount of food foraged from the surrounding countryside was barely enough to supplement the meager provisions being sent by the government.[20]

18. Montgomery Blair to Edward Bates, June 19, 1861, Blair Papers, box 29, LOC; Peckham, *Lyon and Missouri,* 266–67; Francis P. Blair, Sr., to Frank Blair, June 18, 1861, ibid., 265.

19. *Missouri Democrat,* June 24, 26, 1861; Peckham, *Lyon and Missouri,* 282–83; Lyon to George McClellan, June 22, 1861, in *OR,* III, 1:11–12.

20. Adamson, *Rebellion in Missouri,* 137–38; Lurton D. Ingersoll, *Iowa and the Rebellion,* 22; Edward G. Longacre, "A Profile of General Justus McKinstry," 15–16; James S. Clark, *Life in the Middle West,* 57–58.

That every day's delay allowed Jackson and Price to move further away from him frayed Lyon's already-edgy nerves. To make matters worse, on the twenty-sixth, a torrential rain began to fall, and for nearly a week it continued unabated, making roads wholly impassable. Lyon's only hopes were either that Sturgis or Sigel would be able to cut off the retreating columns, or that the rains had swelled the Grand and Osage rivers to the point that Jackson had been stopped before he could cross. Considering the rain, there was little hope that Sturgis could pursue, even if Jackson were bottled up north of either river. It was not until 3:30 A.M. on July 3 that Lyon's force, numbering about 2,350 men, was able to begin pursuit of the State Guard.[21]

However, things elsewhere had not gone as Lyon had hoped. By the time Sturgis left Fort Leavenworth on June 25, Jackson was already at Warsaw, fifty-five miles south of Boonville on the Osage River. After passing hurriedly through Tipton, the column arrived at Cole Camp on the twenty-first, where it was reinforced by a small force of militia. Together, the troops dispersed a group of Home Guards, capturing over 350 muskets. At Warsaw, Jackson received another militia company, together with the four brass cannon taken in April from the Liberty arsenal. Learning there that Price had set out for Arkansas, the governor's column crossed the Osage just prior to the rains, and he started his troops for Lamar, where they would try to meet Price's troops moving from Lexington. His weary, disorganized troops arrived there and established camp, and on July 3 (the day Lyon left Boonville) Rains's force joined them, bringing the total number of troops under the governor's command to 4,900. Although 800 of his men were unarmed, Jackson also possessed seven field pieces.[22]

After leaving the State Guard, and accompanied by his staff and escort, Price rode ahead, gathering recruits as he went. By the time he arrived at Cowskin Prairie, in the extreme southwestern corner of the state, he had accumulated over 1,000 troops, mostly unarmed and completely raw. Leaving his ragtag recruits there, on July 1 he rode to Maysville, Arkansas, for a conference with Brig. Gen. N. Bart Pearce, commanding the Arkansas state troops encamped nearby. Pearce informed Price that McCulloch and his Confederates were currently en

21. Peckham, *Lyon and Missouri,* 280; Special Order no. 3, July 2, 1861, Letters Sent and General Orders Issued, Army of the West, RG 393.

22. Arthur Roy Kirkpatrick, "The Admission of Missouri to the Confederacy," 366–67; McElroy, *Struggle for Missouri,* 130–32.

route from Fort Smith to Maysville and would arrive the next day. Borrowing 600 muskets from Pearce, Price returned to Cowskin Prairie to equip and train his troops.[23]

As Lyon languished in Boonville, Sigel's forces were on the move. The last regiment of the southwest column left St. Louis by rail late on June 15, two days behind the vanguard. After chasing off a group of about 180 State Guard, Sigel's troops occupied Rolla on June 14. He waited there for the balance of his force, then set out immediately for Springfield, where he arrived ten days later. After a short rest, he pushed on toward Neosho. In the meantime, Sweeny managed with great difficulty to arrange for a line of both supplies and transportation to be established through Rolla. On June 23, several days after he sent Lyon's supplies, he himself left St. Louis with 360 troops. Arriving in Rolla that same afternoon, Sweeny was disappointed to find that the supply wagons he had arranged for had not yet arrived. Undaunted, he and his troops left on the next afternoon for Springfield. However, when the column reached Lebanon, he was forced to disarm and disband one of the four Home Guard companies for mutiny. Once done, the rest of the group pushed on toward Springfield, reaching the city on July 1. Three days later, Sweeny issued a proclamation to the residents of the city demanding that all "misled" citizens who "desire to maintain and preserve the best government ever devised by human wisdom" lay down their arms and take an oath of loyalty. "No loyal citizen," it read, "will decline to take such an oath."[24]

On July 3, the same day that Lyon left Boonville, Sigel (who had reached Neosho on July 1, too late to cut off Price but well in advance of Jackson) struck out for Carthage. Simultaneously, Rains's troops met with Jackson's at Lamar. While the "Grand Steeple Chase" (as the *Missouri Democrat* bemusedly called the campaign) moved closer to a climax, one more turn of events occurred that would soon have profound implications for both Lyon and Missouri. By orders of the War Department, the Department of the West was reestablished, to include the state of Missouri. Buttressed by Frank's arrival in Washington, the Blairs had put unrelenting pressure on both the president and the secretary of war and had succeeded in having the old department reinstated. Lyon, how-

23. Shalhope, *Sterling Price*, 167.

24. Peckham, *Lyon and Missouri*, 292–94; Return I. Holcombe and W. S. Adams, *An Account of the Battle of Wilson's Creek . . .* , 6; *Springfield* [Missouri] *Mirror*, July 4, 1861.

ever, was considered too "rash and impolitic" to be appointed as its commander, and for the present the Department of the West existed without one.[25]

The Blairs had someone in mind, however, and since May had lobbied for his appointment. Because they considered Lyon's services in the field too valuable to saddle him with administrative duties, the Blairs selected John Charles Frémont, the celebrated "Pathfinder of the West" and a close personal friend of the Blair family, to head the department. On July 1, Frémont had arrived in New York from France, and with his strong ties to St. Louis (his wife, Jessie, was the daughter of Thomas Hart Benton, Missouri's late political giant, under whose tutelage Frank had learned the craft), the Blairs saw no better choice for their new department commander. More important, the Blairs believed that their public support of Frémont's 1856 presidential campaign would ensure his malleability once he assumed command. They were confident that if Lyon must be subordinate, "the Pathfinder" would at least be of a like mind. On July 9, Frémont was officially offered the appointment, and he gladly accepted. However, delays caused him to remain in New York for two more weeks.[26]

Lyon soon found that the recent downpours would impede his progress even longer. Slowed by mud and continued rains, the column did not reach the Grand River until early on the afternoon of July 7. The river was swollen to flood stage, the road along the river bottom needed to be corduroyed even to get to the river, and the river itself could not be crossed without a pontoon bridge. Sturgis's column, also delayed by the rain, arrived shortly before Lyon's. Once combined, the two forces totaled over 4,500 troops, including a regiment of much-needed cavalry, which Lyon had not had prior to Sturgis's arrival. That night, they began the difficult process of crossing the torrential current.[27]

The Army of the West was able to cross the Grand River during the night and next day, and much of the column was then pushed ahead through recurrent rains toward the Osage. Six men were drowned while crossing the high waters, and Lyon was forced to abandon most of the

25. William E. Parrish, *Turbulent Partnership: Missouri and the Union, 1861–1865,* 49; *Missouri Democrat,* June 25, 1861; Isaac Sherman to Frank Blair, May 29, 1861, Blair Papers, box 18, LOC.

26. Willard Glazier, *Heroes of Three Wars,* 393; Robert L. Turkoly-Joczik, "Frémont and the Western Department," 372.

27. Eugene F. Ware, *The Lyon Campaign,* 159–78.

tents and other equipage at the river. On the morning of July 9, as the last of the troops left the Grand, one of Lyon's spies brought stunning news from the southwest expedition: four days earlier, Jackson's troops had defeated Sigel near Carthage.

While reconnoitering the area west of Springfield, the German had learned of Lyon's victory at Boonville and of Jackson's subsequent retreat. Pushing north toward Lamar, where it was rumored that Jackson was encamped, Sigel did not yet know the size of the host that he sought. Along Coon Creek, just north of Carthage, Sigel engaged the State Guard, who outnumbered him nearly four to one. He was almost surrounded before retiring in surprisingly good order to Mount Vernon. Losses were not heavy, but by the time Lyon received the news it sounded as if Sigel's force would be captured by the combined elements under Jackson and McCulloch if the German were not reinforced within three days. Concerned, Lyon sent word to the German of his position above the Osage and directed him either to move to join Lyon's column or to "hang on Jackson's flank or rear if he advances to meet me." Fearing the worst, Lyon ordered his men to march with all possible haste to save Sigel.[28]

That night, after a forced march of over twenty-five miles, the column reached the Osage River. Like the Grand, it was a raging torrent, and they spent the entire day of July 10 building crossings and moving men carefully over the swift current. Many of the men were able to get some much-needed rest while the river was being spanned, but a fiery sun that had taken the place of the preceding week's heavy clouds made rest difficult. Fearing that the new delay would endanger Sweeny in Springfield, Lyon scrawled a hasty message to him suggesting that he build trenches to defend the city. Because he had heard reports of the inaccurate fire of Sigel's men, he cautioned Sweeny to instruct his men to "fire low and not at random."[29]

Once across the Osage, the column again pushed onward in a rapid march. Lyon sent couriers to the different regiments to speed them up when they began to lag behind, and he personally spurred the troops as he rode by them. The column marched all day through ferocious heat,

28. Ibid., 183–89; Jay Monaghan, *Civil War on the Western Border, 1854–1865*, 150–52; Lyon to John M. Schofield, July 9, 1861, Thomas J. Sweeny Collection, Huntington; Lyon to Franz Sigel, July 10, 1861, Nathaniel Lyon File, SHSM.

29. Ware, *Lyon Campaign*, 190–97; Lyon to Thomas Sweeny, July 1, 1861, Thomas J. Sweeny Collection, Huntington.

then continued into the night without rest. Their only food was the six-day ration of hardtack they carried in their haversacks. Hundreds of stragglers, hopelessly fatigued and many suffering from heat stroke, fell from the line. Most were simply allowed to lie by the sides of the road. Those who continued were ordered to place their blankets in company wagons to lighten their loads and conserve their strength. Lyon knew that if the news about Sigel were true, his entire campaign was in serious jeopardy. He therefore pushed his troops through the entire night and the next morning with only two hours rest.[30]

Early on the afternoon of July 12, Lyon ordered the column to halt and make camp. The men learned then that they had marched over fifty miles in thirty hours and believed jubilantly that they had chased off the rebels threatening Sigel. However, what the men were told and what actually happened following the battle at Carthage were not at all the same story. Sigel had retired in good order to Carthage, and near sunset he took the road that led east to Mount Vernon. Militia horsemen pressed them until dark, but when the light faded and the federal column entered heavy woods, the pursuit ended. Sigel continued his march the entire night and halted the next morning a few miles east of Mount Vernon. Positive that there was no further danger, the German ordered a day's rest. On the eleventh, his troops arrived in Springfield.[31]

Following the battle, Jackson's troops withdrew to Carthage, and while Sigel rested, they marched south triumphantly toward Neosho. On July 6, the governor and General Price joined their jubilant forces. Price had met with McCulloch at Cowskin Prairie on July 2, but the meeting did not go at all well. McCulloch, commander of the Confederacy's Western Division, was very hesitant to use his forces to assist Price. First, he was under specific orders from the Confederate War Department not to enter Missouri. Moreover, he was skeptical of the undisciplined rabble that Price had brought with him. Unarmed and untrained, the ragtag Missourians, whose only distinguishments of rank were small bits of red flannel fastened to sleeves, hardly presented a military bearing on which the former Texas ranger felt that he could rely (which seems ironic, considering McCulloch's insistence upon wearing a velvet civilian's coat rather than a military uniform). However, when McCulloch learned of Sigel's move to cut off Jackson, he took it upon himself to save the

30. Ware, *Lyon Campaign*, 190–97; Lyon to Franz Sigel, July 10, 1861, Nathaniel Lyon File, SHSM.

31. Ware, *Lyon Campaign*, 190–97; Shalhope, *Sterling Price*, 170–71; Monaghan, *Civil War on the Western Border*, 154–56.

Missouri state forces rather than simply return to Arkansas. He marched his forces north and even captured one of Sigel's units in Neosho. When news of Jackson's victory reached the Confederate commander, however, he lost no time leaving the state. Feeling that the Missouri troops were for the moment safe, he and his troops returned to Maysville while Jackson and Price moved to Cowskin Prairie. This was the situation that greeted Lyon when on July 13 he arrived in Springfield.[32]

Having left his troops under Sturgis's command the day before, Lyon rode ahead to Springfield. With a population of two thousand, the Greene County seat represented the largest Missouri city south of St. Louis. When planning his campaign, Lyon had envisioned Springfield as an ending point, a place for jubilant respite after the destruction of Jackson's treasonous rabble. Now, however, he found himself compelled to hold the predominantly pro-Union city against a much stronger army. Lyon met quickly with Sweeny to discuss the situation. Supplies were woefully short; those the Irishman had arranged for still had not arrived. The troops needed shoes and clothing after the hard march from Boonville, and most had not been paid since their enlistment. Particularly distressing was that the ninety-day enlistments of nearly half of his volunteers would soon expire. Many of the Reserve Corps, faced with the harshness and deprivations of campaigning, now grumbled that they desired only to fight for their city and would not reenlist for three years of government service. In a thirty-six-hour span, Lyon had already sent two entire Home Guard regiments back to St. Louis to be mustered out. With ten to twenty thousand secessionists reported south of Springfield, Lyon was visibly worried. Hastily he scratched some messages to Harding, instructing him somehow to have the necessary supplies sent to him. "Governor Jackson will soon have in this vicinity not less than 30,000 men," he wrote to Harding. "I must have at once an additional force of 10,000 men, or abandon my position." Lyon knew that several fully equipped regiments were stationed in southern Iowa and western Illinois, and he saw no better purpose for them than to come to his assistance. Lyon sent several envoys to St. Louis to attend to these crucial matters.[33]

32. Edwin C. Bearss, "Fort Smith Serves General McCulloch as a Supply Depot," 315; Shalhope, *Sterling Price,* 170–71; Peckham, *Lyon and Missouri,* 298.

33. Lyon to Chester Harding, July 13, 1861, in Peckham, *Lyon and Missouri,* 298–99; Adamson, *Rebellion in Missouri,* 163; Special Order no. 11, July 15, 1861, Letters Sent and General and Special Orders Issued, Army of the West, RG 393; Special Order no. 15, July 16, 1861, ibid.; Special Order no. 18, July 16, 1861, ibid.; Special Order no. 21, July 17, 1861, ibid.; Special Order no. 32, July 19, 1861, ibid.; Lyon to Harding, July 15, 1861, in *Congressional Globe,* 37th Congress, 2d sess., 1125–26.

Lyon spent the next several days readying his position for further action. Establishing his headquarters on the north side of College Street, in an unoccupied downtown building belonging to Unionist congressman John S. Phelps, he arranged for his troops to encamp on Pond Creek, near the hamlet of Little York, about fifteen miles west of Springfield. He could not understand why supplies had not been sent; his troops were growing dissatisfied with a constant diet of coffee and corn meal. What he did not know was that McKinstry had not sent any supplies. When Sweeny bypassed him and requisitioned supplies directly from Washington, the indignant quartermaster held that a breach in regulations had occurred and canceled the orders. As a result, Lyon (who had maintained all along that McKinstry was not "in due earnest") received practically none of the supplies that Sweeny had requisitioned. By the time this was discovered, it was far too late. In the meantime, Lyon's troops growled as loudly as their stomachs.[34]

To make matters even worse, on July 16 Lyon received a message from the adjutant general ordering the removal of the five companies of the Second Infantry, including Sweeny himself, from the Department of the West. Lyon was incensed. Desperate for reinforcements, he saw only that the old scoundrel Winfield Scott was taking away his regulars, the pride of his army and the only troops in which he placed any real confidence. Angry that on that same day he had been forced to release an entire regiment of Home Guards because they refused to reenlist, Lyon wrote to Harding that his "misfortunes are greatly due to the rawness of our troops and to the wonton misconduct of many of them. I would not have them in the service if it could be helped."[35]

The order, however, held far deeper implications. By this time, Lyon had begun to feel that the government did not consider his campaign—his cause—important. Though Frémont had been installed as his new commander a full week earlier, he had not yet even arrived at his post. Lyon began to wonder if, for some inexplicable reason, he was being

---

34. Holcombe and Adams, *Account of Wilson's Creek,* 8, 17–18; Adamson, *Rebellion in Missouri,* 122–23, 164–66; Lyon to Chester Harding, July 31, 1861, Letters Received, Department of the West, box 10, RG 393; Lyon to Harding, July 15, 1861, in *Congressional Globe,* 37th Congress, 2d sess., 1125–26.

35. Lyon to E. D. Townsend, July 17, 1861, in Peckham, *Lyon and Missouri,* 303–5; Special Order no. 18, July 16, 1861, Thomas J. Sweeny Collection, Huntington; Lyon to Chester Harding, July 31, 1861, Letters Received, Department of the West, box 10, RG 393.

sacrificed. Angrily, he wrote a long letter to the adjutant general officially acknowledging receipt of the orders and arguing at great length
against the decision. "At Washington," he railed, "troops from all the
northern, middle, and eastern States are available for the support of the
Army in Virginia, . . . and it seems strange that so many troops must go
on from the West, and strip us of the means of defense; but if it is the
intention to give up the West, let it be so . . . ." In a letter to Harding, he
called his old nemesis's intentions "imbecility or malice . . . . Scott will
cripple us if he can." Showing hints of desperation, he sent a plaintive
request for Harding: "See Frémont, if he has arrived. The want of supplies has crippled me so that I cannot move, and I do not know when I
can. Everything seems to combine against me at this point. Stir up
Blair."[36]

Contributing directly to Lyon's despair was the toll that the rigors of
the past month had taken on his strength. In short, Lyon was fatigued.
Normally a light sleeper, he had existed on virtually no rest since before
Camp Jackson. One of his men remembered him during this time as "a
sleepless man" who rose regularly at about 3:00 A.M., while a Cole
Camp resident recalled that on one of the first nights out of Boonville he
and Lyon spent the entire night discussing strategy for the campaign.
The travails encountered in pushing his troops to catch Jackson could
only have advanced his state of physical and mental exhaustion. Though
at this point fatigue affected only his morale, it would soon cause in Lyon
far more serious debilitations.[37]

As Lyon's Army of the West tried to regain its strength in its camp
west of Springfield, it was forced to remain constantly on the alert for
secessionist raids. A sizable number of Southern sympathizers resided in
the area, whose courage was bolstered by the large force of the State
Guard encamped to the south. Pickets exchanged fire on several nights,
but the alerts were for the most part unnecessary. However, they served
to make Lyon and the other officers keenly aware of secessionist activities in the southwestern section of the state. One such operation was a
State Guard recruiting office in the town of Forsyth, about thirty-five
miles south of Springfield. Lyon determined to break up the recruiting
office, and on July 20 he sent Sweeny to the town with 1,200 troops and

36. Lyon to E. D. Townsend, July 17, 1861, in Peckham, *Lyon and Missouri*, 303–5;
Lyon to Chester Harding, July 17, 1861, ibid., 302–3.

37. Ware, *Lyon Campaign*, 227, 339–40; Clark, *Life in the Middle West*, 59; George
S. Grover, "Col. Benjamin Whitehead Grover," 134–35.

a section of artillery. Early on the evening of the twenty-second, the federals arrived at the outskirts of town and after a brief skirmish drove the small force into the broken hills to the south. They then captured the stores that were stockpiled in the village and returned the next day to Springfield, burning what they could not carry with them. Lyon sent similar scouting expeditions to Chesapeake and Greenfield, but neither met resistance nor uncovered any munitions.[38]

Lyon continued to be frustrated by the government's supine attitude toward his efforts. On July 25, however, he received a lengthy letter from Harding that enlightened him somewhat as to the reasons behind the delays. Harding gave news of the still-tenuous situation in northern and eastern Missouri. John Pope, Lyon's old West Point mate, was moving into the northeast corner of the state to secure it, while Benjamin Prentiss was stationed at Cairo with eight regiments. One of the regiments McClellan had approved to be sent to Lyon (the 21st Illinois, commanded by Col. Ulysses S. Grant) had been rerouted to Cairo because of the threat from a large force just south at Columbus, Kentucky. Two regiments, the 7th Missouri, whom Lyon had left at Boonville, and the 13th Illinois, guarding the railroad head at Rolla, could possibly be spared when the situation in the state stabilized. In the meantime, Harding had been granted authority to enlist more troops and was busy doing so.[39]

Although Harding's news held no guarantees, one piece of news Lyon welcomed: Frémont wired on July 23 that he was leaving from New York. At last, Lyon would have a commander who would aid his cause; Blair assured him of that. More immediately important was that Frémont would have the authority to cut through red tape and procure supplies, pay, and reinforcements for Lyon's troops, things Harding proved unable to do while Lyon was in the field. Anticipating Frémont's arrival, Lyon sent Capt. John Cavender to St. Louis on July 25 to see the new department commander. Two days later, he sent Congressman Phelps on the same mission. Lyon's message was emphatic: "*The safety of the State is hazarded;* orders from General Scott strip the entire West of regular forces, and increase the chances of sacrificing it." Within the

38. Thomas Sweeny to Lyon, July 27, 1861, in *OR*, III, 1:44–45; Special Order no. 46, July 23, 1861, Letters Sent and General and Special Orders Issued, Army of the West, RG 393; John Schofield to George Deitzler, July 28, 1861, ibid.: Wilkie, *Pen and Powder*, 24–25.

39. Chester Harding to Lyon, July 21, 1861, in Peckham, *Lyon and Missouri*, 306–11.

week, four more messengers were on their way to see Frémont to implore him to send Lyon aid.[40]

While Lyon cried for relief from Springfield, his adversaries faced problems of their own. At Cowskin Prairie, Price undertook the herculean task of creating an army from his untrained Missourians. Estimating his force to number seven thousand, two thousand of whom were completely unarmed, Price believed somewhat naively that those unarmed troops would be able to pick up dropped arms from those who were either killed or wounded in battle. He also boasted seven small pieces of artillery, though they were woefully short of ammunition. Price was fortunate to be near the Granby mines, an abundant source of both lead and powder. He detailed his men, assisted by blacksmiths and tinsmiths in Carthage, to begin manufacturing small-arms cartridges and artillery shells. Price's greatest hindrance, however, was a lack of trained officers to instruct the equally untrained troops. With only a handful of leaders being skilled in military discipline, many of the officers taught themselves the art of war as they drilled the troops. The situation often created great confusion during drill sessions. Despite the adversities, the troops soon became adept at their duties, and the rabble quickly resembled an army.[41]

Claiborne Jackson did not remain in camp long. Soon after his arrival in Neosho, he learned that the state convention was reconvening on July 22. Certain that one of its first acts would be to depose his government and replace it with another under federal control, the governor sought to counteract the move. Although Jackson realized that he could not prevent any decision the convention might make, he hoped to solicit Confederate assistance with which he could regain a sizable amount of the state. With it, Jackson would regain the allegiance of what he considered a majority of Missouri's citizenry. On July 12, he left the state, accompanied by former U.S. senator David Rice Atchison (who had led a State Guard unit at Carthage), to meet with the Arkansas governor, Henry Rector. They received a favorable reception, and the next day the two traveled to Memphis, Tennessee, where on the twenty-second they met with Gen.

40. Adamson, *Rebellion in Missouri,* 178–80; Lyon to John S. Phelps, July 27, 1861, in Holcombe and Adams, *Account of Wilson's Creek,* 18n; Harding to James O. Broadhead, July 21, 1861, Broadhead Papers, MHS; George B. McClellan to Harding, July 20, 1861, in *Congressional Globe,* 37th Congress, 2d sess., 1126; Lyon to John C. Frémont, July 27, 1861, ibid.

41. Castel, *General Sterling Price,* 28–29.

Leonidas Polk, commanding the Confederacy's Department No. 2. Polk agreed that Missouri was a strategically valuable state and consented to send a force into the southeastern section of the state under the command of Gen. Gideon Pillow. Satisfied with their results thus far, Jackson and Atchison left immediately for Richmond to meet with the Confederate president in hopes of gaining financial aid for the Missouri troops.[42]

By the last week of July, Price felt confident that his troops were ready to take the field. Having heard rumors that Lyon was losing men as enlistments expired, he saw no better opportunity to strike the federals at Springfield and drive them from the southwestern part of the state. Riding into Arkansas, he met again with McCulloch in Maysville and with great difficulty convinced him to join forces again for a movement on Lyon at Springfield. McCulloch, however, consented to the union only after Price agreed to leave behind the unarmed Missourians. Price quickly returned to his troops, and on July 25 they marched from their encampment toward Cassville, where they linked with McCulloch's troops four days later. After waiting two more days for the arrival of Pearce's militia, the 12,700-man column marched toward Springfield on the Telegraph, or Wire, Road. Price brought along his unarmed troops against McCulloch's wishes but issued orders for those Missourians to stay at least one day's march behind the rest of the force.[43]

In Springfield, Lyon was becoming increasingly disconcerted because of his situation. His men had still not been paid, they were dispirited from their lack of clothing, shoes, and food, and squads of soldiers were leaving the ranks daily as their enlistments ran out. Some declared openly that they wanted "a fight or a discharge." His effective force was quickly dwindling, and he had received so many complaints of his troops raiding the local farmers—many of them pro-Union—that he had been forced to issue orders that forbade further "plundering, wanton destruction of property, and disregard of personal rights." Moreover, he had heard from none of his emissaries to St. Louis even though Frémont had arrived in the city on July 25 and had taken up residence in the palatial Brant Mansion. Impatiently, Lyon flooded the telegraph wires with requests for reinforcements.[44]

42. Kirkpatrick, "Admission of Missouri," 368–70; William E. Parrish, *David Rice Atchison of Missouri,* 215–16; Ezra J. Warner, *Generals in Gray,* 242–43.
43. Castel, *General Sterling Price,* 33–35; Edwin C. Bearss, *The Battle of Wilson's Creek,* 21.
44. Lyon to John S. Phelps, July 27, 1861, in *OR,* I, 3:408; General Orders, July 26,

On July 28, Lyon received alarming news that a large force of Confederates had moved from Carthage toward Greenfield and that other smaller groups had been seen both in Sarcoxie and at Bowers' Mills. The forces were reputedly moving on the Dade County Home Guards, stationed in Greenfield, about forty-three miles west of Springfield. Immediately, Lyon sent a regiment to Greenfield, but when they arrived, no rebels could be found. The weary column was forced to retrace its steps.[45]

Just as the Greenfield column arrived back in Springfield, Lyon received two more pieces of distressing news. On the twenty-eighth, Gideon Pillow's Confederates had landed at New Madrid, Missouri, in the Bootheel on the Mississippi. The move threatened the important river junction of Cairo, Illinois, and meant that the forces at Cairo that Lyon hoped would be sent to him would probably stay where they were. At the same time, Lyon received word from his spies that a large force of Confederates was moving north from Cassville. He had been expecting this move since Jackson had escaped his trap, but he worried now that he would be unable to stop it. However, Lyon misinterpreted the Confederates' intentions. He believed that the three columns (McCulloch, Jackson, and the mysterious force reported near Greenfield) were all moving to link somewhere south of Springfield. Once they linked, he estimated that their force would total nearly thirty thousand, far greater than he could combat. Forced into action, Lyon resolved to strike the main column before the three forces converged. He would then turn on the others and defeat each in turn. Undeniably, the plan was risky. Yet Lyon held to his faith in an aggressive offense, and by moving he could at least keep his dissonant troops from leaving the ranks during the move. Haggard and suffering from weight loss—which his slight frame could ill afford— Lyon began preparations to move, not understanding why he had received no word from Frémont.[46]

Unknown to Lyon, his emissaries had indeed reached the department commander, only to be greeted with shocking indifference. Cavender, the first to arrive, received a brief interview with Frémont, then was instructed to return at 9:00 P.M. that evening for a longer session. When

---

1861, ibid., 407; Adamson, *Rebellion in Missouri,* 176–77; Ware, *Lyon Campaign,* 250.

45. Bearss, *Battle of Wilson's Creek,* 14.

46. Ibid., 14–15; E. M. Davis to John C. Frémont, August 3, 1861, in Peckham, *Lyon and Missouri,* 321.

he arrived, the mansion was locked and the windows dark. By chance, Cavender happened to find Frémont's adjutant, Capt. John C. Kelton, who reassured Cavender that the department commander had ordered a paymaster to leave for Springfield the next day and that Frémont had also arranged for Lyon's reinforcements. Cavender left the next day for Springfield. To his credit, Frémont had indeed requested that the War Department send two months' pay for Lyon's troops. However, he sent neither paymaster nor men to Lyon's camp in Springfield.[47]

Phelps, the next to arrive in St. Louis, was granted a personal session with Frémont, only to be told that Lyon's predicament was not as serious as the general believed it to be, that there was no possible way for the Ozark region to yield as many men as McCulloch was purported to have, and that Frémont had no troops to spare as he needed them to turn back Pillow's "Army of Liberation" at New Madrid. Frémont's attitude so outraged Phelps that he decided to travel immediately to Washington and take the matter up with Frank Blair. A "puppet" the Pathfinder had proved most definitely not to be. Lincoln agreed with Blair's and Phelps's concerns and on August 7 directed Cameron to send Lyon reinforcements. His assistance, however, came too late.[48]

Privately, however, Frémont had other thoughts. Overwhelmed by the enormity of his new position, the Pathfinder believed that the potential losses of Cairo and St. Louis were of far greater importance to the federal government than that of the Ozark region. Pillow's army now threatened those cities. For the moment, Lyon needed to act as a defensive force to prevent the Confederates from advancing toward St. Louis. Frémont was convinced that Lyon had enough troops and that he should be able to repel an attack. If he could not, Frémont believed Lyon had the good sense to retire for reinforcements. When Lyon's third messenger, Dr. Frank Porter, arrived to speak with Frémont, the Pathfinder, tired of being badgered, snapped that Lyon would fight at Springfield "only on his own responsibility," for he had his orders to fall back. No record exists of any such direct order. What is clear, however, is that as far as

47. Peckham, *Lyon and Missouri*, 314–17; Assistant Adjutant General, Department of the West, to Simon Cameron, July 29, 1861, Letters Sent, Department of the West, vol. 4, RG 393.

48. Adamson, *Rebellion in Missouri*, 179; Abraham Lincoln to Simon Cameron, August 7, 1861, in *OR*, I, 3:429; John C. Phelps to Hamilton R. Gamble, August 8, 1861, Hamilton R. Gamble Papers, MHS.

Frémont was concerned, Lyon was on his own. Had the department commander known his subordinate better, he would have understood that such caveats would prove small hindrance to Lyon's quest for justice.[49]

49. S. M. Breckinridge to Hamilton R. Gamble, August 3, 1861, Hamilton R. Gamble Papers, MHS; Peckham, *Lyon and Missouri*, 317–18; Edward C. Smith, *The Borderland in the Civil War*, 256–57; Turkoly-Joczik, "Frémont and the Western Department," 371–72.

X

The Punitive Crusade

Late on the afternoon of August 1, Lyon's army moved cautiously south-westward from Springfield. Lyon feared, however, that he did so blindly. "I hardly know how far our situation is hazardous," he wrote to Harding. "We hear of many threats and the scouts of Jackson's forces are heard of to the west of us—where McCullouch's troops are, and whether moving are uncertain." When his cavalry finally informed him that Jackson's vanguard was within eighteen miles of Springfield, he moved only ten miles that day. Sturgis's brigade moved out from their camp at Little York, and that night the two forces combined and encamped in a field along Wilson's Creek, a small tributary of the James River. Lyon liked the Kansans; not only had he lived their fight for many years, but he was also convinced that their deep hatred for the Missourians would prove an asset. However, he deplored their utter lack of discipline, and both he and Sturgis employed stringent measures to prevent them from venting their malice on any local pro-Southern farmers. With them, Lyon had an effective force of 5,868 officers and men, supported by three full batteries.[1]

Upon renewing its march the next morning, the federal column twice met Confederate patrols along the road. Each time, the patrols were quickly beaten back, but Lyon ordered his cavalry to screen the flanks of the lead battalions. The last few days had been oppressively hot, with temperatures reaching as high as 110 degrees. Lyon's troops were straggling badly because of both the heat and the poor rations on which the men had been forced to survive the last three weeks. Also debilitating was the paucity of available water and the choking dust the column kicked up during the march. Late in the morning, the column encoun-

---

1. Lyon to John C. Frémont, August 4, 1861, in OR, III, 1:47–48; Lyon to Chester Harding, July 31, 1861, Letters Received, Department of the West, box 10, RG 393; E. R. Hagemann, ed., *Fighting Rebels and Redskins: Experiences in Army Life of Colonel George B. Sanford, 1861–1892*, 125–26.

tered a sizable force of mounted State Guard just southwest of Dug Springs, an oblong valley broken by projecting spurs forming wooded ridges, through which ran the Wire Road. Because of the wooded terrain, Lyon was unable to ascertain the size of the enemy force and did not attack. Instead, he ordered a battalion of regulars under Capt. Frederick Steele and a company of dragoons under Capt. David S. Stanley to deploy and guard the road. Meanwhile, the rest of the army retired to the northeastern end of the valley.[2]

The mounted troops that the federals met were six companies of James S. Rains's Eighth Division of the Missouri State Guard. Rains was acting as the advance guard of the Confederate forces and was patrolling its "habitual" ten miles ahead of the main column when a patrol bumped into the federal units at Dug Springs. Rains was alerted to the contact early in the afternoon and moved with the rest of his troops and two small mountain howitzers to engage the federals. At about 5:00 P.M., a brisk skirmish ensued between Rains's six hundred horsemen, mostly dismounted, and Stanley's dragoons. The federals had already beaten back two assaults by the Missourians when Stanley ordered his horsemen to charge the retreating Confederates. They thundered down from a commanding spur and cut a swath through Rains's line, sending many into headlong flight. By this time, Lyon, not fully informed of the situation, sent word for Steele to retire, while he formed a portion of his own command and moved forward to relieve him. When Steele pulled back his troops, Rains surmised hastily that the Yankees were retreating and ordered what command he had left to advance. They soon met with close-range artillery fire from Lyon's batteries and fled the field. Many ran the entire ten miles to Crane Creek, where late that night they reached the main force's encampment. The Missourians' embarrassing disorganization disgusted McCulloch, and he determined no longer to act in concert with Price and his damned rabble.[3]

The next morning, August 3, Lyon pushed farther south along the Wire Road, encountering a small Confederate patrol at McCullah's Store, about three miles beyond the end of the Dug Springs valley. After quickly scattering the patrol and occupying their camp, Lyon ordered a halt and for the next twenty hours reconnoitered the surrounding land-

2. Diary of C. M. Chase, July 2 to October 10, 1861, Charles M. Chase Papers, SHSM; Edwin C. Bearss, *The Battle of Wilson's Creek,* 15–17; Return I. Holcombe and W. S. Adams, *An Account of the Battle of Wilson's Creek . . . ,* 11–12.

3. Bearss, *Battle of Wilson's Creek,* 23–27.

scape. However, he was unable to pinpoint the main Confederate force. After receiving alarming news that a large force was moving southeast from Sarcoxie to reinforce Price, Lyon called a council of war. Fearing that the Confederates might use their large number of cavalry to cut the army off from Springfield, and having only one day's worth of rations left, the officers decided to retire.[4]

Lyon grew despondent about the prospect of his glorious campaign coming to an unnecessary and meaningless end. Frémont would not answer his requests for relief, a force was closing in on his rear, and he feared that McCulloch, whom he could not locate, had somehow moved around his own force and was at that very minute closing in on Springfield. On the fourteenth, the entire 1st Iowa was to be mustered out, and with them would go large elements of both the 3rd and 5th Missouri. He would be left with only 3,500 troops, "badly clothed and without prospect of supplies," with which to combat a force of nearly 20,000. Though he had begun to enlist men from around Springfield, Lyon realized they could not replace the numbers he stood to lose. Without a victory to whet their appetites, he feared that most of his force—especially the Germans—would leave at the end of their enlistments. He had all but convinced himself that he had no choice but to retreat, either to Rolla or all the way to St. Louis. Depressed, he wrote a letter to Frémont voicing his opinions and describing his actions over the last several days. The next morning, he ordered his men back to Springfield.[5]

Lyon's apprehensions about McCulloch slipping around his flank were unfounded. While Lyon searched futilely for the main Confederate force, his adversaries had not moved from their camp south of Dug Springs. An ostensible rift had developed between the two Confederate commanders, jeopardizing the future of their entire campaign. Price was convinced that the entire federal army was in their front and that their chance for victory was at hand. On August 3, he pleaded with McCulloch to advance with him immediately to defeat Lyon's force. McCulloch balked. Thoroughly disgusted with the Missouri troops and their com-

4. Hardy Kemp, *About Nathaniel Lyon, Brigadier General, United States Volunteers and Wilson's Creek,* 190–91; Bearss, *Battle of Wilson's Creek,* 27–28; Jared Lobdell, ed., "Civil War Journal and Letters of Colonel John V. DuBois, Part II," 23. Also known as Curran Post Office and McCullah's Chapel, the "Store" was actually a small settlement established in the late 1840s by Alexander McCullah. It contained both a trading post and a small church and served the locals as a mail stop along the Wire Road.

5. Lyon to John C. Kelton, August 4, 1861, in *OR,* III, 1:47–48.

manders, he refused to cooperate with them in any concerted effort unless Price granted him overall command.

The Missourian was appalled at the notion. He was older than McCulloch and believed that he had far more military experience (he had been a brigadier general with an independent command in the war with Mexico, when McCulloch was only a captain of scouts). Moreover, this was *his* state, he had far more troops than the Texan, and Price was a major general while McCulloch was but a brigadier. When McCulloch refused to recognize Price's volunteer militia rank, Price stormed out of the meeting. He later realized, however, that he could not defeat Lyon's force without the Texan's troops. The next day, Price returned to McCulloch's tent and, after a pompous reiteration of all the reasons why he was far more fit for the overall command, submitted to McCulloch's demand if he would participate in the attack. McCulloch agreed but was so angered by Price's overbearing attitude that their relations during the rest of the operation were irrevocably strained.[6]

The delay caused by the Price-McCulloch disagreement gave Lyon's troops enough time to slip back to Springfield. In addition, Rains's Missourians had bungled their surveillance duties and allowed Lyon to do so unnoticed, enraging McCulloch even further. In scorching weather, the Southern column began a forced march to overtake the Federals, but the weather proved too exhausting for the troops. On August 6, the Confederate vanguard encamped at the point where the Wire Road crossed Wilson's Creek, ten miles southwest of Springfield. A number of fields of ripening corn were in the immediate vicinity, and McCulloch's troops were beginning to run short of provisions. Without knowing exactly where Lyon was positioned or whether he had fortified, McCulloch was hesitant to attack, and he saw Wilson's Creek as a good site from which to reconnoiter Springfield.[7]

For the next several days, while he waited for his supply train, McCulloch probed Lyon's position without success. Price was exasperated. He had given the Texan his command but could not get him to attack. Just after daybreak on August 9, Price confronted McCulloch heatedly about his intentions. In an effort to appease Price, McCulloch called a general meeting of the officers for that afternoon. At the council of war, McCul-

---

6. Robert E. Shalhope, *Sterling Price: Portrait of a Southerner,* 173.

7. Ibid., 173–74; Bearss, *Battle of Wilson's Creek,* 33–34; Eugene F. Ware, *The Lyon Campaign,* 287.

loch made the officers aware of his own reservations about attacking the federals in Springfield. Impatiently, Price threatened to reassume command of the Missourians and lead an attack himself, with or without the assistance of either McCulloch or his troops. Confronted with the ultimatum, McCulloch acquiesced. He issued marching orders for 9:00 P.M. that night and scheduled an attack for daybreak the next morning, August 10.[8]

While the Confederates commanders were unable to make decisions, Lyon was experiencing difficulties of his own in Springfield. The column had retreated hastily from Dug Springs, arriving in the city on August 5 about sundown. Convinced that an attack would come soon, Lyon left Sturgis with a force of two thousand about four miles south of the city to protect the main avenue of approach. Upon reaching his headquarters, he ordered that all roads leading into Springfield be posted with sentries. Although any individual would be permitted to enter the city, none could leave without a signed pass. He wanted no news of his plans or the condition of his troops to leak to the Confederates, who would soon reach Springfield, he thought. He then ordered his troops to sleep on their arms until further notice in case of attack.[9]

Shortly after Lyon's return, John Cavender greeted him with the story of Frémont's inexplicable behavior. Since so much time had passed since Frémont's arrival in St. Louis, Lyon was not surprised, especially after hearing reports that the department commander had personally led troops to Cairo. Somberly, he now realized that he would receive no assistance from Frémont. All signs pointed sadly toward an immediate retreat to Rolla. It was the only logical course of action. Yet Lyon could not resign himself simply to retreat; he had come too far. Moreover, he was gripped by indecision, a state that he had seldom before experienced. He had never been one to change his mind once he had set it on a certain purpose, even under extreme adversities. And the purpose that he was now fulfilling was the most important of his life. He could not retreat until he was sure that there was no other way. Lyon decided to wait until the next day to see if any new developments had taken place that might aid his position. Only then would he accept the prospect of retreat, which in his mind was the same as defeat.

On the morning of August 6, a wagon train finally reached Spring-

8. Bearss, *Battle of Wilson's Creek,* 37–38.
9. Ibid., 41; Ware, *Lyon Campaign,* 296.

field, providing Lyon's men with rations and clothing. The provisions succeeded in lifting their sunken spirits somewhat, and for the first time in over two weeks the men received full rations. Lyon took this as a good sign and put retreat out of his mind for the time being. That afternoon, he learned from his spies that McCulloch's Confederates were encamped on Wilson's Creek. Convinced that circumstances were improving, he hatched an impetuous plan calling for the combined elements of two brigades to make a night attack on the encamped Confederates. He gave marching orders for 6:00 P.M. that night.[10]

Almost immediately after Lyon had sent his orders, an excited courier rushed in carrying a message from Capt. Job Stockton of the Springfield Home Guards. One of his patrols had clashed with a party of rebel cavalry at Grand Prairie, just west of town. The horsemen were reputed to be Price's. Lyon now wondered if all three of the shadow columns had joined and were encamped at Wilson's Creek. He decided that the best way to find out was to carry out the attack on the Confederate camp. Sending two companies to assist Stockton, Lyon ordered a number of his forces to be ready to march in support of Sturgis. He postponed the night march until 10:00 P.M.[11]

By now, Lyon was running on sheer adrenaline. Though never one to share pleasantries with his command, he was increasingly cross and irritable from both lack of rest and the constant pressure upon him. His office was deluged by local residents, mostly Unionists, who complained of soldiers having stolen horses and livestock. Lyon was continually forced to send couriers to help find the stolen property, if possible, or to promise restitution, though he knew none was forthcoming. Moreover, the city was flooded with refugees fleeing the Confederates and looking to him for protection. Schofield recalled that Lyon was overwhelmed by a "morbid sensitiveness" to the inevitable disaster that would befall the residents of southwestern Missouri if the army were forced to retreat. He found it terribly difficult to face those loyal citizens who depended upon him when he himself was so unsure of the future.[12]

To make matters worse, there was growing unrest among the volunteers over what they saw as a lack of direction in the high command and a

---

10. Bearss, *Battle of Wilson's Creek*, 42.

11. Ibid.; James Peckham, *General Nathaniel Lyon and Missouri in 1861*, 325.

12. Jared C. Lobdell, ed., "Civil War Journal and Letters of Colonel John V. DuBois, April 12, 1861, to October 16, 1862, Part I," 456; Ware, *Lyon Campaign*, 296–97; John M. Schofield, *Forty-six Years in the Army*, 39.

lack of respect for their efforts. They had been marched from Springfield to find the enemy, yet inexplicably had returned to base without giving battle. They were constantly on the alert while holed up in town and were formed at all hours of the night, only to have their positions shifted slightly and be told again to sleep on their arms. They believed the "little red-headed cuss" had meager gratitude for all their efforts, and when they sent word to him that many would ignore their enlistment expirations to stay for the fight, they were told that it was their duty to do so. One Iowa volunteer private, angered by Lyon's callousness, remarked, "I never liked him, nor did any of us as far as I ever could see . . . . He struck us as a man devoted to duty, who thought duty, dreamed duty, and had nothing but 'duty' on his mind." The volunteer troops held none of the blind adoration for Nathaniel Lyon that the Germans had for Sigel.[13]

The combined pressures cut deeply into Lyon's capacity for leadership. He had lost the mental sharpness that had characterized his entire military career, and he began to depend more and more on the decisions of his subordinates. Though he ordered an attack that would pit only half of his troops against the entire Confederate camp, he was so oblivious of time that he did not arrive at his troops' camp until 2:00 A.M., a full four hours late. Inexplicably, he waited another hour without giving any orders. At 3:00 A.M., he finally looked at his pocketwatch and realized his misjudgment of the time. He then canceled the attack and returned to Springfield. On the ride back, his mental fatigue prompted him to confess to Schofield "that he had a premonition that a night attack would prove disastrous, and yet he had felt impelled to try it once, and perhaps should do so again, 'for my only hope of success is in a surprise.'"[14]

Throughout the day of August 7, reports reached Lyon of an imminent attack on Springfield. He kept his troops on alert the entire day, under a blistering sun, while federal cavalry skirmished repeatedly with Confederate horsemen. That night, Lyon held a council of war at his headquarters on College Street. The session lasted until midnight, and the group discussed at length the options of merely evacuating the city or abandoning the entire section of the state, retreating either to Rolla or to

13. Ware, *Lyon Campaign*, 291–92, 296–97, 339–40.
14. Lobdell, "DuBois Journal, Part II," 24; Holcombe and Adams, *Account of Wilson's Creek,* 20.

Fort Scott, Kansas. Although Lyon wanted to hold on, his subordinates appeared to agree that the situation was too tenuous to remain in Springfield.

Suddenly, Sweeny rose, and with a flushed face he began to exhort the others in his thick Irish brogue. Gesticulating with his left arm (he had lost the right at Churubusco), he grew more excited as he spoke. He disagreed strongly with the idea of a retreat without battle. The rebels would boast of their easy victory and terrorize the loyal residents who did not leave. The result would be that the region's Unionists would become wholly discouraged. More important, the soldiers would lose all morale and would no doubt leave the ranks at the end of their enlistments. As a final, dramatic stance, Sweeny exclaimed, "Let us eat the last bit of mule flesh and fire that last cartridge before we think of retreating."

Sweeny's pluck, as well as his theatrics, seemed to enliven the federal commander. Because Lyon held the Irishman in such high regard, his empassioned speech stirred Lyon to action. Although the night's meeting ended with an agreement to wait the situation out and leave only if compelled by the Confederates, by the next morning Lyon appeared to have regained his lost conviction. When asked if the army would retreat, he snapped, "Not until we are whipped out!"[15]

On Thursday, August 8, another warning came of an imminent Confederate attack. The federal troops drew up in line of battle at the edge of town while teamsters rolled their wagons to the center of Springfield for protection. Officers took roll calls every hour to keep the men in position. It had not rained for over two weeks, and the troops suffered from the day-long exposure to the torrid heat. No attack came, and Lyon lost patience with waiting idly in Springfield. He determined to attack himself. That evening, he called another council of war. As soon as his officers seated themselves, Lyon began speaking:

> Gentlemen, there is no prospect of our being re-enforced at this point; our supply of provisions is running short; there is a superior force in front; and it is reported that Hardee is marching with 9,000 men to cut our line of communication.[16] It is evident that we must retreat. The question arises, what is the best method of doing it. Shall we endeavor to retreat without giving the enemy battle beforehand, and run the risk of having to fight every inch along

15. Holcombe and Adams, *Account of Wilson's Creek,* 21; Bearss, *Battle of Wilson's Creek,* 42–43; Holcombe and Adams, *Account of Wilson's Creek,* 21–22.

16. In early August, Confederate general William J. Hardee made an abortive drive on Ironton, Missouri, from Pitman's Ferry, Arkansas.

our line of retreat, or shall we attack him in his position, and endeavor to hurt him so that he cannot follow us. I am decidedly in favor of the latter plan. I propose to march this evening with all our available force, . . . throw our whole force upon him at once, and endeavor to rout him before he can recover from his surprise.[17]

It was an audacious plan, but one that Lyon was convinced was essential to his campaign's success. Moreover, it could not be delayed. Many of his volunteers were scheduled to leave in only five days, and only one regiment had agreed to stay long enough for a fight. If he withdrew, they would simply disappear. He had no chance for reinforcements, he had no fortifications, and although he was still in possession of his beloved regulars, even they remained under orders to go East unless Lyon received countermanding instructions. Any day he might receive orders recalling them. No, Lyon thought it better to attack now rather than wait for his entire command to be withdrawn. But there was a far greater reason for ordering an attack. In his own mind, Lyon would not retire without punishing the secessionists, and that conviction was so all-consuming that he cast to the wind all sound military judgment. He was willing to risk his entire force for that purpose.

Had Lyon's mental vigor been at normal strength, the attack would have taken place that night. However, he was visibly drained, and objections were voiced by other commanders. Several of their regiments had just returned from a nine-mile reconnaissance mission and were not fully rested, and they had not yet received their provisions from the supply train. Surprisingly, Lyon succumbed to their remonstrances and agreed to postpone the attack until the next night.[18]

The next morning, August 9, Lyon received his only correspondence from Frémont, dated August 6. Hoping for news of reinforcements, Lyon ripped open the envelope, only to be sadly disappointed. Imperiously worded, the dispatch informed him that the department commander believed Lyon had grossly overestimated the force in his front and that he would be sent no reinforcements. Frémont then requested that his subordinate report any future movements as soon as possible and that "if Lyon was not strong enough to maintain his position as far in advance as Springfield, he should fall back toward Rolla until reinforcements should meet him." Frémont had not directly ordered Lyon to

17. Ware, *Lyon Campaign,* 303–4.
18. Ibid.

retreat; however, he had made it clear that any fight Lyon might find in Springfield would be solely his own responsibility.[19]

Frémont's message was bitter medicine indeed. Throwing the paper on the desk, Lyon cried out, "God damn General Frémont! He is a worse enemy to me and the Union cause than Price and McCulloch and the whole damned tribe of rebels in this part of the State!" Frustrated, he ordered Schofield to respond to Frémont's enraging note. He then fired off a letter to the commander of the Dallas County Home Guard directing that he move his command immediately to Springfield and that his men should wear strips of white cloth on their hats so they would not be mistaken for State Guard. When Schofield finished the letter to Frémont, Lyon read it and found that he wished some of the wording changed to reflect the precarious position he believed the department commander had placed him in. After inserting his own wording, Lyon told Schofield to send it to St. Louis. The last paragraph reveals Lyon's desperation:

I find my position extremely embarrassing, and am at present unable to determine whether I shall be able to maintain my ground or be forced to retire. I can resist any attack from the front, but if the enemy moves to surround me I must retire. I shall hold my ground as long as possible, *though I may without knowing how far* endanger the safety of my entire force with its valuable material, *being induced by the important considerations involved to take this step* . . . . [Lyon's changes in italics][20]

At 9:00 A.M., Sigel came to Lyon's office. The two had a long private conference. Impetuous himself, and vainglorious to a fault, Sigel posed an alternative to Lyon's plan of attack. Whereas Lyon had intended to attack Price's left flank with the entire federal force, Sigel advocated a different strategy, one that contradicted the most basic of military principles. The German suggested dividing the attacking force into two assaults. One, under Lyon, would attack as per the original plan. The other, under Sigel, consisting of two regiments of volunteers (Germans, of course) totaling 1,100 men, would circle to the southeast of the Confederate camp and launch a simultaneous assault on the unsuspect-

19. Schofield, *Forty-six Years in the Army,* 39–40; Holcombe and Adams, *Account of Wilson's Creek,* 23–24.

20. Holcombe and Adams, *Account of Wilson's Creek,* 19; Lyon to M. B. Edwards, August 9, 1861, Civil War Collection, MHS; Schofield, *Forty-six Years in the Army,* 40–41.

ing rear of the camp. If the plan worked, the entire camp would be a mass of confusion and would flee before the combined federal assaults.[21]

The plan was even riskier than Lyon's. Sigel proposed dividing a heavily outnumbered force in the very face of the enemy. The plan was preposterous, yet Lyon accepted it—he believed he had no choice. Because of his dire troop situation, Lyon was forced to rely ever more heavily upon his remaining German recruits. As their leader, Sigel's importance to Lyon's campaign was only magnified; "I fights mit Sigel" had become a password among the proud German troops. Because so many of them were nearly ready to leave, Lyon needed desperately to maintain Sigel's unqualified support. In short, Lyon felt he must assent to Sigel's plan to maintain that support. At a meeting of the commanders at 4:00 P.M. that afternoon, Lyon unveiled his decision to use Sigel's plan of attack. Despite vehement opposition from the other commanders, the troops would march at 6:00 P.M. that evening. When later questioned on the reasons for the decision, Lyon replied, "Frémont won't sustain me. Sigel has a great reputation, and if I fail against his advice it will give Sigel command and ruin me. Then again, unless he can have his own way, I fear he will not carry out my plans."[22]

Sweeny had not been present at the conference, and when he heard of the new plan he rode immediately to Lyon's personal quarters. Along with Florence M. Cornyn, surgeon of the 1st Missouri, he attempted to talk Lyon out of the two-pronged attack. Neither advocated aborting the attack altogether, but they questioned the propriety of the new plan. Lyon conversed with them on the rear piazza, which was slightly cooler than his quarters, but would not change his mind. Genuinely fatigued, he dismissed them and retired to his room.[23]

Lyon had been a military man too long not to understand that his most obvious course was retreat. However, he could not face the humiliation of failure. He had worked so hard and come too far for it to come to such an ignominious end. By pulling back to Rolla, he would admit that Frémont had bested him, that his enemies in Washington knew what they were doing when they continued to hamper Blair's efforts to have Lyon

21. Holcombe and Adams, *Account of Wilson's Creek,* 27; Lobdell, "DuBois Journal, Part II," 27; Schofield, *Forty-six Years in the Army,* 43.

22. Lobdell, "DuBois Journal, Part II," 27–28; Bearss, *Battle of Wilson's Creek,* 47; Lyon to Chester Harding, July 31, 1861, Letters Received, Department of the West, box 10, RG 393.

23. Peckham, *Lyon and Missouri,* 329.

put in command of the western theater. However, if he could deal the secessionists a stunning blow, he would prove the verity of his campaign. A quick, hard attack, followed by an orderly withdrawal, would not be misconstrued as a defeat. And in the case of a victory, the results would speak for themselves. Either way, Lyon would fulfill his campaign of punishment and still maintain his credibility. As he related to one acquaintance, "To abandon the Southwest without a struggle would be a sad blow to our cause, and would greatly encourage the Rebels. We will fight, and hope for the best." If his cause, the government's cause (by now the two were in his mind inextricably fused), was right, then Lyon would receive his reward of victory and the secessionists their punishment. The supreme being would see to that. If there truly were a God, one that doled out such rewards and punishments, then Lyon's campaign—God's campaign—could not fail. It was his duty to try.[24]

Lyon reached Phelps Grove, where Sturgis had been stationed since his return from Dug Springs, shortly before 6:00 P.M. The troops had already been issued cartridges and two days' rations. Before commencing the march, he addressed each of his regiments individually. Delivered softly yet deliberately, his message was hard for the companies on either end of the line to hear, and many of those who did hear were disappointed with Lyon's uninspiring message. To each regiment, he said, "Men, we are going to have a fight. We will march out in a short time. Don't shoot until you get orders. Fire low—don't aim higher than their knees; wait until they get close; don't get scared; it's no part of a soldier's duty to get scared."[25]

When rain developed, the Confederate command aborted the attack they had scheduled for that same evening. Both Lyon's and Sigel's columns, however, trudged southward through the wet night. The artillery wrapped their wheels with blankets to muffle the noise, and the cavalry used gunny sacks on their horses' hooves. Despite all of their precautions, the march was still noisy. The rain was the only factor that maintained Lyon's element of surprise. By 1:00 A.M., his guides led the column to within sight of the fires of the northernmost enemy pickets, and Lyon ordered the men to halt there and wait for dawn. At about midnight, Sigel's "brigade" moved into position astride the Wire Road south of the

24. Thomas W. Knox, *Camp-Fire and Cotton Field: Southern Adventure in Time of War*, 68.

25. Bearss, *Battle of Wilson's Creek*, 50; Ware, *Lyon Campaign*, 310.

Confederate camps, placing his four pieces of artillery to command the cornfield in which the southernmost elements of the Confederates were encamped. He waited for morning and the first sounds that would erupt from Lyon's guns, the signal to begin his own attack.[26]

As Lyon and Schofield lay in the light rain, sharing a rubber blanket, Lyon appeared more disconsolate than ever. He was not hopeful for victory and muttered repeatedly about being abandoned by his superiors. As his aide-de-camp remembered, Lyon "was oppressed with the responsibility of his situation, with anxiety for the cause, and with sympathy for the Union people in that section." Turning to Schofield, he remarked morbidly, "I am a believer in presentiments, and I have a feeling that I can't get rid of that I shall not survive this battle." A bit later, he added, "I will gladly give my life for a victory."[27]

At dawn, Lyon brought his troops into a line of advance. They moved to within a thousand yards of the Confederate camp before running into its pickets. Firing commenced immediately, and the pickets quickly withdrew. Lyon's infantry moved forward slowly, crossing a ravine and ascending a steep ridge, where they engaged a hastily formed skirmish line. As the firing increased, Lyon ordered up his two batteries of artillery. The Confederate skirmishers gave ground quickly. As the federal line spread out west of and perpendicular to Wilson's Creek, Lyon sent a battalion of infantry under Capt. Joseph Plummer across to the east side of the creek. After fording the stream, Plummer's men advanced into a hilltop cornfield owned by John A. Ray, where they immediately engaged the 3rd Louisiana, one of McCulloch's regiments of Confederates. As Lyon's troops gradually pushed the Confederate line back, they moved up the northern slope of the battlefield's dominant hill. The firing intensified as more of the Confederate forces, mostly Price's, came into line and advanced to the south slope of that hill. The two lines pushed back and forth across its crest.[28]

Meanwhile, Sigel launched his own attack. As soon as the sound of

26. John R. Gratiot to "Friend," August 12, 1861, Civil War Collection, MHS; Holcombe and Adams, *Account of Wilson's Creek,* 26–30; Franz Sigel to Walter L. Howard, July 30, 1895, in "Letter of Gen. F. Sigel," 147–48.

27. William H. Wherry, "Wilson's Creek, and the Death of Lyon," in *Battles and Leaders of the Civil War,* ed. Robert U. Johnson and Howard L. Conard, 1:292–93; Albert R. Greene, "On the Battle of Wilson's Creek," 117; Schofield, *Forty-six Years in the Army,* 43.

28. Holcombe and Adams, *Account of Wilson's Creek,* 31–34; Knox, *Camp-Fire and Cotton Field,* 69.

Lyon's musket fire crackled through the creek valley, Sigel ordered his cannon to open fire on the rebel camps in the fields west of the creek. The surprised Confederates quickly scattered to the north, and Sigel advanced the length of the fields and reformed his line at the north end near the Sharp farmhouse. Having captured some of the panicky Confederates, Sigel was misinformed that Lyon was routing Price's troops. The German saw a chance to bag the entire Confederate army as it ran southward on the Wire Road. He moved his troops quickly to a position straddling the road and awaited the retreating rebels. At this point, Sigel was convinced that his plan had worked to perfection and that he would soon be regaled as the battle's hero.[29]

At the northern end of the battle, the 3rd Louisiana drove Plummer from the Ray cornfield, and the federals recrossed the creek in disorder. By now, Lyon had engaged his entire line and was being subjected to a galling fire from the Pulaski Arkansas Battery, planted on a high hill on the east side of the creek. One of Lyon's batteries, under the direction of Lt. John V. DuBois, hastened forward and with incredibly accurate fire effectively neutralized the Confederate guns. Another section of DuBois's battery then pushed back McCulloch's Louisianans before they could press Plummer's retreating battalion. The fighting on the slope, soon known as "Bloody Hill," became intense; in some places the lines were separated by only a few yards.[30]

By mid-morning, the heat had become frightful. Bloody Hill had at this time few trees of any consequence, mostly short scrub oaks, and in the open terrain men fell from both wounds and heat stroke. Lulls settled periodically over the battlefield, marred only by desultory firing, as if both armies needed to catch their breath and take water before resuming the desperate struggle. Then the great crash of musketry and the thunder of cannon fire would resume almost spontaneously, to continue with wavelike intensity until another respite mysteriously occurred. While the 3rd Louisiana cleared the Ray cornfield of Plummer's men, Price was beaten back in two assaults on Bloody Hill. Upon hearing that Sigel was in his rear, McCulloch ordered the Louisianans to reform and double-quick on the Wire Road to the southern end of the battlefield to meet Sigel's advance.[31]

29. Holcombe and Adams, *Account of Wilson's Creek,* 40–41.
30. Bearss, *Battle of Wilson's Creek,* 84–86.
31. Ibid., 85–87; Holcombe and Adams, *Account of Wilson's Creek,* 34–35.

Meanwhile, Sigel's men enjoyed a long rest at the Sharp farmhouse. At about 8:30 A.M., Dr. S. H. Melcher spied a body of men moving down the valley from the north and crossing Skegg's Branch. Because they had last heard Lyon's guns emanating from that direction, he believed the troops to be federals. Melcher confirmed the sighting when he saw the line dressed in gray coats similar to those worn by the 1st Iowa. Sigel held his fire until it was too late, then was greeted with a devastating, close-range volley from the 3rd Louisiana. The German troops fled in horror from the Louisianans' point-blank fire. Within minutes, Sigel and his entire command were routed from the battle, chased incessantly by the Confederate cavalry. Those not captured, including Sigel, stopped only when they reached Springfield.[32]

On Bloody Hill, Lyon's troops were holding up well under the withering fire and intense heat. Their commander, however, was not faring as well. Having dismounted from his gray steed, he was directing the troops movements on foot, leading his mount by the reins. When once he moved dangerously close to the front lines, a rifle ball creased the outer portion of his right calf, causing him great pain and requiring attention to stop the flow of blood. Shortly thereafter, his dapple-gray horse was struck, and without plunging or rearing it expired immediately. Although he valued the horse greatly, he had no time to grieve and continued onward, waving his drab felt hat and sword to rally his troops.[33]

Despite the already stifling heat, Lyon kept his well-worn captain's tunic (no doubt more comfortable than the stiff, heavy brigadier's uniform) buttoned to his chin. Pale and dazed, he was soon struck again, this time grazed on the right side of the head. Blood ran down his cheek and matted his sweaty hair and beard as he limped toward the rear and sat down. An officer spied his wounded commander and bound a handkerchief around his head. Lyon was again despondent. Totten noticed his commander's head wound and offered him some brandy from his canteen. Lyon somberly declined. A short time later, Schofield happened by and sat next to Lyon. "It is as I expected," Lyon moaned; "I am afraid the day is lost." "No, General," Schofield replied, "let us try once more."[34]

Encouraged by Schofield's enthusiasm, Lyon stood up. He determined now to send his remaining reserves into the fray. Sturgis, who happened

32. Bearss, *Battle of Wilson's Creek,* 87–92.

33. Holcombe and Adams, *Account of Wilson's Creek,* 35–36, 99.

34. Ibid.; Report of James Totten, August 19, 1861, in *OR,* I, 3:74; Schofield, *Forty-six Years in the Army,* 44.

to be nearby, dismounted one of his orderlies and offered Lyon his mount. Lyon refused, saying, "I do not need a horse." He then ordered Sturgis to rally a portion of the 1st Iowa, one of the reserve units already committed, which had broken. When Sturgis went to the rear to rally the broken unit, other members of the regiment who were still in good order called for a leader since theirs was not in sight. Believing this his last chance for victory, Lyon determined to lead a fresh assault. Needing help to climb into the orderly's saddle, Lyon dripped blood from the heel of his right shoe. When his aides attempted to dissuade him from exposing himself so precariously to fire, Lyon replied firmly, "I am but doing my duty." Directing Sweeny, who had just ridden up, to lead the Iowans, Lyon rode closely to the right of the regiment. When an opposing party of horsemen emerged almost perpendicular to the Iowans, Lyon believed that he recognized one as Price himself. He ordered his escort to "draw pistols and follow," but an aide, Lt. William Wherry, convinced him that the move was far too rash. Lyon acceded and moved to the left rear of the line.[35]

Spying a gap in the line, Lyon twice called for the 2nd Kansas, the other reserve regiment, to move to the front. As they advanced in columns of platoons, Lyon ordered them deployed on the right of the 1st Iowa. Determined to drive from the crest the enemy regiment directly in his front (the 3rd Arkansas), he directed two companies of the 1st Iowa to join the Kansans' charge. Astride the orderly's horse, Lyon grasped the reins in his left hand and turned to the right. Waving his hat with his right hand, he attempted to rally the Kansans as they came near. "Come on, my brave boys," he barked, "I will lead you! Forward!"[36]

A murderous sheet of fire erupted from the thick brush in Lyon's immediate front. As he was turned to lead on the Kansans, Lyon was struck in the left breast. A large-caliber bullet, fired from only a few yards, entered below his fourth rib, tore through his heart and both lungs, and exited the right rear of his torso, just below the shoulder blade. Stunned, Lyon attempted to dismount but quickly began to fall. His personal orderly, Pvt. Albert Lehmann, rushed up and caught Lyon

35. Holcombe and Adams, *Account of Wilson's Creek,* 36; Wherry, "Wilson's Creek, and the Death of Lyon," 295; *Oration of Hon. B. Gratz Brown . . . ,* 7.

36. Holcombe and Adams, *Account of Wilson's Creek,* 99; Wherry, "Wilson's Creek, and the Death of Lyon," 295; Bearss, *Battle of Wilson's Creek,* 115–16; John R. Gratiot to "Friend," August 12, 1861, Civil War Collection, MHS; *Missouri Democrat,* September 10, 1861.

in his arms as he slumped. Cradling his fallen commander's limp form as he lowered him to the earth, Lehmann allowed Lyon's uncovered head to rest against his shoulder while he tried to stop the profuse flow of blood. Fighting to remain conscious, Lyon gasped for breath. After several agonizing minutes, Lyon found one last surge of consciousness and opened his eyes. Barely audible, he whispered hoarsely, "Lehmann, I am going."[37]

A moment later, he expired, amid the smoke and din of battle. Few of the troops even realized it. Although the charge of the 2nd Kansas succeeded in driving their foes from the hill after a twenty-minute struggle, the battle continued to rage. Lt. Gustavus Schreyer found the fallen general a few minutes later; Lyon's orderly was clutching his commander's hat and bemoaning his death. Taking charge, Schreyer, aided by Lehmann and two members of Schreyer's company of the 2nd Kansas, transported Lyon's body to the rear. Wherry and the rest of Lyon's staff soon learned the news. Fearing that word of the general's death would have an adverse effect on the troops, Wherry pulled Lyon's coattails over his face, and they placed the body in the shade of a small blackjack oak. Wherry quickly found Schofield and informed him of Lyon's death. Schofield rode over to view the body, then sought Sturgis and passed to him the army's overall command. The battle continued for about another hour, during which Price mounted one final grand assault upon Bloody Hill, only to be repulsed for a third time. The firing stopped almost immediately after Price's last assault. As the Confederates fell back a short distance to regroup for another assault, Sturgis made use of the time to order a hasty retreat to Springfield. The exhausted Confederates ordered no pursuit; the battle of Wilson's Creek had ended. The Lyon campaign was over as well. With its leader had died its purpose.[38]

37. Holcombe and Adams, *Account of Wilson's Creek,* 99; *Oration of Hon. B. Gratz Brown,* 7; Bearss, *Battle of Wilson's Creek,* 116; Wherry, "Wilson's Creek, and the Death of Lyon," 295.

38. Bearss, *Battle of Wilson's Creek,* 116–21; Wherry, "Wilson's Creek, and the Death of Lyon," 295–96.

Epilogue

The battle at Wilson's Creek was bloodier than anyone had imagined. In the brief six hours of fighting, the federal army suffered 1,317 killed, wounded, and missing, while the Confederates lost 1,230, a staggering 16 percent casualty rate that would stand eventually as one of the highest of the war. When viewed in light of the fact that the battle was fought between forces consisting overwhelmingly of untried recruits, of which nearly half were armed with no more than shotguns or fowling pieces, and of which several thousand were completely unarmed and never took part in the battle, the statistics are particularly amazing. As one participant aptly remembered the battle, it was one "mighty mean-fowt fight."[1]

News of Wilson's Creek and of Lyon's death made headlines across the country, evoking conflicting responses. Despite the initial banner in the *New York Times* proclaiming the battle a "Great National Victory in Missouri," the actual results soon became known. Barton Bates wrote his father, "General Lyon's death cost us much popular strength throughout the state." However, because the campaign had driven so many of those of questionable allegiance into the ranks of the secessionists, Bates believed that "we are really better off having them avowed against us than as pretended neutrals." While many Unionists were discontented with Frémont's apparent abandonment of Lyon's campaign, others questioned Lyon's rash strategy. "We all feel for Gen Lyon's death," wrote one resident, "but it seems as tho' our commander was very fond of attacking the enemy with the odds against them. I shall feel much better satisfied with Gen Sigel as command."[2]

1. Edwin C. Bearss, *The Battle of Wilson's Creek,* 136; Bruce Catton, *Terrible Swift Sword,* 20.

2. *New York Times,* August 14–15, 1861; Barton Bates to Edward Bates, September 8, 1861, Bates Family Papers, MHS; William F. Broadhead to James O. Broadhead, August 14, 1861, James O. Broadhead Papers, MHS; H. Everett to Abiel Leonard, August 17, 1861, Abiel Leonard Collection, SHSM.

Still others rejoiced at the news. James Thomas, a free black barber in St. Louis, recalled that his first knowledge of Lyon's death came from a young Southern sympathizer whose hair Thomas was cutting. "Hurry up and let me out of here," the man said to him; "I'm told Lyons [*sic*] was killed and I want to get drunk." J. D. McKown, another St. Louis resident, was more demonstrative. "*Lyon, the king of the beasts*," he wrote, "the *Camp Jackson HERO,* the murderer of innocent women and children and as I believe under the displeasure of God, he has met his just reward."[3]

For a time following the battle, it appeared as if Nathaniel Lyon's importance had eluded even his own troops. During the last minutes of the battle, Sturgis ordered the late general's body to be taken to the rear and placed in a wagon for transportation to Springfield. Shortly after this was done, a sergeant, not realizing that the body dressed in captain's garb was Lyon's, ordered it removed from the wagon so that wounded might be transported in it. In the haste of the army's ensuing retreat, the body of the first Union general to die in the war was completely forgotten.[4]

Upon its discovery by the Confederates, a State Guard lieutenant had the body placed in a small ambulance and taken to Price's headquarters. About noon it was turned over to Dr. S. H. Melcher, the surgeon of the 5th Missouri who had mistaken McCulloch's advance on Sigel for Lyon's troops. Dr. Melcher took the body to the Ray house, the only nearby structure he knew of, and examined it on the bed in the front room. Afterward, James Rains furnished an armed escort of State Guard to transport the corpse to Springfield. It rested briefly at Lyon's former headquarters office, but when Sturgis began his march to Rolla, he discovered that Lyon's body had again been forgotten. Sturgis sent an armed guard back to Springfield to retrieve the body so it could be moved to Rolla with the army. Because no metallic coffin was available, Chief Surgeon E. F. Franklin attempted to embalm the general's body. However, the massive heart wound prevented any retention of fluids, and Franklin canceled the effort. Sturgis sent word to the chief surgeon to dispose of the body in the best manner possible.[5]

    3. Loren Schweninger, ed., *From Tennessee Slave to St. Louis Entrepreneur: The Autobiography of James Thomas*, 162; J. D. McKown to "Dear Children," August 18, 1861, McKown Family Papers, SHSM.
    4. Return I. Holcombe and W. S. Adams, *An Account of the Battle of Wilson's Creek . . . ,* 97–98.
    5. Ibid.; J. F. Snyder to O. W. Coller, January 8, 1883, John F. Snyder Collection,

The next morning, August 11, Franklin ordered the construction of a black walnut coffin, encased in zinc, for the general's corpse. Hearing that Lyon's remains lay downtown in a charnel house, Mary Phelps, the wife of Congressman John Phelps, sent a wagon and had the body removed to her farm, placing it in her ice house. By this time, elements of the Confederate army had arrived in Springfield, and some of the soldiers learned where Lyon's remains were being held. Those in Mosby M. Parson's division, encamped nearby, actually went to the Phelps house in hopes of viewing their late adversary. One officer was reported to have said to a horrified Mrs. Phelps, "There is quite a contrast betwixt the resting place of old Lyon's body and his soul, isn't there Madame? The one is in the ice house; the other in hell!"[6]

As the days passed, many more idle soldiers came to the Phelps home. On August 13, after some drunken soldiers threatened to "cut the damned heart" out of Lyon's body for a relic, a panicky Mrs. Phelps sent word to Price requesting a burial detail. Some of the State Guard volunteered, and that evening they buried Lyon's corpse in a cornfield on the Phelps farm. While tamping down the dirt, several of the soldiers were reported to have gleefully jumped up and down on the grave while an Irish Confederate quipped, "Be jabers, we shtompted him good!" Ironically, only the day before, Frémont had released two regiments from Jefferson Barracks, per Lincoln's wishes, to reinforce Lyon.[7]

A week later, a four-mule ambulance arrived at the Phelps home, bearing a large iron coffin. In the wagon were Danford Knowlton, John B. Hasler, Capt. George P. Edgar, of Frémont's staff, and George N. Lynch, a St. Louis undertaker. After receiving the shocking telegraph message relating Lyon's death, Knowlton and Hasler had made the long trip to Missouri at the expense of the state of Connecticut. Once in St. Louis, the two, escorted by Edgar, secured a pass from Frémont to go

MHS; S. H. Melcher to Martin J. Hubble, August 17, 1910, Hubble Family Papers, SHSM.

6. S. H. Melcher to Martin J. Hubble, August 17, 1910, Hubble Family Papers, SHSM; Holcombe and Adams, *Account of Wilson's Creek*, 102–3; *Missouri Democrat,* August 28, 1861; W. H. Rogers to "Custodian of Historical Events that took place in Springfield, Missouri," February 16, 1947, Nathaniel Lyon File, SHSM. The federal government paid Mary Phelps twenty thousand dollars for her services.

7. Holcombe and Adams, *Account of Wilson's Creek,* 103; *San Joaquin* [California] *Republican,* September 14, 1861; *Missouri Democrat,* August 26, 1861; Assistant Adjutant General, Department of the West, to Samuel Curtis, August 12, 1861, Letters Sent, Department of the West, vol. 4, RG 393; Diary of C. M. Chase, August 14, 1861, Charles M. Chase Papers, SHSM.

through the lines and retrieve Lyon's body from Springfield. They reached the Phelps house on the afternoon of August 22, and that evening disinterred the body, placing it in the large casket. Packing the coffin in ice, the party left the next morning for Rolla. On the evening of August 26, the entourage arrived by train in St. Louis.[8]

Lyon's body lay in state for two days at Frémont's headquarters. Thousands came to view the casket, while the department commander published a special order "lament[ing], in sympathy with the country, the loss of the indomitable General Nathaniel Lyon . . . . Let us all emulate his prowess and undying devotion to duty." Frémont authorized regiments present at Wilson's Creek to emblazon "Springfield" on their colors "as a distinguished memorial to their services to the nation." On August 28, a military funeral procession wound its way through the city's streets, the flag-draped casket followed by the riderless horse Lyon had been riding when fatally struck. Stores and dwellings alike were draped in mourning as the procession moved to the levee, where the casket was taken across the river to a waiting train, bound for the East.[9]

Flags flew at half-mast as the procession made stops in Cincinnati, Philadelphia, New York, and Hartford. At each, the body of the North's first war hero lay in state for public viewing, although the coffin remained closed due to its advanced stage of decay. Eastern newspapers soon picked up a patriotic but incorrect report that Lyon had bequeathed his entire estate, reputedly worth over thirty thousand dollars, to the federal government "to be used in the prosecution of the war." The funeral train left Hartford on September 4, and after disembarking at Willimantic late that afternoon, the cortege traveled on to Eastford. Though it arrived well after dark, the streets were illuminated by the flames of hundreds of candles and lanterns held by those standing outside their homes, lit in anticipation of the arrival of the village's most famous son. As the church bell tolled and a band played various dirges,

8. Holcombe and Adams, *Account of Wilson's Creek,* 103–7; Allen B. Lincoln, ed., *A Modern History of Windham County, Connecticut,* 1:392–93; W. A. Buckingham to Hamilton R. Gamble, August 14, 1861, Hamilton R. Gamble Papers, MHS; John C. Frémont to Franz Sigel, August 19, 1861, Letters Sent by Major Gen. Frémont, RG 393; *Missouri Democrat,* August 27, 1861; *Missouri Republican,* August 27, 29, 1861; George P. Rawick, ed., *The American Slave: A Composite Autobiography,* 11:149–50.

9. Lyon, *Last Political Writings of General Nathaniel Lyon, U.S.A.,* 237; *Missouri Republican,* August 28, 1861; *Missouri Democrat,* August 29, 1861.

the long line of carriages climbed the steep hill to the Congregational Church, where the body rested overnight, guarded by a squad of Lyon's troops who had accompanied it from St. Louis. The next morning, amid the brilliance of a New England fall, thousands of onlookers attended a magnificent five-hour service, including the governors of both Connecticut and Rhode Island, their staffs, three members of Congress (including former Eastford resident Galusha A. Grow), the mayors of both Providence and Hartford, numerous army officers, and Lyon's remaining family. The large numbers forced most to remain on the steep front lawn of the church during the service.[10]

At 3:30 P.M., the funeral procession, one and a half miles in length, wound its way to the small, hillside cemetery below the nearby village of Phoenixville, two and a half miles south of Eastford. Under a large stand of weeping willows, two miles from his birthplace, Nathaniel Lyon was lowered into a grave in the family plot, next to his parents and two brothers. As the honor guard formed a hollow square around the grave, the City Guard fired three volleys, their reports echoing down the valley of the Natchaug River on the still September afternoon. The large crowd then slowly dispersed, leaving the graveyard to those charged with covering the casket with the rocky Connecticut earth.[11]

The turmoil in Missouri over the army command continued even after Lyon's death. Though Frémont continued as department commander for a time, once news of Wilson's Creek and Lyon's death reached the nation, he received vehement criticism for what many considered a needless sacrifice. And although Frank Blair had believed initially that the responsibility for Lyon's death lay with "red tape and the Quartermasters Department," he and the other Blairs soon reversed their view and led the storm of protest raging against the Department of the West's controversial commander. The Pathfinder further raised the ire of the president by issuing an unauthorized emancipation proclamation for Missouri's slaves, which Lincoln himself was forced to rescind. Opposition to Fré-

---

10. Lyon, *Last Political Writings,* 239–66; *New York Times,* September 1, 1861; *Hartford Courant,* September 4, 1861, July 21, 1929; James M. McPherson, *Battle Cry of Freedom,* 292; Estate Inventory of Nathaniel Lyon, Eastford Township Probate Records, CSL; *Speech of Charles H. Howland, Inaugural Proceedings of the Lyon Monument Association . . . ,* 42; Diane Maher Cameron, *Eastford: The Biography of a New England Town,* 171; Susan J. Griggs, *Folklore and Firesides in Pomfret and Hampton,* 159; Jeremiah Burns, *The Patriot's Offering,* 43–45. Lyon died intestate; therefore, he could not have left his estate to the government.

11. Lyon, *Last Political Writings,* 267–69.

mont grew so pronounced that on November 2 Lincoln removed him from command of the department for gross mismanagement of his office.[12]

Two days after Lyon's death, as the federal forces withdrew to Rolla, Price issued a proclamation from Springfield to the people of Missouri assuring them that his army, "organized under the law of this state, for the protection of your homes and firesides, and the maintainance of the rights, dignity and honor of Missouri," would remain in the field to protect them from "subjugation and enslavement" by the "usurpers in Washington." Three weeks later, Price was leading ten thousand Missourians northward—without McCulloch, who had returned to Arkansas—toward the Missouri River, hoping to spark a popular uprising against federal rule. Though he forced the surrender of a Union garrison at Lexington, the rebellion failed to materialize, and Price was forced to retreat to southwestern Missouri when Frémont concentrated his forces near the river and threatened to cut off Price's army. In February 1862 a federal force of twelve thousand under the command of Samuel R. Curtis drove Price from the state. With the exception of another of Price's forays into the upper section of the state, Missouri remained for all intents and purposes in Union hands. Just prior to Lyon's death the Missouri state convention had replaced Jackson's secessionist government with a provisional government that unequivocally supported the Union. Though often strained, Missouri's bond with the Union held up for the duration of the war.[13]

For his actions, Lyon has since been known as the "savior of Missouri." His eternal sobriquet, however, is somewhat misleading. To his credit, he provided the St. Louis Arsenal with the defenses needed to ensure its protection against the machinations of the city's secessionists. Moreover, his move on the state capital allowed time for the replacement of the secessionist legislators with ones loyal to the Union. Yet his decision to declare war on Missouri was based upon neither military nor political necessity. Even without his efforts, it is unlikely that Missouri would ever have seceded, despite her governor's efforts to the contrary. And in securing the Missouri River, Lyon had provided all that was

12. Frank Blair to Montgomery Blair, August 21, 1861, Blair Papers, box 3, LOC; James M. McPherson, *Ordeal by Fire*, 158.

13. "Proclamation to the people of Mo.," August 12, 1861, Sterling Price Papers, SHSM; Albert Castel, "A New View of the Battle of Pea Ridge," 137; Catton, *Terrible Swift Sword*, 49–51; Jay Monaghan, *Civil War on the Western Border, 1854–1865*, 182–205 passim; McPherson, *Battle Cry of Freedom*, 292–93.

needed to defend the state from future invasion, if the federals chose to fortify it. However, Lyon chose not to stop there.

Perhaps most dramatic were the effects of Lyon's campaign and Wilson's Creek upon the Missouri populace. By polarizing the state, Lyon and Blair provided guerrilla bands with a cause célèbre for which they subjected large areas of Missouri to three years of rampant bushwhacking, sniping, hit-and-run raiding, arson, and murder. The truest meaning of the term *civil war* was nowhere more apparent than in Missouri. Men such as William Quantrill, "Bloody Bill" Anderson, and George Todd gained notoriety by unleashing bloodthirsty attacks upon Unionist residents, while "Jayhawkers" like James H. Lane and Charles Jennison led retaliatory raids that often equaled their rivals in their destructive fury. Missouri, more than any other state, suffered the nightmare of internecine warfare, which, almost as Lyon had predicted, touched every man, woman, and child living there in some way during the next three years and beyond. And more than any other single individual, Nathaniel Lyon bore responsibility for this fratricidal tragedy.[14]

On a different level, however, the emergence of men such as Lyon and Blair represented a tragedy on even a grander scale: the ascendancy of radicalism in the nation as a whole. In an atmosphere charged by sectional strife, exacerbated by the events of the turbulent decade following the war with Mexico, agitators both North and South found by 1860 especially receptive ears when asserting the irreconcilable differences between the two regions. Yet the extremism that contributed to the outbreak of war reached far beyond a "blundering generation" of overzealous politicians; it reflects the mood of an entire nation caught amid rapid economic and social changes yet not fully understanding either. When the political system—with its only workable vehicle for change being compromise—failed to keep pace with the country's growth, this lack of understanding gave rise to anger. With such prevailing sentiment, radicals found their words—and actions—not only accepted but encouraged by large segments of the population. And by taking the initiative, they helped lead an excitable nation into a war of such magnitude no one could have envisioned. Lyon's actions in Missouri could never have occurred without such widespread passion.[15]

Yet Lyon's war was more than political extremism; it was a personal

14. James G. Randall and David Donald, *The Civil War and Reconstruction,* 235–36; McPherson, *Battle Cry of Freedom,* 292; Richard S. Brownlee, *Gray Ghosts of the Confederacy,* 3–5.

15. Randall and Donald, *Civil War and Reconstruction,* 106–8.

vendetta, wrought by a blind hatred of the nation's secessionists that obfuscated all other possible consequences beyond the fulfillment of his own personal vengeance. Instead of saving the state, Lyon actually started a war that otherwise might not have erupted. His decision to pursue the State Guard to Springfield and then attack at Wilson's Creek epitomized his entire life; it was made with a single-mindedness from which he would not compromise. Though advised to retreat, Lyon was obsessed by an overweening vow to punish the secessionists. He viewed himself as the state's supreme arbiter, and once he acquired the power to act as such, he would not relinquish it. It was his duty, it was his crusade, and, as he predicted while still stationed in Kansas, it cost him his life. But to Nathaniel Lyon, that was mere justice.

Bibliography

PRIMARY SOURCES
Manuscript Collections

Bates Family Papers. Missouri Historical Society, St. Louis.
Blair Family Papers. Library of Congress, Washington, D.C.
Broadhead, James O. Papers. Missouri Historical Society, St. Louis.
Camp Jackson Collection. Missouri Historical Society, St. Louis.
Chase, Charles M. Papers. Joint Collection—Western Historical Manuscript
   Collection/State Historical Society of Missouri Manuscripts, Columbia.
Civil War Collection. Missouri Historical Society, St. Louis.
Cooper County [Missouri]. Papers. Joint Collection—Western Historical Manu-
   script Collection/State Historical Society of Missouri Manuscripts, Columbia.
Dick, Franklin A. Papers. Library of Congress, Washington, D.C.
Eads, James B. Papers. Missouri Historical Society, St. Louis.
Fordyce Family Papers. Missouri Historical Society, St. Louis.
Gamble, Hamilton R. Papers. Missouri Historical Society, St. Louis.
Gibson, Charles. Papers. Missouri Historical Society, St. Louis.
Gilbert, Cass. Papers. Library of Congress, Washington, D.C.
Graham, Richard. Papers. Missouri Historical Society, St. Louis.
Henry, Mrs. Jesse P. Papers. Missouri Historical Society, St. Louis.
Hubble Family Papers. Joint Collection—Western Historical Manuscript Col-
   lection/State Historical Society of Missouri Manuscripts, Columbia.
Jefferson Barracks Papers. Missouri Historical Society, St. Louis.
Lane, William Carr. Papers. Missouri Historical Society, St. Louis.
Leonard, Abiel. Papers. Missouri Historical Society, St. Louis.
———. Papers. Joint Collection—Western Historical Manuscript Collection/
   State Historical Society of Missouri Manuscripts, Columbia.
Love, James E. Papers. Missouri Historical Society, St. Louis.
Lyon, Nathaniel. Papers. Eastford Historical Society. Eastford (Connecticut)
   Town Hall.
———. Papers. Connecticut Historical Society, Hartford.
———. Papers. Archives, History and Genealogy Unit, Connecticut State
   Library, Hartford.
———. Papers. Harry N. Ensign Autograph Collection. Yale University
   Library, New Haven, Conn.
———. Papers. Chicago Historical Society.

————. Papers. Kansas State Historical Society, Topeka.

————. West Point Diploma. Chester C. Corbin Public Library, Webster, Mass.

————. Papers. American Antiquarian Society, Worcester, Mass.

————. Papers. Joint Collection—Western Historical Manuscript Collection/ State Historical Society of Missouri Manuscripts, Columbia.

————. Personal Account Book. Wilson's Creek National Battlefield Park Archives and Library, Springfield, Mo.

————. Papers. New-York Historical Society, New York.

————. Papers. United States Military Institute Archives and Library. West Point, N.Y.

————. Papers. South Dakota Historical Society, Pierre.

McKown Family Papers. Joint Collection—Western Historical Manuscript Collection/State Historical Society of Missouri Manuscripts, Columbia.

Missouri Militia Collection. Missouri Historical Society, St. Louis.

Porter, V. Mott. Papers. Missouri Historical Society, St. Louis.

Price, Sterling. Papers. Joint Collection—Western Historical Manuscript Collection/State Historical Society of Missouri Manuscripts, Columbia.

Reavis, Logan U. Papers. Chicago Historical Society. Reynolds, Thomas C. Papers. Missouri Historical Society, St. Louis.

Schofield, John M. Papers. Library of Congress, Washington, D.C.

Scott, Elvira A. W. Manuscript. Joint Collection—Western Historical Manuscript Collection/State Historical Society of Missouri Manuscripts, Columbia.

Smith, Anthony W. Papers. Missouri Historical Society, St. Louis.

Snyder, John F. Papers. Missouri Historical Society, St. Louis.

Stearns, George L. Papers. Kansas State Historical Society, Topeka.

Sweeny, Thomas J. Papers. Henry E. Huntington Library, San Marino, Calif.

Thompson, Sallie Yeatman. Papers. Ovenshine Family Collection. United States Army Military History Institute. Carlisle Barracks, Penn.

Documents: Government and Church Records

Ashford, Connecticut, Congregational Church Records, 1712–1941. 5 vols. Archives, History and Genealogy Unit, Connecticut State Library, Hartford.

Ashford District Probate Records. Ashford (Connecticut) Town Hall.

Connecticut Headstone Inscriptions. Charles R. Hale Collection. RG 72:1, Durham, Eastford, and East Granby. Archives, History and Genealogy Unit, Connecticut State Library, Hartford.

Connecticut Vital Records. Ashford and Eastford Townships. Barbour Collection. Archives, History and Genealogy Unit, Connecticut State Library, Hartford.

Eastford, Connecticut, Congregational Church Records, 1777–1941. 5 vols. Eastford (Connecticut) Town Hall.

Eastford District Probate Records. Archives, History and Genealogy Unit, Connecticut State Library, Hartford.

General Orders of the Department of the West, January 1858 to November

1861. Record Group 393, Records of the United States Army Continental Commands. National Archives, Washington, D.C.

Letters Received by the Department of the West, 1853–1861. Record Group 393, Records of the United States Army Continental Commands. National Archives, Washington, D.C.

Letters Sent by the Department of the West, 1853–1861. Record Group 393, Records of the United States Army Continental Commands. National Archives, Washington, D.C.

Letters Sent and General and Special Orders Issued, Army of the West, 1861. Record Group 393, Records of the United States Army Continental Commands. National Archives, Washington, D.C.

Letters Sent by Maj. Gen. Frémont, Commanding the Department of the West, 1861. Record Group 393, Records of the United States Army Continental Commands. National Archives, Washington, D.C.

Orders and Special Orders of the Department of the West, December 1853 to December 1857. Record Group 393, Records of the United States Army Continental Commands. National Archives, Washington, D.C.

Pomfret District Probate Records. Archives, History and Genealogy Unit, Connecticut State Library, Hartford.

Post Files of Fort Pierre, Nebraska Territory, 1854–1856. Record Group 94, Records of the Adjutant General's Office, 1780s–1917. National Archives, Washington, D.C.

Register of Deliquencies, 1838–1842. United States Military Academy Library and Archives, West Point, N.Y.

Register of the Officers and Cadets of the United States Military Academy, 1818–1850. United States Military Academy Library and Archives, West Point, N.Y.

Reports of the Adjutant General's Office. Record Group 94, Records of the Adjutant General's Office, 1780s–1917. National Archives, Washington, D.C.

Returns of the Second Infantry Regiment. Record Group 94, Records of the Adjutant General's Office, 1780s–1917. National Archives, Washington, D.C.

Special Orders of the Department of the West, January 1858 to November 1861. Record Group 393, Records of the United States Army Continental Commands. National Archives, Washington, D.C.

Transcripts of the Court Martial of Second Lieutenant Nathaniel Lyon, December 28, 1842, to January 7, 1843. Record Group 153, Records of the Judge Advocate General [Army]. National Archives, Washington, D.C.

Transcripts of the Court Martial of Brevet Colonel William R. Montgomery, September to December 1855. Record Group 153, Records of the Judge Advocate General [Army]. National Archives, Washington, D.C.

U.S. Census Office. 1st Census of the United States, 1790: Population Schedules. Windham County, Conn.

———. 2nd Census of the United States, 1800: Population Schedules. Windham County, Conn.

————. 3rd Census of the United States, 1810: Population Schedules. Windham County, Conn.
————. 4th Census of the United States, 1820: Population Schedules. Windham County, Conn.
————. 5th Census of the United States, 1830: Population Schedules. Windham County, Conn.
————. 6th Census of the United States, 1840: Population Schedules. Windham County, Conn.
————. 7th Census of the United States, 1850: Population Schedules. Windham County, Conn.
————. 8th Census of the United States, 1860: Population and Slave Schedules.
St. Louis County, Mo.
U.S. Military Academy Library Circulation Records, 1836–1841. U.S. Military
Academy Library and Archives, West Point, N.Y.

Published Sources

*Address on the Death of Gen. Nathaniel Lyon, Delivered at Manhattan [Kan-
sas], September 26th, 1861, by George D. Henderson, Chaplain at Fort
Riley.*
Executive Documents of the Senate of the United States. Second Session of the
Thirty-first Congress. Washington, D.C.: Union Office, 1851.
Hoadly, Charles J., ed. *The Public Records of Connecticut.* 26 vols. Hartford:
Case, Lockwood and Brainard Co., 1887.
*Inaugural Proceedings of the Lyon Monument Association of the State of Mis-
souri, Had in the Hall of the House of Representatives at Jefferson City,
January 11, 1866.* St. Louis: R. P. Studley and Co., Printers, 1866.
Jameson, E. H. E., ed. *A Memorial Wreath Containing an Address from the
Lyon Monumental Association of St. Louis, Together with the Oration of
Gov. B. Gratz Brown, Delivered January 11, 1866; and Remarks on the Life
and Services of Gen. Nathaniel Lyon, by Gen. W. T. Sherman, Hon. Daniel
S. Dickinson, and Others.* St. Louis: R. P. Studley and Co., Printers, 1871.
*Oration by Hon. B. Gratz Brown, Before the General Assembly of Missouri, at
the Inauguration of the Lyon Monument Association, in Jefferson City, Mis-
souri, January 11, 1866.* Washington, D.C., 1866.
Rawick, George P., ed. *The American Slave: A Composite Autobiography.* 19
vols. Westport, Conn.: Greenwood Press, 1972.
*Report of the Commission Appointed to Improve the Burial Place of General
Nathaniel Lyon at Eastford, Conn.* Willimantic, Conn.: The Hall and Bill
Printing Company, 1909.
*The War of the Rebellion: A Compilation of the Official Records of the Union
and Confederate Armies.* 4 ser., 128 vols. Washington, D.C., 1881–1901.

Newspapers

Daily Missouri Democrat.
Daily Missouri Republican.
Harper's Weekly.

Hartford Courant.
San Joachin [California] *Republican.*
Springfield [Missouri] *Mirror.*
New York Daily Tribune.
New York Herald.
New York Times.

SECONDARY SOURCES
Books, Articles, Theses, and Dissertations

Adamson, Hans Christian. *Rebellion in Missouri, 1861: Nathaniel Lyon and His Army of the West.* New York: Chilton Company, 1961.

Ambrose, Stephen E. *Duty, Honor, Country.* Baltimore: Johns Hopkins University Press, 1966.

———. "The Monotonous Life." *American History Illustrated* 8 (August 1971): 22–32.

Anderson, Galusha. *A Border City During the Civil War.* Boston: Little, Brown and Company, 1908.

"A Soldier's Account of the Battle of Boonville." *Missouri Historical Review* 19 (July 1925): 725–26.

Athearn, Robert G. *Forts of the Upper Missouri.* Englewood Cliffs, N.J.: Prentice-Hall, 1967.

Barber, John W., and Henry Howe, eds. *Historical Collections of the State of New York.* New York: S. Tuttle, Publishers, 1844.

Barnes, John. "Boonville: The First Land Battle of the Civil War." *Infantry Journal* 35 (December 1929): 601–7.

Barry, Louise. "Kansas Before 1854: A Revised Annals—Part 22." *Kansas Historical Quarterly* 33 (Spring 1967): 1–213.

Bauer, K. Jack. *The Mexican War, 1846–1848.* New York: Macmillan Publishing Co., 1974.

Beale, Howard K., ed. *The Diary of Edward Bates.* Washington, D.C.: U.S. Government Printing Office, 1933.

Bearss, Edwin C. *The Battle of Wilson's Creek.* Bozeman, Mont.: Aircraft Printers, 1975.

———. "Fort Smith Serves General McCulloch as a Supply Depot." *Arkansas Historical Quarterly* 24 (Winter 1965): 315–47.

Berwanger, Eugene H. *The Frontier Against Slavery.* Urbana: University of Illinois Press, 1971.

Bierbaum, Milton E. "The Rhetoric of Union or Disunion in Missouri, 1844–1861." Ph.D. diss., University of Missouri–Columbia, 1965.

Biographical Directory of the American Congress, 1774–1961. Washington, D.C.: U.S. Government Printing Office, 1961.

Blum, Virgil C. "The Political and Military Activities of the German Element in St. Louis, 1859–1861." *Missouri Historical Review* 42 (January 1948): 103–29.

Boatner, Mark M. *The Civil War Dictionary.* New York: David McKay Co., 1959.

Britton, Wiley. *Civil War on the Border.* New York: G. P. Putnam's Sons, 1899.

Brown, William Wells. *Narrative of William W. Brown, a Fugitive Slave.* Boston: Anti-Slavery Office, 1848.

Brownlee, Richard S. *Gray Ghosts of the Confederacy.* Baton Rouge: Louisiana State University Press, 1958.

Burns, Jeremiah. *The Patriot's Offering; or, The Life, Services, and Military Careers of the Noble Trio, Ellsworth, Lyon, and Baker.* New York: Baker and Godwin, Printers, 1862.

Cain, Marvin C. "Edward Bates and Hamilton R. Gamble: A Wartime Partnership." *Missouri Historical Review* 56 (January 1962): 146–55.

———. *Lincoln's Attorney General: Edward Bates of Missouri.* Columbia: University of Missouri Press, 1965.

Cameron, Diane Maher. *Eastford: The Biography of a New England Town.* Danielson, Conn.: Eastford Historical Society, 1976.

Castel, Albert. *A Frontier State at War: Kansas, 1861–1865.* Ithaca, N.Y.: Cornell University Press, 1958.

———. "A New View of the Battle of Pea Ridge." *Missouri Historical Review* 62 (Fall 1967): 136–51.

———. *General Sterling Price and the Civil War in the West.* Baton Rouge: Louisiana State University Press, 1968.

Catton, Bruce. "Lincoln's Difficult Decisions." *Civil War History* 2 (June 1956): 5–12.

———. *Terrible Swift Sword.* Garden City, N.Y.: Doubleday and Company, 1963.

———. *The Coming Fury.* Garden City, N.Y.: Doubleday and Company, 1961.

———. *This Hallowed Ground.* Garden City, N.Y.: Doubleday and Company, 1963.

Child, Martha F. "The Lionhearted General." *New-England Galaxy* 12 (Summer 1970): 40–48.

Clark, James S. *Life in the Middle West; Reminiscences of J. S. Clark.* Chicago: The Advance Publishing Co., 1916.

Clow, Richmond L. "General William S. Harney on the Northern Plains." *South Dakota History* 16 (Fall 1986): 229–48.

Coffman, Edward M. *The Old Army: A Portrait of the American Army in Peacetime, 1784–1898.* New York: Oxford University Press, 1986.

Connelly, Thomas L. *The Marble Man: Robert E. Lee and His Image in American Society.* New York: Alfred A. Knopf, 1977.

Covington, James W. "The Camp Jackson Affair, 1861." *Missouri Historical Review* 55 (April 1961): 197–212.

Craig, Douglas L. "An Examination of the Reasons for Missouri's Decision Not to Secede in 1860." M.A. thesis, University of Missouri–Kansas City, 1969.

Crisler, Robert M. "Missouri's 'Little Dixie.'" *Missouri Historical Review* 42 (January 1948): 130–39.

———. "Republican Areas in Missouri." *Missouri Historical Review* 42 (July 1948): 299–309.

Cullum, George W. *Biographical Register of the Officers and Graduates of the*

U.S. Military Academy at West Point, N. Y. 3 vols. New York: Houghton, Mifflin and Company, 1891.

Daniels, Bruce C. *The Connecticut Town: Growth and Development, 1635–1790.* Middletown, Conn.: Wesleyan University Press, 1979.

Davis, William Heath. *Seventy-five Years in California.* San Francisco: John Howell, Publisher, 1929.

DeLand, Charles E. "Editorial Notes on 'Old Fort Pierre and Its Neighbors.'" *South Dakota Historical Collections* 1 (1902): 317–79.

Dictionary of American Biography. 20 vols. New York: Charles Scribners' Sons, 1928–1937.

"Documentary History of Kansas—Governor Denver's Administration." *Collections of the Kansas State Historical Society* 5 (1896): 502–43.

Dry, Camille N., and Richard J. Compton. *Pictorial St. Louis.* St. Louis: Compton and Company, 1876.

Duke, Basil W. *Reminiscences of General Basil W. Duke, C.S.A.* Garden City, N.Y.: Doubleday, Page and Co., 1911.

"Extinct Geographical Locations." *Collections of the Kansas State Historical Society* 12 (1912): 471–90.

Foner, Eric. *Free Soil, Free Labor, Free Men: The Ideology of the Republican Party Before the Civil War.* New York: Oxford University Press, 1970.

Fuller, Robert C. *Mesmerism and the American Cure of Souls.* Philadelphia: University of Pennsylvania Press, 1982.

Gannon, Gerald. "The Harney-Price Agreement." *Civil War Times Illustrated* 23 (December 1984): 40–45.

Glazier, Willard. *Heroes of Three Wars.* Philadelphia: Hubbard Bros., Publishers, 1879.

Goetzmann, William H. *Army Exploration in the American West, 1803–1863.* New Haven: Yale University Press, 1959.

Goodlander, Charles W. *Memoirs and Recollections of C. W. Goodlander.* Ft. Scott, Kans.: Monitor Printing Co., 1900.

Gray, O. W. *Atlas of Windham and Tolland Counties, Connecticut.* Hartford: C. G. Keeney, 1869.

Greene, Albert R. "On the Battle of Wilson's Creek." *Collections of the Kansas State Historical Society* 5 (1896): 116–27.

Griess, Thomas E., and Jay Luvaas, eds. *The Centennial of the United States Military Academy at West Point, New York.* 2 vols. New York: Greenwood Press, 1969.

Griggs, Susan J. *Folklore and Firesides in Pomfret and Hampton.* By the Author, 1950.

Grover, George S. "Col. Benjamin Whitehead Grover." *Missouri Historical Review* 1 (January 1907): 129–39.

Hagemann, E. R., ed. *Fighting Rebels and Redskins: Experiences in Army Life of Colonel George B. Sanford, 1861–1892.* Norman: University of Oklahoma Press, 1969.

Hammond, William A. "Brigadier-General Nathaniel Lyon, U.S.A.—Personal Recollections." *Magazine of American History* 13 (March 1885): 237–48.

————. "Recollections of General Nathaniel Lyon." *Annals of Iowa* 4 (July 1900): 414–70.

Harvey, Charles M. "Missouri from 1849 to 1861." *Missouri Historical Review* 2 (October 1907): 23–40.

Hendrick, Burton J. *Lincoln's War Cabinet.* Garden City, N.Y.: Doubleday and Company, 1946.

Henry, Robert Selph. *The Story of the Mexican War.* Indianapolis: Bobbs-Merrill, 1950.

Hesseltine, William B. *Lincoln and the War Governors.* New York: Alfred A. Knopf, 1948.

Hickman, Russell K. "Reeder Administration Inaugurated—Part I." *Kansas Historical Quarterly* 36 (Autumn 1970): 305–40.

Holcombe, Return I., and Adams, W. S. *An Account of the Battle of Wilson's Creek, or Oak Hills, Fought Between the Union Troops, Commanded by Gen. N. Lyon, and the Southern, or Confederate, Troops, Under Command of Gens. McCulloch and Price, on Saturday, August 10, 1861, in Greene County, Missouri.* Springfield, Mo.: Dow and Adams, Publishers, 1883.

Horsman, Reginald. *Race and Manifest Destiny: The Origins of American Racial Anglo-Saxonism.* Cambridge: Harvard University Press, 1981.

Howard, Robert P. *Illinois: A History of the Prairie State.* Grand Rapids, Mich.: William E. Eerdmans Publishing Company, 1972.

Humphrey, James. "The Country West of Topeka Prior to 1865." *Collections of the Kansas State Historical Society* 4 (1900): 283–300.

Hutchinson, William. "Sketches of Kansas Pioneer Experiences." *Collections of the Kansas State Historical Society* 7 (1902): 392–407.

Ingersoll, Lurton D. *Iowa and the Rebellion.* Philadelphia: J. B. Lippincott and Co., 1866.

Irwin, Ray W., ed. "Missouri in Crisis—The Journal of Captain Albert Tracy, 1861." *Missouri Historical Review* 51 (October 1957 and January 1958): 8–21 and 151–64.

Johannsen, Robert W. *Stephen A. Douglas.* New York: Oxford University Press, 1973.

Johnson, Robert Underwood, and Howard L. Conard, eds. *Battles and Leaders of the Civil War.* New York: Thomas Yoseloff, 1956.

Kemp, Hardy. *About Nathaniel Lyon, Brigadier General, United States Army Volunteers and Wilson's Creek.* By the Author, 1978.

Kennedy, Joseph C. G. *Preliminary Report on the Eighth Census, 1860.* Washington D.C.: U.S. Government Printing Office, 1862.

Ketchum, Richard, ed. *The American Heritage Book of the Revolution.* New York: American Heritage Publishing Co., 1958.

Kirkpatrick, Arthur Roy. "The Admission of Missouri to the Confederacy." *Missouri Historical Review* 55 (July 1961): 366–86.

————. "Missouri in the Early Months of the Civil War." *Missouri Historical Review* 55 (April 1961): 235–66.

————. "Missouri on the Eve of the Civil War." *Missouri Historical Review* 55 (January 1961): 99–108.

———. "Missouri's Secession Government, 1861–1865." *Missouri Historical Review* 45 (January 1951): 124–37.

Knapp, Joseph G. *The Presence of the Past.* St. Louis: St. Louis University Publications, 1979.

Knox, Thomas W. *Camp-fire and Cotton Field: Southern Adventure in Time of War.* Philadelphia: Jones Brothers and Company, 1865.

Krug, Mark M., ed. *Mrs. Hill's Journal: Civil War Reminiscences, By Sarah Jane Full Hill.* Chicago: R. R. Donnelley and Sons Company, 1980.

Lademann, Otto. "The Capture of Camp Jackson—St. Louis, Missouri, Friday, May 10th, 1861." *War Papers . . . Wisconsin Military Order of the Loyal Legion* 4 (1941): 69–75.

Larson, James. *Sergeant Larson, 4th Cav.* San Antonio, Tex.: Southern Literary Institute, 1935.

Lathrop, David. *The History of the Fifty-ninth Regiment Illinois Volunteers.* Indianapolis: Hall and Hutchinson, 1865.

Laughlin, Sceva B. *Missouri Politics During the Civil War.* Salem, Oreg.: By the Author, 1930.

"Letter of Gen. F. Sigel." *Missouri Historical Review* 1 (January 1907): 147–48.

Lincoln, Allen B., ed. *A Modern History of Windham County, Connecticut.* 2 vols. Chicago: The S. J. Clarke Publishing Co., 1920.

Lobdell, Jared, ed. "Civil War Journal and Letters of Colonel John V. DuBois, April 12, 1861, to October 16, 1862." Parts I and II, *Missouri Historical Review* 60 and 61 (July and October 1966): 425–59 and 22–39.

Longacre, Edward G. "A Profile of General Justus McKinstry." *Civil War Times Illustrated* 17 (July 1978): 14–21.

Lyman, William. "Origin of the Term 'Jayhawker.'" *Collections of the Kansas State Historical Society* 14 (1918): 203–7.

Lyon, Nathaniel. *Last Political Writings of General Nathaniel Lyon, U.S.A.* New York: Rudd and Carleton, 1861.

Lyon, William H. "Claiborne Fox Jackson and the Secession Crisis in Missouri." *Missouri Historical Review* 58 (July 1964): 422–41.

Martin, George W. "The Territorial and Military Combine at Fort Riley." *Collections of the Kansas State Historical Society* 7 (1902): 361–73.

Martin, Sidney Walter. *Florida During the Territorial Days.* Athens: University of Georgia Press, 1944.

Mattes, Merrill J., ed. "Patrolling the Santa Fe Trail: Reminiscences of John S. Kirwan." *Kansas Historical Quarterly* 21 (Winter 1955): 569–85.

———. "Report on Historic Sites in the Fort Randall Reservoir Area, Missouri River, South Dakota." *South Dakota Historical Collections* 24 (1949): 470–577.

McClure, James. "Taking the Census in 1855." *Collections of the Kansas State Historical Society* 8 (1904): 230–40.

McDonough, James L. *Schofield: Union General in the Civil War and Reconstruction.* Tallahassee: Florida State University Press, 1972.

McElroy, John. *The Struggle for Missouri.* Washington, D.C.: The National Tribune Co., 1909.

McFeely, William S. *Grant: A Biography.* New York: W. W. Norton and Co., 1981.

McPherson, James M. *Battle Cry of Freedom.* New York: Oxford University Press, 1988.

———. *Ordeal By Fire.* New York: Alfred A. Knopf, 1982.

Meyers, Augustus. "Dakota in the Fifties." *South Dakota Historical Collections* 10 (1920): 130–94.

———. *Ten Years in the Ranks; U.S. Army.* New York: The Stirling Press, 1914.

Middlekauff, Robert. *The Glorious Cause.* New York: Oxford University Press, 1982.

Miller, Robert E. "'One of the Ruling Class': Thomas Caute Reynolds, Second Confederate Governor of Missouri." *Missouri Historical Review* 80 (July 1986): 422–48.

Monaghan, Jay. *Civil War on the Western Border, 1854–1865.* Lincoln: University of Nebraska Press, 1955.

Moore, Frank, ed. *Rebellion Record: A Diary of American Events.* New York: Arno Press, 1977.

Morse, Jarvis M. *A Neglected Period of Connecticut History, 1818–1850.* New Haven: Yale University Press, 1933.

Mowry, Duane, ed. "A Statesman's Letters of the Civil War Period." *Illinois State Historical Journal* 2 (July 1909): 42–53.

National Cyclopedia of American Biography. 15 vols. New York: James T. White and Company, 1904.

Neely, Mark E., Jr. *The Abraham Lincoln Encyclopedia.* New York: McGraw-Hill, 1982.

Nichols, Alice. *Bleeding Kansas.* New York: Oxford University Press, 1954.

Nute, Grace Lee, ed. "A Nathaniel Lyon Letter." *Mississippi Valley Historical Review* 9 (September 1922): 139–44.

Oates, Stephen B. "Nathaniel Lyon—A Personality Profile." *Civil War Times Illustrated* 6 (October 1968): 15–25.

———. *To Purge This Land with Blood: A Biography of John Brown.* New York: Harper and Row, 1970.

———. *With Malice Toward None: The Life of Abraham Lincoln.* New York: Harper and Row, 1977; Mentor Books, 1978.

O'Connor, Thomas H. *The Disunited States: The Era of Civil War and Reconstruction.* New York: Harper and Row, 1978.

"Official Correspondence Relating to Fort Pierre." *South Dakota Historical Collections* 1 (1902): 381–440.

Parrish, William E. *David Rice Atchison of Missouri: Border Politician.* Columbia: University of Missouri Press, 1961.

———. "General Nathaniel Lyon—A Portrait." *Missouri Historical Review* 49 (October 1954): 1–18.

———. *Turbulent Partnership: Missouri and the Union, 1861–1865.* Columbia: University of Missouri Press, 1963.

Peckham, James. *General Nathaniel Lyon and Missouri in 1861.* New York: American News Company, 1866.

Peterson, Norma L. *Freedom and Franchise: The Political Career of B. Gratz Brown*. Columbia: University of Missouri Press, 1965.

Phillips, Christopher W. "The Court Martial of Lieutenant Nathaniel Lyon." *Missouri Historical Review* 81 (April 1987): 296–308.

―――. "The Noble Lyon? The Life and Death of Union General Nathaniel Lyon." M.A. thesis, Illinois State University, 1986.

Plattenburg, Cyrus B. "In St. Louis During the 'Crisis.'" *Illinois State Historical Journal* 13 (April 1900): 16–22.

Plummer, Mark A. *Frontier Governor: Samuel J. Crawford of Kansas*. Lawrence: University of Kansas Press, 1971.

Prucha, Francis P. *Guide to the Military Posts of the United States, 1789–1895*. Madison: State Historical Society of Wisconsin, 1964.

Purcell, Richard J. *Connecticut in Transition, 1775–1818*. Middletown, Conn.: Wesleyan University Press, 1963.

Radin, Max, ed. "The Stone and Kelsey 'Massacre' on the Shores of Clear Lake in 1849: The Indian Viewpoint." *California Historical Society Quarterly* 11 (September 1932): 266–73.

Randall, James G., and David Donald. *The Civil War and Reconstruction*. Lexington, Mass.: D. C. Heath and Company, 1969.

Reavis, Logan Uriah. *The Life and Military Services of Gen. William Selby Harney*. St. Louis: Bryan, Brand and Co., 1878.

Robbins, Peggy. "The Battle of Camp Jackson." *Civil War Times Illustrated* 20 (June 1981): 34–43.

Roed, William. "Secessionist Strength in Missouri." *Missouri Historical Review* 72 (July 1978): 412–23.

Rogers, Fred B. "Bear Flag Lieutenant—The Life Story of Henry L. Ford (1822–1860)." Part 4. *California Historical Society Quarterly* 30 (March 1951): 49–55.

―――. "Early Military Posts of Mendocino County, Calif." *California Historical Society Quarterly* 27 (September 1948): 215–28.

Rolle, Andrew F. "William Heath Davis and the Founding of American San Diego." *California Historical Society Quarterly* 31 (March 1952): 33–48.

Rombauer, Robert J. *The Union Cause in St. Louis in 1861*. St. Louis: Nixon-Jones Printing Co., 1909.

Rorvig, Paul. "The Significant Skirmish—The Battle of Boonville, June 17, 1861." Unpublished paper presented at the Missouri Conference on History, March 17, 1989.

Rowan, Steven, and James Neal Primm, eds. *Germans for a Free Missouri: Translations from the St. Louis Radical Press, 1857–1862*. Columbia: University of Missouri Press, 1983.

Ruhlen, George. "San Diego Barracks." *Journal of San Diego History* 8 (April 1967): 7–15.

Russel, Robert R. *Economic Aspects of Southern Sectionalism, 1840–1861*. New York: Russell and Russell, 1960.

Ryle, Walter H. *Missouri: Union or Secession*. Nashville: George Peabody College for Teaching, 1931.

Scharf, J. Thomas. *History of Saint Louis City and County.* 2 vols. Phila-
    delphia: Louis H. Everts and Co., 1883.
Schofield, John M. *Forty-six Years in the Army.* New York: The Century Co.,
    1897.
Schweninger, Loren, ed. *From Tennessee Slave to St. Louis Entrepreneur: The
    Autobiography of James Thomas.* Columbia: University of Missouri Press,
    1984.
Shalhope, Robert E. *Sterling Price: Portrait of a Southerner.* Columbia: Univer-
    sity of Missouri Press, 1971.
Sherman, Edwin A. "Sherman Was There—The Recollections of Edwin A.
    Sherman." Part 2. *California Historical Society Quarterly* 24 (March 1945):
    42–72.
Sherman, William T. *Memoirs of W. T. Sherman.* New York: D. Appleton and
    Co., 1875.
Shindler, Henry. "First Capital of Kansas." *Collections of the Kansas State
    Historical Society* 12 (1912): 331–37.
Shoemaker, Floyd C. *A History of Missouri and Missourians.* Columbia, Mo.:
    Walter Ridgway Publishing Co., 1922.
Singletary, Otis A. *The Mexican War.* Chicago: University of Chicago Press,
    1960.
Smith, Donnal V. "The Influence of the Foreign-Born of the Northwest in the
    Election of 1860." *Mississippi Valley Historical Review* 19 (September
    1932): 192–204.
Smith, Edward C. *The Borderland in the Civil War.* New York: Macmillan,
    1927.
Smith, George Winston. "New England Business Interests in Missouri During
    the Civil War." *Missouri Historical Review* 41 (October 1946): 1–18.
Smith, William E. *The Francis Preston Blair Family in Politics.* New York:
    Macmillan, 1933.
Snead, Thomas L. *The Fight for Missouri from the Election of Lincoln to the
    Death of Lyon.* New York: Charles Scribner's Sons, 1886.
Starr, Stephen Z. *Jennison's Jayhawkers.* Baton Rouge: Louisiana State Univer-
    sity Press, 1973.
"Statement of Theo. Weischselbaum, of Ogden, Riley Cty., July 17, 1908."
    Collections of the Kansas State Historical Society 11 (1915): 561–71.
Sunder, John E. "The Early Telegraph in Rural Missouri, 1847–1859." *Mis-
    souri Historical Review* 51 (October 1956): 42–53.
Tanner, A. H. "Early Days of Kansas." *Collections of the Kansas State Histor-
    ical Society* 14 (1918): 224–34.
Taylor, Robert J. *Colonial Connecticut: A History.* Millwood, N.Y.: KTO
    Press, 1979.
Treadway, William E. "The Guilded Age in Kansas." *Kansas Historical Quar-
    terly* 40 (Spring 1974): 1–37.
Turkoly-Joczik, Robert L. "Fremont and the Western Department." *Missouri
    Historical Review* 82 (July 1988): 363–85.
United States Military Academy, West Point. *The Centennial of the United*

States Military Academy at West Point, New York. 2 vols. Washington, D.C.: U.S. Government Printing Office, 1904.

Ware, Eugene F. *The Lyon Campaign.* Topeka, Kans.: Crane and Company, 1907.

Warner, Ezra J. *Generals in Blue.* Baton Rouge: Louisiana State University Press, 1959.

———. *Generals in Gray.* Baton Rouge: Louisiana State University Press, 1959.

Weems, John Edward. *To Conquer a Peace.* Garden City, N.Y.: Doubleday and Company, 1974.

White, Mrs. S. B. "My First Days in Kansas." *Collections of the Kansas State Historical Society* 11 (1910): 550–60.

Wilentz, Sean. *Chants Democratic: New York City and the Rise of the American Working Class, 1788–1850.* New York: Oxford University Press, 1984.

Wilkie, Franc B. *Pen and Powder.* Boston: Ticknor and Company, 1888.

Wilson, Frederick T. "Fort Pierre and Its Neighbors." *South Dakota Historical Collections* 1 (1902): 263–311.

Woodward, Ashbel. *Life of General Nathaniel Lyon.* Hartford, Conn.: Case, Lockwood and Company, 1862.

Wurthman, Leonard B., Jr. "Frank Blair: Lincoln's Congressional Spokesman." *Missouri Historical Review* 64 (April 1970): 263–88.

———. "Frank Blair of Missouri, Jacksonian Orator of the Civil War Era." Ph.D. diss., University of Missouri–Columbia, 1969.

Wyman, Mark. *Immigrants in the Valley: Irish, Germans, and Americans in the Upper Mississippi Country, 1830–1860.* Chicago: Nelson-Hall, 1984.

Index